BEGINNING

Drupal®

Jacob Redding

WILEY

Wiley Publishing, Inc.

Beginning Drupal®

Published by
Wiley Publishing, Inc.
10475 Crosspoint Boulevard
Indianapolis, IN 46256
www.wiley.com

Copyright © 2010 by Wiley Publishing, Inc., Indianapolis, Indiana

Published by Wiley Publishing, Inc., Indianapolis, Indiana

Published simultaneously in Canada

ISBN: 978-0-470-43852-7

Manufactured in the United States of America

10 9 8 7 6 5 4 3 2 1

For general information on our other products and services please contact our Customer Care Department within the United States at (877) 762-2974, outside the United States at (317) 572-3993 or fax (317) 572-4002.

Wiley also publishes its books in a variety of electronic formats. Some content that appears in print may not be available in electronic books.

Library of Congress Control Number: 2009930281

This book is first and foremost dedicated to the Drupal community, a melting pot of some of the most talented and intelligent people I have had the pleasure of working with. Equally important is Diana Kuan. She stuck by me while I wrote this book, pulled incredible hours with the Drupal Association, traveled to countless Drupal events and went crazy trying to keep up with the intense development of Drupal 7. Thank you Diana.

CREDITS

EXECUTIVE EDITOR
Carol Long

PROJECT EDITOR
Ed Connor

TECHNICAL EDITOR
Joshua Brauer

PRODUCTION EDITOR
Kathleen Wisor

COPY EDITOR
Kathi Duggan

EDITORIAL DIRECTOR
Robyn B. Siesky

EDITORIAL MANAGER
Mary Beth Wakefield

MARKETING MANAGER
Ashley Zurcher

PRODUCTION MANAGER
Tim Tate

VICE PRESIDENT AND EXECUTIVE GROUP PUBLISHER
Richard Swadley

VICE PRESIDENT AND EXECUTIVE PUBLISHER
Barry Pruett

ASSOCIATE PUBLISHER
Jim Minatel

PROJECT COORDINATOR, COVER
Lynsey Stanford

COMPOSITOR
Jeff Lytle, Happenstance Type-O-Rama

PROOFREADER
Carrie Hunter, Word One, New York

INDEXER
Robert Swanson

COVER DESIGNER
Michael E. Trent

COVER IMAGE
© Jim Jurica/istockphoto

ABOUT THE AUTHOR

 **JACOB REDDING** got his start in Drupal in 2005 after 10 years in the IT industry building custom software with everything from Microsoft to Linux and UNIX technologies. He has since become heavily involved in the Drupal association and Drupal communities around the world, speaking and leading classes in not only New York, San Francisco, Boston, and Washington DC, but also far-flung locales such as China and Jordan. An enthusiastic advocate of open-source, he currently spends most of his time providing project management and training on Drupal-based websites.

ACKNOWLEDGMENTS

DIANA KUAN DESERVES the top spot here. Serving as a part-time editor, proofreader, supporter, and impromptu student she helped set the flow of the book, proofread nearly every page, and tested many of the exercises. Without her assistance and support this book would have taken yet another year, an outcome that would have surely sent the publisher's henchmen out to get me.

Jason Chinn, Mr. Magicspark, helped me through the rough spots of theming including building the nice Drupal chocolate theme used in Chapter 13. Without him the theming chapter would have been a rambling mess.

My students: To those in China: 你们帮我很多,我想说非常感谢你们。 我希望我们可以在来见面。 My students in Jordan caught me during a critical time of this book and unknowingly tested several of the exercises in the book, thank you for secretly helping to create this book. I can't leave out those in my home country of the United States, thank you for listening to me ramble about in class. I hope that I have been a useful part of your Drupal journeys.

Joshua Brauer: My technical editor. Although we have never met and I'm not entirely sure how we were paired together, the odd in-book synergy somehow worked. I was able to see through his trying-to-be-nice commentary that brow beat me into thoroughly revising the chapters into something useable.

Carol Long and Ed Connor at Wiley/Wrox: Oh boy. These two had no idea what they signed up for. The book started on very early versions of Drupal 7 and was revised too many times for them to count. Their patience and tolerance of my "I'll get it to you soon-ish" (heavy emphasis on –ish) and "by the way Drupal 7 changed so I have to rewrite the entire chapter" is much appreciated.

The entire Drupal community: You gals and guys are amazing. From small meetups in Beijing, large DrupalCamps in Los Angeles, collaborative working sessions in New York and the awesome DrupalChix group, you (the Drupal community) are amazing individuals to know and to collaborate with. With the book finally complete I hope to see you all in IRC more often.

CONTENTS

INTRODUCTION

OVER THE PAST FEW YEARS, the Web has undergone dramatic changes. What originally started as a handful of static web pages with a few e-commerce sites in the mix has now turned into a frenzy of collaboration and information sharing. New websites are expected to meet a certain level of interactivity and information-sharing. RSS feeds, blogs, and podcasts are just a few of the current standards. Photo uploads with auto-resizing and cropping, video and audio embedding, and even web APIs are quickly becoming the new standard-website functions.

Years ago, when I started creating dynamic websites, I began as most developers did, by writing my own custom content management system (CMS). My experience was not unlike that of others who followed the same path. The system was light and fast, and did everything that I, and my clients, asked — until a new feature emerged on the Web, and my software had to play catch-up. Soon I was buried under a pile of feature requests and bug fixes, which left me with no time to innovate. My quest for a better solution led me through a maze of software packages, until a friend told me about Drupal.

According to him Drupal has two really great things going for it. The first is that it's built on a modular structure, so it can quickly adapt to custom and unique scenarios. The second is that it is built around a community that is growing every day. When a new feature emerges on the Web, chances are someone has already gotten it to work within Drupal. The community factor is what sold me.

Now that I have been working with Drupal for a few years, I am in awe at how well the community has organized itself and, as a result, kept itself and the Drupal project on the cutting edge of web technology. Drupal has moved from being a piece of software that modularized the latest Internet technologies, to a platform that creates the latest technologies. The community made this happen.

You are now a part of this awesome community. Welcome.

Who This Book Is For

This book was written for people who want a robust website and aren't afraid to get their hands dirty.

Maybe you're the leader of a nonprofit who wants to organize your constituency through a community-driven website. You have a bit of prior experience in creating HTML pages by hand or with another CMS. You're now ready to dig in and create your community's website, and Drupal is your tool of choice, but you want to be on the fast track.

Perhaps you're an established developer and possess the skills to create your own custom CMS or have experience with other software packages. You're looking for definitions and examples on Drupal's terminology and structure so that you can take advantage of Drupal's fast development cycle that you hear so much about.

To get the most out of this book, you should already possess or have a strong desire to obtain experience in web development with HTML, JavaScript, or PHP. I did not set out to write a book that guides you step-by-step through building a specific website such as one for a restaurant or bakery. Instead, I set out to write a book that will help you understand how you can use Drupal to take the vision in your head and apply it to the Web. For example, when you understand that you need a new form of content, flip to Chapter 6, "Content," which discusses all aspects of content in depth, including creating, administering, moderating, and controlling that content.

Experienced developers who are looking to propel themselves on the fast track to custom module development might find it useful to skim Chapters 2 through 4, and then skip forward to the later chapters on module development. I would suggest that you spend a bit of time on Chapter 6, "Content," and Chapter 10, "Workflow and Actions," and Chapter 11, "Views." A good understanding of these chapters may save you countless development hours.

What This Book Covers

This book focuses on Drupal 7, but the changes since Drupal 6 are highlighted where appropriate. This book walks you through the entire process of creating a Drupal website. It starts with the installation, moves to administration and configuration, and then covers users and permissions. The book also discusses content (including nodes, users, and blocks), Drupal's infamous taxonomy system, tips on how to make your site not look like a Drupal site, and instructions on expanding your site with contributed and/or custom modules.

How This Book Is Structured

I often train others on how to use Drupal, so this book is structured similar to a training manual. The chapters are ordered in a manner that builds upon the topics of the previous chapter. For example, the chapter on Views is after the chapters on users, content, and taxonomy, because a view works with all of these items. I believe this order will help you understand the overall flow and structure of Drupal. Each chapter, however, is a thorough examination of its topic.

I don't expect you to read the book cover to cover before building your website. You should read this book alongside your development and use it as an aid or reference.

If you are new to Drupal, I recommend that you read at least the first parts of each chapter, but you can move to the next chapter if the topic becomes too complex or just plain boring. You can then revisit each chapter when you need clarification or more information.

Experienced developers or those with previous Drupal experience may find it beneficial to skip to the chapters that matter most to them. Each chapter is designed to be independent, although the examples in one chapter may build upon the examples in the previous chapter. If you find this to be the case, simply flip back one chapter and follow the last example to catch up.

What You Need to Use This Book

The book covers Drupal version 7, which has the following requirements:

- ➤ Webserver: Apache 1.3 or 2.x or IIS 6+
- ➤ Database server: MySQL 5+ or Postgres 8.3+
- ➤ PHP 5.2 or higher

The XAMPP project for Microsoft Windows, Linux, and Mac OS X as well as the MAMP project for Mac OS X contain all of these requirements in a single downloadable package.

Please visit `http://drupal.org/requirements` for up-to-date system requirements.

CONVENTIONS

To help you get the most from the text and keep track of what's happening, I've used a number of conventions throughout the book.

Exercises that you can try out for yourself generally appear in a box like this:

TRY IT OUT   What You Will Be Doing in this Exercise

Each *Try It Out* consists of an exercise you should work through, following the text in the book.

1. They usually consist of a set of steps.

2. Each step has a number.

3. Follow the steps using your copy of the database.

How It Works

After each *Try It Out*, the code you've typed will be explained in detail.

> **WARNING** Boxes like this one hold important, not-to-be forgotten information that is directly relevant to the surrounding text.

> **NOTE** Notes, tips, hints, tricks, and asides to the current discussion are offset and placed in italics like this.

This book also uses the following styles to set apart non-standard text:

➤ New and important terms are *italicized*.

➤ A combination of two or more keyboard strokes is presented like this: Ctrl+A.

➤ File names, URLs, and code within the text are shown in a monofont, like so: `persistence.properties`.

➤ Separate lines of code are formatted in the following ways:

```
Monofont type with no highlighting is used for most code examples.
Bold is used to emphasize code that's particularly important in the present
context.
```

SOURCE CODE

As you work through the examples in this book, you may choose either to type in all the code manually, or to use the source code files that accompany the book. All the source code used in this book is available for download at http://www.wrox.com. When at the site, simply locate the book's title (use the Search box or one of the title lists) and click the Download Code link on the book's detail page to obtain all the source code for the book. Code that is included on the Web site is highlighted by the following icon:

**Available for
download on
Wrox.com**

Listings include the filename in the title. If it is just a code snippet, you'll find the filename in a code note such as this:

code snippet filename

> **NOTE** *Because many books have similar titles, you may find it easiest to search by ISBN. This book's ISBN is 978-0-470-43852-7.*

Once you download the code, just decompress it with your favorite compression tool. Alternately, you can go to the main Wrox code download page at http://www.wrox.com/dynamic/books/download.aspx to see the code available for this book and all other Wrox books.

ERRATA

We make every effort to ensure that there are no errors in the text or in the code. However, no one is perfect, and mistakes do occur. If you find an error in one of our books, like a spelling mistake or faulty piece of code, we would be very grateful for your feedback. By sending in errata you may save another reader hours of frustration and at the same time you will be helping us provide even higher quality information.

To find the errata page for this book, go to http://www.wrox.com and locate the title using the Search box or one of the title lists. Then, on the book details page, click the Book Errata link. On this page you can view all errata that has been submitted for this book and posted by Wrox editors. A complete book list including links to each book's errata is also available at www.wrox.com/misc-pages/booklist.shtml.

If you don't spot "your" error on the Book Errata page, go to www.wrox.com/contact/techsupport.shtml and complete the form there to send us the error you have found. We'll check the information and, if appropriate, post a message to the book's errata page and fix the problem in subsequent editions of the book.

P2P.WROX.COM

For author and peer discussion, join the P2P forums at p2p.wrox.com. The forums are a Web-based system for you to post messages relating to Wrox books and related technologies and interact with other readers and technology users. The forums offer a subscription feature to e-mail you topics of interest of your choosing when new posts are made to the forums. Wrox authors, editors, other industry experts, and your fellow readers are present on these forums.

At http://p2p.wrox.com you will find a number of different forums that will help you not only as you read this book, but also as you develop your own applications. To join the forums, just follow these steps:

1. Go to p2p.wrox.com and click the Register link.

2. Read the terms of use and click Agree.

3. Complete the required information to join as well as any optional information you wish to provide and click Submit.

4. You will receive an e-mail with information describing how to verify your account and complete the joining process.

> **NOTE** You can read messages in the forums without joining P2P but in order to post your own messages, you must join.

When you join, you can post new messages and respond to messages other users post. You can read messages at any time on the Web. If you would like to have new messages from a particular forum e-mailed to you, click the Subscribe to this Forum icon by the forum name in the forum listing.

For more information about how to use the Wrox P2P, be sure to read the P2P FAQs for answers to questions about how the forum software works as well as many common questions specific to P2P and Wrox books. To read the FAQs, click the FAQ link on any P2P page.

1

Introducing Drupal

WHAT YOU WILL LEARN IN THIS CHAPTER:

➤ History of Drupal

➤ Drupal's community

➤ How to find and participate in the community, including: IRC, Meetups, Camps, and Drupal conferences

➤ Professional Drupal support

➤ The Drupal Association

What is Drupal? If this is your first time using Drupal, you're probably trying to answer this yourself, and you may have heard conflicting answers. Often Drupal is described as a content management system, whereas other times, it's called a content management framework. So is it a system or a framework? Here's a simple definition:

> Drupal is an open source software application that manages the content of and builds websites and web applications. It can be used to create a web blog, e-commerce store, photo gallery, or social networking website.

That seems straightforward, right? In fact, it sounds a lot like Joomla!, Wordpress, Zope, and many other content management systems (CMSs). So why do people use the term content management platform or content management framework?

The use of the terms *platform* and *framework* is an attempt to describe Drupal as a base or a foundation onto which you build your desired websites or web applications. Out of the box, Drupal can be used to instantly create a website with users, articles, blogs, comments, and a forum. With a few modules from http://drupal.org it can be transformed into an e-commerce site, a group photo gallery, and more. Drupal is also built around a modular core and a strong application programming interface (API) so you can quickly and easily extend Drupal to build the site of your dreams. This leads to the following, more technical definition:

> *Drupal is a modular framework written in the PHP scripting language that contains a CMS, a module system, and an API for rapid development of websites and web applications.*

An example I've used often is Lego systems. You can purchase the race car Lego set and build the provided example race car. You could also build a luxury car with the same Lego set. If you purchase the rocket ship Lego set, you could combine the two and build a luxury rocket race car. After all, it's only a set of blocks that you put together using your imagination. Drupal is built on the same idea — it's a set of modules that you mix and match to build your perfect website or web application.

HISTORY OF DRUPAL

In 2000, Dries Buytaert, a student at the University of Antwerp, needed a method to communicate with his classmates and friends. He built a small web application so that he and his friends could leave notes for each other. After Dries graduated he moved the software over to drop.org and used it to experiment with new web technologies such as syndication, rating, and distributed authentication. Dries also made the software freely available and licensed it under the GPL. It didn't take long before the software's unique modular structure gained notice and attracted a community of developers and users.

Why is the Name Drupal?

When searching for domain names Dries accidentally misspelled the Dutch word dorp (meaning village) as drop. Accepting his mistake he registered and started to use the drop.org domain. In 2001 the project officially adopted the name Drupal. The Dutch word for drop is druppel, which changed to Drupal (pronounced "droo-puhl") for easier pronunciation.

Who is Drupal?

As of this book's writing, thousands of developers have contributed to the Drupal project. Many have contributed by adding modules and themes, providing support on drupal.org and the Internet Relay Chat (IRC) channels, and participating at meetups, DrupalCamps, and conferences around the world. Drupal has been recorded as having a developer base in almost every country in the world. It truly is an international open source project.

THE DRUPAL COMMUNITY

Drupal is not just software — it's a community! The Drupal community is one of the largest and most supportive communities in the open source world. In fact, the community is so strong that it should be a major deciding factor when you're choosing whether or not to use Drupal. Imagine building a site that requires a certain piece of functionality. You found a module that does 90 percent of the work but isn't quite right. You can decide to code this functionality on your own or you could work with the current module owner to modify and build in the functionality you need. If you code it yourself, you will have to maintain it in perpetuity, but if you work with the current module owner and the community, you are sharing maintenance with the community. The latter result is a more sustainable, longer lasting website and web application.

There is no formal agreement with the community. The agreement is much more tacit. A user providing support one day may expect to receive support another day. Likewise, other module developers will maintain their module if you maintain yours, so that everyone's site can grow and expand.

You do not have to be a developer to participate in the community. There are groups of designers, users, administrators, and others at all levels working together to build great sites. The worst thing you can do when starting out with Drupal is to ignore the community.

WHERE IS THE COMMUNITY?

The Drupal community meets online and, better yet, in the real world. Here are a few places where you can find them:

➤ Forums on Drupal.org (`http://drupal.org/forum`)

  Installation, configuration, migration, translation, upgrading, and module development are just some of the topics covered in the forums. Forums are a great place to start when first learning about Drupal and its community.

➤ IRC channels

  Because it functions in real time, IRC can provide the fastest support, communication, and collaboration. IRC can be accessed using IRC software such as Mirc (Windows), Colloquy (Mac OS X), or xChat (Linux). The server is `irc.freenode.net` and the top three channels are (note that many more exist):

  ➤ `#drupal-support` — Provides general support for installation, configuration, and site administration. When starting out with Drupal this is the channel to use.

  ➤ `#drupal-themes` — Provides support for the creation and modification of Drupal themes (most often on custom themes).

  ➤ `#drupal` — Hosts high-level development discussions on Drupal core and modules. Once you have used Drupal for a while and are developing modules, use this channel to collaborate with other developers.

  You can find more channels and the rules to IRC etiquette at `http://drupal.org/irc`.

➤ Drupal Groups at `http://groups.drupal.org`

  The Drupal Groups website is the Grand Central station of the Drupal community. Like-minded users and developers meet and collaborate on common topics and projects on this website. Regional groups from New York City, Paris, Wisconsin, Peru, and Texas schedule regular meetups. Topic-based groups such as High Performance and Drupal in Education are great for finding others who are in similar situations as you. At the time of this writing, there were over 360 active groups. Find a local group and get involved!

➤ Regional and language-based websites

There are several regional websites that enable users to communicate in their local language or connect within a geographic region. Examples include `drupalchina.org`, `drupaltaiwan.org`, `drupalitalia.org`, and `ladrupal.org`. Language-based communities can be found at `http://drupal.org/language-specific-communities`, and geographic communities can be found at `http://groups.drupal.org/groups`.

➤ Camps and conferences

Drupalcon brings together developers, designers, users, and other Drupal professionals from all over the world. Currently Drupalcon is held once a year in Europe and North America but is quickly expanding to other parts of the world. Check `http://drupalcon.org` for the latest event schedule.

Drupalcon may be the biggest Drupal-based conference, but it is not the only one. DrupalCamps, meetups, and other community-organized events happen daily around the world. Check `http://groups.drupal.org/events` for the most recent events.

PROFESSIONAL SUPPORT

The Drupal community forums and IRC channels are filled with wonderful volunteers working day and night to help each other build and troubleshoot their websites. Although working with the community is the best way to learn Drupal quickly, you may or may not have your questions answered or problems fixed in a timely manner; these channels can require patience. Fortunately the companies of the Drupal community are there to help you.

Drupal is a software application that runs on a server platform, meaning a host. For this reason support packages are divided into three general categories: Drupal-only, server-only, Drupal + server. Many hosting companies provide server-only support and do not support the Drupal software, whereas Drupal professionals may provide Drupal-only support. When purchasing support it is best to ask what is and what is not supported to find the right combination for your project and budget.

You can find a list of hosting companies that specialize in Drupal at `http://drupal.org/hosting` and a list of companies providing support, consulting, and development at `http://drupal.org/services`. To help get you started here a few of the more popular options:

➤ Acquia Drupal

Created by the founder of Drupal, Dries Buytaert, this company provides a distribution of Drupal that bundles some of the most popular contributed modules and a custom Acquia module to connect your website to Acquia's automated monitoring and support network. Because Acquia's distribution is built on top of Drupal, it is 100 percent compatible with all of Drupal's modules, themes, translations and other items, including every exercise in this book. In fact, you can use Acquia's Drupal distribution with this book.

Acquia Drupal can be found at `http://acquia.com`.

➤ Hosted Drupal solutions

A hosted Drupal solution is different from a regular host. A hosted Drupal solution is a host that installs, configures, and fine-tunes Drupal for you. Often these companies will continually monitor your installation for updates to Drupal and its modules. Although Drupal is compatible with many hosts the difference is the specialty in Drupal, which you'll appreciate when your site goes down in the middle of the night. Many other Drupal companies will only host sites they build or help you build. But a hosted Drupal solution takes your site, your code, and your system and makes sure it's rock-solid.

Check out the following hosted Drupal solutions:

- ➤ Hot Drupal (`http://hotdrupal.com`)
- ➤ Workhabit (`http://workhabit.com`)
- ➤ Acquia Drupal (`http://acquia.com`)

For high availability, high traffic websites check out Acquia, Four Kitchen's Pressflow Drupal distribution `http://pressflow.org`, Pantheon, an EC2/Cloud computing distribution (`http://getpantheon.com`), or Firehose at `http://stationindustries.com`.

You can browse many more hosted Drupal solutions or Drupal-compatible web hosts at `http://drupal.org/hosting`.

➤ Drupal professionals

The Drupal community is teeming with dedicated professionals that are ready to help you build your website, provide a bit of custom development, or give you advice. Companies exist for customers with nearly any budget, from the hobbyist to the Fortune 500 enterprise customer. If you choose to hire a professional be sure to inquire about their launch and on-going support options.

You can browse a list of Drupal professionals at `http://drupal.org/services`.

Confused? Don't be. The community is there to help you. If you have questions simply log into IRC channel #drupal-support, ask your question in the Drupal forums at `http://drupal.org/forums`, or pick up your phone and talk to one of the many Drupal professionals listed at `http://drupal.org/services`.

Of course you don't need to hire a professional to build, support, or even host your website. Keep reading to become your own Drupal professional.

THE DRUPAL ASSOCIATION

Standing to the side of the community and directed to support and protect your rights as a community member is the Drupal Association. Originally created to purchase hardware to support the drupal.org infrastructure, the Association quickly became a defender of the Drupal trademark from an erroneous claim against it. This all community- and volunteer-run nonprofit works to ensure that Drupal continues to be free and available for everyone to enjoy. A few of the activities that the Association performs are:

- ➤ Purchasing infrastructure (servers, etc.) that the drupal.org websites use
- ➤ Protecting the Drupal trademark
- ➤ Defending Drupal against GPL infringements
- ➤ Working with the community to organize the annual Drupalcon conference

➤ Redesigning and creating functional upgrades to the drupal.org website

➤ And many other supporting activities!

The Association does not write or maintain the Drupal software or control the content on any of the drupal.org websites. The Drupal project is solely owned and run by the community. As a community-run organization all users are able and encouraged to participate in the Drupal Association to help Drupal continue as one of the greatest open source projects!

The Drupal Association can be found at `http://association.drupal.org`.

SUMMARY

It should be clear that Drupal is much more than great software; it is also a great community. The Drupal software, built upon a modular architecture, allows you to build great websites with relative ease. And the community of users, designers, and developers, as well as great Drupal companies, are all there to help you support your website both now and in the future. You need no special skills or invitation to join the Drupal community, just a bit of time to participate in it. Drupal is more than software. Drupal is you!

Welcome to the community!

In the next chapter you'll explore Drupal's installation process and begin your Drupal journey.

EXERCISES

1. What website can you use to connect with other Drupal users, developers, and professionals with similar interests or located near you?

2. Where can you communicate with other Drupal users or developers in real time over the Internet?

3. What nonprofit organization helps to protect the Drupal community's code from GPL copyright infringement, protects the Drupal trademark, and supports the `http://drupal.org` infrastructure?

4. Drupal is a great CMS, but developers also love it because of its great _____? (three letter acronym)

Answers to the Exercises can be found in the Appendix.

▶ WHAT YOU LEARNED IN THIS CHAPTER

- ➤ Drupal is not only a CMS but also a framework and an API for building great websites and applications.

- ➤ Drupal's modular structure allows you to plug in the pieces you need to build the website of your dreams.

- ➤ Drupal is pronounced "droo-puhl" and comes from the Dutch word for drop.

- ➤ Drupal is not just software. It is a living and thriving community of developers, designers, and users.

- ➤ The Drupal community meets online in the drupal.org forums and IRC channels as well as in-person at locations around the world. Find out more at http://groups.drupal.org.

- ➤ From the hobbyist to the Fortune 500, companies exist at all levels to give you professional service.

- ➤ You are now part of the Drupal community!

2

Installing Drupal

WHAT YOU WILL LEARN IN THIS CHAPTER:

➤ Installing a Drupal website

➤ Installing Drupal using the Acquia Distribution

➤ Exploring the files, folders and structure of Drupal

➤ Reviewing the sites folder

➤ Exploring inheritance and overrides

➤ Overriding Drupal's default theme with one of your own

Now that you have decided to use Drupal the next step is to download and install it. In fact you might have already installed one or more Drupal websites. Even if you have already installed Drupal, a quick read through this chapter will help to clarify the process and help you better understand Drupal.

This chapter reviews the installation process of a single Drupal website. You will explore the files and folders of Drupal to better understand its structure and to learn what you can and cannot modify. You'll explore Drupal's system of inheritance and overrides and learn how to install Drupal in a language other than English.

After completing this chapter you can continue on in the book or skip over to Chapter 18, which covers advanced Drupal installations. Chapter 18 covers installing multiple websites with a single download of Drupal, sharing users between multiple Drupal websites, explores the settings.php file, and how to use CVS to simplify updates to your Drupal website.

GETTING STARTED WITH DRUPAL

The first step to getting started with Drupal is to make sure that you meet all of the requirements. Drupal 7 requires the following:

➤ Web server: Apache 1.3/2.x or IIS 6+

➤ Database server: MySQL 4.1+ or Postgres 7.4+

➤ PHP 5.2 or higher

➤ PHP memory limit that is higher than 16MB (recommended 32MB)

> **NOTE** *Please visit* `http://drupal.org/requirements` *for more details on Drupal's requirements.*

If you are using a web host that advertises compatibility with Drupal, most of these are likely already set up. Be aware however that many hosts use PHP 4 by default and not PHP 5. Often a quick call to their support line is all that is needed to get them to switch your account over to PHP 5.

To use Drupal locally on your computer you will need to install these items separately. I highly recommend the XAMPP software for Windows (`http://apachefriends.org`) or the Mac OS X equivalent, MAMP (`http://mamp.info`). These free software packages provide everything you need in a single download. This chapter and the remainder of the book will assume that you are using XAMPP or MAMP for your Drupal website. The chapters and exercises will work the same if you choose to use a web host instead.

Another option that is great for evaluating Drupal is Acquia's DAMP stack installer (DAMP = Drupal, Apache, MySQL, PHP). Discussed later in this chapter Acquia's stack installer provides a ready-to-go Acquia Drupal website with only a few clicks. You may use the Acquia Drupal distribution to follow along in this book.

INSTALLING A SINGLE DRUPAL WEBSITE

You'll start with a generic installation of Drupal and then take a look at each step and explore how it all works. To begin you need to have a database as well as a username and password with access to this database. If you are working with XAMMP or MAMP, you can use the included `phpMyAdmin application` to create the database as well as a username and password. phpMyAdmin is a popular open source application for managing the databases and users of a MySQL server. If you are using a web host, consult their documentation to determine how to create these items.

The following set of activities will walk you through creating a database and a username/password for use with Drupal. If your host has supplied you with these items you may skip ahead.

TRY IT OUT Creating a Database using phpMyAdmin

This exercise walks you through creating a database for Drupal by using phpMyAdmin included with XAMPP/MAMP.

1. With the XAMPP/MAMP application running navigate to phpMyAdmin with your web server; `http://localhost/phpMyAdmin`.

2. Login to phpMyAdmin using the credentials provided with your XAMPP/MAMP installation.

3. Click Databases from the front menu.

4. At the bottom of the Database page type "drupal" into the Create new database form then click Create as shown in Figure 2-1.

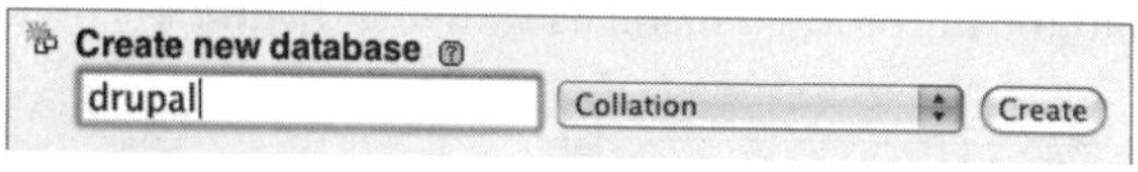

FIGURE 2-1

How It Works

The phpMyAdmin application makes it easy to create a new database on a MySQL database server. If you created your database from a tool provided by your web host or if your web host simply gave you the name of a database the result is the same as creating one with phpMyAdmin. You only need a few items in order to install Drupal.

➤ A Database name

➤ A Database username and password

➤ The type of Database server (MySQL, PostgreSQL, etc.)

➤ The URL of the database server

TRY IT OUT Creating a Username and password for your Database

This exercise walks you through creating a username and password for Drupal.

1. Navigate back to the front page of `phpMyAdmin`, then click Privileges.

2. On the Privileges page click "Add a new user" near the middle of the page, shown in Figure 2-2.

3. Fill in a username and password, as shown in Figure 2-3, then near the bottom right of the screen click Go.

FIGURE 2-2

Do not assign permissions on this page. The permissions listed on this page are global permissions and will apply to all databases.

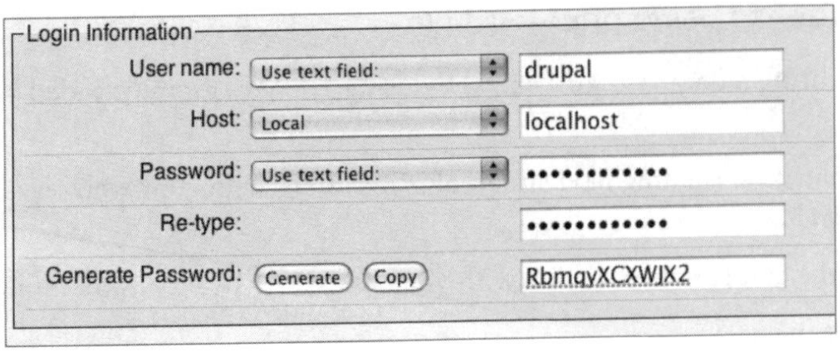

FIGURE 2-3

4. On the resulting page, the user's property page, find the Database-specific privileges form in the middle of the page and choose Drupal from the drop-down menu as shown in Figure 2-4.

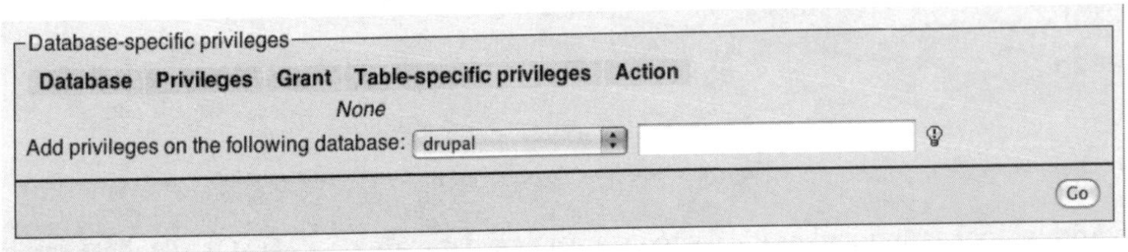

FIGURE 2-4

5. Select the following permissions, as shown in Figure 2-5, SELECT, INSERT, UPDATE, DELETE, CREATE, ALTER, INDEX, DROP, CREATE TEMPORARY TABLES, and LOCK TABLES, then click Go.

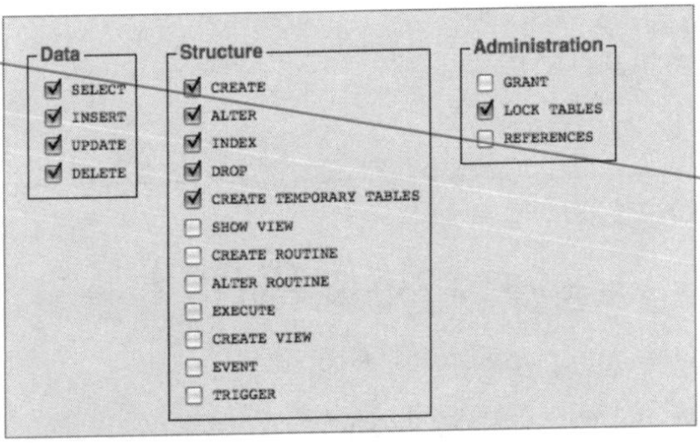

FIGURE 2-5

You now have a new user for your Drupal database and you are ready to move onto installing your first Drupal website.

How It Works

In the previous exercise you created a database and in this exercise you created a user account with access to that database. Web hosts often combine these two actions using the same name for the user and the database but it is important to understand that these are separate items. A user may have access to multiple databases and multiple users may be able to access a single database.

Note that the permissions granted in step 5 (Figure 2-5) are the bare minimum permissions required by Drupal. It is a good security practice to only grant the permissions that are necessary for Drupal. Never use the phpMyAdmin account for your Drupal website as this could cause a security breach.

During the installation you may have noticed an option to create a database for the user as shown in Figure 2-6. This can be useful and will save you an extra step but be aware that it will automatically grant all permissions to the newly created user, which are more than what is necessary for Drupal to function.

INSTALLING DRUPAL

Installing Drupal is as simple as placing the files in the web directory, copying a settings .php file, and then navigating to the Drupal website. Drupal will automatically detect if the database is not configured and prompt you to install your first Drupal website. The site will be configured and ready for use within a few minutes.

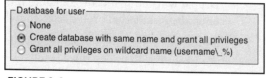

FIGURE 2-6

TRY IT OUT   Installing Drupal

In this exercise you will be installing your first Drupal site.

1. Download the latest version of Drupal from `http://drupal.org` and place it within your web root directory and decompress it. If you are using MAMP (Mac) your web root directory is `/Applications/MAMP/htdocs`, if you are using XAMPP (windows) use a web root directory at `C:\XAMPP\htdocs`.

2. Within the newly created Drupal folder copy the file `/sites/default/default.settings.php` to `/sites/default/settings.php` as shown in Figure 2-7.

3. Open your web browser and navigate to your new Drupal website that is located at `http://localhost/Drupal7`. Substitute the word Drupal 7 for the name of the folder you created in step 1.

4. Drupal will automatically detect that you are installing a new site and ask you to select an Installation profile as shown in Figure 2-8. Select Drupal and then click Save and continue.

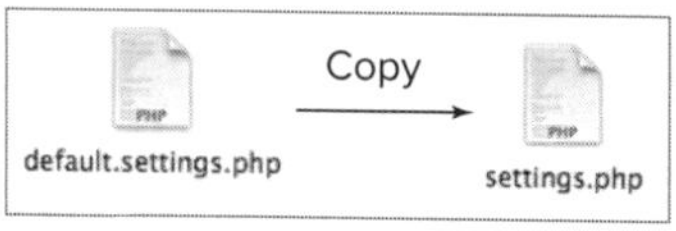

FIGURE 2-7

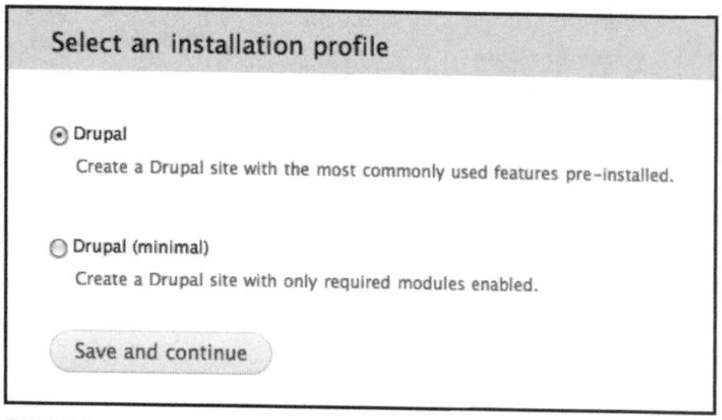

FIGURE 2-8

5. Click the Install Drupal in English link.

> **NOTE** At this point in the installation you may be presented with a Requirements problem screen. Commonly this is due to not copying the settings.php file, described in step 2, or a problem with the file or folder permissions. Simply follow the instructions on this screen to continue.

6. On the Database Configuration screen, type the database name, username, and password that you created earlier as shown in Figure 2-9 then click the Save and continue button located at the bottom of the page.

> Drupal will automatically configure the database as well as a default set of modules based upon the installation profile selected, which in this case is Drupal.

7. After Drupal has configured the database your next step is to configure your basic site information as show in Figure 2-10 as described below.

> ➤ **Site name** — Also known as a site title, this will appear on the header of a web browser.

> ➤ **Site e-mail address** — This address is the sender e-mail address used for all e-mails sent by the website, which includes new user notifications and password requests.

8. Below the Site information, configure the first administrator account as shown in Figure 2-11.

This administrator account is a security sensitive account as it bypasses all permissions available in Drupal, this account has an all-access pass to your website that can not be taken away. Be sure to set a strong password on this account and place it in a safe place.

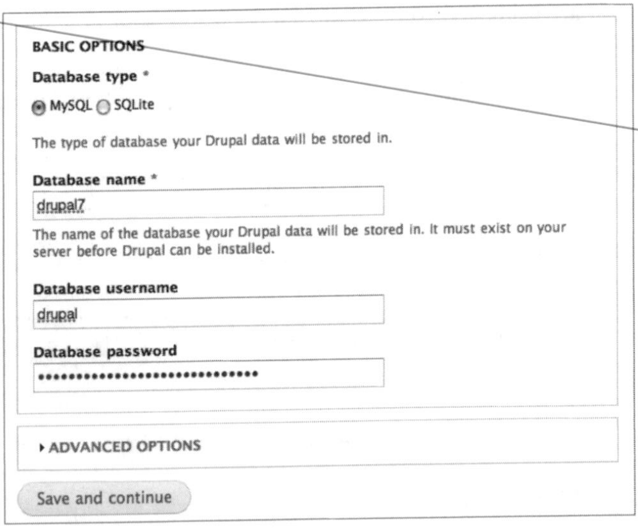

BASIC OPTIONS

Database type *

◉ MySQL ◯ SQLite

The type of database your Drupal data will be stored in.

Database name *

```
drupal7
```

The name of the database your Drupal data will be stored in. It must exist on your server before Drupal can be installed.

Database username

```
drupal
```

Database password

```
••••••••••••••••••••••••••••••
```

▸ ADVANCED OPTIONS

[Save and continue]

FIGURE 2-9

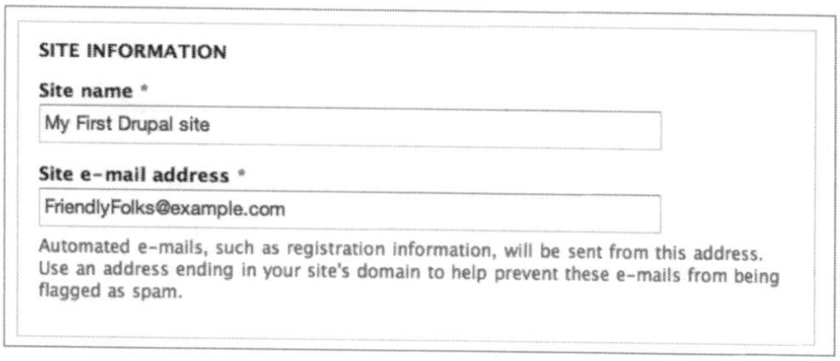

SITE INFORMATION

Site name *

My First Drupal site

Site e-mail address *

FriendlyFolks@example.com

Automated e-mails, such as registration information, will be sent from this address. Use an address ending in your site's domain to help prevent these e-mails from being flagged as spam.

FIGURE 2-10

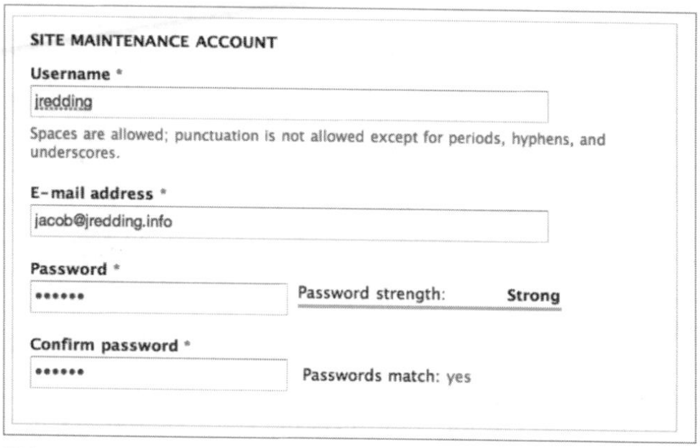

SITE MAINTENANCE ACCOUNT

Username *

jredding

Spaces are allowed; punctuation is not allowed except for periods, hyphens, and underscores.

E-mail address *

jacob@jredding.info

Password *

●●●●●●   Password strength: **Strong**

Confirm password *

●●●●●●   Passwords match: yes

FIGURE 2-11

9. The last settings on Configure site screen are your default site settings. Configure the following server settings:

➤ **Default country** — Defines the country for your site.

➤ **Default time zone** — This setting is the site default for users who have not yet chosen a time zone to match their geography.

➤ **Update notifications** — This keeps your site up-to-date by checking with `drupal.org` for updates to both core and contributed modules.

➤ **Receive e-mail notifications** — When an update is found for your website Drupal will send an e-mail to the e-mail address you entered earlier.

10. Click the Save and Continue button.

Congratulations — you now have a new Drupal website!

How It Works

Drupal's installation automates as much of the process as possible. The database is automatically installed and populated and many of the most commonly used modules are enabled. On the last page you configure your site's name, date and time settings, as well as set the first administrator account. In the next chapter you'll explore how to change these settings after installation.

> **NOTE** Downloads from drupal.org are compressed tar.gz files. If you have SSH command line access to your server you can use the command tar -zxvf drupal-7-x.tar.gz to uncompress and unpack the files. If you only have FTP or SCP access to your server you will need to uncompress and unpack them before uploading by using an application such as WinZip on Windows or by double-clicking the files on a Mac OS X.

Installation Profiles

The first page you encountered during the installation process asked you to choose an installation profile. In a default Drupal package you are presented with two options: Drupal and Drupal (minimal). An install profile is an automated way to install a customized Drupal website that includes themes, modules and a preset configuration. For example you could create an install profile for your local little league teams or the Boy/Girl scout troops in your region.

Read more about Install profiles at `http://drupal.org/project/installation+profiles`.

Installing Drupal in Different Languages

One of the many reasons why people choose the Drupal platform is for its multiple language support. Drupal has been translated into many languages and includes built-in support for Chinese/Japanese/Korean (CJK) character set languages as well as Right to Left (RTL) languages such as Hebrew or Arabic. To install Drupal in a different language first visit `http://drupal.org/project/translations` to download the appropriate translation. Extract the contents into Drupal's root directory and then begin the installation process as normal. You'll be able to select the new language during installation.

Don't worry, however, if you did not select a translation during the installation process. You can install a translation or translate your website at anytime.

ACQUIA'S STACK INSTALLER

Although a repeat of what you have already done in this chapter it would be a crime to not mention Acquia's drop-dead simple Drupal installer. Acquia's stack installs Acquia Drupal + Apache + MySQL + phpMyAdmin. The Stack also known as DAMP provides a very quick and easy local installation of Acquia Drupal. Acquia Drupal is a distribution of Drupal that comes preloaded with selected themes and modules from `http://drupal.org` as well as a few custom items from Acquia to connect in with Acquia's support network. It is 100 percent compatible with Drupal as well as this book but keep in mind that Acquia's default theme might differ from what is shown in this book.

You can download the DAMP stack from Acquia at `http://acquia.com/downloads`. Once downloaded run, the installer and you'll be greeted with a welcome screen as shown in Figure 2-12. The defaults provided are sane so you can whip through the installation accepting the defaults. After the legal agreement you'll be asked where to place the files (Figure 2-13), what ports to use (Figure 2-14), and finally for a username and password (Figure 2-15).

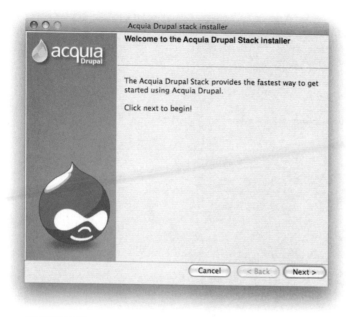

FIGURE 2-12

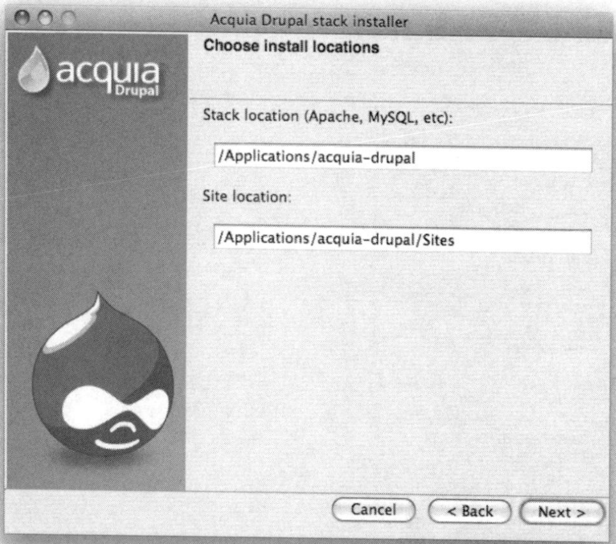

FIGURE 2-13

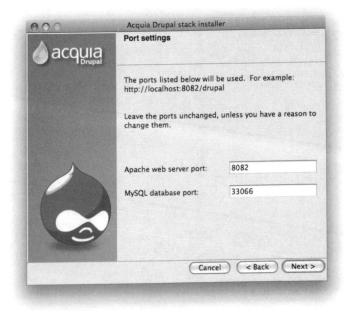

FIGURE 2-14

FIGURE 2-15

Once installed you can stop and start Apache and MySQL (and thus Drupal) by using the provided Acquia control panel as shown in Figure 2-16.

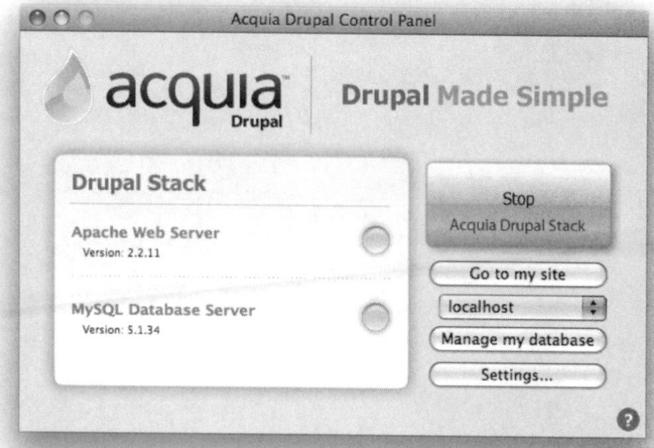

FIGURE 2-16

NOTE *You can use both MAMP/XAMPP and Acquia's DAMP on the same computer because they each use different default port settings for Apache and MySQL. This can allow you to easily explore and compare Drupal and Acquia Drupal. Note that you can also use Acquia Drupal on MAMP/XAMPP.*

Breaking It Down

Now that you have a basic installation of Drupal up and running take a closer look at how it all works. Figure 2-17 shows the default Drupal folder structure. Notice that all folders and files have locks over them except for the Sites folder. These locked folders and files are collectively known as Drupal's core. The Drupal community has agreed upon a Golden Rule known as "Don't hack core." This means that you should never add files, remove files, or modify any files outside of the Sites folder.

Don't Hack Core

Modifying files within the core folders is considered taboo because it makes your site hard to maintain and troubleshoot. Drupal provides an API and a method of overrides allowing you to fully customize your site without the need to modify any core files. The exercise in the Inheritance and Overrides section of this chapter demonstrates how this works. All customizations are to be kept within your site's folder.

Utilizing the Sites folder for all of your customizations is to your advantage. The idea is simple: Whenever an update of Drupal is released, you download, unpack, and replace the default Sites folder with yours. A Sites folder can contain multiple websites, which enables you to update one, two, or hundreds of websites at the same time.

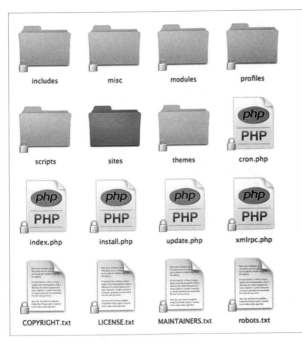

FIGURE 2-17

Core Files

Curiosity killed the cat but it shouldn't kill your website. To help you along with deciphering Drupal here is a brief list and description of the files and folders you should never modify.

➤ **Includes** — This folder contains common functions used in Drupal, such as the bootstrap process, caching, database, and session management. Collectively, this folder contains the central nervous system of the Drupal system. One wrong move in this folder and your entire system can be paralyzed.

➤ **Misc** — This folder is used to store core image files as well as JavaScript files (such as `jquery`).

➤ **Modules** — This folder contains the core modules that make Drupal tick. Additional modules should not be added here — place those in your site's folder.

➤ **Profiles** — This folder contains installation profiles, which are sets of modules, themes, and instructions to automate the installation of Drupal to a preconfigured state. These files are used during Drupal's installation process.

➤ **Scripts** — This folder is used to store a few administrative command-line scripts for cleaning up code, running cron, and testing Drupal core. These files are not part of Drupal's execution cycle but are useful for advanced administration.

➤ **Themes** — This folder contains core themes that are included with the Drupal download to make getting started with Drupal easier. If you'd like to modify a core theme you can copy it to your site's Themes folder or consider creating a sub-theme. The Theming chapter has all the information you need to start customizing your site's theme.

Sites Folder

The Sites folder is where your Drupal website stores database settings, modules, themes, files, and any other items specific to your website. This is also the folder that makes it possible for Drupal to handle multiple websites. The multi-site functionality is handled by bundling each site's information into a unique site folder. When Drupal loads a website it searches Sites for a folder named after the website. For example, if the URL is `http://mysite.com` then Drupal would look for the folder `sites/mysite.com`. If one is not found the Default folder is used.

A much broader example is contained in `settings.php`. Consider the URL `http://www.drupal.org/mysite/test`. The search order would be as follows:

1. `sites/www.drupal.org.mysite.test`

2. `sites/drupal.org.mysite.test`

3. `sites/org.mysite.test`

4. `sites/www.drupal.org.mysite`

5. `sites/drupal.org.mysite`

6. `sites/org.mysite`

7. `sites/www.drupal.org`

8. `sites/drupal.org`

9. `sites/org`

10. `sites/default`

Note that the default folder is last in the list and therefore will only be used when no other folder matches the requested URL. If you will not be hosting multiple sites with Drupal it is appropriate to use the default folder, this is the folder used by Drupal's installation process.

You will also notice an All folder within Sites. This folder contains only modules and themes that are shared amongst all websites. The All folder does not contain a `settings.php` file, because it is not site-specific. If you would like to share a single theme or module across multiple website this is the place to put it.

What's in a Site's Folder?

Figure 2-18 depicts a typical site's folder.

The items within a Site's folder are as follows:

➤   **Themes** — This is a manually created folder that contains downloaded or custom themes specific to a website.

➤   **Modules** — This is a manually created folder that contains downloaded or custom modules specific to a website.

➤   **Files** — This folder is created by Drupal during installation. It contains uploaded images, documents, and other files that are available on the website.

➤ **Private** — New to Drupal 7 this folder will contain any files that are restricted to members only and not available to the general public for download. This is great for sites that require users to login before they can view or download a file.

➤ **settings.php** — This is automatically managed by Drupal's installation and contains database connection settings as well as advanced PHP and Drupal settings. You can read more about this file in the Advanced installation chapter of this book.

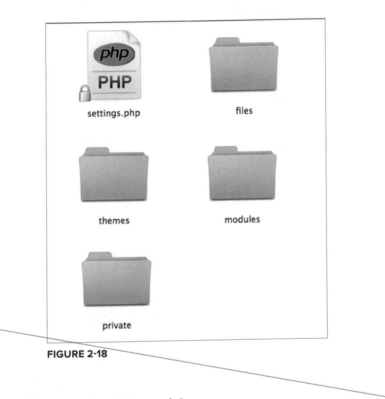

FIGURE 2-18

Inheritance and Overrides

Drupal is designed to give individual websites ultimate control. When Drupal is looking for modules and themes it first searches the core folders, then `sites/all`, and finally the individual site's folder. In Drupal, modules and themes must be uniquely named eliminating the possibility of having two versions of the same module or theme installed.

For example, consider the core theme Garland. If you copy this theme from `/themes/garland` to `/sites/all/themes`, then Drupal will use the version in `/sites/all/themes/garland` and not the core version. If you then copy this to your individual site's folder (ex. `sites/default/themes/garland`), Drupal will use that version instead of the version in `/sites/all/themes`. Ultimately your individual site is the winner. This is how Drupal allows you to customize without having to modify the core files. Remember Drupal's golden rule is "Don't hack core".

TRY IT OUT   Overriding Drupal's Core Garland Theme

Follow this exercise to learn how to override Drupal's default theme with your own theme.

1. Copy the folder `/themes/garland` to `sites/default/themes/garland`.

2. Visit the theme administration page by clicking Administer ⇨ Appearance or selecting Appearance from the top administration bar, shown in Figure 2-19.

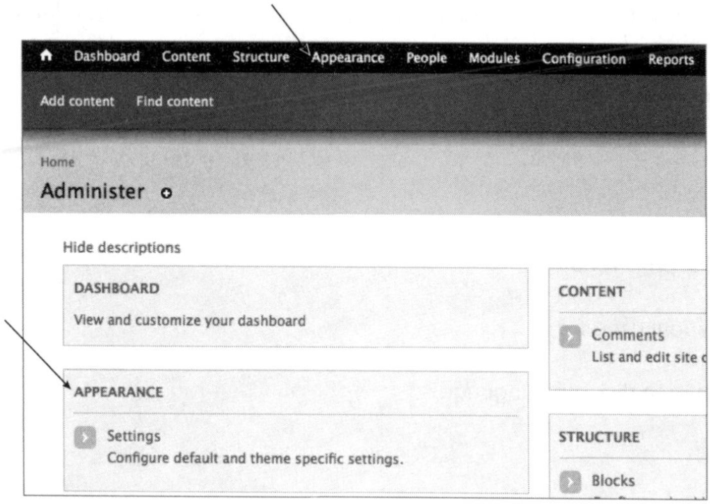

FIGURE 2-19

Verify that the theme location has moved by checking the URL path of the theme's screenshot. You can do this by right clicking on the screenshot and choosing Open/View image. The URL to the image should read `/sites/default/themes/garland/screenshot.png`. This indicates that the core theme is no longer being used.

How It Works

Drupal allows individual websites to override any of Drupal's core modules or themes. When you copied the core theme to your site's folder, Drupal recognized the change and switched to using your copy of the theme instead of the version in core. The hierarchy of inheritance in order of use is:

➤ Your site's folder (for example: `sites/example.com`)

➤ The sites/all folder

➤ Drupal core

A theme in sites/all/themes will override Drupal core and the same theme in your site's folder will override all of them.

SUMMARY

At this point you have walked through a basic installation of Drupal and explored Drupal's folder structure. You learned that Drupal's core includes everything outside of the Sites folder and that these core items should never be modified. This unsaid rule is known as "don't hack core." The remainder of this chapter dives even deeper into the installation of Drupal exploring multi-site installations, sharing users and content between sites, and harnessing the power of settings.php. If this is your first Drupal website it is recommended that you skip this section and revisit it later once you are familiar and comfortable with Drupal.

In the next chapter you will configure your new website by adding content to it, adding users, configuring permissions and adding a contact form so that site visitors can get in touch with you.

EXERCISES

1. What version of PHP does Drupal 7 require?

2. What is the Sites folder in Drupal used for?

3. How do you install Drupal using a different language?

4. What is Core?

5. Why should you not modify Core?

6. If your Drupal site is at the URL `http://www.wiley.com` what is the name of your Site's folder?

7. Why is setting a strong password on the first user account created important?

Answers to the Exercises can be found in the Appendix.

▶ **WHAT YOU LEARNED IN THIS CHAPTER**

➤ Drupal's installer will automatically install and configure your database.

➤ Drupal can be installed in a language other than English by simply downloading a translation from http://drupal.org/project/translation.

➤ Your site's database settings, modules, themes, and uploaded files are stored within the sites folder.

➤ Your site's folder should be named are your site's URL without the http:// (for example: example.com).

➤ If Drupal does not find a folder for your site's URL it will use the settings found in the default folder.

➤ The word "Core" represents all files and folders outside of Drupal's sites folder.

➤ You should never modify Core.

Your First Drupal Website

WHAT YOU WILL LEARN IN THIS CHAPTER:

➤ How to create an Article (news story or blog entry)

➤ How to create an About Us page

➤ Adding the RSS (Syndication) block to your sidebar

➤ Enabling and configuring your Contact Form

➤ Modifying site permissions to create a members-only website

➤ How to create new user accounts

➤ Selecting a new theme

➤ Downloading and installing a new theme

➤ Configuring Cron

Quickly get up to speed on your new Drupal website by following along with this chapter. In this overview, you will create content, enable the contact form, add blocks to the left and right side-bars, and explore your site's permissions. At the end of this chapter, you'll have a fully functional website. You will also have explored the most common administrative functions and settings.

The topics covered in this chapter are done at a high level to quickly introduce you to the various administrative areas of Drupal. Once you feel comfortable with the exercises performed in this chapter, you'll be ready to move on to the subsequent chapters that cover these areas, functions, and settings in greater depth.

ADDING CONTENT

You have a message. You want to be heard, or maybe your client does. In either case, one of your first steps will be to add content to your site. Drupal's default installation provides two types of content: Articles and Pages. Both of these items are known as *nodes* in Drupal's terminology. The concept of a node is important to understand because nodes share a common set of attributes and features. For example, all nodes can receive comments and be available in RSS feeds. Also, other modules can add features to nodes, extending a node's functionality. An example of this is the contributed Fivestar module, which adds the ability to rate content.

In the following two exercises, you'll explore the differences between an Article node and a Page node. One of the first things you should notice is that the Article and Page creation page look nearly identical, with just a few differences. After the exercises, it should be apparent why this is.

TRY IT OUT Creating an Article Entry

This exercise walks you through the steps to create an article entry.

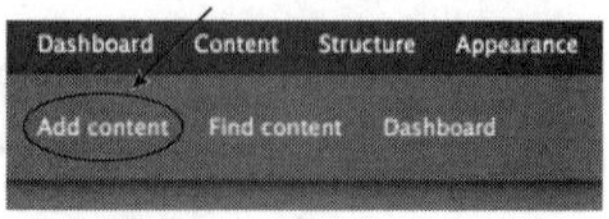

1. Log into your website as an Administrator.

FIGURE 3-1

2. Click Add Content in the top menu as shown in Figure 3-1.

3. Click Article under Add New Content.

4. On the Create Article screen, type in the following information as shown in Figure 3-2:

➤ Title: `Hello world!`

➤ Tags: `first post, introduction`

➤ Body: `Hello world this is my first article. How are you?`

➤ (optional) Upload an image to be shown within the article.

5. Click the Save button at the bottom of the page.

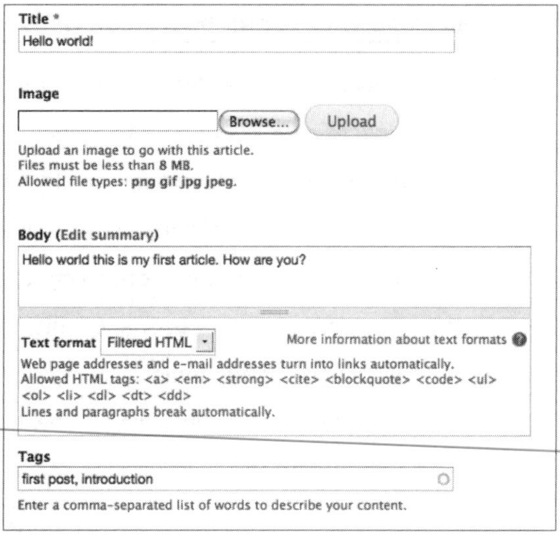

How It Works

An Article is a node type, also known as a content type in Drupal. Articles are typically used

FIGURE 3-2

for news, updates, and other constantly changing content. Articles, like all nodes, are created through the Add Content screen. Every node type shares a common set of attributes, although they vary in their defaults and where and how they appear on the website. This will become more apparent after the second exercise.

TRY IT OUT Creating an About Us Page

This exercise walks you through the steps to create an About Us page.

1. Click Add Content in the top menu as shown previously in Figure 3-1.

2. Click Page under Add New Content.

3. On the Create Page screen, type in the following information as shown in Figure 3-3:

➤ Title: `About Us`

➤ Body: `As a new website we provide our readers with excellent and fresh content.`

4. Click the Save button at the bottom of the page.

How It Works

Pages are the static pieces of your website that are typically reserved for site necessities such as About Us, Directions, or a copyright notice. The Add Content screen is similar to that of an Article, because both items are nodes.

Title *
About Us

Body (Edit summary)
As a new website we provide our readers with excellent and fresh content.

FIGURE 3-3

Differences between Articles and Pages

If you compare the Create Article screen (Figure 3-2) and the Create Page screen (Figure 3-3), the first difference you will see is that an Article has an image upload form and allows for Tags (categorization). Pages only have a title and body. This is simply a Drupal default. A Page can be modified to have Tags or its own categorization system, pages can also accept images or file uploads. You will learn how to modify these settings in Chapter 6, "Content."

Now compare the lower portion of each screen as shown in Figure 3-4 and Figure 3-5.

Create Article

Title *
Hello World!

Tags
first post, introduction,

Enter a comma-separated list of words to describe your content.

Full text (Edit summary)
Hello world this is my first article. How are you?

Menu settings Not in menu	**Menu link title**
Revision information No revision	The link text corresponding to this item that should appear in the menu. Leave blank if you do not wish to add this post to the menu.
URL path settings No alias	
Comment settings Open	**Parent item** <Main menu>
Authoring information By jredding	The maximum depth for an item and all its children is fixed at 9. Some menu items may not be available as parents if selecting them would exceed this limit.
Publishing options Published, Promoted to front page	**Weight** 0 Optional. In the menu, the heavier items will sink and the lighter items will be positioned nearer the top.

Save   Preview

FIGURE 3-4

Create Page

Title *
About us

Full text (Edit summary)
As a new website we provide our readers will excellent and fresh content.

Menu settings Not in menu	**Menu link title**
Revision information No revision	The link text corresponding to this item that should appear in the menu. Leave blank if you do not wish to add this post to the menu.
URL path settings No alias	
Comment settings Closed	**Parent item** <Main menu>
Authoring information By jredding	The maximum depth for an item and all its children is fixed at 9. Some menu items may not be available as parents if selecting them would exceed this limit.
Publishing options Published	**Weight** 0 Optional. In the menu, the heavier items will sink and the lighter items will be positioned nearer the top.

Save   Preview

FIGURE 3-5

Note that the Comment settings on an Article are set to Open, whereas the settings for a Page are set to Closed. The Publishing options also differ, with Article set to Published and Promoted to Front Page, and Page set only to Published. These defaults reflect how you want the respective pieces of content to appear on your site.

Nodes Are Content

If it hasn't become clear by now that Articles and Pages are both based on nodes, let it resound in your memory forever. Understanding the concept of a node is important when you want to add new types of content such as events, images, or videos to your website. In Drupal, you look for the functionality that you want to add, instead of a module that provides you with a specific content type. For example, the embedded media field module (`http://drupal.org/project/emfield`) adds the ability to insert Flickr photos, YouTube videos, Last.fm music, and many other forms of media directly into any node (i.e., content type) on your website. In Chapter 6, you will learn more about nodes, including how to modify their defaults and create your own content types.

Content Summaries

When creating your first article, you may have noticed the Edit Summary button (shown previously in Figure 3-1). A Summary is also known as a teaser, the part of the node that is shown on your site's front-page. It is also used in your site's RSS feeds, tempting the user to click the Read More link. Clicking this link will display a new Summary box above the Full Text box as shown in Figure 3-6.

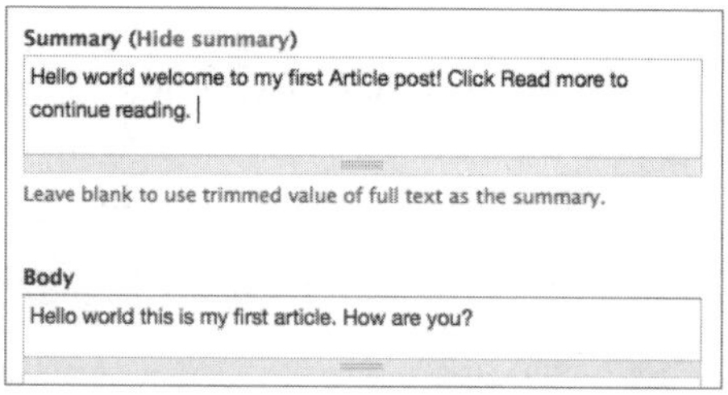

If you do not enter a Summary, the default set for each content type will automatically create one for you. By default, the summary is the first 600 characters of your Article.

FIGURE 3-6

Modifying the Defaults

So far this chapter has stated that you can change the defaults for nearly everything. But where should you start?

You can modify the defaults for each content type at Structure ⇨ Content Types, as shown in Figure 3-7. Select Edit to the right of the content type you want to modify.

The following screen will display all the default options available for that content type. For example, you can configure the length of the summary under Display Settings, as shown in Figure 3-8.

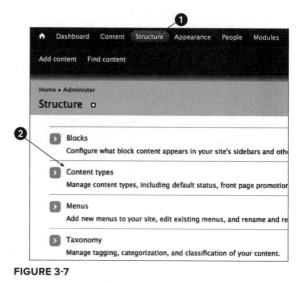

FIGURE 3-7

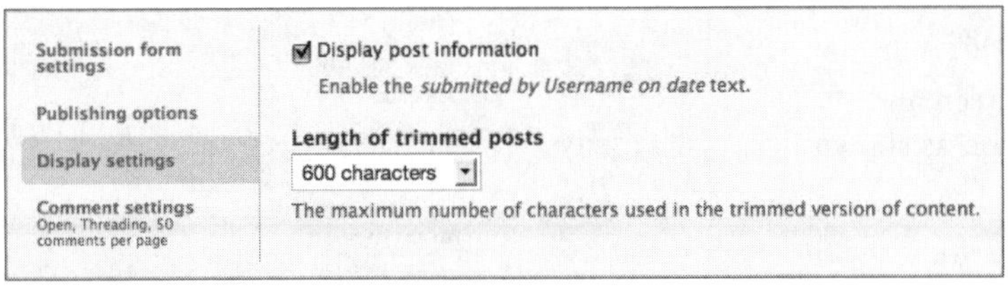
Submission form settings
Publishing options
Display settings
Comment settings
Open, Threading, 50 comments per page
Display post information
Enable the submitted by Username on date text.
Length of trimmed posts
600 characters
The maximum number of characters used in the trimmed version of content.

FIGURE 3-8

The default options and instructions on creating custom content types are covered in Chapter 6

> ***NOTE*** *Changes to the Display Settings will take effect on all new content created after the setting change, in other words this setting is not retroactive.*

MODIFYING YOUR MENUS

Now that you have an About Us page, follow the next exercise to place a link in your top menu (Figure 3-9), to provide easy access for your site's visitors.

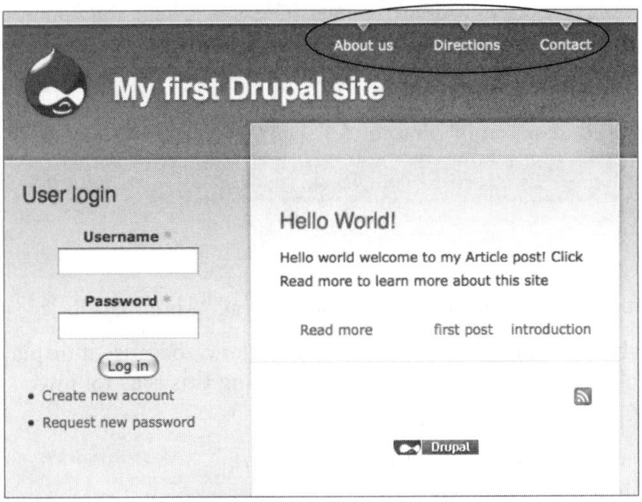
About us
Directions
Contact
My first Drupal site
User login
Username
Password
Log in
Create new account
Request new password
Hello World!
Hello world welcome to my Article post! Click Read more to learn more about this site
Read more
first post
introduction
Drupal

FIGURE 3-9

TRY IT OUT Modifying the Top Menu

This exercise walks you through adding the About Us page to the Administration menu.

1. Navigate to the About Us page you created in the previous Try It Out exercise. If you cannot locate this page, click Content in the upper-left corner.

2. Click Edit on the About Us page.

3. Scroll to the bottom of the screen and enter the following information as shown in Figure 3-10:

➤ Menu Link Title: **About us**

➤ Parent Item: Select <Main menu>

➤ Weight: Select 0

4. Click the Save button.

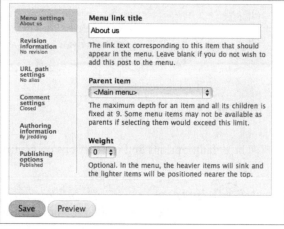

How It Works

To save you time, Drupal provides a method to directly add a Menu link when you create or edit the node. You can also add new

FIGURE 3-10

Menu items by clicking Structure in the Administration menu. Go to Administer ➪ Menus (under Structures) ➪ Add Link next to the respective menu (in this case, the Main menu).

A WORD ON MENUS

Drupal contains several menus by default, and you can create many more. As you have already seen, the Main menu is the menu displayed at the top of your site. Menus are also provided for administration, management, site navigation, and user account links. These are all explored in-depth in Chapter 5, "Administration— Blocks, Menus and Themes."

Review the following items shown in Figure 3-10:

Menu Link Title: The text that will appear to the site visitor (such as "About Us").

Parent Items: This drop-down box can be a bit confusing at first glance because it displays every menu and every menu link on your site. The key to deciphering this is as follows:

➤ *<menu name>*: The < > indicates that this item is a separate and independent menu. Figure 3-11 displays two menus: Main Menu and Management.

➤ -- : Two dashes indicate that the item is located underneath a menu. Each subsequent two dashes indicate than the item is a child of a parent. Article and Page are children of Add New Content and are located within the Management menu.

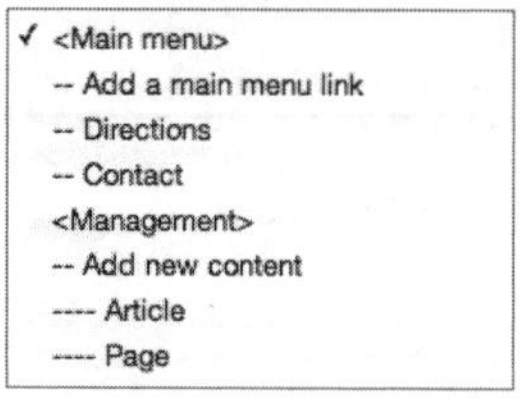

```
✓ <Main menu>
-- Add a main menu link
-- Directions
-- Contact
<Management>
-- Add new content
---- Article
---- Page
```

FIGURE 3-11

Weight: Every link in a menu is first ordered by its weight and then alphabetically. Links with lower numbers are listed higher than the higher (heavier) numbers. To reorganize your links, just use the drag and drop interface in the Menu administration page.

ADDING BLOCKS TO YOUR WEBSITE

Blocks are the pieces of content that typically flank the left or right side of a website. Recent comments, latest users, a navigational menu, advertisements, or a box of RSS feeds are all examples of blocks. Figure 3-12 displays two blocks in the left sidebar region of Drupal's default theme: Search and User Login.

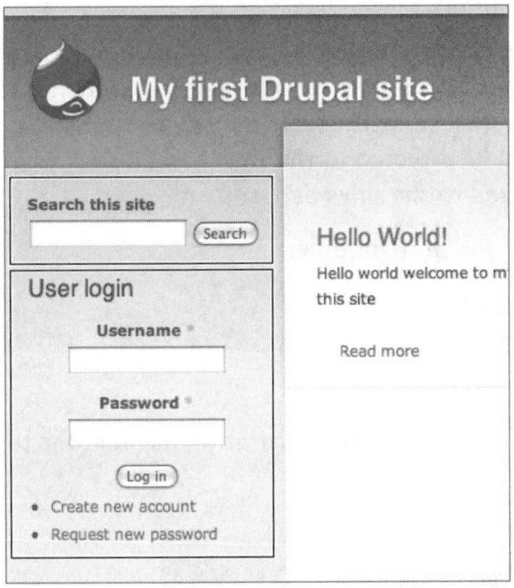

FIGURE 3-12

TRY IT OUT   **Enabling the Recent Comments and Syndication Blocks**

In this exercise, you enable a few useful blocks and explore the concept of Drupal's regions and blocks.

1.   Log into your website as an Administrator. Click Structure in the Administration menu at the top of the screen, and then click Blocks.

2.   Drag the Recent Comments block from the Disabled section to underneath the Right Sidebar. Do this by clicking and holding the cross symbol to the left of the block's name.

3.   Drag the Syndicate block from the Disabled section to underneath the Right Sidebar. Figure 3-13 displays how this should look.

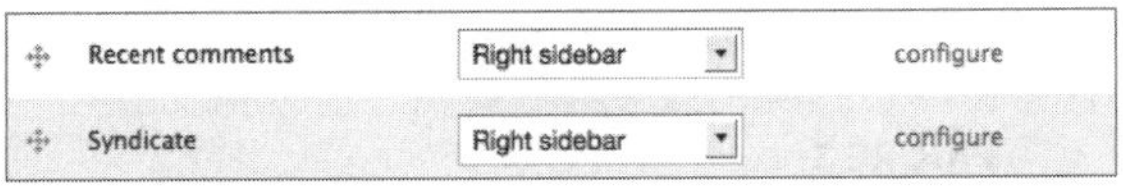

FIGURE 3-13

4.   Click the Save button at the bottom of the page.

How It Works

Blocks are placed within Regions on your site. A Region is defined by the site's theme, so each website may not have the same regions. Drupal's default regions are Header, Footer, Left Sidebar, Right Sidebar, Content, Highlighted Content, and Help. When you are on the Blocks admin page, you can see that each region is highlighted by a dotted border box with the name of the region (see Figure 3-14).

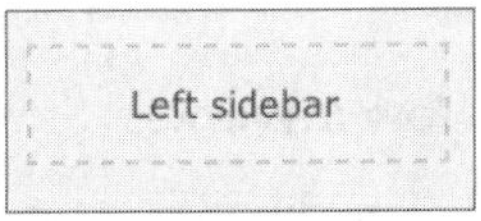

Left sidebar

FIGURE 3-14

Dragging the blocks from the Disabled area to the Right Sidebar region enables the block and sets its order. You can reorder blocks by simply dragging them up or down on the screen. The order in which they appear on the Block admin page is the order in which they will appear to the user.

GETTING IN CONTACT

Allowing site visitors to contact you is an essential piece of any website. Drupal's Contact module (which is disabled by default) provides a quick and simple mechanism for site users to contact one or a group of e-mail addresses. Users may also select from a list to direct their inquiry to the right person. For example, inquires to "Report a bad link" could be directed to the site's webmaster, whereas inquires to "Contact us about advertising" can be directed to the sales department.

In the following exercises, you enable and configure the Contact module.

TRY IT OUT   **Enabling the Contact Module**

In this first exercise, you enable the Contact module.

1. Log into your website as an Administrator. Click Modules in the Administration menu at the top of the screen, as shown in Figure 3-15.

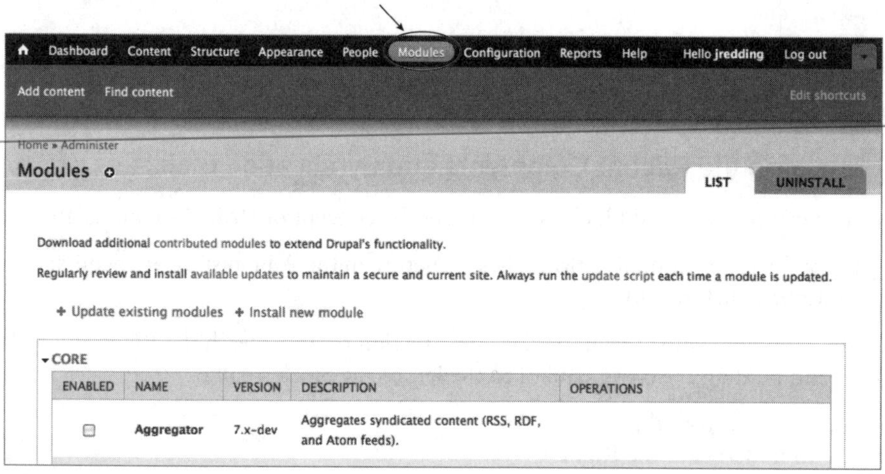

FIGURE 3-15

2. Under the Core module category, enable the Contact module by checking the box to the left of the name.

3. Click the Save Configuration button at the bottom of the page.

How It Works

Before the Contact module can be used, it must be enabled. Enabling a module in Drupal is as simple as checking the box next to it and saving the page.

TRY IT OUT Configuring the Contact Module

In this exercise, you configure the `Contact` module to send e-mails to your sales team.

1. Log into your website as an Administrator. Click Structure in the Administration menu at the top of the screen, and then click Contact Form.
2. Click Add Category at the top of the page.
3. Fill in the following information as shown in Figure 3-16:
   - Category: **`Advertise with us`**
   - Recipients: **`sales@localhost.com`** (better yet, enter your own e-mail address)
   - Auto-reply: **`Thank you for contacting our sales department. We will respond to your inquiry as soon as possible.`**
   - Weight: Select 0
   - Selected: Select Yes
4. Click the Save button at the bottom of the page. Your Contact form settings should look similar to Figure 3-17.

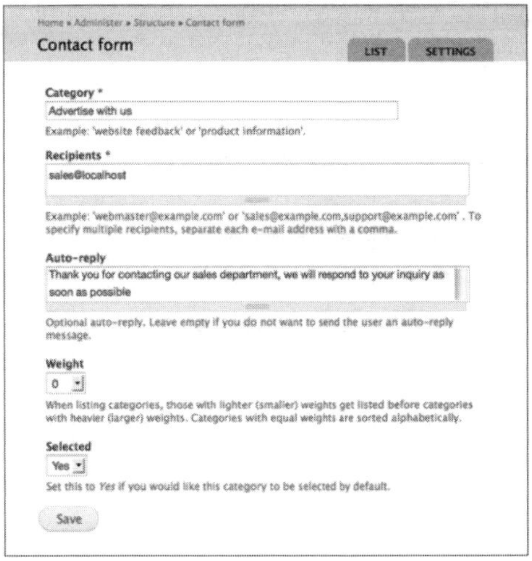

FIGURE 3-16

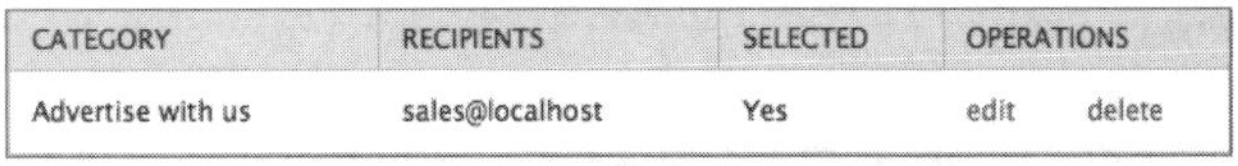

CATEGORY	RECIPIENTS	SELECTED	OPERATIONS	
Advertise with us	sales@localhost	Yes	edit	delete

FIGURE 3-17

TRY IT OUT Testing the Contact Module

Now that the `Contact` module is enabled and configured, you'll test it out by sending a sample message.

1. Navigate your browser to `http://localhost/contact`.
2. Fill out the Contact form similarly to Figure 3-18 and click the Send E-mail button.

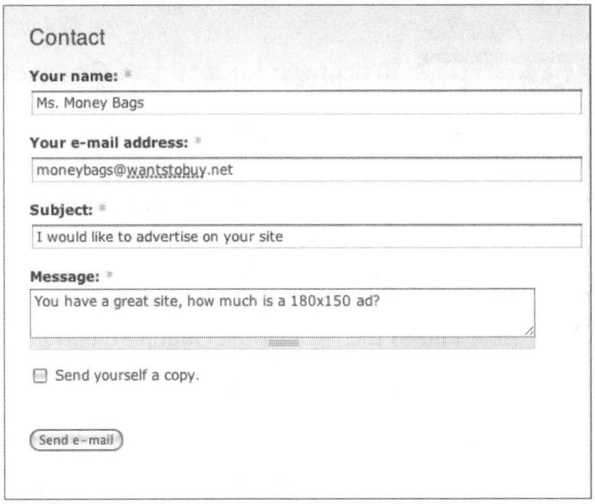

FIGURE 3-18

How It Works

The Contact form works by creating a simple e-mail (with a subject and message) that is redirected to one or more e-mail addresses. You might have noticed that the Category name you filled out in the Contact form settings does not appear on the contact form located at `http://localhost/contact`. If only one category exists, Drupal presents a single form and ignores the Category name and the selected setting. When multiple categories are enabled, the form looks like Figure 3-19. Note that the addition of the Category drop-down list is not included if only a single category exists (as was the case in Figure 3-18).

FIGURE 3-19

Adding the Contact Form to Your Main Menu

The Contact form makes it easy for site visitors to contact you. Unfortunately, you have to make its presence known. The Contact form adds a new menu entry but it is disabled by default. Follow the next exercise to place a link to the Contact form in your Main menu right next to the About Us link.

TRY IT OUT   Adding a Link to the Contact Form in the Menu

In this exercise, you make it easier for your site visitors to contact you by placing a link in your site's Main menu.

1. Log into your website as an Administrator. Click Structure in the Administration menu at the top of the screen, and then click Menus.

2. Click List Links to the right of the Navigation menu.

3. Click Edit to the right of the Contact menu link.

4. Modify the form with the following information as shown in Figure 3-20:

➤ Menu Link Title: `Contact`

➤ Description: `Contact us to advertise on our site or to report a problem.`

➤ Enabled: Check this box

➤ Parent Link: Select <Main menu>

➤ Weight: Select 1

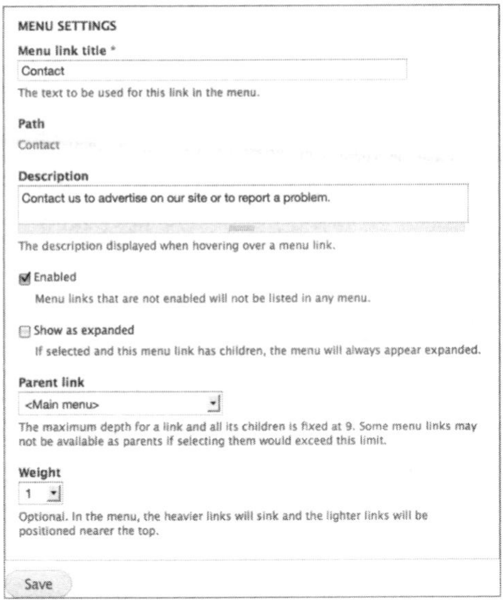

FIGURE 3-20

> **NOTE** The Weight is 1, placing it to the right of the About Us link, which has a weight of 0.

5. Click the Save button at the bottom of the page.

How It Works

The Contact module automatically creates a link to the Contact form and places it in the Navigation menu. The Navigation menu is a catchall menu for automatically created links provided by the modules you enabled. You need to move links from this menu into one of the visible menus — in this case, the Main menu.

Summing Up the Contact Form

Drupal's Contact module is a great way to quickly add a simple contact form to your website. Multiple categories can be used to send inquires to different groups of people. The auto-reply feature is also nice to let site visitors know that their e-mail has been received. Once enabled the contact form is always available at http:// localhost/contact. However, the menu link is not enabled by default, so be sure to add a link to the contact form in your menu.

> **NOTE** Want a little more complexity on your Contact form? Try out the Webform contributed module available at http://drupal.org/project/webform.

EXPLORING YOUR SITE'S PERMISSIONS

Permissions in Drupal are similar to having a bouncer at a fancy nightclub: users are denied access unless explicitly allowed. This creates a default secure environment but requires you to remember to grant access when you have enabled a new feature, added a new content type, or enabled a new module. To underscore this point, the `Contact` module you just enabled is available only to site administers and not to anonymous users. Obviously, this is a problem. Follow the next exercise to enable the Contact form for all site visitors.

TRY IT OUT   Enabling Anonymous Users to Use the Contact Form

After you complete this exercise, anonymous users will be able to use the Contact form to send you an e-mail.

1.   Log into your website as an Administrator. Navigate to Configuration, and then click Permissions as shown in Figure 3-21.

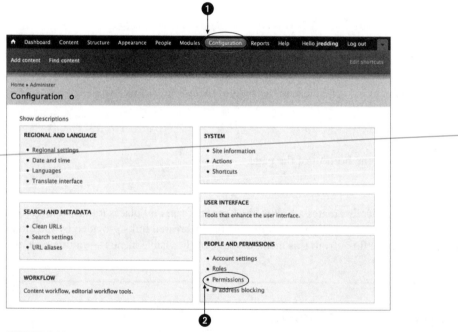

FIGURE 3-21

2.   Grant the anonymous user access to the site-wide contact form by checking the corresponding box in the Anonymous User column, as shown in Figure 3-22.

PERMISSION	ANONYMOUS USER	AUTHENTICATED USER	ADMINISTRATOR
Contact			
Administer site–wide contact form	☐	☐	☑
Access site–wide contact form	☑	☐	☑

FIGURE 3-22

3. Click the Save Permissions button at the bottom of the screen.

How It Works

When the `Contact` module was enabled, it added a few new permissions but did not automatically grant them to any users except for Administrators. In this exercise, you allowed Anonymous Users access by explicitly granting it to them. Drupal assumes everyone is denied access unless they have a specific permission allowing them access. There are no permissions that deny access, just permissions that grant access.

CREATING A MEMBERS-ONLY SITE

To further explore Drupal's permissions, you will now modify your site to be a members-only site, restricting access to all of your content unless the user has an account and is logged in. In Drupal, there are many ways of doing this, but for your initial approach, you'll begin with the simplest method. In later chapters, you'll explore more complex and robust methods.

Exploring Roles

A Drupal website may have hundreds or thousands of users. Drupal grants permissions to a *role* to which users are added. Permissions are not granted to individual users. A user that is a member of multiple roles will be granted a cumulative set of permissions. Examples of roles include titles such as Administrators, Content Editors, Paid Members, and Article Writers.

For Members Only

In the following exercises, you'll create your members-only site by first revoking access to the Anonymous User role, and then granting access to users with an account.

TRY IT OUT   Restricting Access to Your Site's Content

After completing this exercise, anonymous users will be denied access to your site's content.

1. Log into your website as an Administrator. Navigate to Configuration, and then click Permissions as shown in Figure 3-21.

2. Uncheck the Access Content permission for the Anonymous User role (left-most) located under the Node group, as shown in Figure 3-23.

PERMISSION	ANONYMOUS USER	AUTHENTICATED USER	ADMINISTRATOR
Node			
Administer content types	☐	☐	☑
Administer nodes	☐	☐	☑
Access content	☐	☑	☑

FIGURE 3-23

3. Click the Save button at the bottom of the page.

4. Test the permission by logging out of your website. You should see an `Access denied` message. If not, verify the permissions.

How It Works

Users who are not logged in are part of the Anonymous User role. By default, the Anonymous User role is granted access to your site's content. Content is defined as all nodes, which includes Articles and Pages. When you revoked (unchecked) this permission in this exercise, anonymous users were instantly denied access to your content.

Access Denied? Create an Account

At this point, users are being redirected to an Access Denied page that is not very informative. In the following exercise, you will make your site a little more user-friendly by redirecting users to the registration screen so that they can sign up for access to your site.

TRY IT OUT | **Directing Denied Users to the Create Account Page**

In this exercise, you direct users to the Create New Account page.

1. Log into your website as an Administrator. Navigate to Configuration, and then click Site Information (under System) as shown in Figure 3-24.

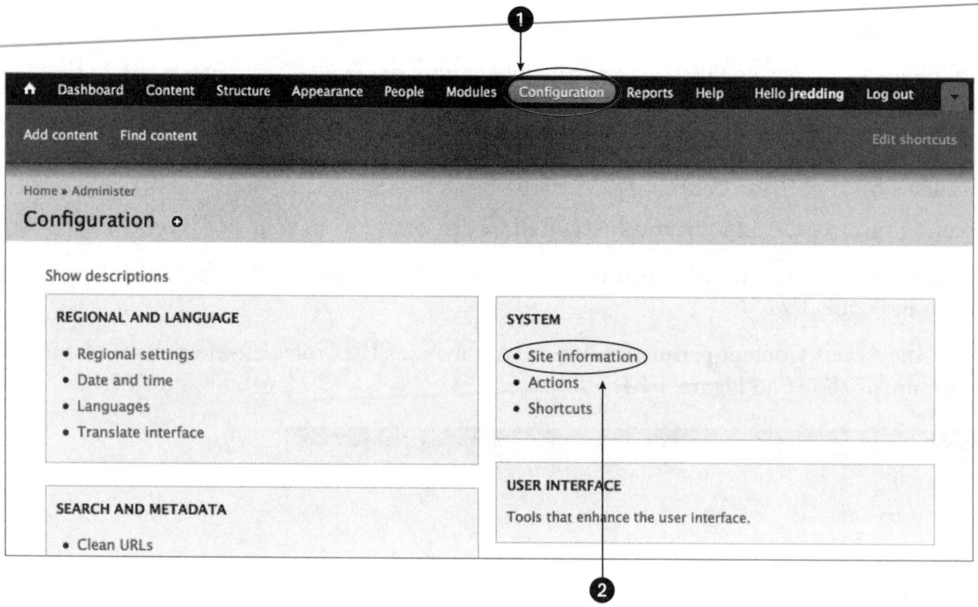

FIGURE 3-24

2. In the URL entry box under Default 403 (Access Denied) Page, type **user/register** as shown in Figure 3-25.

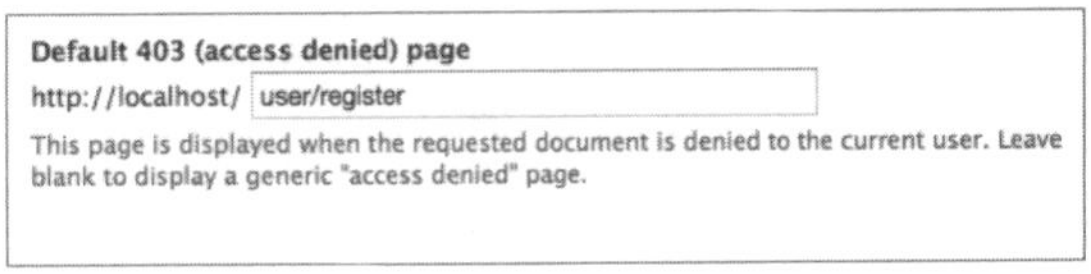

> Default 403 (access denied) page
> http://localhost/ [user/register]
> This page is displayed when the requested document is denied to the current user. Leave blank to display a generic "access denied" page.

FIGURE 3-25

3. Click Save Configuration at the bottom of the screen.

How It Works

Whenever a user encounters a page they are restricted from, Drupal will look at the value in the Default 403 (Access Denied) Page setting and redirect the user to that page. This could be any valid URL within Drupal that the user has access to. In this exercise, you redirected users to the Create Account page located at `user/register`, but you could have led them to the Contact page by entering **contact** in the URL box instead.

Lonely? Add a Few Users

At this point, you have a great members-only website. But you are the only member, making for a rather lonely website. In the next exercise, you will create another user so that you have some company on the website.

TRY IT OUT Creating a New User

In this exercise, you create a new user account to share access to your site.

1. Log into your website as an Administrator. Click People in the Administrator menu at the top of the screen, as shown in Figure 3-26.

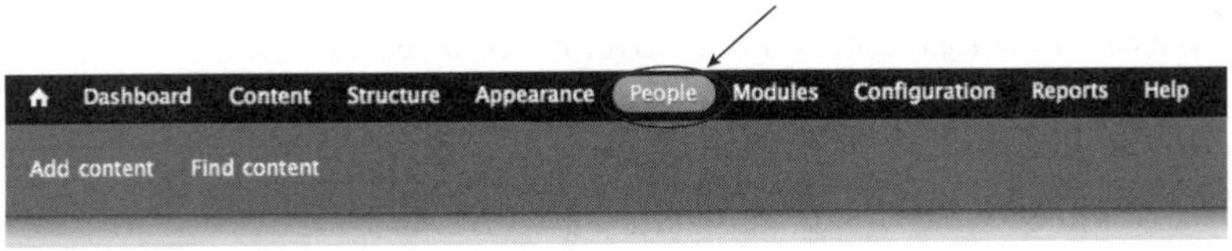

🏠 Dashboard Content Structure Appearance (People) Modules Configuration Reports Help

Add content   Find content

FIGURE 3-26

2. Click Add User at the top of the People management page as shown in Figure 3-27.

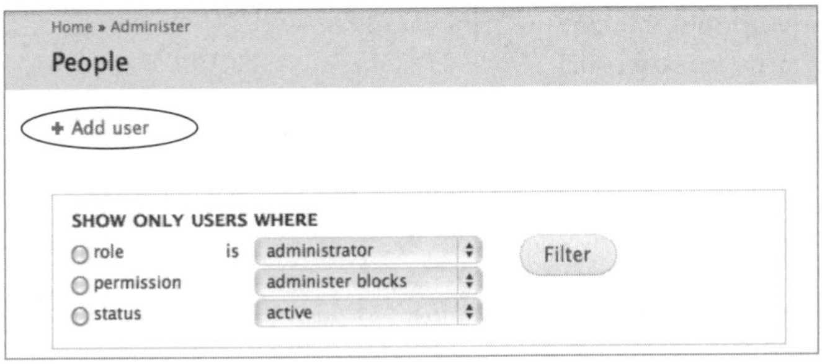

Home » Administer
People

(➕ Add user)

SHOW ONLY USERS WHERE
- ○ role   is [administrator ▾]   [Filter]
- ○ permission   [administer blocks ▾]
- ○ status   [active ▾]

FIGURE 3-27

3. Fill in the following information as shown in Figure 3-28:

➤ Username: `a_friend`

➤ E-mail Address: `afriend@localhost` (better yet, enter your e-mail address)

➤ Password: `123!@#qweASD` (Note that Drupal provides password recommendations as shown in Figure 3-28. Users should strive to match the criteria for a strong password.)

➤ **Status:** Click the Active radio button

➤ **Notify User Of New Account:** Check this box

ACCOUNT INFORMATION

Username *

`a_friend`

Spaces are allowed; punctuation is not allowed except for periods, hyphens, apostrophes, and underscores.

E-mail address *

`afriend@localhost`

A valid e-mail address. All e-mails from the system will be sent to this address. The e-mail address is not made public and will only be used if you wish to receive a new password or wish to receive certain news or notifications by e-mail.

Password *   Confirm password *

●●●●●●   ●●●●●●

Password strength: ▓▓▓▓ Passwords match: yes

Provide a password for the new account in both fields.

Status

○ Blocked

◉ Active

Roles

☑ authenticated user

☐ administrator

☑ Notify user of new account

[Create new account]

FIGURE 3-28

How It Works

Adding a new user account is as simple as filling out a username, an e-mail address, and a password. Because you are an Administrator, you can also assign the user to a role and have Drupal send out a notification e-mail. The notification e-mail welcomes the user to the site, includes their username and password, and links to your site so that they can get started right away. You can modify this notification message at Configuration ➪ Account Settings (located under People and Permissions).

Blocked Accounts

User accounts can be set to one of two states: Blocked or Active. Blocking an account is useful if you think the account may not be used right away, if you want to temporarily ban a user, or if a user decides to leave but may return in the future. Blocking an account leaves everything intact but prevents the user from logging in. Blocking takes effect immediately.

A Word on Strong Passwords

To enhance security, Drupal introduced a password strength meter. This meter watches a user's proposed password and evaluates it based upon the criteria outlined in Figure 3-29. Each time a user makes a suggestion, it is removed from the list and the password meter increases. You should encourage each of your users to create strong passwords.

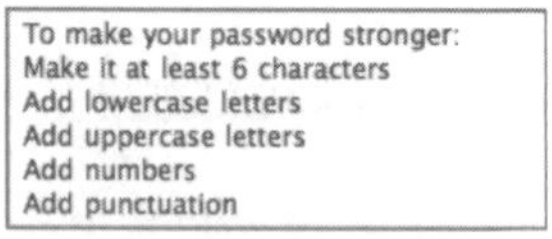

To make your password stronger:
Make it at least 6 characters
Add lowercase letters
Add uppercase letters
Add numbers
Add punctuation

FIGURE 3-29

> **NOTE** *The LoginToboggan contributed module (*`http://drupal.org/project/`*`logintoboggan`*) provides many useful login-related features, such as increasing the flexibility of how users log in and offering a direct login when a user is denied access.*

Wrapping up Users and Permissions

Although you have only made a basic members-only website, the exercises should have helped you understand how Drupal assigns permissions and how you can use them effectively. User accounts are assigned into roles, and roles are granted permissions. Drupal uses only grant-based permissions, defaulting to deny access to any user without an explicitly granted permission. When enabling new modules, be sure to check the permissions to ensure that the correct roles have the access they need. Remember that if you are logged in as the first user account created (the Site Maintenance account), you automatically bypass all permissions.

In Chapter 7, "User Management," you'll explore users and permissions in-depth, including site e-mails, user profiles, and the consequences if you delete an account.

TIME FOR A NEW LOOK

Now that you have spent a bit of time on your site, you are probably tired of looking at the same blue screen. A site that looks like every other site isn't very exciting, nor does it express your (or your client's) personality. Themes are the answer you are looking for. A theme controls exactly how a Drupal site looks and feels. The placement of text, blocks, menus, and comments along with their colors, backgrounds, fonts, and images are all controlled by the theme.

Follow the next exercise to modify the colors of your default theme.

TRY IT OUT | **Modify your theme's settings**

After you complete this exercise, your site will be draped in new colors.

1. Logged into your website as an Administrator, select Appearance from the Administration menu at the top of the screen as shown in Figure 3-30.

FIGURE 3-30

2. Edit the Settings of the Garland theme, shown in Figure 3-31.

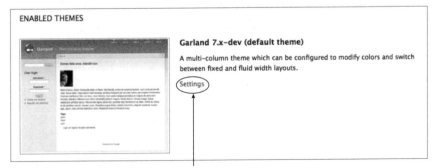

FIGURE 3-31

3. Select Belgian Chocolate as the Color set, as shown in Figure 3-32, then click Save configuration.

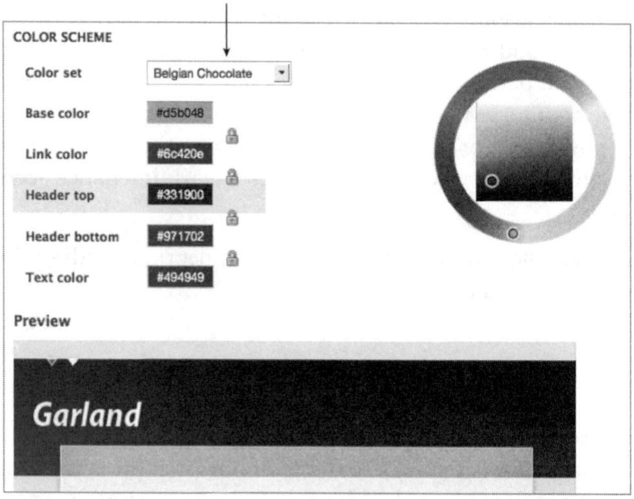

FIGURE 3-32

How It Works

Before you can set up a new theme, it must first be enabled for use, and then set as the default.

Time for Something Different

As you probably noticed, Minnelli and Garland are almost identical themes, except that that Minnelli is set to a fixed width instead of fluid width. The last exercise didn't exactly work miracles. The default themes that are shipped with Drupal only give you an idea of what a theme can do. In fact, the Stark theme is specifically designed to give you a foundation on which to build your theme. By itself, it's plain and very boring.

What if you don't want to build a theme? Fortunately, the Drupal community has created numerous themes that are freely available for download at `http://drupal.org/project/themes`. In the next exercise, you'll choose one of these themes and install it.

TRY IT OUT Downloading and Installing a New Theme

After completing this exercise, you will understand how to download and install themes from `http://drupal.org` and other Drupal theme sites.

1. Point your browser to `http://drupal.org/project/themes` and select a theme that is compatible with Drupal 7. A great example is the Mulpo theme available at `http://drupal.org/project/mulpo`.

2. Download the 7.x version of the theme to your site's themes directory located at `sites/default/themes`. Uncompress the `.tar.gz` file. If the `themes` directory does not exist, simply create it. Your `sites` directory should look like Figure 3-33.

default.settings.php

files

private

settings.php

themes

mulpo

mulpo-7.x-1.0.tar.gz

FIGURE 3-33

3. Enable your new theme as demonstrated in the previous exercise.

How It Works

As described in Chapter 2, "Installing Drupal," new themes are placed within your site's respective folder (`sites/default/themes`). Alternatively, you can place themes in the `sites/all/themes` folder, making them available to every site in a multi-site configuration (described in Chapter 18, "Advanced Drupal Installations"). There is no limitation to the number of themes that can be installed on a Drupal installation, so go wild trying out new themes. After you decide to not use a theme, simply disable and delete it.

You learn more about themes in Chapter 5, "Theming." When you are ready to create your own theme, jump to Chapter 13.

CRON

Before a site can go live, its Cron jobs must be set up and verified to be running well. Cron (short for chronograph) is based on the UNIX system that automates tasks called *cron jobs*. Drupal's cron system helps to keep your site active, up to date, and running optimally. For example, if your site aggregates data from RSS feeds, the data will be updated only if cron is run. More importantly, Drupal uses cron to check for new releases, updates your site's search index, and clears out old data such as caches and log files. If this data is not removed, Drupal may run slower over time.

Running Drupal's cron is a straightforward process. Follow the next exercise to learn how.

TRY IT OUT   **Running Drupal's Cron**

This exercise walks you through running Drupal's cron manually.

1. Log into your website as an Administrator. From the Administration menu at the top of the screen, choose Reports ➪ Status Report. Or if you're on the Administration page, select Status Report, as shown in Figure 3-34.

2. Locate the Cron Maintenance Tasks line as shown in Figure 3-35.

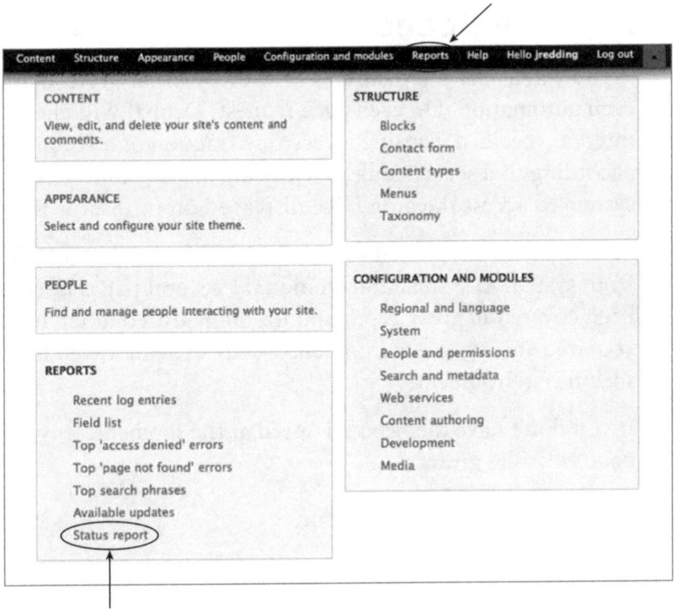

FIGURE 3-34

> ✓ **Cron maintenance tasks**   Last run 4 sec ago
>
> You can run cron manually.
> To run cron from outside the site, go to http://localhost/cron.php?cron_key=ceafe92a328d10123071d4ff7622c5d6

FIGURE 3-35

3.   Click the `run cron manually` link.

How It Works

When the `run cron manually` link is clicked, Drupal kicks off a process that informs all modules that cron is being run. These modules can then choose to run a process during this cron cycle or wait until the next one. Drupal also checks the log files and cache records for old or stale data and flushes it out if necessary.

Manually? No Way! Let the Computer Do It

Of course a site isn't very automated if you have to manually run cron every day. By default, Drupal will run cron jobs every three hours if your site is accessed at least once every three hours. You can modify this interval at Configuration ⇨ Site Information ⇨ Automatically Run Cron, as shown in Figure 3-36. From drop-down menu under Automatically Run Cron, you can select an interval; the choices range from 1 Hour to 1 Week to Never.

> **Automatically run cron**
>
> 3 hours ⬍
>
> When enabled, the site will check whether cron has been run in the configured interval and automatically run it upon the next page request. For more information visit the status report page.

FIGURE 3-36

A Need for Speed

If you run a very busy site and need every bit of performance, it is best to disable Drupal's built-in cron automation. On each page request, Drupal will check to see if cron has been run within the interval specified, causing a very tiny fraction of a second difference in speed. You can run cron according to a set schedule, such as during the non-peak hours of your site, by utilizing an external system to access the cron URL displayed on the Status Report (shown previously in Figure 3-35).

Setting up an automated cron task is a very simple procedure that unfortunately can vary wildly from system to system and would take several pages to cover properly. Fortunately, this topic has been covered in great depth and for many different environments at `http://drupal.org/cron`. If you are running an environment locally or with a web host, chances are that this page covers your specific environment.

If you don't have the need for speed at the moment, leave Drupal's defaults alone and revisit them once your site grows.

SUMMARY

In this chapter, you explored many of the most commonly used areas of Drupal in a high-level overview. The basics of nodes (Articles and Pages), blocks, users, and user permissions were covered as well as exploring several parts of Drupal's backend administrative interface. At this point, you are probably bursting with questions and want to explore some of these areas more in-depth. If you are, then you're in luck. The next several chapters explore the nuances of all these topics.

The next few chapters build upon the topics introduced in this chapter and Chapter 2, leaving no Drupal administration stone unturned. In Chapter 4, "Administration—Configuration, Modules, and Reporting," you'll revisit the foundation settings of your website, including its name, where your files are stored, how your frontpage appears, and other foundation items. These items should to be set up correctly before you launch to avoid any potential issues.

EXERCISES

1. What is the difference between the Article and Page content types?

2. How does the contact form use categories?

3. What is cron?

4. How can you deny access to your site's content?

5. What is a theme?

Answers to the Exercises can be found in the Appendix.

▶ **WHAT YOU LEARNED IN THIS CHAPTER**

➤ Creating content

➤ Modify your site's settings, including:

   ➤ Site name

   ➤ Default frontpage

   ➤ Site slogan, Page Not Found message, and the Access Denied page

➤ Modifying your theme's settings

➤ Configure cron's frequency

4

Administration — Configuration, Modules, and Reporting

WHAT YOU WILL LEARN IN THIS CHAPTER:

➤ Configuring your site's title, e-mail address, and slogan

➤ Modifying the Page not found (404) and Access denied (403) error messages

➤ Adjusting the date/time formats and default server time

➤ Enabling Clean URLs

➤ Reviewing and adding text formats

➤ Setting your public and private file system preferences

➤ Maintenance mode (taking your site temporarily offline)

In the previous chapter you configured your new website in a rapid-fire fashion making the rounds to the most common administrative functions. Now it is time to get down and dirty exploring these administrative areas in depth over the next four chapters. In this chapter you will explore the foundation settings of your website that should be configured before you put your site into production to avoid any potential issues down the road. Although Drupal's defaults are sane, reviewing and understanding them will help you create a top notch website.

For example, your site's name is used when people bookmark your website or view your RSS feeds. If you decide to change the name later, those who have already bookmarked your website will not receive the update.

Drupal's administration is separated into six main sections: Content, Appearance, People, Structure, Configuration, Modules, and Reports. Additional modules you install will expand these sections with more settings. The following four chapters dissect each of these areas helping you to understand what is there now and what might be there in the future. Your journey begins by reviewing Configuration and Reports.

CONFIGURATION

Once you have visited all the fun parts of your site covered in Chapter 3 you should find yourself at Configuration and modules (Figure 4-1). Here you tweak and fine-tune your website, polishing it and preparing for prime-time.

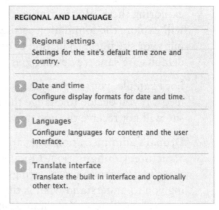

FIGURE 4-1

Many of these settings you will only visit once but a solid understanding of them will help you keep a top-notch and well-running site.

Start by visiting the settings that were automatically configured during installation. This is your chance to undo any of the gnarly mistakes you might have made. Navigate to Configuration by clicking its title in the top administration bar, shown in Figure 4-1.

Home » Administer

Configuration ⚬

Hide descriptions

REGIONAL AND LANGUAGE

▷ Regional settings
Settings for the site's default time zone and country.

▷ Date and time
Configure display formats for date and time.

▷ Languages
Configure languages for content and the user interface.

▷ Translate interface
Translate the built in interface and optionally other text.

SYSTEM

▷ Site information
Change basic site name, e-mail address, slogan, default front page, number of posts per page, error pages and cron.

▷ Actions
Manage the actions defined for your site.

▷ Shortcuts
List the available shortcut sets and switch between them.

USER INTERFACE
Tools that enhance the user interface.

SEARCH AND METADATA

▷ Clean URLs
Enable or disable clean URLs for your site.

▷ Search settings
Configure relevance settings for search and other indexing options.

▷ URL aliases
Change your site's URL paths by aliasing them.

PEOPLE AND PERMISSIONS

▷ Account settings
Configure default behavior of users, including registration requirements, e-mails, and user pictures.

▷ Roles
List, edit, or add user roles.

FIGURE 4-2

As you can see in Figure 4-2 this area is also divided into several subcategories most of which are self-explanatory. Keep in mind that these subcategories will expand when new modules are installed/enabled. Knowing and understanding these categories will help you to find the configuration for the new modules you install. For example enabling the core Locale module (used for site translation) will add Languages and Translate interface to the Regional and Language subcategory as shown in Figure 4-3.

REGIONAL AND LANGUAGE

▷ Regional settings
Settings for the site's default time zone and country.

▷ Date and time
Configure display formats for date and time.

▷ Languages
Configure languages for content and the user interface.

▷ Translate interface
Translate the built in interface and optionally other text.

FIGURE 4-3

SYSTEM — SITE INFORMATION

Site information is located under System and consists of many of the items that you configured during installation.

The most commonly adjusted item in this area is the default frontpage setting. Top to bottom, the settings are as follows:

➤ **Site name** — The site's name appears in the title bar of the web browser to the right of the vertical line (|) (shown in figure 4-4) and is often displayed on the top of every web page (shown in figure 4-5). Keep in mind that this name is used when users bookmark your site and is often displayed in search engine results. You'll want to set it to the right name before going live with your site.

➤ **E-mail Address** — All automatically generated e-mails (new user welcome e-mail, password resets, etc.) from your Drupal site will use this e-mail address for the "from" and "reply-to" addresses. Commonly this is set to noreply@example.com or mr-roboto@example.com.

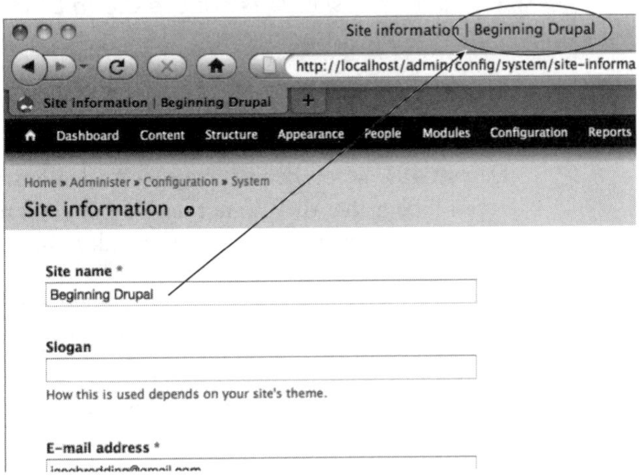

FIGURE 4-4

FIGURE 4-5

➤ **Slogan** — A one-line statement about your website. Often displayed just after or below the site title at the top of the page as shown in Figure 4-5, although its placement (if it appears at all) is determined by the theme. Drupal's initial theme (Garland) does not display the Slogan by default, enable it at Appearance ⇨ Garland: Configure.

> **NOTE** *The theme decides where and how the site name and slogan appear. Some themes may not implement either of the items.*

➤ **Default Frontpage** — What appears on the frontpage. By default this is node, which means that it will chronologically display the summaries of the latest published nodes with the

Promoted to frontpage publishing option. Control the number of posts with the Number of posts on frontpage setting directly below.

The frontpage can be changed to any accessible path in Drupal. For example, if you would like the article at `http://localhost/node/1` to be the frontpage then you enter `node/1` here. Drupal does not do a redirect so the URL would remain `http://localhost`. Keep in mind that standard Drupal permissions still apply so if the anonymous user does not have permission to this page they will be denied (as demonstrated in Chapter 3).

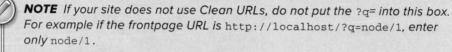

> **NOTE** If your site does not use Clean URLs, do not put the `?q=` into this box. For example if the frontpage URL is `http://localhost/?q=node/1`, enter only `node/1`.

➤ **Default 403 (access denied) page** — As demonstrated in Chapter 3, when a user attempts to access a page that they do not have permission to this page is displayed. Set it in the same manner as the frontpage setting. If left blank a simple "Access denied" message is displayed.

> **NOTE** The Login Toboggan module (`http://drupal.org/project/logintoboggan`) can be used to redirect a user to the login page when they encounter an access-denied page. After logging in they will be redirected to the originally requested page.

➤ **Default 404 (not found) page** — When a user comes across a page that does not exist, this page is displayed. If left blank, a very basic "Page not found" page is displayed.

> **NOTE** The search 404 module (`http://drupal.org/project/search404`) can be used to replace your 404 error pages with a search page for the keywords found in the URL. With a little luck your user will be redirected to the page they wanted instead of seeing an error message.

➤ **Automatically run cron** — Discussed in Chapter 3, this setting instructs Drupal how often to run the Cron jobs.

> **NOTE** In previous versions of Drupal a footer message (ex. Copyright) was set on this page. In Drupal 7 footers have been implemented as blocks and are available at Structure ➪ Blocks and discussed in Chapter 5. "Blocks, Menus, and Themes."

System — Actions

Actions are responses to a triggering event such as sending an e-mail to an author when a comment has been posted on their article or an e-mail to a site administrator when a new user has registered. Actions and the required triggers are discussed in Chapter 10, "Triggers, Actions, Workflow and Rules."

Regional and Language — Settings

Across from your Site information is another important area, Regional and Language — Settings and Date and time. Change your site's default country and time zone in the Regional Settings and modify how the date and time appears in Date and time, shown in Figure 4-6. Modify these to reflect the format most famil-

FIGURE 4-6

iar with your site visitors. The Medium format is used for content and comment posts. Long and short formats may be used by contributed modules or by customizing your theme (see Chapter 13, "Theming").

Time Zone Issues

To overcome time zones issues, Drupal stores dates and time using a UNIX epoch timestamp, which is based on Universal Time Coordinated (UTC) and dynamically translates these times to either the

site's default time zone or the user's personal time zone. This means that if you are located in New York but your site's default time is set to Los Angeles, posts will appear to have been posted three hours earlier. Change your user profile to override the site default.

The site default is configured here as shown in Figure 4-7. Provide users the ability to specify their time zone by checking the User may set their own time zone box, shown in Figure 4-7.

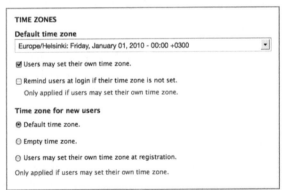

FIGURE 4-7

Time Zones When Creating Content

When you post content on your site, the date and time is based on your account setting. If you are a frequent traveler this may not be the correct time zone for your posting. In order to be reflective of the actual time you posted, you can either adjust your account's setting before writing the article or modify the recorded time manually. Users with the `Administer nodes` permission can modify the time zone of any post within the `Authoring information` of the node as shown in Figure 4-8.

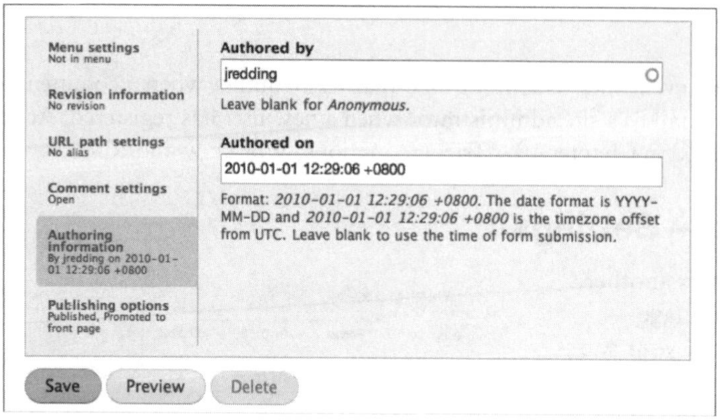

FIGURE 4-8

The time zone is set to the far right of the time using the offset from UTC. Figure 4-8 demonstrates a post written on January 1st, 2010 at 12:29 pm UTC+8 (China).

Although this is a great option for recording the actual time the post was written, the fact that it requires the `Administer nodes` permission does not make it a good option for a site with more than a handful of trustworthy users.

Regional and Language — Translate

If you are running a multi-lingual site you may see the options shown in Figure 4-9 provided by the Locale module. These items provide options for translating or importing a translation of your site. Chapter 12, "Internationalization" covers how to create and manage a multi-lingual site.

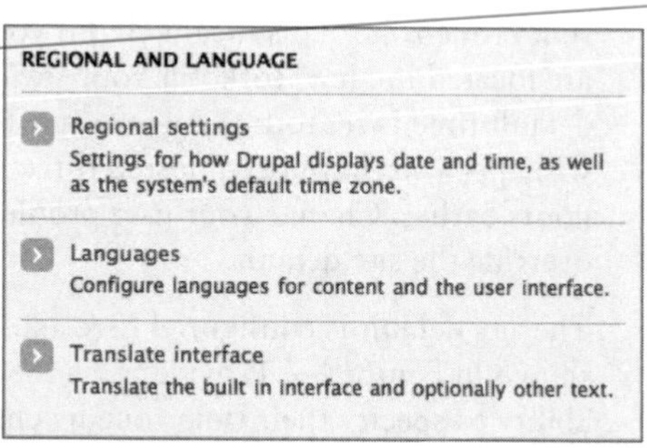

FIGURE 4-9

Media

Before you begin to upload content to your website you should take a few minutes to learn where that content is going and how it is being treated. During installation Drupal automatically created a few directories for your files. Is this the best place for your data? Quite possibly but it pays to understand where your valuable images, videos, and documents are being stored.

Begin with the File system settings shown in Figure 4-10; Configuration and modules ➪ Media ➪ File system.

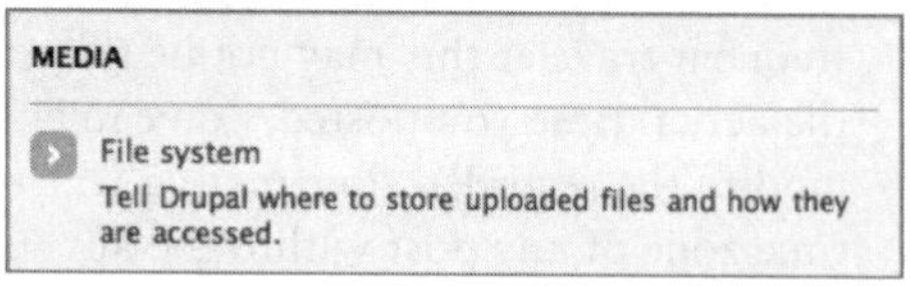

FIGURE 4-10

Media — File System

This section defines where your images, videos, documents and other uploads will be stored. Although Drupal defines a few defaults to get your site up and running you should take a few minutes to understand how and where Drupal stores your files.

Public vs. Private Files

The first two settings on this page are the locations of your public files and your private files as shown in Figure 4-11. Public files are considered files that are accessible to the entirety of the Internet for unlimited, unrestricted download. Private files are the exact opposite. Downloading private files may require a user to log in or a user might be restricted to only a single download or a limited number of downloads in a day. Whatever your requirement, a private file is guarded by Drupal whereas a public file is not.

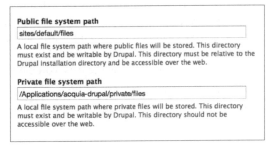

Public file system path

sites/default/files

A local file system path where public files will be stored. This directory must exist and be writable by Drupal. This directory must be relative to the Drupal installation directory and be accessible over the web.

Private file system path

/Applications/acquia-drupal/private/files

A local file system path where private files will be stored. This directory must exist and be writable by Drupal. This directory should not be accessible over the web.

FIGURE 4-11

Consider the following example of a file named `budget.pdf`. Using the Public or Private file type, the following URLs would be used respectively:

➤ **Public** — `http://localhost/sites/default/files/budget.pdf`

➤ **Private** — `http://localhost/system/files/budget.pdf`

The difference between the two is immense. The public file URL points directly to the file on your server's hard drive. To reduce system resources, Drupal will not be informed of this request and the file will be sent directly to the client. In comparison, the Private file is preceded by `/system/files`, a pseudo path that Drupal manages. When this file is requested Drupal starts up and enforces the security restrictions on the file.

The Private File Tax

As with any middle-tier there is a tax for this interception and it is the performance of your server. Public files are dramatically faster than private files. Fortunately in Drupal 7 you can host both public and private files side by side. You will learn more about this in Chapter 6, "Content."

Put Your Files on Lock Down

If you decide to use private files, be sure to change the private file system directory shown in Figure 4-11 to a location outside of your web server directory. Drupal will prevent direct access to this directory by using a `.htaccess` file, but a poorly configured server could ignore this directive allowing access by a crafty visitor. Placing these files in a location that is not web accessible will force Drupal to always retrieve them, thwarting those crafty site visitors.

Set It and Forget It

Modifying the public or private file system directories after files have been uploaded will not move any of the existing files although it will modify the URLs to those files. This will cause every file uploaded before the system directory change to result in a 404 page not found until you manually move the files to the new directory.

Temporary Directory

The temporary directory is necessary for Drupal to function and is periodically cleaned out by the modules that use it. Proper cleaning of the temp directory requires a properly running Cron so be sure that it is functioning correctly (Chapter 3). The temporary directory should not be placed in a folder that is accessible over the Web as several modules use this space to temporarily store uploaded files. Crafty visitors may search for any sensitive or forgotten files in the temporary folder as an attempt to circumvent any security you have.

This is often set to /tmp or to a directory located with private file's parent directory. Figure 4-12 shows MAMP's temporary directory.

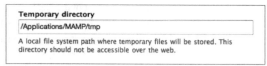

FIGURE 4-12

> ✎ **NOTE** *The file field discussed in Chapter 6, "Content" can be used to implement custom file upload fields on content types. These custom fields may use different public and private settings, folder settings, allowed file types, and maximum file size settings.*

PHP File Size Limitations

The maximum file size users can upload is ultimately limited by the amount of memory allocated to Drupal and a maximum PHP upload size. Fortunately it is easy to increase the size. Unfortunately each server and web host has a different method. A few of the most common methods are outlined here in preferred order. You will only need to use one of the methods.

settings.php

Within your site's settings.php file find the lines that begin with `ini_set` (approximately line 220). These lines modify your PHP configuration. Enter the following information to increase your maximum file size to 40MB; adjust as necessary, maintaining a memory limit that exceeds the file size.

```
ini_set('memory_limit', '60M');
ini_set('post_max_size', '40M');
ini_set('upload_max_filesize', '40M');
```

.htaccess

The `.htaccess` file is a hidden file located within Drupal's root directory; this file contains instructions for the Apache web server. Find the line that reads `<IfModule mod_php5.c>` (approximately line 33) directly below enter the following.

```
php_value memory_limit 60M
php_value post_max_size 40M
php_value upload_max_filesize 40M
```

php.ini or php5.ini

If the above items fail you may have to add a custom php.ini or php5.ini file to your web root. Although not complicated each web host has a different method making it impossible to clearly outline in a book.

Fortunately the Drupal community has already covered this is great depth over at `http://drupal.org/node/147534`.

Media — Image Toolkit

You won't see many options here. The first line informs you which toolkit is installed and if it is working correctly; by default this is the GD toolkit. Here you can adjust the image quality of all processed images (resized, scaled, etc.) as shown in Figure 4-13. The setting is used for all installed modules that do not explicitly use a separate processing engine, which is very unusual. User profile pictures are resized according to this quality setting.

The GD toolkit is a fast and simple toolkit that satisfies the needs of most websites, so it shouldn't need to be changed. However you might consider switching to improve image quality and performance. The ImageMagick toolkit is said to produce higher quality images as well as reduced CPU processing time. Of course technology changes rapidly so be sure to check the latest status on GD, ImageMagick, or any other image toolkit you want to try.

Information on GD toolkit can be found at `http://php.net/gd`. You can read more about ImageMagick at `http://imagemagick.org`.

> **Image toolkit**
>
> The GD toolkit is installed and working properly.
>
> **JPEG quality**
>
> `75` %
>
> Define the image quality for JPEG manipulations. Ranges from 0 to 100. Higher values mean better image quality but bigger files.
>
> Save configuration

FIGURE 4-13

People and Permissions

This section encapsulates all user related settings and functions including user registration requirements, account e-mails, profile settings, and user permissions. This section is covered in Chapter 7, "Users."

Web Services

Web Services (Figure 4-14) include items such as your RSS feed, the import of external RSS feeds, RDF, Atom, XML services, and other potential site APIs you enable from third-party modules.

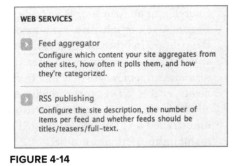

> **WEB SERVICES**
>
> Feed aggregator
> Configure which content your site aggregates from other sites, how often it polls them, and how they're categorized.
>
> RSS publishing
> Configure the site description, the number of items per feed and whether feeds should be titles/teasers/full-text.

FIGURE 4-14

Web Services — RSS Publishing

Really simply syndication (RSS) is so easy to setup in Drupal that you don't even have to lift a finger. Drupal automatically creates a site-wide RSS feed for you at `http://localhost/rss.xml` and additional custom RSS feeds can be created by using taxonomy, discussed in Chapter 8, "Taxonomy." The settings here, shown in Figure 4-15, will affect every RSS feed on your site with the exception of those created by contributed modules such as views (`http://drupal.org/project/views`). By default your RSS feed will mimic your site's frontpage with the setting of Titles plus teaser.

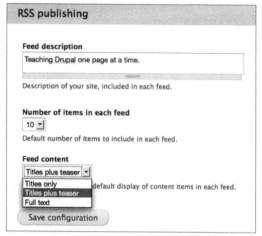

FIGURE 4-15

> **NOTE** The Views module (`http://drupal.org/project/views`) can create custom RSS feeds based upon a very flexible set of criteria. RSS feeds for comments? Yup! Custom feeds per author? Of course! Flip over to Chapter 11, "Views" to learn more.

Web Services — Feed Aggregator

When you want to display content from external sites on your site, the Aggregator module is what you need. Included with core but disabled by default, flip over to Configuration and modules ⇨ Modules and enable it under the Core section. Once enabled it will appear as a setting under Web Services as shown in Figure 4-14.

Content Authoring — Text Formats

Text formats are the front line defense that not only keeps your site free of malicious code but also keeps it looking good. Text formats can remove, add, modify, or interpret the text entered into an Article or Page body, comment (Figure 4-16), or into any text area on your Drupal site. In other words it can modify the appearance of your content. For example, text formats can remove curse words from comments, enable WIKI syntax in blog entries, or add BBCode to your forum. You can set up unrestricted text formats for trusted users and maintain restrictions for others.

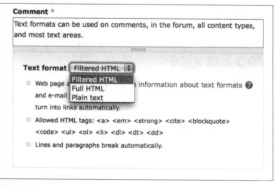

FIGURE 4-16

Access Text formats at Configuration and modules ⇨ Content Authoring ⇨ Text formats. Drupal's default installation contains three formats, shown in Figure 4-17, Filtered HTML, Full HTML, and Plain text.

NAME	ROLES	OPERATIONS	
Filtered HTML	anonymous user, authenticated user, administrator	configure	delete
Full HTML	administrator	configure	delete
Plain text	All roles may use this format	configure	

FIGURE 4-17

Text formats consist of a collection of filters that sift through and process the text you entered. When a user submits a comment or node, Drupal stores their text unmodified, then when the text is used (i.e., viewed), it is passed through the text format chosen for the text. Drupal never modifies the text entered, allowing you to change and adjust the formats knowing that you are not permanently modifying the data.

EXPLORE THE FILTERED HTML TEXT FORMAT

Take a look at the filters used in the `Filtered HTML` text format, shown in Figure 4-18, by click-

ing `configure` to the right of the format (Figure 4-17) to see how this format will modify the appearance of your text.

With these filters in place the text format will modify, remove, add, or interpret text.

Modify Text

The `Convert URLS into links` filter converts words that begin with `http://` or contain @ into clickable links. The `Correct broken HTML` filter ensures that all postings contain properly closed HTML tags inserting corrections as necessary.

FIGURE 4-18

Add Text

The `Convert line breaks` filter automatically inserts `<br>` and `<p>` tags based on the line breaks (the return key) entered by the user. This keeps your site's HTML well formatted and consistent across browsers.

Remove Text

The `limit allowed HTML tags` filter strips unwanted HTML tags as well as JavaScript and CSS. This filter keeps your site safe by removing malicious code and keeps it looking good by removing unwanted HTML.

As you can see the `Filter HTML` text format adds, removes, and modifies the text of your site. If you compare this format to the `Full HTML` format you'll notice that the only difference is the absence of the `Limit allowed HTML tags` filter.

Interpreting Text

Filters can also interpret text. Examples of interpretation would be enabling WIKI or BBCode syntax, which can interpret text such as *bold* to **bold**. Many contributed modules provide this functionality as well as the core PHP filter module, which is disabled by default for security reasons (read tip).

> **WARNING** The core module `PHP filter` adds an input filter that allows you to add custom PHP code to textboxes throughout your site (nodes, comments, etc.). Although this makes Drupal extremely powerful it is a high security risk. Enable the PHP filter only for those users that are highly trusted. PHP code executed on your server allows full access to your database, your content, and files. Crafty users may also gain access to other sites in a Drupal multi-site installation.
>
> Don't trust them with your dog? Don't trust them with the PHP filter!

Choosing Roles and the Importance of the Order

The filter list on the main Text formats page displays filters in their preferred order. The first listed format that the user has permission for is chosen as their default format. As demonstrated in Figure 4-16 users can select any other format they have permission for from the drop-down box. Consider the order presented in Figure 4-19, which is a convenient order for highly trusted administrators that need complete flexibility on your site.

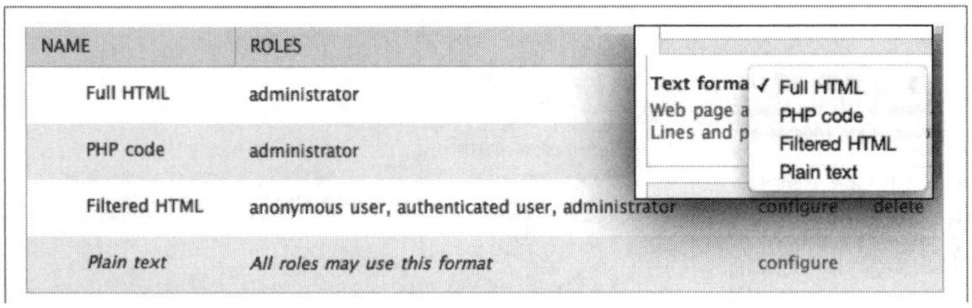

NAME	ROLES	
Full HTML	administrator	
PHP code	administrator	
Filtered HTML	anonymous user, authenticated user, administrator	configure delete
Plain text	All roles may use this format	configure

Text forma ✓ Full HTML
Web page a   PHP code
Lines and p   Filtered HTML
Plain text

FIGURE 4-19

Be selective when choosing the roles that can use each format. For example, the `Full HTML` format allows tags such as `<font>` or `<table>`, which could significantly alter the appearance of your site. It also allows the `<script>` and `<form>` tags which could allow malicious users to engage in cross-site scripting attacks or forge password entry forms compromising your site's security.

> **NOTE** The roles that may use a text format can select within each text format or by granting the appropriate permission at Configuration and modules ⇨ Permissions ⇨ Filter Section.

Configuring the Filters

As you've seen, each format consists of one or more filters. Each filter can be uniquely configured per format by clicking the `Configure` tab within the format. This allows you to use one filter to remove nearly all HTML within one format and the same filter in a different format to remove only a few HTML tags. Note that not all filters have configurable settings, as demonstrated by the `Filtered HTML` format, displayed in Figure 4-20; some filters lack configurable settings for the `Convert line breaks` and `Correct broken HTML` filters.

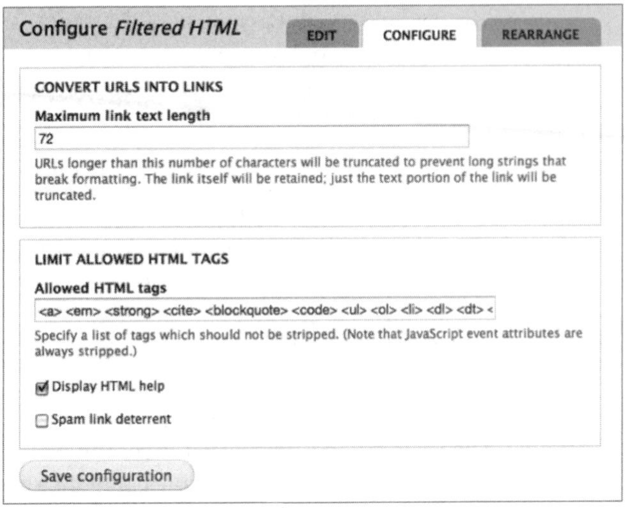

FIGURE 4-20

The Order Matters

As if on an assembly line, the text is processed through a series of filters in the order they are presented on the Rearrange tab. Each filter operates independently of the others and thus can modify the work of the preceding filter. For example, if the `Convert URLS into links` filter creates several links (`<a>` tags) and the `Limit allowed HTML tags` strips all `<a>` tags the result will be text devoid of links. Figure 4-21 shows the default filter order for the *Filtered HTML* text format.

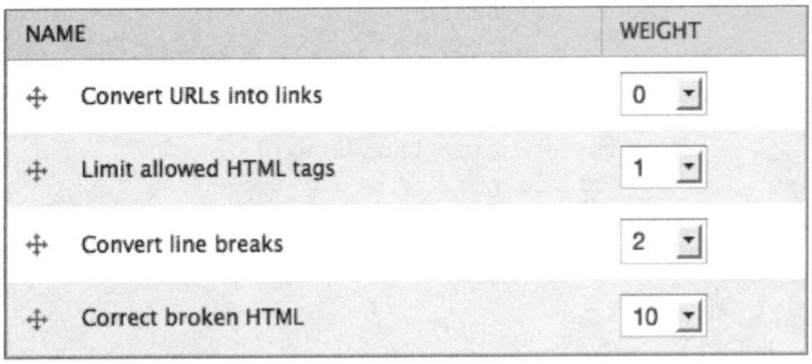

FIGURE 4-21

Additional Filters

Once you get used to input formats you may find that the default filters don't provide you with the functionality you want. Don't worry, there is a large assortment of filters ready for download on Drupal.org; simply navigate to `http://drupal.org/project/Modules/category/63`. Here are a few filters to get you started.

> ➤ **BBCode** — (`http://drupal.org/project/bbcode`) A very popular module useful for forum administrators. BBCode, short for Bulletin Board Code, provides a simplified method for writing HTML. Example:
>
> `[b]bold text[/b]` will be transformed into the HTML `<strong>bold text</strong>`.

➤ **Markdown syntax** — (http://drupal.org/project/markdown) Similar in concept to BBCode but with different syntax. Markdown allows users to use a simplified set of tags to modify the look of their content. Example:

#header1 would create <h1>header1</h1>

##header2 would create <h2>header2</h2>

➤ **Pirate** — (http://drupal.org/project/pirate) On international Talk Like A Pirate Day, September 19th, this module will modify appropriate English phrases into pirate-speak. Argh matey this module be more fun than a bottle of rum.

Writing Your Own Filter

In Chapter 15, "Custom Modules" you'll learn how to write your own custom module. To jump start that process and get you excited take a look at how simple it is to write your own custom module. The Drupal API (Application Programming Interface) provides the function hook_filter_ info. Using this function, your module can tell Drupal how you will be filtering the text.

Available for download on Wrox.com

```
function bd_chp4_filter_filter_info() {
  $filters['bd_chp4_filter'] = array(
    'title' => t('Beginning Drupal Chapter 4 sample filter'),
    'description' => t('A very basic demonstration filter'),
    'process callback' => 'bd_chp4_filter_eval',
  );
  return $filters;
}

function bd_chp4_filter_eval($text) {
  $output = strip_tags($text);
  return $output;
}
```

code snippet bd_chp4_filter Module

Search and Metadata - Clean URLs

Using a bit of magic this setting takes an ugly URL such as http://localhost/index.php?q=blog and cleans it up to be http://localhost/blog. These URLS not only look better but they help your visitors remember (or guess) your URLS. Take the following example:

http://localhost/shoes/black/running/mens

without Clean URLS this might be http://localhost/?q=shoes&c=black&t=running&g=mens

As you can see the first URL is easier to tell your friends about or modify to select different shoes. Clean URLs is commonly a part of search engine optimization (SEO) helping search engines more easily find your data, which may lead to high search engine ranking. Regardless of if it helps your search ranking it simply looks better.

During installation Drupal tests for support of Clean URLs and automatically enables this option if it's available. If your server fails the test don't fret because you can still get it working. The first step is to determine the type of web server you are using. The Apache web server is the most common and is used by XAMPP/MAMP. Microsoft's IIS web server is also used on some web hosts. If you are unsure, contact your web host. Based on the web server you are using, follow the appropriate instructions below.

APACHE

Drupal requires that `mod_rewrite` is enabled and that `.htaccess` is available. If you are using XAMP/MAMP ensure that `mod_rewrite` is enabled within the `httpd.conf` file located in the `conf/Apache` folder of XAMP/MAMP. The file should have a line that reads:

```
LoadModule rewrite_module modules/mod_rewrite.so
```

This line should not have a # in front of it, which would indicate that the line is commented out and inactive. If you are using Apache 2 on a dedicated server, `mod_rewrite` can be enabled through the use of the a2enmod command:

```
a2enmod mod_rewrite
```

The next piece of magic is the `.htaccess` file located within Drupal's root folder. Note that the file name begins with a "`.`" (period) indicating that it is a hidden file on Linux and Mac OS X. If the `.htaccess` file is missing or if `.htaccess` support is disabled, this will not work. The magic lines in the `.htaccess` files are as follows:

```
RewriteEngine on

#Rewrite URLs of the form 'x' to the form 'index.php?q=x'.
RewriteCond %{REQUEST_FILENAME} !-f
RewriteCond %{REQUEST_FILENAME} !-d
RewriteCond %{REQUEST_URI} !=/favicon.ico
RewriteRule ^(.*)$ index.php?q=$1 [L,QSA]
```

Within XAMP/MAMP .htaccess support is enabled with the line:

```
AllowOverride All
```

This line is placed within a directive for your website's home directory such as the following, which indicates that the website is located at `/Applications/MAMP/htdocs` (the default location):

```
<Directory "/Applications/MAMP/htdocs">
    Options All
    AllowOverride All
    Order allow,deny
    Allow from all
</Directory>
```

A NEED FOR SPEED

For performance reasons `.htaccess` is often disabled in Apache. This increases performance when enabled for every page request Apache searches for and if found reads the `.htaccess` file causing your server to do quite a bit of extra work. Clean URLs will work without a `.htaccess` file by placing these lines directly into your site's main configuration file.

Your configuration file would look similar to the following:

```
<Directory "/Applications/MAMP/htdocs">
    Options Indexes FollowSymLinks
    AllowOverride All
    Order allow,deny
    Allow from all

    #Rewrite URLs of the form 'x' to the form 'index.php?q=x'.
    RewriteEngine on
    RewriteCond %{REQUEST_FILENAME} !-f
    RewriteCond %{REQUEST_FILENAME} !-d
    RewriteCond %{REQUEST_URI} !=/favicon.ico
    RewriteRule ^(.*)$ index.php?q=$1 [L,QSA]
</Directory>
```

IIS

If you are using Microsoft's IIS web server you need to configure the IIS server before you can enable Drupal's Clean URLs. Details on how to configure your IIS web server can be found at `http://drupal.org/node/3854`. Note that if you are using a web host you will need to work with them to enable this support.

Search and Metadata — URL Aliases

A function of the core `path` module a URL alias is for you to take a nondescript URL and make it more informative. For example modifying `http://localhost/node/2` to be `http://localhost/about`.

With the `path` module enabled you have two methods to add these friendly URLs. The first is at Configuration ⇨ Search and Metadata ⇨ URL Aliases as shown in Figure 4-22.

The second method is conveniently located directly on the node edit form. Simply type in the alias you want and Drupal will do the rest as shown in Figure 4-23.

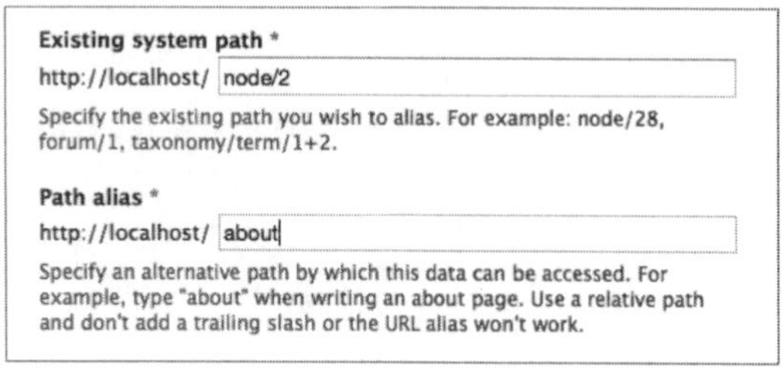

Existing system path *

http://localhost/ node/2

Specify the existing path you wish to alias. For example: node/28, forum/1, taxonomy/term/1+2.

Path alias *

http://localhost/ about

Specify an alternative path by which this data can be accessed. For example, type "about" when writing an about page. Use a relative path and don't add a trailing slash or the URL alias won't work.

FIGURE 4-22

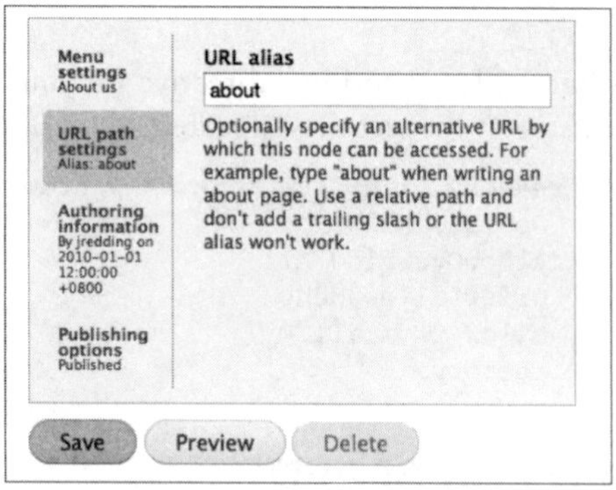

Menu settings	URL alias
About us	about
URL path settings	Optionally specify an alternative URL by which this node can be accessed. For example, type "about" when writing an about page. Use a relative path and don't add a trailing slash or the URL alias won't work.
Alias: about	
Authoring information	
By jredding on 2010-01-01 12:00:00 +0800	
Publishing options	
Published	

Save   Preview   Delete

FIGURE 4-23

Alias Your Way to a Better Search Ranking

It is a generally assumed best practice that having a well organized and aliased website will better your search engine rank. The voodoo magic that is SEO changes rapidly so whether or not this is actually true is another matter. Regardless, a well aliased site simply looks better. Here are a few tips to help keep your site looking good and give it a leg up on the search engine front.

➤ **Pathauto** — As you can probably guess aliases are highly recommended but manually aliasing every piece of your content is extremely tedious. The pathauto module (`http://drupal.org/project/pathauto`) does all of this aliasing for you which automatically includes creating aliases such as `http://localhost/2010/Jan/01/your-blog-post`.

➤ **One alias per node** — Multiple aliases for the same node may lead search engines to believe that you are a spam site with little valuable content. The Global Redirect module (`http://drupal.org/project/globalredirect`) can help to ensure that this doesn't happen to you.

➤ **Organization** — A well thought out and organized website is easier to navigate and helps users, and search engines, understand your content. For example, place news at `/news`, blogs at `/blogs`, and your store at `/store`.

➤ **Consistency** — When creating aliases, be consistent in your naming and be sure to mind your organization patterns. `Pathauto` can be an immense help here.

➤ **Avoid spaces** — Unfortunately web browsers are still behind the times and don't know how to effectively deal with spaces. Your URLs will end up with a %20 instead of a space causing a difficult to read and ugly URL.

➤ **Dashes not underscores** — Instead of a space use a — (dash) and not _ (underscore). Again `pathauto` can help you with this.

> **NOTE** *If you are not using Clean URLS you can still use aliases but they will be preceded with* `?q=` *or* `index.php?q=`. *For example* `http://localhost/?q=about`. *When entering your existing path or the new alias do not enter the* `?q=` *portion.*

Maintenance Mode

While you are preparing your site for launch you may want to make it inaccessible to the general public. Or perhaps you are implementing a new feature or theme on your existing site. In either case you want to temporarily stop users from adding new comments, stories, blog entries, or other content to your site. Place your site into offline mode to kick off currently logged in users and put up a Site under maintenance page at Configuration ⟳ Development — Maintenance mode.

TRY IT OUT   Taking Your Site Offline Temporarily

This exercise walks you through temporarily taking your site offline by placing it in maintenance mode.

1.   Log into your website as an administrator.

2.   Navigate to Configuration ⇨ Development — Maintenance mode.

3.   Check the Put site into maintenance mode.

4.   Modify the Maintenance mode message (Optional).

5.   Click Save configuration.

6.   Log out.

At this point your website is within maintenance mode and all non-administrative users will be prevented from viewing the website; instead they will be presented with your maintenance mode screen.

TRY IT OUT   Log into Your Offline Website

1.   Manually navigate your browser to `http://localhost/user` or `http://localhost?q=user` if you site is not using clean URLs.

2.   Log in with an administrator account.

How It Works

Drupal maintenance mode is designed to restrict your users from adding new content such that you have perform maintenance on the site. Once a site is set to offline, administrators will stayed logged in and can perform all functions on the site. Non-administrators will be presented with the maintenance mode screen.

> **NOTE** The theme's template file `maintenance-page.tpl.php` can be used to custom the look of the maintenance page. See Chapter 13, "Theming" for more information on how to use this file.

IP Address Blocking

Unfortunately, site administrators still have to deal with malicious users and automated bots. Spammers can flood a site with thousands of requests per second in an attempt to create one comment or a single piece of content. Each request is received and processed, which eats up valuable server time. Excessive abuse can cause your site to respond slowly or grind to halt. Once you know the IP address of the spammer, enter it at Configuration ⇨ People and permissions ⇨ IP address blocking. Requests originating from any listed IP will be immediately blocked. This will save precious system resources because Drupal will not process the requests.

You can often obtain the IP address of the abuser through the web server logs or Drupal's logs located at Reports ⇨ Recent log entries.

An IP can also be blocked within `settings.php` for an even faster block that saves even more system resources at the cost of manageability. See Chapter 18 for an explanation of how to do this.

> **NOTE** IP address blocking is used to combat abusive computers known as spam bots that are attacking your site. The contributed module Mollom (`http://drupal.org/project/mollom`) can be used to protect your site against spam comments or content. The troll module may also help you root out and block the pesky users on your site (`http://drupal.org/project/troll`).

SUMMARY

This chapter guided you through the most common configuration settings for a new Drupal site. Many of these settings are "set 'em and forget 'em" items. Although you may only visit a handful of times they are very important settings for any top-notch website. At this point you should have a fully configured website that is ready for content, a new theme, and blocks placed in their appropriate places.

In the next chapter you'll move away from the one-time configuration settings and onto the aspects of your sites that are more public facing such as settings blocks, creating menus, and enabling new themes. In later chapters you'll add content, users, and create your site's taxonomy strategy. All of these culminate into Chapter 9, "Prepare for Launch," where you will review and configure all of the necessary settings to make your website public.

EXERCISES

1. Why is it important to set your site's name before you launch?

2. The post date of your content is based on what time zone?

3. What is the difference between a public and a private file?

4. Where should private files be stored?

5. What is the purpose of a text format?

6. In order for clean URLs to function what file must exist in Drupal's root directory?

7. What is a URL alias?

Answers to the Exercises can be found in the Appendix.

▶ **WHAT YOU LEARNED IN THIS CHAPTER**

➤ Modifying the site's title, slogan, e-mail address, and other items

➤ Setting your site's default country, timezone, and date/time

➤ Customizing the 404 Page not found and 403 Access denied pages

➤ Setting the location of your uploaded public and private files

➤ Enabling and configuring your text formats to preserve the security and visual integrity of your site

➤ Enabling Clean URLs

➤ Creating URL Aliases and maintaining a proper path strategy

➤ Putting your site into maintenance mode

5

Administration — Blocks, Menus, and Themes

WHAT YOU WILL LEARN IN THIS CHAPTER:

➤ Configuring your site's blocks

➤ Creating new blocks

➤ Explore a block's visibility settings

➤ Creating and configuring your site's menus

➤ Primary and Secondary menus

➤ Enhancing SEO with custom URL aliases

➤ Setting a new site theme

➤ Allow your users to select their own theme

In this chapter you'll review the major building blocks of your site that give it structure; blocks, menus and themes. Blocks are the pieces of content that generally flank the left and right side of a site offering helpful information such as the latest blog posts, recent comments, or the ads that help pay your bills. Menus provide crucial site navigation and are commonly shown horizontally across the top of the site as well as vertically on the side. A theme is one of the most important parts of your site as it controls your site's appearance including all colors, fonts, and layout.

Blocks and menus are added, configured and managed through the Structure section. Themes are appropriately kept under the Appearance section.

BLOCKS

The pieces of content that appear on the left or right side of your website are called *blocks* in Drupal. Examples include the User login block, the administrative menu, or the help block that you enabled in Chapter 3. Blocks are either supplied by an enabled module or manually created perhaps to display a twitter widget or embed a YouTube video.

As you experienced in Chapter 3, blocks are placed within a region of your theme. Each theme can choose to use custom regions or utilize the default regions; Left sidebar, Right sidebar, Content, Header, Footer, Highlighted content, Help, Dashboard main, and Dashboard sidebar. You can see where each of these regions is located in your theme by visiting the block administration page at Administer ⇨ Structure ⇨ Blocks then clicking the Demonstrate block regions as shown in Figure 5-1, with the result in Figure 5-2. Remember that each theme may have different regions so be sure to switch to the appropriate theme before viewing the regions as demonstrated in Figure 5-1.

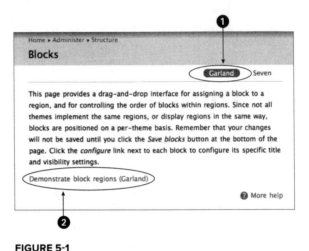

FIGURE 5-1

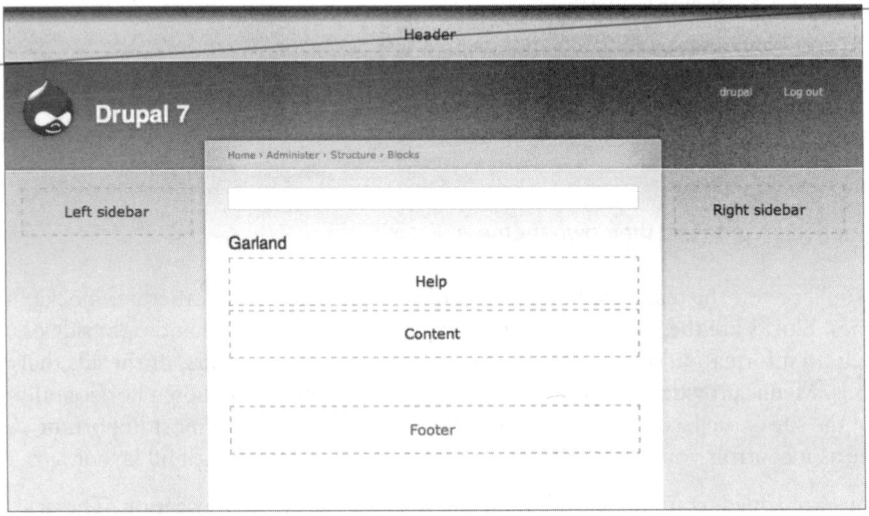

FIGURE 5-2

Note that a region may not appear on all pages. For example the default regions, Dashboard Main and Dashboard sidebar, only appear on the Dashboard pages. It is common however, that most regions will appear so the demonstration page shown in Figure 5-2, which is a good guide.

In Chapter 3 you explored regions and block ordering when you enabled the help and syndication blocks. In the following exercise you will create your own custom block. Custom blocks are often used to display widgets, for example a twitter or YouTube widget.

TRY IT OUT   **Create a Custom Block**

In this exercise you will create a custom block that tells the world how much you enjoy Drupal.

1.   Logged in as an administrator navigate to Administer ⇨ Structure ⇨ Blocks as shown in Figure 5-3.

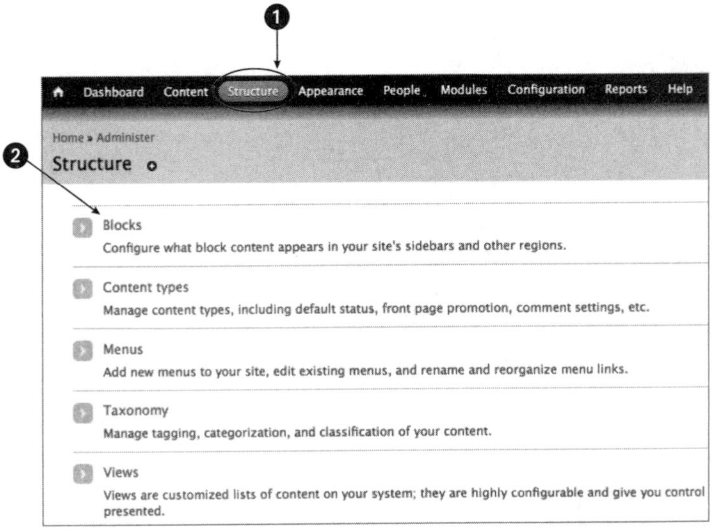

FIGURE 5-3

2.   Click Add block at the top of the page.

3.   Enter the following information as shown in Figure 5-4.

> ➤   Block description: My first custom block

> ➤   Block title: Drupal rocks!

> ➤   Block body:

```
<strong>Drupal rocks!</strong>
```

Home » Administer » Structure » Blocks

Blocks

Use this page to create a new custom block. New blocks are disabled by default, and must be moved to a region on the blocks administration page to be visible.

▾ BLOCK SPECIFIC SETTINGS

Block description *

My first custom block

A brief description of your block. Used on the blocks administration page.

Block title

Drupal rocks!

The title of the block as shown to the user.

Block body *

<strong>I love the power of Drupal!</strong>

Text format Filtered HTML ▾   More information about text formats ❓
Web page addresses and e-mail addresses turn into links automatically.
Allowed HTML tags: <a> <em> <strong> <cite> <blockquote> <code> <ul> <ol> <li>
<dl> <dt> <dd>
Lines and paragraphs break automatically.

The content of the block as shown to the user.

FIGURE 5-4

4. Under `Region settings` place the block into the left region for the Garland theme as demonstrated in Figure 5-5.

▾ REGION SETTINGS
Specify in which region this block is displayed.

Garland region
Left sidebar ▾

Seven region
Disabled ▾

5. Click `Save block` leaving all other options at their defaults.

FIGURE 5-5

6. Confirm your block is working by navigating to your site's frontpage, shown in Figure 5-6.

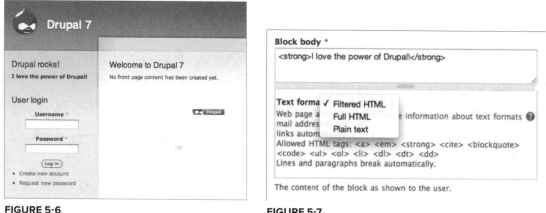

FIGURE 5-6

Block body *

<strong>I love the power of Drupal!</strong>

Text forma ✓ Filtered HTML
Web page a   e information about text formats ❓
mail addres   Full HTML
links autom   Plain text
Allowed HTML tags: <a> <em> <strong> <cite> <blockquote>
<code> <ul> <ol> <li> <dl> <dt> <dd>
Lines and paragraphs break automatically.

The content of the block as shown to the user.

FIGURE 5-7

How It Works

Manually created blocks are bits of content similar to a node or a comment. The content can be text, HTML, an image, or a widget from an external or even custom PHP code provided that the Text format allows the content. As shown in Figure 5-7 the Text format is set at Filtered HTML, which automatically strips certain HTML tags to help ensure your site is safe. If you are sure of the content you are adding in you can set this to Full HTML and Drupal will allow all content to be added, this is often necessary to include widgets from an external site.

Block Visibility

By default blocks appear for all users on all pages. This is not always desirable. For example you wouldn't want the administrative menu appearing for anonymous users. Also you may want the recent comments block to only appear on the blog page or advertisements displayed for anonymous users but not for logged in users, giving people incentive to sign up. Drupal provides four methods for you to control the visibility of your blocks as shown in Figure 5-8, Page specific, Role specific, Content Type specific, and User specific.

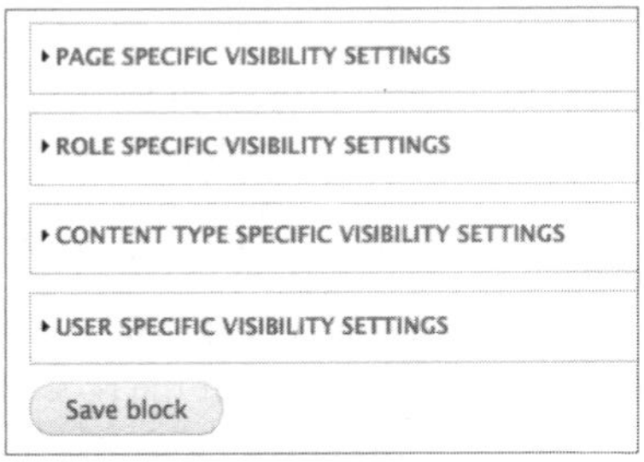

▸ PAGE SPECIFIC VISIBILITY SETTINGS

▸ ROLE SPECIFIC VISIBILITY SETTINGS

▸ CONTENT TYPE SPECIFIC VISIBILITY SETTINGS

▸ USER SPECIFIC VISIBILITY SETTINGS

Save block

FIGURE 5-8

Visibility settings are controlled from the block configuration page, accessed by clicking configure to the right of the block.

> **Page specific** — Although the title is Page specific it may be easier to look at it as path specific. Two options are provided "Every page except those specified below" and the negation "only the pages specified below." Pages are listed one per line and allow for the * wildcard character. Here are some examples:
>
>   user
>
> This will apply when the user is located at `http://localhost/user` but will not apply when they are at `http://localhost/user/register`. To have it apply to both URLs simply add in a second page like the following and as shown in Figure 5-9:
>
>   user
>   user/register
>
> OR
>
>   user
>   user/*

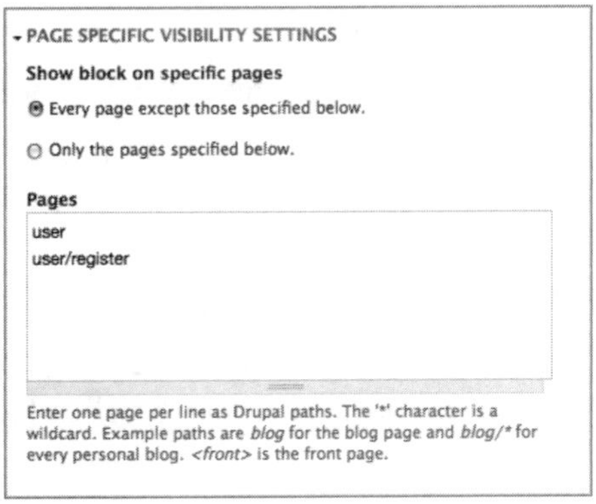

▾ PAGE SPECIFIC VISIBILITY SETTINGS

Show block on specific pages

◉ Every page except those specified below.

○ Only the pages specified below.

Pages

    user
    user/register

Enter one page per line as Drupal paths. The '*' character is a wildcard. Example paths are *blog* for the blog page and *blog/** for every personal blog. *<front>* is the front page.

FIGURE 5-9

The latter will apply to all URLs after `http://local-host/user` such as `http://localhost/user/login`, `http://localhost/user/password`, etc.

The last example gives it away that pages truly means path because you can use wildcards to match the URL path. This is particularly true if a piece of content is made available via multiple paths (also known as aliases) as each of the paths will be evaluated and used to determine the block's visibility.

> NOTE *Pages are listed in the clean URL fashion even if you are not using clean URLs. For example if your site's URL looks like* `http://localhost/index.php?q=user/register` *you only need to enter* `user/register`*.*

➤ **Role specific** — Users must exist in one or more of the checked roles in order to see this block. If no roles are checked then the block is available to all users. In the example shown in Figure 5-10 only anonymous users will see this block, which may be great if you remove advertising for authenticated users (i.e., those logged in).

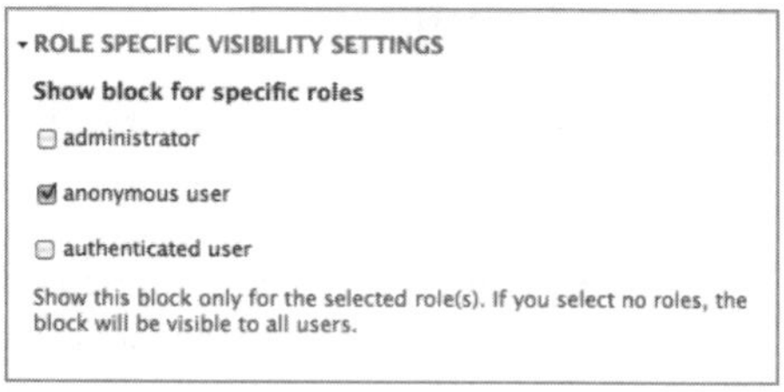

FIGURE 5-10

➤ **Content Type specific** — This is a great control that looks at the type of content the user is browsing. For example you can post the latest comments block when a user is browsing your Blog and post the Latest Blog entries block when a user is browsing a Page such as your about page.

➤ **User specific** — By default you have control over what a user can or cannot see. This setting allows you to give control over to your users. For example, setting a block to Hide this block by default lets individual users show it; you can create a members-only block that requires a user account to see. If you have set a Role specific setting the user must also be a part of the respective role.

➤ **Personalize blocks** — Users can control their personal block settings within their user account as shown in Figure 5-11.

FIGURE 5-11

TRY IT OUT **Configure Block Visibility**

This exercise walks you through configuring your custom block to be visible only for authenticated users that are browsing user profiles, as shown in Figure 5-12.

1. On the Block administration page at Administer ➪ Structure ➪ Blocks click configure to the far right of the My first custom block.

2. Near the bottom of the page under `Role specific visibility settings` check Authenticated user, as shown in Figure 5-13.

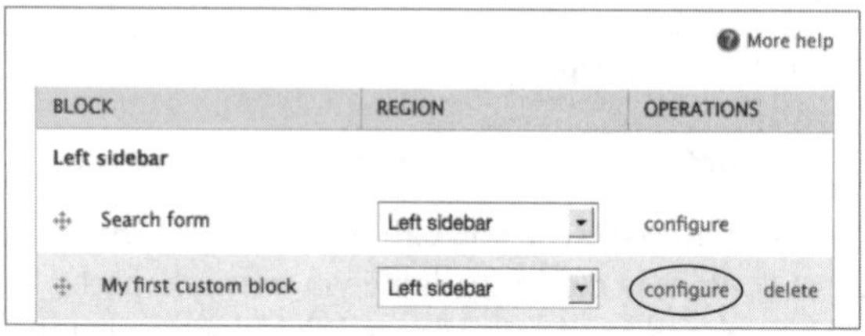

BLOCK	REGION	OPERATIONS
Left sidebar		
⊕ Search form	Left sidebar ▾	configure
⊕ My first custom block	Left sidebar ▾	configure delete

FIGURE 5-12

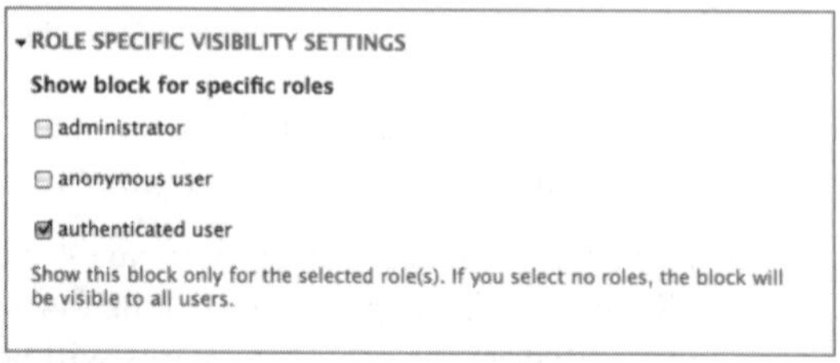

▾ ROLE SPECIFIC VISIBILITY SETTINGS

Show block for specific roles

☐ administrator

☐ anonymous user

☑ authenticated user

Show this block only for the selected role(s). If you select no roles, the block will be visible to all users.

FIGURE 5-13

3. Under `Page specific visibility settings` set the following, as shown in Figure 5-14:

➤ Only the pages specified below

➤ Under Pages enter:

```
user
user/*
```

4. Click the `Save block` button at the bottom of the page.

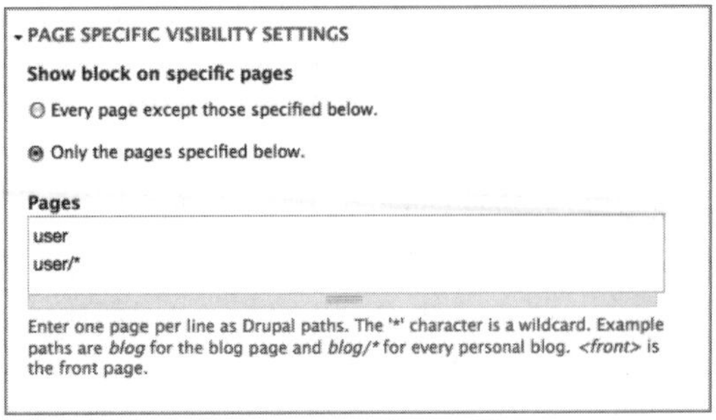

FIGURE 5-14

Verify that the block only appears on the user pages for authenticated users by clicking your username in the top administration menu or navigating to `http://localhost/user`. Check for the presence of the block, then log out and view the same page. The block should not appear when you are logged out.

How It Works

Block visibility is determined by a combination of all visibility settings. In this case the user must be an authenticated user as well as visiting the user pages. If you had also set a Content type visibility setting then Drupal would check that the Content type matched.

Block Visibility Using PHP

The visibility settings described above provide quite a bit of flexibility but you may find that you want to set visibility based on a unique custom criteria. With the PHP filter module enabled, an option to use PHP to control visibility settings will appear under the Page specific visibility settings as shown in Figure 5-15.

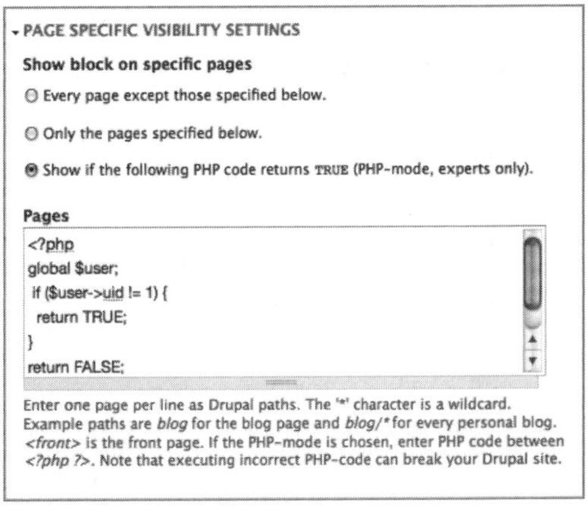

With a bit of PHP you can set visibility based on almost anything. Here are two examples to help get you started.

This example will display the block when the time on the server is in the am:

FIGURE 5-15

```
<?php
if (format_date(time(), 'custom', 'a') == 'am') {
  return TRUE;
}
else {
  return FALSE;
}
?>
```

This example will show the block only on the user pages if the user account being viewed is not the currently logged in user and is not an anonymous user. For example if user 1 is visiting the profile of user 2 at `http://localhost/user/2`:

```php
<?php
  global $user;
  $path = arg(1);
  $uid = arg(2);
  if ($path == 'user' && $uid != $user->uid && $user->uid > 0) {
    return TRUE;
  }
  else {
    return FALSE;
  }
?>
```

> **WARNING** *Using PHP for block visibility requires the* `Allow PHP for block visibility` *permission. This is an advanced feature and should only be allowed to trusted users as poorly written PHP can disable a website or open it up to security vulnerabilities.*

TRY IT OUT Use PHP to Control Block Visibility

This exercise sets your custom block to appear when an authenticated user is browsing the user profile pages. The block does not appear when a user is browsing their own profile.

1. Log in as an administrator and enable the PHP filter module at Administer ➪ Configuration and modules ➪ Modules.

2. Configure your custom block by navigating to the Block administration page at Administer ➪ Structure ➪ Block and clicking configure to the far right of the `My first custom block` block.

3. Under Page specific visibility settings choose `Show if the following PHP code returns true` and enter the following code:

```php
<?php
  global $user;
  $path = arg(0);
  $uid = arg(1);
  if ($path == 'user' && $uid != $user->uid && $user->uid > 0) {
    return TRUE;
  }
  else {
    return FALSE;
  }
?>
```

How It Works

Each time Drupal displays a page it will evaluate the PHP code entered within the Pages box. If the PHP code returns TRUE then the block is displayed, otherwise Drupal assumes the block is not to be displayed (i.e., return FALSE). Technically the trailing bit of code shown below is unnecessary but having this bit of code enhances readability.

```
else {
    return FALSE;
}
```

> ⊗ **WARNING** *Malformed or incorrect PHP syntax can cause your site to malfunction if entered incorrectly so be sure to double check your code before saving the block. Take note of the URL of your custom block's configuration page. You can use it if your site is rendered unusable by a bug in your code.*
>
> *Example:* `http://localhost/admin/structure/block/configure/block/1`

MENUS

Menus are collections of links to help users navigate your site. Navigate to Structure ⇨ Menus to view your site's menus. Drupal defines several default menus to help get you started but you are free to create as many menus as you see fit. All menus are also blocks thus they can be placed on your site according to the block settings you learned earlier in this chapter.

Drupal's default menus include:

➤ **Main menu** — By default this menu is located horizontally across the top of your site and it is typically used as the site's main form of navigation. In Chapter 3 you added a link to your About page in this menu, shown in Figure 5-16.

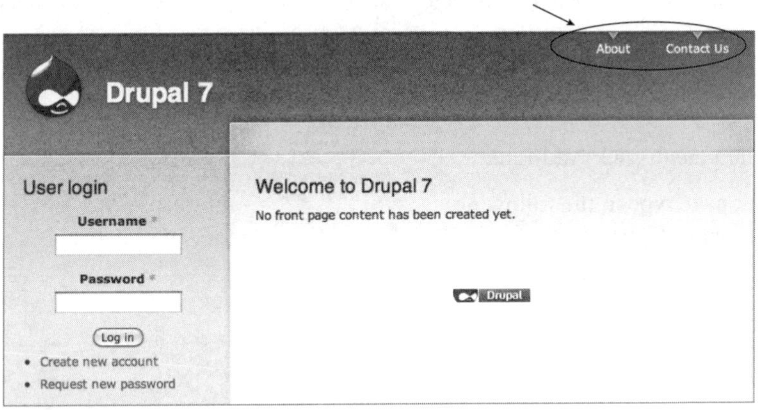

FIGURE 5-16

➤ **Management** — A set of links to all of your sites's administration areas.

➤ **Navigation** — This menu can also be thought of as a repository of links. New modules will place their non-administrative links within this menu by default. You can, and often will, move links from this menu to other menus.

➤ **Secondary menu** — This menu is provided as an example of how menus can be used. Typically it is used for lesser-used links and may not be very prominent on your site. Links such as your legal copyright notice, business information, etc. are only displayed on certain pages.

➤ **User menu** — My account, Logout, and other user-specific links are located in this menu and displayed when a user logs in. The menu is generally user specific providing links to the user's profile, their recent blog posts, etc., as shown in Figure 5-17.

FIGURE 5-17

As with many things in Drupal these menus are only defaults, you are free to define new menus and move links between each of these menus. In the following exercises you will create new links, move links between menus, and create your own custom menu.

TRY IT OUT | **Add a New Link to the Main Menu**

This exercise walks you through adding new links to the main menu. You will add a link to the first article node you added in Chapter 3.

1. Log in as an administrator and navigate to Administer ➪ Structure ➪ Menus.

2. To the right of Main menu click Add Link.

3. On the Create link page type in the following information as shown in Figure 5-18:

➤ Menu link title: My first article

➤ Path: node/1

➤ Description: My first Drupal article

➤ Enabled: checked

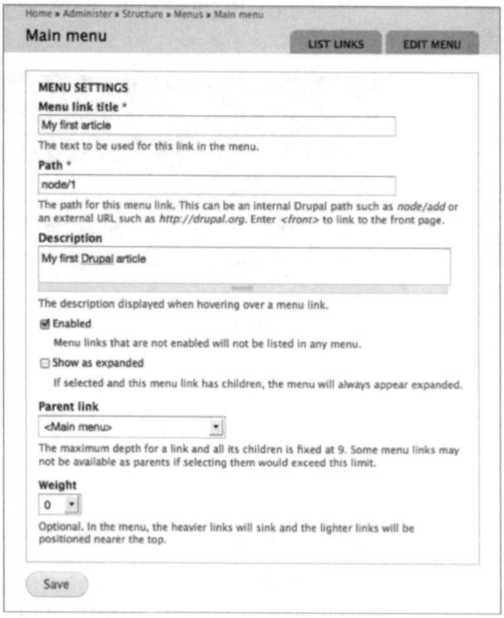

FIGURE 5-18

➤ Show as expanded: unchecked

➤ Parent link: <Main menu>

➤ Weight: 0

How It Works

Menu links can point to either a local path or an external website. When entering the path you omit your website's URL and the non-clean portion. For example, if the URL is `http://localhost/index .php?q=node/1` simply enter `node/1` for the path. If the link is external be sure to include the `http://`, example `http://www.wrox.com` not `www.wrox.com`.

Reviewing Menu Links

Take a few minutes to understand the other features of a menu link.

➤ **Enabled** — If unchecked the item will not appear in the menu. This allows you to temporarily remove links from a menu without having to delete it. If the link has child links they are also disabled.

➤ **Expanded** — Menu items may have child links up to nine levels deep. Expanded links display the first level of child links. If this link is also a child its parent will also be expanded. Figure 5-19 shows the administrative menu and you can see that the Structure menu item is expanded. The Content Types and Menus links also have children, as denoted by the arrow, but they are not expanded.

➤ **Parent link** — Links are created independently of a menu and are placed within the menu. This is nice because you can easily move links in between menus. The < > (for example: `<Management>`) indicates a separate and independent menu. Two dashes `--` indicate that the item is located underneath a menu and each subsequent two dashes indicate that an item is a child of a parent.

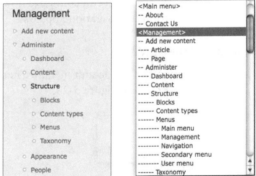

FIGURE 5-19   **FIGURE 5-20**

Figures 5-19 displays the resulting menu for the menu hierarchy created in Figure 5-20. You can see the two menus in Figure 5-20, Main menu and Management.

➤ **Weight** — Menu links are ordered by weight and then sorted alphabetically, lighter numbers float to the top of the menu (left in a horizontal menu). You can also rearrange the menu by dragging and dropping links on the List links page of each menu.

Adding a Menu Link Directly on Content

To save time you can add a link to your content when creating or editing it. In Chapter 3 you added the About page to the Main menu using this method. Users with the Administer menus permission will see a Menu settings option at the bottom of the node edit page as shown in Figure 5-21.

A Word On Permissions

In order to add, edit, or modify a menu or menu link a user must have the `Administer menu` permission. It is also the permission needed to use

FIGURE 5-21

the menu settings directly on a node (Figure 5-21). Users with only this permission will not, however, see the Administration menu as shown in Figure 5-19. Grant users the `Access administration pages` permission in order for them to navigate to the Menu administration pages.

Menu Settings

At the top of the menu administration page, Administer ⇨ Structure ⇨ Menu, is a settings tab (Figure 5-22) wherein you can configure how your site's primary form of navigation appears.

FIGURE 5-22

Default Content Menu

This first option sets the default menu users are presented when adding a new piece of content to a menu, demonstrated in Figure 5-23.

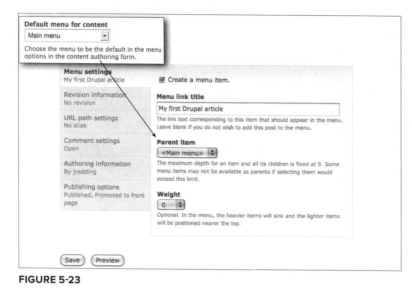

FIGURE 5-23

Main and Secondary Links

Themes generally provide a special section for the main and secondary links. Drupal's Garland theme places these both at the top right of the theme as shown in Figure 5-24.

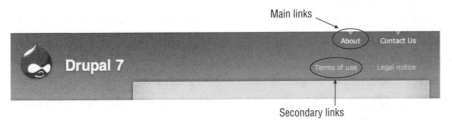

FIGURE 5-24

If you set the main and secondary menus to the same menu Drupal will expand the children in the secondary menu location when the parent is selected in the main menu. In the example shown in Figure 5-25 the Add new content link has been added to the Main menu, which has been set for both Main and Secondary links. Add new content has two child links, Article and Page. When Add new content is selected the child links appear in the secondary menu, otherwise the secondary menu is empty.

FIGURE 5-25

Related Modules

Thousands of modules have been contributed to the Drupal project. Here are a few menu related modules that you might find useful:

- ➤ **DHTML menu** (http://drupal.org/project/dhtml_menu) — A menu containing a high number of nested child links can cause navigation to be slow, because each expansion of a parent link requires a full-page refresh. DHTML Menu can speed up your site by using client-side JavaScript to expand the parent link exposing the child links.

- ➤ **Taxonomy Menu** (http://drupal.org/project/taxonomy_menu) — Plan to use taxonomy to categorize your content? If so, this module will make automatic menus based on your site's categorization strategy.

URL ALIASES AKA CUSTOM PATHS

Diamonds may be a girl's best friend but URL aliases are a search engine's best friend. SEO begins here by providing a much clearer path to your content. For example, a URL alias can change http://localhost/node/1 into http://localhost/about.

The path module creates URL aliases; which is disabled by default. Follow the exercise to learn how to use this important module.

TRY IT OUT   Create a Custom Path for the About Page

This exercise walks you through enabling and using the path module to make the about page, created in Chapter 3, accessible at `http://localhost/about`.

1.   Enable the path module.

> ➤   Log in as an administrator and navigate to Administer ➪ modules ➪ Modules.

> ➤   Check the box to the left of the Path module and click Save configuration at the bottom of the page.

2.   Navigate to Administer ➪ modules ➪ URL aliases.

3.   Click Add alias at the top of the page and enter the following information as shown in Figure 5-26.

> ➤   Existing system path: node/2

> ➤   Path alias: about

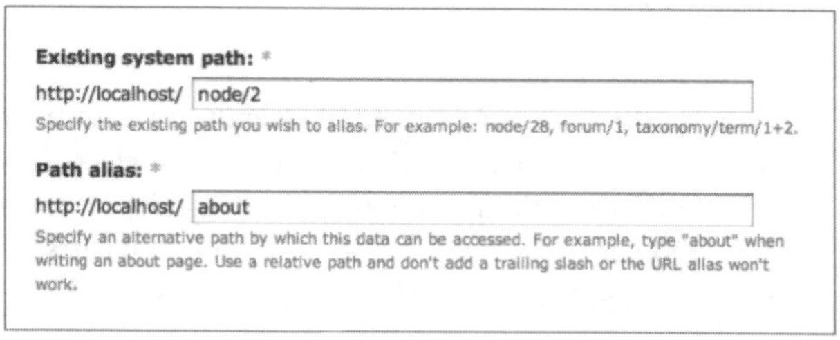

Existing system path: *

http://localhost/ `node/2`

Specify the existing path you wish to alias. For example: node/28, forum/1, taxonomy/term/1+2.

Path alias: *

http://localhost/ `about`

Specify an alternative path by which this data can be accessed. For example, type "about" when writing an about page. Use a relative path and don't add a trailing slash or the URL alias won't work.

FIGURE 5-26

When user navigates to `http://localhost/about` they will see `http://localhost/node/2`.

How It Works

The path manages the URLs of your website allowing you to alias existing paths to something more user and search engine friendly. With the path module enabled you can also add paths directly on the node edit page as shown in Figure 5-27.

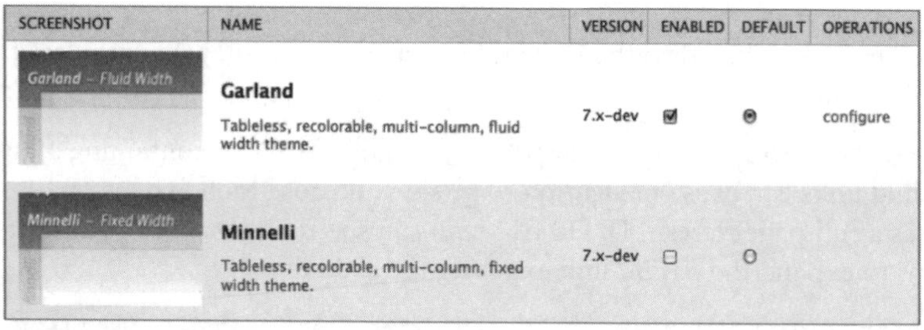

SCREENSHOT	NAME	VERSION	ENABLED	DEFAULT	OPERATIONS
Garland – Fluid Width	**Garland** Tableless, recolorable, multi-column, fluid width theme.	7.x–dev	☑	◉	configure
Minnelli – Fixed Width	**Minnelli** Tableless, recolorable, multi-column, fixed width theme.	7.x–dev	☐	○	

FIGURE 5-27

> **NOTE** *Managing URL aliases can quickly become a chore. Fortunately the Path auto module uses a bit of magic to automatically set aliases for your content. For example* `http://localhost/2010/01/01/happy-new-year` *or* `http://localhost/your-awesome-blog-entry`. *It is a must have module for SEO purposes. Get it at* `http://drupal.org/project/pathauto`.

A Word on Permissions

Users need the `Create URL aliases` permission in order to alias content on your site. This permission only allows them to add aliases, not delete or edit. The `Administer URL aliases` permission allows them to modify any and all aliases on the website including deleting existing aliases.

THEMES

A theme defines how your site is laid out and appears to your site visitors. Themes define the colors and fonts used on your site as well as if your site uses one, two, three, or more columns. Themes are highly configurable in Drupal and can be fully customized by a web designer. The Drupal community is filled with designers that have created many custom themes. They are freely available for download at `http://drupal.org/project/themes`.

Often people complain that using a common system, such as Drupal, is that your site will look like every other site. You will lose your individuality and uniqueness. In Drupal nothing could be further from the truth. The theme has ultimate control over how the site looks and every aspect of your site can be modified by the theme. In this section you'll learn how to use and configure existing themes. In Chapter 13 you'll dig into the specifics on how to fully customize your website.

> **NOTE** *Want to see what a completed Drupal site looks like? Check out the Drupal showcase at* `http://drupal.org/forum/25` *or the Drupal section of CMS design* `http://drupal.cmsdesigns.org/`.

Theme Administration

The central place of management for all themes is at Administer ➪ Appearance or by clicking Appearance in the top Administration bar. Themes are enabled and configured in this section, including any custom theme settings, with the exception of theme-specific block settings, which are managed with blocks Administer ➪ Structure ➪ Blocks (covered earlier in this chapter).

One of the first things you will notice on this page is that multiple themes are listed. Drupal can utilize multiple themes on the same website. You may have multiple themes installed and enabled to allow users to select their own custom theme, flip between a mobile theme and full browser theme, or set custom themes based on the content being viewed.

All installed themes are listed on the theme administration page, however, before a theme can be used it must be enabled. Enable a theme by clicking the Enabled checkbox to the right of the theme's name as shown in Figure 5-27. A default theme must also be selected by using the Default radio button.

> **NOTE** *If your site displays unusual or erratic behavior you should switch to a core theme before you begin troubleshooting to eliminate the possibility of a broken theme. A core theme is one included with Drupal's main download. Garland is the best choice.*

Theme Global Settings

In Chapter 3 you downloaded and installed the `Mulpo` contributed theme, in this chapter you'll review the theme specific settings.

Themes share a common collection of settings called the global settings. Global settings are used for newly enabled themes that haven't been configured. After a theme is configured its settings override the global settings. Click Configure at the top of the Themes page to modify the Global or individual theme settings, shown in Figure 5-28.

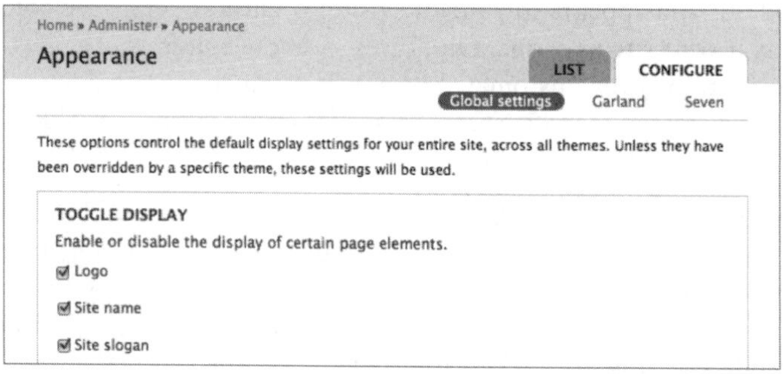

FIGURE 5-28

Global settings include an on/off toggle for the following display items.

➤ **Logo** — A site's logo is uploaded via the Logo image settings form near the bottom of the Global setting's page. If no logo is uploaded the theme's default logo will be used. One uploaded logo can apply across multiple themes.

➤ **Site name** — The text is modified in the Site Settings located at Administer ➪ Configuration ➪ Site information. The Site name is typically displayed next to or underneath the logo.

➤ **Site slogan** — A site's slogan is typically only a few words such as "The best kitten pictures on the Web" and is generally displayed just below the site's logo. The text is modified in the Site Settings located at Administer ➪ Configuration ➪ Site information.

➤ **User pictures in posts** — Toggles if a user's picture will be displayed alongside their posts. This requires picture support to be enabled at Administer ➪ Configuration ➪ Account settings (under People and Permissions).

➤ **User pictures in comments** — Toggles if a user's picture will be displayed alongside their comments. This requires picture support to be enabled (see above).

➤ **User verification status in comments** — When site visitors post comments they can optionally leave a name. To distinguish between posters that have legitimate user accounts and those that are simply leaving a name Drupal adds `(not verified)` to their name, shown in Figure 5-29. Simply uncheck the box here if you prefer to leave this off.

FIGURE 5-29

➤ **Shortcut icon** — Also known as the *favicon*, shown in Figure 5-30, it is uploaded via the Shortcut icon settings form near the bottom of the settings page. If no image is uploaded the theme's default will be used.

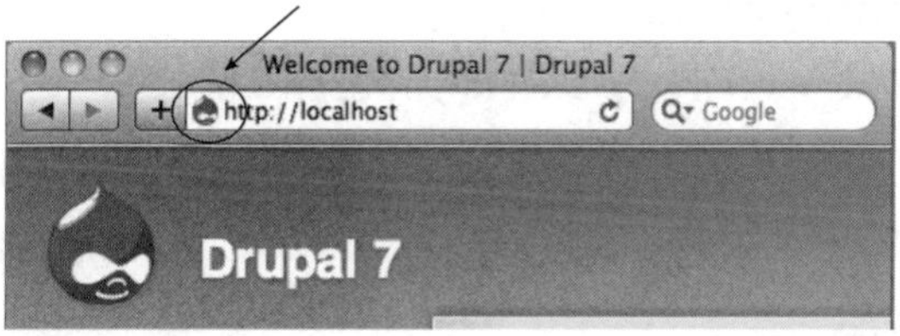

FIGURE 5-30

➤ **Main menu** — Commonly this is a site's top tabs or links although the display varies greatly depending on the theme. Its links are configured in the site's menus located at Administer ➪ Site building ➪ Menus. Previously this was called Primary links.

➤ **Secondary menu** — Commonly a second smaller set of tabs or links located just below the main menu. Its links are configured in the site's menus located at Administer ➪ Site building ➪ Menus. Both Main menu and Secondary menu were discussed under Menus in this chapter.

Theme Settings Summary

Each theme controls it own settings and can vary from what appears in the global settings. If a theme does not implement a feature the setting may be removed to avoid confusion. Themes may also provide custom settings such as the color configuration available with the Garland theme, shown in Figure 5-31.

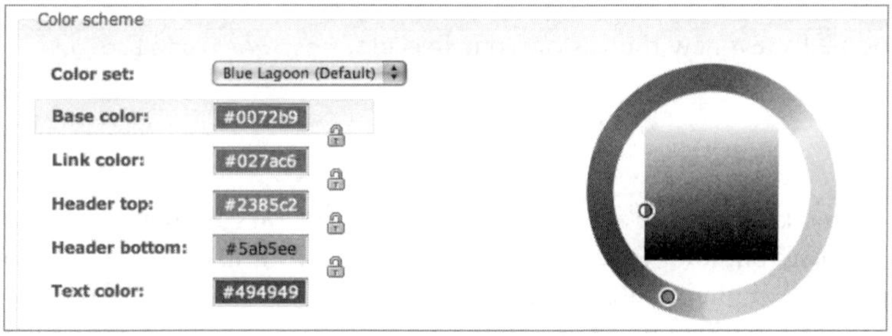

FIGURE 5-31

Installing New Themes

A site can have an unlimited number of themes installed allowing you to test out themes, allow your users choose a personal theme, or set a mobile site theme. You could even set a theme based on time of day, the referring site people used or for the individual page being viewed. When installing new themes mind just a few rules.

Watch the Version

Drupal themes are written to a specific version of Drupal core and are not backward or forward compatible. This means that if you are using Drupal 7 you will need a Drupal 7 theme, Drupal 5 or Drupal 6 themes will not work.

Theme Location

Themes can be placed in one of two places.

➤ `sites/all/themes`

➤ `sites/example.com/themes` (for example: sites/localhost/themes)

When Drupal searches for installed themes it begins with the core themes at `/themes` then it searches `sites/all/themes` and finally your site's folder either at `sites/default/themes` or `sites/example.com/themes`. If the same theme is found in multiple locations Drupal will use the location that you have the most control over (i.e., your site's theme will always be used before a core theme). You should never place or modify a theme inside `/themes`. If you'd like to modify a core theme copy it from `/themes` to your site's directory.

Review the inheritance and overrides section and exercise in Chapter 2 to better understand this directory hierarchy.

User Specific Themes

Previous versions of Drupal had a permission entitled `Select different theme` that allowed users to select a theme different than the site's default. Due to its low use and wonderful ability to create a confusing interface it was removed. Many site builders used this permission in order to test out new themes on the live site before setting it as the site's default.

Use the `Theme developer` module to test new themes on your live site, `http://drupal.org/project/devel`.

Custom Theme per _____

Fill in the blank. Drupal can set a custom theme for nearly every scenario you can imagine. Perhaps users see one theme on the blog posts but another when they are viewing your articles. Maybe you change themes based on the visitor's language. Whatever your requirement is chances are there is a contributed module to help you. Review them by browsing the Theme related module category at `http://drupal.org/taxonomy/term/73`.

Start with the Theme key module at `http://drupal.org/project/themekey`. Although not available for Drupal 7 at the time of writing it shouldn't be far behind.

Administrative Theme

Custom themes are often very flashy and constrained to specific dimensions. Unfortunately a flashy theme can make a site hard to administer by squishing the administrative areas to something that is unusable or simply annoying. Fortunately Drupal allows you select a different theme for the administrative interface. By default the administrative theme is set to the Seven theme. The Administrative theme is used for any items accessible under the URL `http://localhost/admin`. You can also use the administrative theme when adding or editing nodes by checking the Use administration theme for content editing box as shown in Figure 5-32.

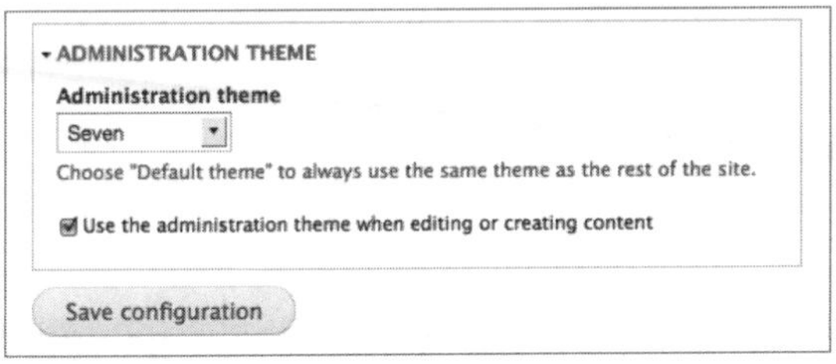

FIGURE 5-32

Post Information

Although not a theme setting it is often thought of as one. Post information is the byline under each node that, by default, reads Submitted by *username* on *datetime*. The date and time is displayed based on the site's medium date format, which is configured at Administer ⇨ Configuration ⇨ Date and time. You can toggle Post information on or off for each content type at Administer ⇨ Structure ⇨ Content types then selecting edit for the respective content type and modifying the Display settings as shown in Figure 5-33.

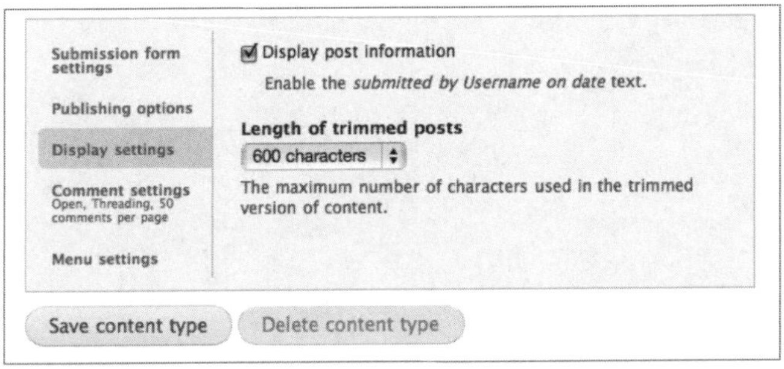

FIGURE 5-33

SUMMARY

In the previous chapter you covered the basic site configuration settings. This chapter covered blocks, menus, custom URL paths, and your site's theme. You may think that blocks are just small bits of information that flank the left and right site of your site but they can take on many forms and can be extremely versatile. Experiment with them in your footer or header regions or flip over to Chapter 13, "Theming" to learn how to implement your own custom regions.

Don't forget to enable the Path module to create custom URL paths for your content. A custom URL path is one of many SEO settings. Make your life easy by installing the Pathauto module (http://drupal.org/project/pathauto).

In the next chapter you will revisit the content creation pages and learn how to create new types of content as well as how to customize the display of your content.

1. What is a block?

2. How many regions does a theme have?

3. If you want a block to appear only on the blog section at `http://localhost/blogs`, how would you accomplish this?

4. Why would you set the Main links and Secondary links to the same menu?

5. What is a URL alias?

Answers to the Exercises can be found in the Appendix.

▶ **WHAT YOU LEARNED IN THIS CHAPTER**

> ➤ Blocks are either supplied by a module or manually created.

> ➤ Blocks are placed within a region and a theme defines what regions are available and where they appear.

> ➤ Visibility settings for a block can be set per user, role, content type, or URL path. If the PHP filter module is enabled you can use PHP to control a block's visibility setting.

> ➤ The PHP Filter is an extremely powerful module and should only be granted to highly trusted site administrators (hint: malformed PHP code can disable your website).

> ➤ Menus are collections of links to internal pages or external websites. All menus are blocks.

> ➤ Use the path module to set a custom URL for a node.

> ➤ The Pathauto module automatically creates URL aliases for all of your content.

6

Content

WHAT YOU WILL LEARN IN THIS CHAPTER:

➤   What are nodes?

➤   Creating new node types

➤   Setting default node options

➤   Managing fields

➤   Content Construction Kit (CCK)

➤   Administering nodes including moderation

➤   Comment moderation

➤   Controlling spam

The heart, and purpose, of any website is its content. It may be videos or music uploaded by your users, news stories written by reporters, the products in your online store, or comments left behind by site visitors. This chapter covers two of Drupal's main forms of content; nodes and comments. Nodes are the most prominent pieces of content and, by default, include Pages and Articles. Nodes are limitless in options and can include videos, mp3s, blog entries, and more. Comments, often equally as important, are responses to nodes.

Drupal's vast set of contributed modules freely available on drupal.org contains many modules that provide other types of content for your site. For example the Twitter module (`http://drupal.org/project/twitter`) displays the tweets of your site's users on your website. Although this is content that can be placed around your site the tweets are not nodes and thus have different attributes than a node. A good understanding of the concept of a node and how it differs from other pieces of content is a vital piece to gaining clarity to Drupal.

This chapter reviews the node; walking you through the concept and purpose, creating your own custom node types, and administering your site's nodes. After a thorough review of the node system you will explore the comment system as well as how to administer your site's comments and handle comment spam.

The exercises in this chapter build on top of each other and should be done in succession. You will start with a simple node type and then expand upon it to allow anonymous users to add content, upload files and have these pieces of content placed in a moderation queue awaiting review by a site administrator.

NODES

Also known as content types, nodes are the basic building blocks of a Drupal site and construct the major pieces of your site's content. Static content such as an About or a Directions page as well as dynamic content such as a blog entries, news stories, podcasts, reports, and store products are all nodes. In a default installation, Drupal enables two node types: Article and Page. Forum, Blog, and Poll content types are also available by enabling their similarly named modules.

What is a Node?

The concept of a node is one of the unique things in Drupal that sets it apart from other systems. When Dries Buytaert created Drupal, he noticed that a website's content tended to have similar attributes. For example, a blog entry and a news article both have a title, creation date, author name, and several other items. After a lot of research and several major versions later, Drupal has defined a set of common attributes upon which all nodes are built. These attributes include the following:

➤ **NID (Node ID)** — Every node is given a unique ID within the Drupal system. If you create a `page` node with an `id` of 1 and subsequently create an `article` node, it would be given an `id` of 2, and the next `page` node receives an `id` of 3. All nodes, regardless of type, can be accessed at `http://localhost/node/<id>` (for example, `http://localhost/node/1`).

➤ **Title** — All nodes are required to have a title.

➤ **UID (User ID)** — Nodes are explicitly tied to the User that created the node by their ID (UID). Anonymous users use an ID of 0 (zero).

➤ **Status** — A node may be Published or Unpublished. These two states allow you to create a new piece of content but keep it offline until you are ready for it to be public.

➤ **Created and Changed** — These two items are time stamps that record when the node was created and when it was last modified.

➤ **VID (Version ID)** — All node types are automatically eligible for revision control. If enabled Drupal keeps track of all changes to a node and provides a mechanism wherein previous versions can be reviewed and rolled back.

➤ **Language** — Drupal is multi-language friendly and maintains a language setting for all nodes. This makes it easy to translate a site's content.

In addition to these attributes, nodes may also have comments, be promoted to the frontpage, or set to Sticky so that they appear at the top of lists. All nodes also have five permissions: Create, Edit Any, Edit Own, Delete Any, and Delete Own.

The node system is one of the key reasons why development on Drupal is faster than other systems. Modules do not have to create custom types of content but instead can create a node and piggyback on all of the built-in node functionality. Moreover modules that add new features or attributes to a node can be used for all node types.

For example, if you wanted to create a podcast, you could use the Audio module (`http://drupal.org/project/audio`), which creates an Audio node type. Because Audio is a type of node it automatically has commenting, revision control, permissions, and is multilingual-ready. Moreover, it will work perfectly with other node based modules such as the Content Construction Kit (CCK) and Views.

One way to think of a node is to consider that of a Mr. Potato head toy. At the center of Mr. Potato head is just a lumpy potato; by itself it is nothing spectacular. When you add a nice set of lips, big eyes, and funny ears the potato comes to life. Think of the potato as the node and the lips, and eyes and ears as the addition of commenting, file uploads, and custom fields such as links to YouTube videos, Flickr photos, or a category dropdown.

Why Nodes?

The purpose of the node system is that it allows for nearly limitless flexibility. Contributed modules can attach themselves to a node extending its functionality. Major subsystems (comments, permissions, etc.) are reused, keeping consistency throughout your site, while also maintaining a lightweight system that can be built very quickly.

Modules are able to easily attach new functionality to a node because of Drupal's Application Programming Interface (API). If you are a developer or would like to learn skip over to Drupal's API documentation at `http://api.drupal.org`. Custom development is also covered in Chapters 15, 16, and 17.

With a basic understanding of what a node is move onto creating your own custom nodes.

CREATING CUSTOM CONTENT TYPES

In Chapter 3 you were introduced to and created both an Article and a Page node, Drupal's default content types. You can add new content types to your site by either enabling modules, such as the blog, book, forum or poll module, or by creating it yourself. The following exercise will walk you through the steps to create a new content type.

Before You Begin Consider Your Options

New users to Drupal often make the mistake of creating a new content type in order to separate or categorize content. For example an international news website might create several content types such as News – Europe, News – North America, News – South America, News – Africa, and News – Asia. Content types should not be used in this manner; instead create a single content type, News, then use Taxonomy to categorize them correctly. Learn more about this in Chapter 8, "Taxonomy."

When would you create a new content type? Here are a few reasons:

> **Different default settings** — Individual content types maintain distinct default settings for Published state, revision control, promotion to the frontpage, commenting, post information (byline), moderation, and others. A unique content type can aid your specific workflow.

➤ **Permissions** — Each content type has multiple permissions; Create, Edit own, Edit all, Delete own, and Delete all. For example, you can grant a Blogger the ability to add Blog posts but not add or edit Pages.

➤ **Theming** — Content types can styled and themed independently of each other. The theme can make the Article node appear vastly different that Page nodes. Theme elements, such as the author byline, can also be toggled per content type. This feature is especially important when you consider an online-store. You would probably want your store products to appear different than your blog posts.

You'll learn more about this in Chapter 13, "Theming."

➤ **Unique fields** — As you will learn in this chapter, content types can be as simple as a single field or contain complex multiple field data entry forms. For example, Audio nodes (i.e., podcasts) not only have a title and a description of the podcast but they also have a link to download the MP3 and quite possibly other fields for multiple download files (ogg, wav), the lyrics/transcript, links to related websites, or other content.

Follow along in the next exercise to create your own custom content type.

TRY IT OUT Creating a New Content Type

Follow these steps to create a new Gossip content type to allow your users to upload all the juiciest gossip from around the globe:

1. Navigate to Content types by clicking Structure in the top administration menu, then Content types as shown in Figure 6-1.

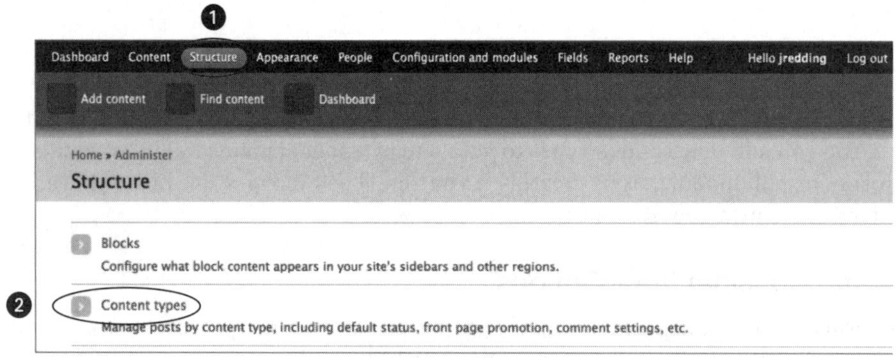

FIGURE 6-1

2. In the Content Types area, click Add Content Type at the top of the page, as shown in Figure 6-2.

3. In the Identification area, type the following as shown in Figure 6-3.

➤ Name: `Gossip`

➤ Description: `Got a hot story? Heard a celebrity rumor? Tell us and if it's good we'll make you famous!`

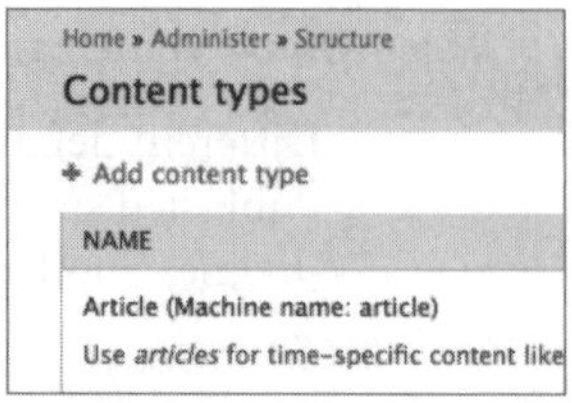

FIGURE 6-2

4. Under Publishing uncheck Published and Promoted to frontpage as shown in Figure 6-4.

5. Click Save content type at the bottom of the page.

6. Navigate to the Create Content page by clicking Add content in the top Administration bar to see the new content type.

IDENTIFICATION

Name *

Gossip   Machine name: gossip [Edit]

The human-readable name of this content type. This text will be displayed as part of the list on the *add new content* page. It is recommended that this name begin with a capital letter and contain only letters, numbers, and **spaces**. This name must be unique.

Description

Got a hot story? Heard a celebrity rumor? Tell us and if its good we'll make you famous!

FIGURE 6-3

How It Works

When building a new content type you start by building around the node core. As it is a node you're provided with several basic foundation items such as a title and description, and published, promoted, and revision options. In this exercise you unchecked Published and Promoted to frontpage because this content type should be reviewed before it is displayed on your website.

Submission form settings	**Default options**
Publishing options	☐ Published
Display settings	☐ Promoted to front page
Comment settings Open, Threading, 50 comments per page	☐ Sticky at top of lists
	☐ Create new revision
Menu settings	Users with the *administer nodes* permission will be able to override these options.

Save content type

FIGURE 6-4

Machine Name

Take another look at the Name field and notice that underneath it is an automatically created field Machine name, as shown in Figure 6-5.

The Machine name field is used in modules as well as when theming. In Chapter 13 you'll see that when theming a node you can create a template file

IDENTIFICATION

Name *

Gossip   Machine name: gossip [Edit]

The human-readable name of this content type. This text will be displayed as part of the list on the *add new content* page. It is recommended that this name begin with a capital letter and contain only letters, numbers, and **spaces**. This name must be unique.

FIGURE 6-5

entitled node-machinename.tpl.php. In this example, the Machine name is gossip, so your template file would be named node-gossip.tpl.php. Renaming the Machine name after its been created will cause issues with any modules or themes that explicitly refer to this node type.

Individual content types have a number of other configuration options. These are described over the next few pages.

Submission Form Settings

A node must have a Title field although you may change the label that appears on the node creation form. For example, if you have a node type for file uploads you may change this label to File Name.

The Body field is optional. If this node type will not have a body, simply leave this field blank. This setting will affect future nodes as well as any node edits. This means that if you create a node type with a body and later remove the Body field, all previously created nodes will still maintain their body text, but the text will not be editable.

Text Formats

A body field is known in Drupal as a filtered text area. This means that the user can enter text that contains HTML, Wiki syntax, BBcode or other interpretative text. A Text Format either selected for or chosen by the user will control how their text is interpreted or filtered. For example, will their bolded HTML display as bold text or as bold text. Text formats can also strip out harmful HTML or JavaScript. Flip back to Chapter 4 to learn more about Text formats.

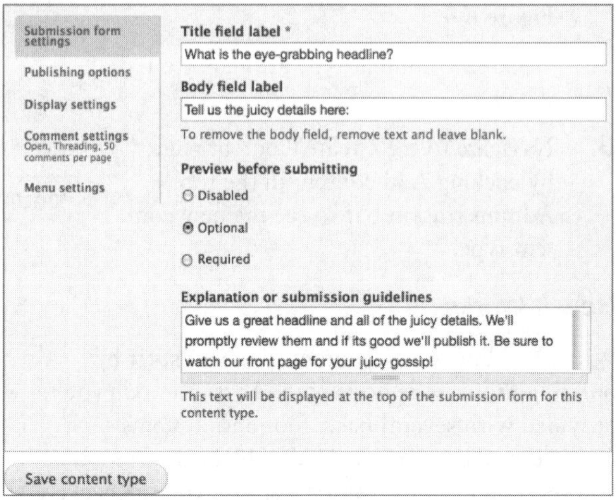

FIGURE 6-6

Publishing Options

Publishing options comprise a set of default options that each newly created node will have. You can use these options to force certain options to always occur. For example, ensuring that revisions are tracked by checking Create new revision. Users with the Administer nodes permission can modify these when creating or editing a node. Other users will not be presented with the options.

The Publishing options are as follows:

➤ **Published** — A node is not visible until it is published. This is a great option if you need time to revise a piece of content before it is available to the general public.

➤ **Promoted to frontpage** — This option flags the node content so that it will appear on the site's default frontpage. This is a common default for blog entries but is less common for pages (for example: About Us, Directions, Contact Us, etc.).

➤ **Sticky at Top of Lists** — A sticky node always appears at the top of lists, regardless of how the list is sorted.

➤ **Create New Revisions** — If this option is enabled, whenever a node is edited, a new revision will be kept along with the old one. This is a great option to track the changes of a node over time. Set it here to force a revision to always be created.

➤ **Multilingual Support** — If the locale module is enabled this option will be available. Enabling this option will place a drop-down menu with your site's languages on each node allowing you to specify what language the node is written in. This is one of the steps to creating a multilingual site. Add and enable languages at Administer ➪ Configuration ➪ Languages (Regional and Languages).

Display Settings

Toggle the Post information (byline) on or off with this setting. The Post information is shown in Figure 6-7.

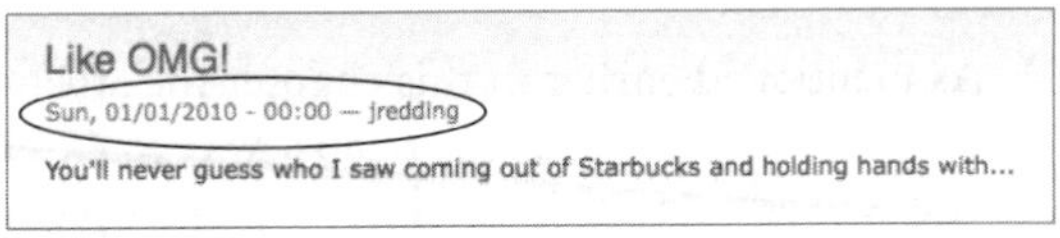

FIGURE 6-7

Comment Settings

This area contains settings that are configured *per node* and *per node type*, with *type* being the operative word here. The Default comment setting for new content (shown in Figure 6-8) is a default for and can be configured on each individual node. The other settings are set for all nodes of this type. Users with the Adminster nodes permission can modify the default comment setting on individual nodes.

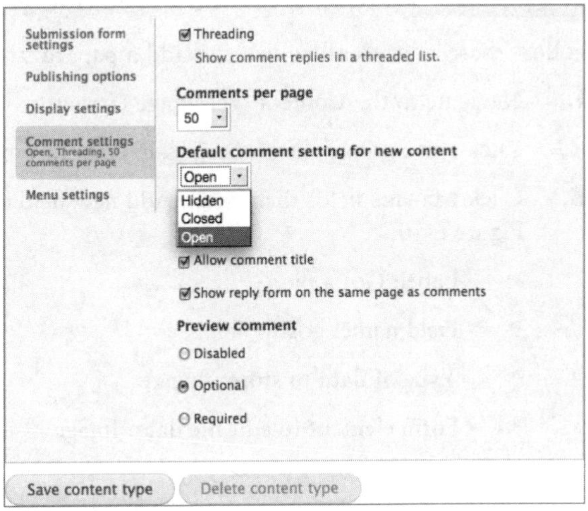

The Comment Settings per node options are as follows:

➤ **Hidden** — No comments, including existing comments, are displayed. No new comments can be added, and the comment form doesn't display. This is a great setting for the About Us and Contact Us pages.

FIGURE 6-8

➤ **Closed** — If comments become unruly, you may set the comments to Read Only (i.e. Closed). Existing comments will be displayed, but no new comments can be added.

➤ **Open** — Let the users go wild. Any user with the Post Comments permission may leave a comment.

The remaining settings are configured *per node type*, which means that all nodes of this type will adhere to these settings. These settings are self-explanatory, so they are not covered here.

Menu Settings

Users with the Administer menus permissions can directly add their newly created content to one of the menus checks in the Menu settings, Figure 6-9. Optionally you can help them along by setting a default parent menu item with the selected menu(s).

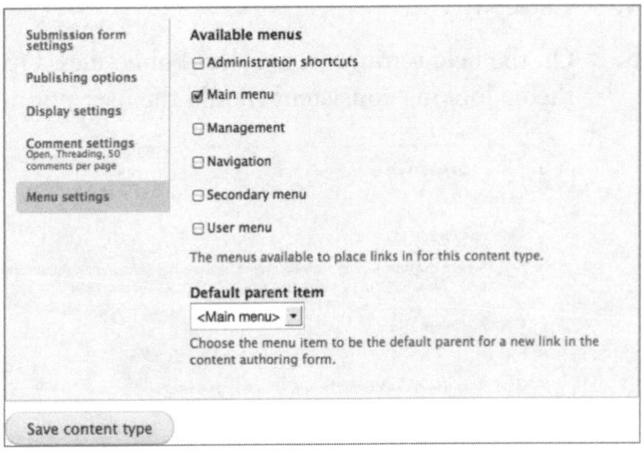

FIGURE 6-9

ADDING AN IMAGE UPLOAD FIELD

As mentioned earlier in this chapter the advantage of using a node model is that nodes can be extended. This first and foremost way to extend a node is to modify its fields. In the next exercise you will add an image field to your Gossip content type allowing users to upload a picture of the celebrity they are gossiping about.

TRY IT OUT   Adding an Image Field to your Gossip Content

Follow these steps to allow users to add a paparazzi shot to go along with their celebrity gossip.

1.   Navigate to the Content types page (Structure ⇨ Content types).

2.   Click edit to the right of the Gossip content type.

3.   Click Manage fields then under Add new field enter the following information, as shown in Figure 6-10.

> ➤   **Label:** Got a pic?

> ➤   **Field name:** gossip_image

> ➤   **Type of data to store:** Image

> ➤   **Form element to edit the data:** Image

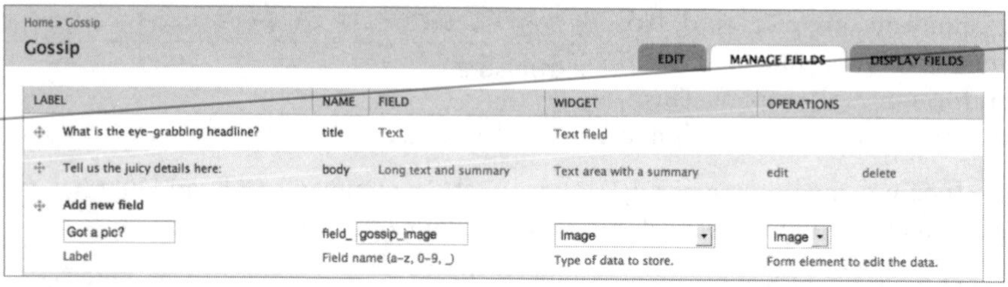

FIGURE 6-10

4.   Click Save.

5.   On the field settings page select Public files. Optionally upload a default image to help keep your theme looking consistent should the user not provide a picture.

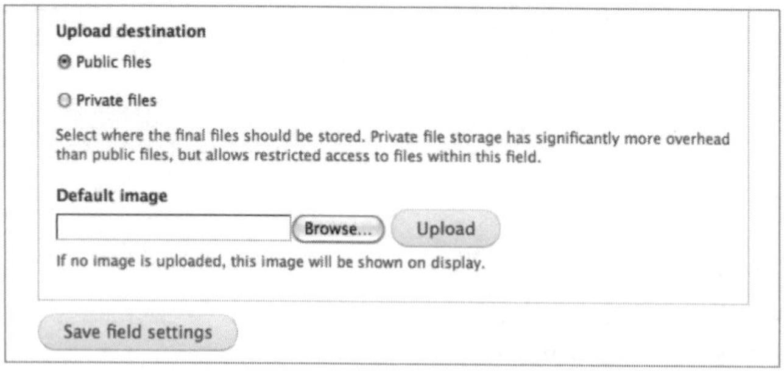

FIGURE 6-11

> **NOTE** *Public files are accessible to the general public whereas private files might require user registration or additional restrictions (perhaps they have to be purchased). Public and Private files are discussed in Chapter 4 – Administration and Configuration.*

6. Click Save field settings.

7. Navigate to Add content ⇨ Gossip to see your new field.

How It Works

Content types can contain any number of custom fields. As you saw each field has a type such as File, Image, Text, Number, etc. Depending on the type of field selected the form element may vary. For example the Boolean type (True/False or Yes/No) can be set to either a drop-down selection or a single checkbox, as shown in Figure 6-12.

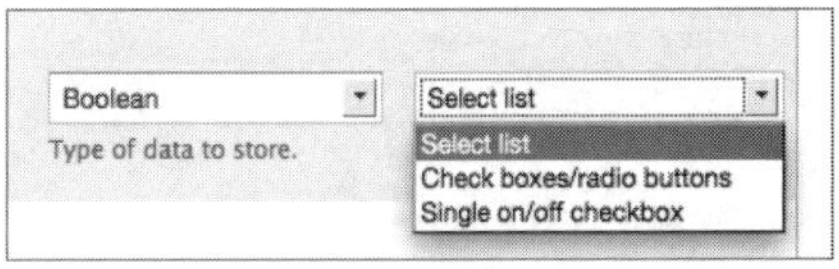

FIGURE 6-12

Multiple Fields for Multiple Images?

No. Each field added to a content type has the option to be restricted to only a single entry or allow for multiple entries. With a simple setting you can allow a user to upload up to 3, 5, or 10 images. You can even set it to unlimited to all your users to go crazy. Set the limit within each field's settings.

The Power of Image Field

As first glance the image field seems rather basic allowing a user to simply upload an image. Image field, however, is quite powerful with a few built-in features that can help your site looking good by automatically cropping, resizing, rotating, or even converting them to black and white. Each field is configured individually so begin by navigating to the Gossip Content type and clicking the edit operation for your image field, as shown in Figure 6-13.

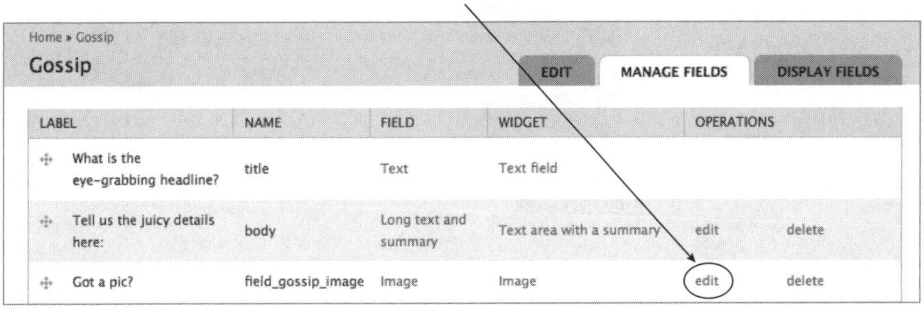

FIGURE 6-13

At the top of the settings page you'll notice that on this page you can modify the field's label or add help text. You can also restrict the file types that can be uploaded by extension and set minimum and maximum image sizes, as shown in Figure 6-14. Files under the minimum are rejected whereas files above the maximum resolution are automatically resized to the maximum image resolution. Continue on to the section on Image styles to learn more about automatically resizing your images.

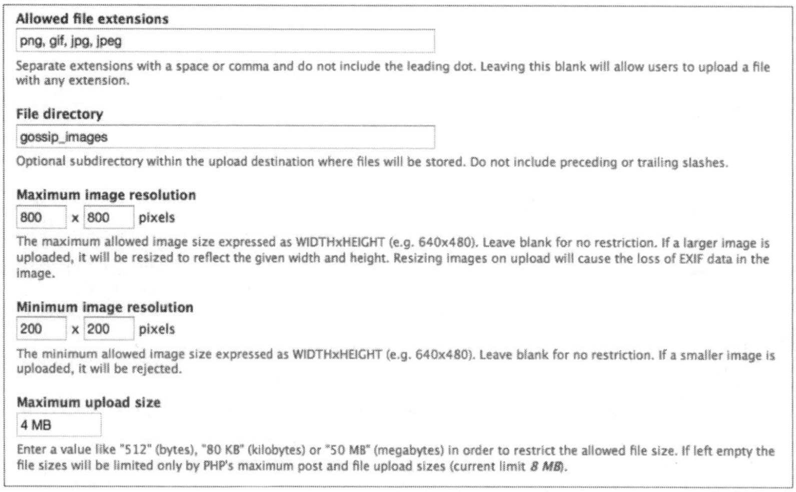

Allowed file extensions
png, gif, jpg, jpeg
Separate extensions with a space or comma and do not include the leading dot. Leaving this blank will allow users to upload a file with any extension.
File directory
gossip_images
Optional subdirectory within the upload destination where files will be stored. Do not include preceding or trailing slashes.
Maximum image resolution
800 x 800 pixels
The maximum allowed image size expressed as WIDTHxHEIGHT (e.g. 640x480). Leave blank for no restriction. If a larger image is uploaded, it will be resized to reflect the given width and height. Resizing images on upload will cause the loss of EXIF data in the image.
Minimum image resolution
200 x 200 pixels
The minimum allowed image size expressed as WIDTHxHEIGHT (e.g. 640x480). Leave blank for no restriction. If a smaller image is uploaded, it will be rejected.
Maximum upload size
4 MB
Enter a value like "512" (bytes), "80 KB" (kilobytes) or "50 MB" (megabytes) in order to restrict the allowed file size. If left empty the file sizes will be limited only by PHP's maximum post and file upload sizes (current limit 8 MB).

FIGURE 6-14

Modifying the file directory is useful to separate the image files on your server's hard drive, which can help with scalability issues if your site will be using lots of image fields across numerous content types. This directory will be created either under the Public or Private files folder depending on the field's setting.

Image Styles

One of the most powerful features of the Image field is tucked away near the bottom of the settings page.

The Preview image style, Figure 6-15, allows you to process an image so that it better fits your website. For example, you can use it to:

original (view actual size)
600px
800px
black-n-white-thumbnails (view actual size)
89px
105px

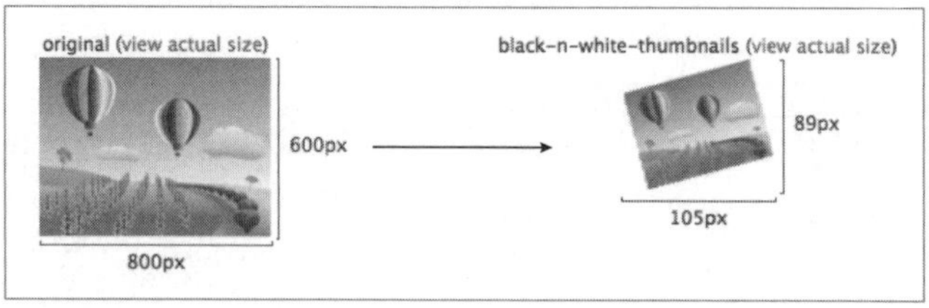

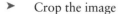

FIGURE 6-15

- Create 75x75 square images
- Rotate images to give them a new look
- Crop the image
- Convert the image to black and white

You can also combine these effects such that you can crop, resize, give a slight rotation, and convert to black and white (shown in Figure 6-15). All of this happens automatically and without user interaction.

You can select an Image type on each individual image field. You create Image styles at Administer ⇨ Configuration ⇨ Image styles (Media).

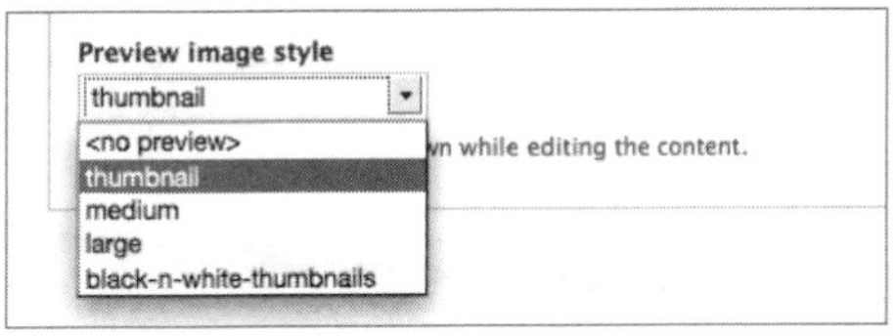

FIGURE 6-16

Follow the next exercise to create the image style shown in Figure 6-16.

TRY IT OUT   **Adding a new Image style for your Gossip Images**

In this exercise you will add a new image style that will be used for the preview image shown on the Gossip content type. This style will not modify the original file only create a new preview image.

1.   Navigate to Configuration ⇨ Image styles (under Media), as shown in Figure 6-17.

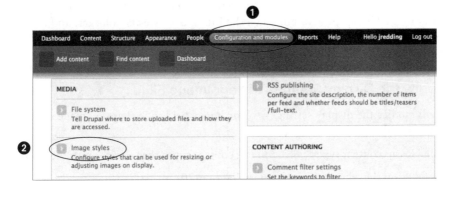

FIGURE 6-17

2.   Click Add style at the top of the page and enter `black-n-white-thumbnails` as the style name.

3.   At the bottom of the page choose Scale, then click Add, as shown in Figure 6-18.

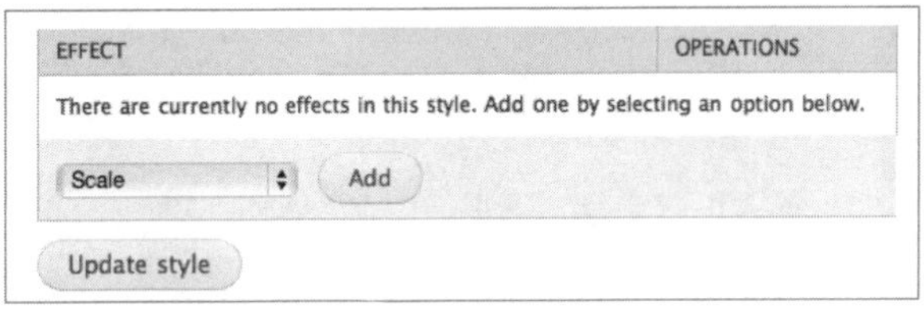

4.   Enter 90 pixels for the Width and 90 pixels for the Height then save the effect.

FIGURE 6-18

5.   Add the Desaturate effect.

6.   Add a rotate effect with a -15 degree angle and a background color of #FFFFFF (White).

7. After you have added the three effects click `Update style`. Your style should look similar to Figure 6-19.

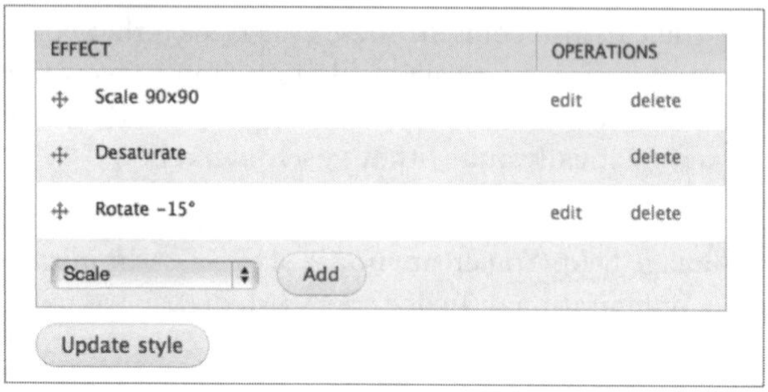

How It Works

Image styles are used to automatically modify images. The styles can be used with the Image field within Views or other contributed modules. Styles work by creating and modifying a copy of the original image the first time the styled image is viewed. If you later modify a style the previous images created with the style will be flushed and recreated.

EFFECT	OPERATIONS	
⊹ Scale 90x90	edit	delete
⊹ Desaturate		delete
⊹ Rotate −15°	edit	delete
Scale ⇕ Add		
Update style		

FIGURE 6-19

One of the great things about styles is that you can use them in multiple places or use different styles for different situations. For example, you can set the small, rotated, black and white photo when displaying the teaser to the Gossip content but when the full node is viewed a larger, and color version of the photo is displayed. You can retain the original but only show it when users specifically request it. In the next exercise you will setup your gossip content type in this manner.

TRY IT OUT **Modify the Display Settings of Your Image Field**

In this exercise you will modify the display settings of your image field such that the image appears differently in the teaser than in the full-node view.

1. Navigate to your Gossip content type at Structure ⇨ content types then click edit to the far right.

2. Choose Display fields on the edit page as shown in Figure 6-20.

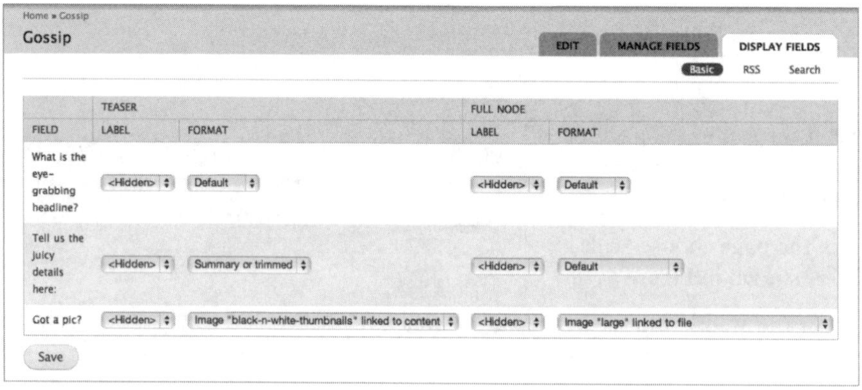

Home » Gossip

Gossip   EDIT   MANAGE FIELDS   **DISPLAY FIELDS**

Basic   RSS   Search

FIELD	TEASER		FULL NODE	
	LABEL	FORMAT	LABEL	FORMAT
What is the eye-grabbing headline?	<Hidden> ⇕	Default ⇕	<Hidden> ⇕	Default ⇕
Tell us the juicy details here:	<Hidden> ⇕	Summary or trimmed ⇕	<Hidden> ⇕	Default ⇕
Got a pic?	<Hidden> ⇕	Image "black-n-white-thumbnails" linked to content ⇕	<Hidden> ⇕	Image "large" linked to file ⇕

Save

FIGURE 6-20

3. Note that the screen is split into two sides; Teaser (left) and Full node (right).

4. Set the Teaser to:

 ➤ **Label:** Hidden

 ➤ **Format:** Image "black-n-white-thumbnails" linked to content.

5. Set the Full node:

 ➤ **Label:** Hidden

 ➤ **Format:** Image "large" linked to file.

 Figure 6-20 displays the results.

6. Click Save.

7. Verify the results by navigating to the teaser of a Gossip content type (for example by promoting one to the frontpage) and also to the Full page.

How It Works

Each field maintains its only display settings. These settings allow you to define the placement of the label as well as how the content appears to the user. As you saw in this exercise Image fields allow you to define what Image style you would like to use. Note that you can define a separate style for Teasers, Full node view, RSS feeds, and search results.

Image Style Requirements

Image styles require an image toolkit. PHP 5 includes the GD toolkit although it is possible that a host has disabled it use. You can check to see what toolkit is installed by navigating to Administer ➪ Configuration ➪ Image toolkit (under Media). Alternatively you can use the ImageMagick toolkit to process images.

Imagemagick is considered to provide higher quality pictures and uses less server resources (i.e. faster and better). It is a replacement for PHP's GD processor. If you have installed ImageMagick on your server you can use the `ImageAPI` module to unlock its use for your Drupal site.

 ➤ ImageAPI — `http://drupal.org/project/imageapi`

 ➤ ImageMagick — `http://imagemagick.org`

Maximum Upload Size

You may have noticed that the maximum upload size of your image or file fields has a limit. Commonly this is only 8mb, as shown in Figure 6-21.

This is a PHP imposed limitation. Fortunately it is easy to increase the limit. Unfortunately each server and web host has a different method. A few of the most common methods are outlined here in preferred order. You will only need to use one of the methods.

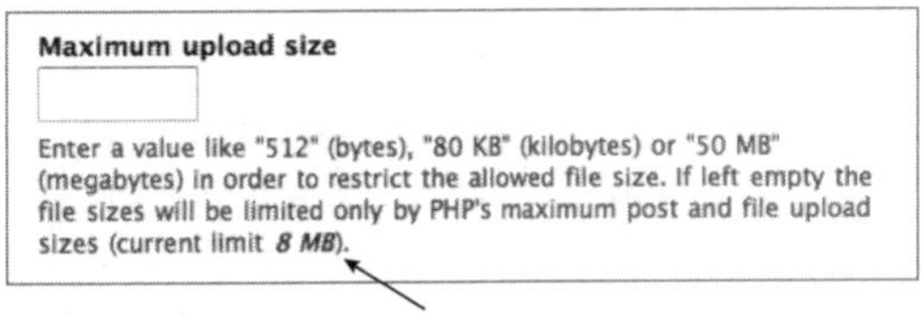

Maximum upload size

Enter a value like "512" (bytes), "80 KB" (kilobytes) or "50 MB" (megabytes) in order to restrict the allowed file size. If left empty the file sizes will be limited only by PHP's maximum post and file upload sizes (current limit *8 MB*).

FIGURE 6-21

settings.php

Within your site's settings.php file find the lines that begin with `ini_set` (approximately line 220), these lines modify your PHP configuration. Enter the following information to increase your maximum file size to 40MB. Adjust as necessary maintaining a `memory_limit` that exceeds the `post_max_size`.

```
ini_set('memory_limit', '60M');
ini_set('post_max_size', '40M');
ini_set('upload_max_filesize', '40M');
```

.htaccess

A hidden file located within Drupal's root directory; this file contains instructions for the Apache web server. Find the line that reads `<IfModule mod_php5.c>` (approximately line 33) and directly below it enter the following:

```
php_value memory_limit 60M
php_value post_max_size 40M
php_value upload_max_filesize 40M
```

php.ini or php5.ini

If the above items fail you may have to add a custom php.ini or php5.ini file to your web root. Although not complicated, each web host has a different method, making it impossible to clearly outline in this book.

Fortunately the Drupal community has already covered this is great depth over at `http://drupal.org/node/147534`.

PERMISSIONS

At this point in configuring your Gossip content type the only users that can add content are administrators (i.e., you). Anonymous users do not have permission to add content or upload files as originally intended. In this section you will correct this.

Each individual content type has five permissions; Create, Edit own, Edit all, Delete own, Delete all. In additional to individual content type permission you can grant the following global permissions:

➤ **Administer content types** — Grant users the ability to create new and modify existing content types. Users cannot create content with this permission. You will probably also want to grant them the `Access administration pages` permission (under System) so that they can navigate to the content types pages. Otherwise you will need to link them directly to the content creation page at `http://localhost/admin/structure/types`.

➤ **Administer nodes** — This permission allows a user to modify nearly every aspect of a node. This includes modifying the published status, promoting it to the frontpage, or modifying the comment settings. Users will also need permission to edit one or more content types. For example, if you would like a user to promote Gossip content to the frontpage, grant them the `Administer nodes` permission and the `Edit all Gossip content` permission; this user would not be able to promote Article content as they do not have the edit ability.

> ➤ **Access content** — By default granted to anonymous and authenticated users. In Chapter 3 you removed this permission to create a members-only website.

> ➤ **Bypass node access** — An incredibly powerful permission that allows users nearly unfettered access to all of your site's content. Grant this permission only to highly trusted users.

Revisions

Revisions are an automatic part of every node and a user needs no additional permission to create a revision. The only requirement is that the *Create new revision* checkbox is selected when the node is being edited as shown in Figure 6-22. The rub, however, is that a user must have the *Administer nodes* permission in order to select this checkbox. Fortunately this is easy to get around by simply setting the content type's default to *create a new revision* at Structure ⇨ Content types. With this set revisions will be automatically stored.

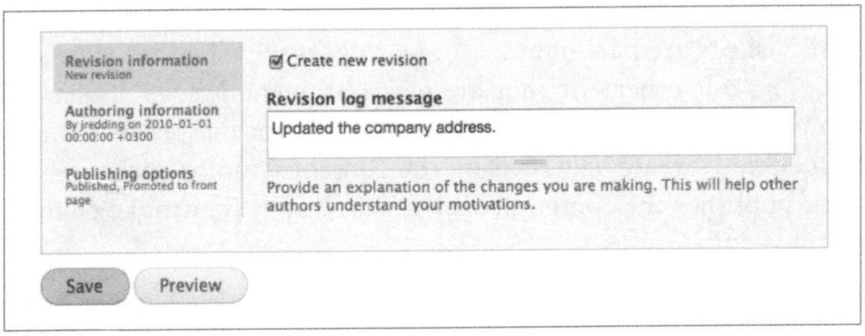

Revision information New revision	☑ Create new revision
Authoring information By jredding on 2010-01-01 00:00:00 +0300	**Revision log message** Updated the company address.
Publishing options Published, Promoted to front page	Provide an explanation of the changes you are making. This will help other authors understand your motivations.

Save   Preview

FIGURE 6-22

You can grant your users permission to view, revert, or delete revisions. Note that these permissions apply to all content types.

Complete the next exercise to allow anonymous users to submit new gossip to your site and automatically track revisions to the submissions.

TRY IT OUT   **Allow Anonymous Users to Submit Gossip Content and Track Edits.**

In this exercise you'll modify the permission and the content types defaults.

1. Navigate to Administer ⇨ Configuration ⇨ Permissions (under People and Permissions).

2. Check to grant the Create Gossip content permission for anonymous users as shown in Figure 6-23.

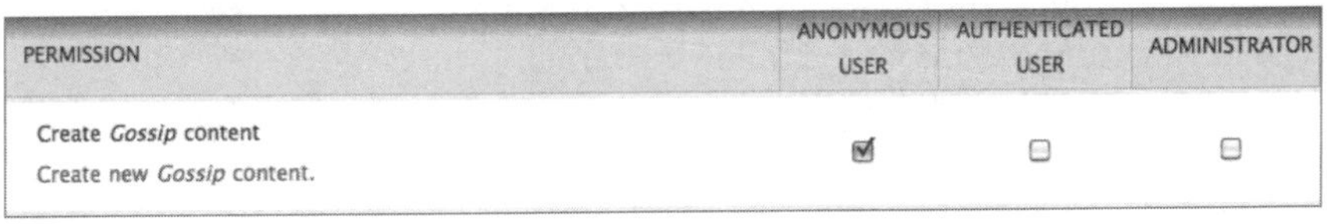

PERMISSION	ANONYMOUS USER	AUTHENTICATED USER	ADMINISTRATOR
Create *Gossip* content Create new *Gossip* content.	☑	☐	☐

FIGURE 6-23

4. Click Save permissions at the bottom of the page.

    With a permission in place set the defaults of the content type to always save a revision.

5. Navigate to the Gossip content type configuration page at Administer ⇨ Structure ⇨ Content types, then click edit to the right of the Gossip content type.

    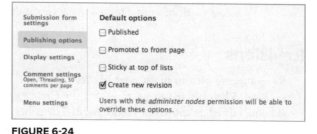

6. Under `Publishing Options` check `Create new revision` as shown in Figure 6-24.

7. Click Save content type at the bottom of the page.

FIGURE 6-24

How It Works

Permissions are granted to roles and all visitors are part of at least one role. If they log into your site they are part of the `Authenticated users` role otherwise they are part of the `Anonymous users` role. In this exercise you granted Anonymous users the ability to submit gossip content but because the Publishing options are set to Unpublished and Create new revision the content will not appear on your site. When an administrator/moderator publishes the content it will appear and if they make changes to the content they'll be tracked within a revision.

Enabling anonymous user submissions on a site that is live on the Internet will quickly become overrun with spam content coming from automated spam bots. Continue on to the Spam section to learn how to curtail any spam abuse on your site.

> **NOTE** The Diff module (`http://drupal.org/project/diff`) can show you the differences between two versions of a node, allowing you to easily see what was modified. The functionality is similar to the Track changes functionality in Microsoft Word.

DIGGING DEEPER INTO FIELDS

Understanding the terminology used in Drupal will help when you want to extend Drupal's core functionality. There are quite a number of modules that extend Drupal's core field functionality. This functionality is also known as Content Construction Kit (CCK), the reason for this is explained at the end of this section. Review the following terms.

Fields

A *field* is an area on the content type wherein the user can add in information. Earlier in this chapter you added an Image field. You can also add in fields for file uploads, text fields, numeric field, taxonomy terms, or selection lists. A field has a specified type as well as a widget that determines how it appears on your site.

Field Types (Type of Data to Store)

Although it would be easy to create all fields as simple text fields it is not very user friendly. A *field type* allows you to control what the user can or should enter. For example, if you add a field that asks a user for the sales price you most likely want them to enter it numerically (i.e., 40 and not forty). Specific field types are often created for items such as postal codes, phone numbers, addresses, etc. to verify that the data entered is correct before it is saved and presented on the website. You created an image field type earlier in this chapter.

The field type concerns the type of data being entered and not necessarily its presentation. Widgets control how the data is requested/presented from the user.

Widgets (Form Element)

A *widget* is used for the display of the field during node creation or editing and is specific to the field type. For example, a list field type contains two widgets; checkboxes/radio buttons or a select list. The results of each are the same, that is the user can choose one or one or more options, but the presentation of the field differs.

Returning to your Gossip content type consider if you added a field for the Gossip's truthiness allowing users to select one or more options that describe how accurate the gossip may be. In the following four figures (Figure 6-25 to Figure 6-28) the field and field type remains the same but the field's widget and the widget's options are different.

	ALLOW ONE VALUE	ALLOW MULTIPLE VALUES
Checkboxes/ radio buttons	How accurate would you say this gossip is? : * ○ Solid fact! ○ My BFF told me ○ It must be true ○ Celebrity gossip is always true **FIGURE 6-25**	How accurate would you say this gossip is? : * ☐ Solid fact! ☐ My BFF told me ☐ It must be true ☐ Celebrity gossip is always true **FIGURE 6-26**
Select list	How accurate would you say this gossip is? : * [My BFF told me ▼] **FIGURE 6-27**	How accurate would you say this gossip is? : * Solid fact! My BFF told me It must be true Celebrity gossip is always true **FIGURE 6-28**

As you can see a widget can dramatically alter the presentation of the field. The data collected remains the same.

Follow the next exercise to add this field to your Gossip content type.

TRY IT OUT Add a CCK Field to Your Gossip Content Type

Follow these steps to add a new field to your Gossip content type to ask users about the validity of their gossip.

1. Navigate to your Gossip content type at Structure ⇨ Content types, click `edit` then `manage fields`.

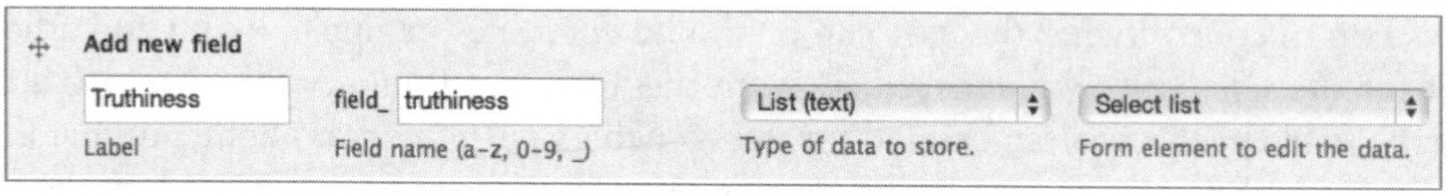

✛ **Add new field**			
Truthiness	field_ truthiness	List (text) ⬍	Select list ⬍
Label	Field name (a–z, 0–9, _)	Type of data to store.	Form element to edit the data.

FIGURE 6-29

2. Add a new field with the following information:

➤ Label: `How accurate would you say this gossip is?`

➤ Field name: `accuracy`

➤ Type of date to store (field type): `List`

➤ Form element to edit the data: `Select list`

3. Click Save at the bottom of the page.

4. On the next page under the Allowed values list type in the text as shown in Figure 6-30.

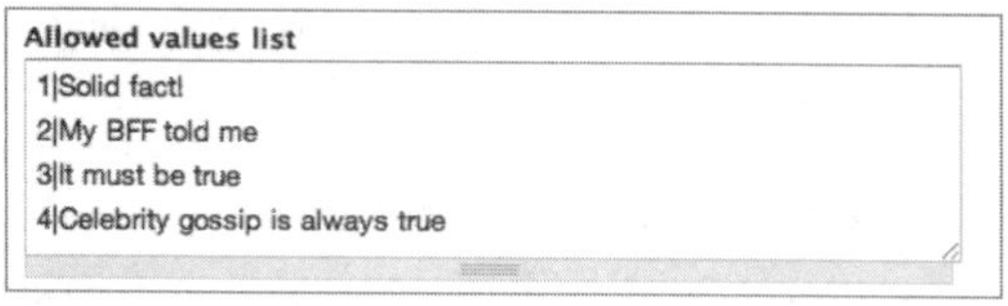

Allowed values list
```
1|Solid fact!
2|My BFF told me
3|It must be true
4|Celebrity gossip is always true
```

FIGURE 6-30

5. Click Save field settings at the bottom of the page.

At this point use a different browser to navigate to the Add content page. Your Gossip content type should now contain a field similar to that shown in Figure 6-31.

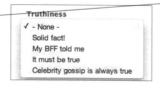

Truthiness
✓ - None -
Solid fact!
My BFF told me
It must be true
Celebrity gossip is always true

FIGURE 6-31

6. On the `Manage fields` page of your Gossip content type click on the `Select` link under Widget. Change the widget type to `Checkboxes/radio buttons`, as shown in Figure 6-32.

7. The widget should now appear similar to Figure 6-33.

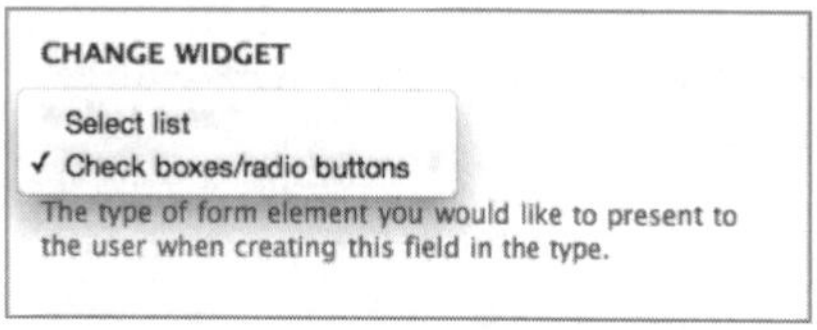

CHANGE WIDGET
Select list
✓ Check boxes/radio buttons
The type of form element you would like to present to the user when creating this field in the type.

FIGURE 6-32

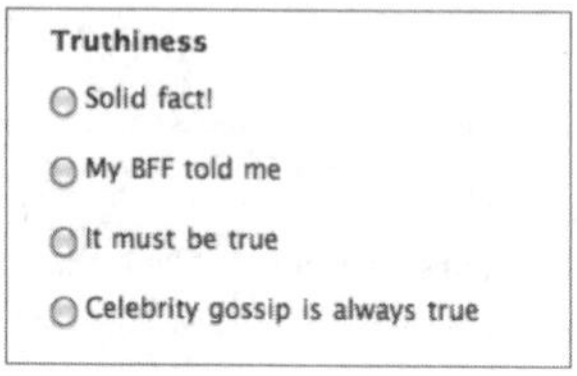

Truthiness
◯ Solid fact!
◯ My BFF told me
◯ It must be true
◯ Celebrity gossip is always true

FIGURE 6-33

How It Works

Field types are used to define a certain type of data such as text, numbers, images, files, etc. The widget presents the field to the user in a way that most represents how the user should enter the data. In this example you modified the look from a drop-down box to a radio button. If you further modify the field to allow multiple fields each widget will subsequently morph accordingly.

Contributed modules can add field types or new widget. For example, the date module not only adds a date field type but also a date picker/calendar selection widget.

Allowed Values List

The syntax used for the allowed values list in the last exercise might have looked a bit odd. It is odd but for good reason. The | is a delimiter separating the database value and the presented value, known as key and label respectively. This syntax is important because when using a key you can change the label at anytime without modifying your results. You can omit the key but any change to the label will cause a new and different database entry and will skew your results. For example consider the following scenario.

In January you set the values as in the exercise. Over the course of six months your website collects 100 items of Gossip that were marked as "Solid fact!" Then in June you decide to change the wording from "Solid fact!" to "This is no lie!" The meaning was the same but the descriptive wording changed. At this point you want to display a page showing all Gossip marked as "This is no lie!" if you did not use a key then the page will only display content added since June but if you used a key (i.e., `1|This is no lie!`) then you will see the submitted Gossip for the entire year as the key did not change; "Solid fact!" and "This is no lie!" were both stored in the database as a numeric 1.

> **NOTE** *This Accuracy field described here is an example to demonstrate how fields work. The taxonomy system provides a better mechanism to categorize your content instead of this list field type. List field types are great for small items such as agreements but not for categorization. Example: Do you agree to these terms and conditions? Yes/No*

CONTENT CONSTRUCTION KIT (CCK)

If you have done a bit of research into Drupal you probably have heard this name. Although you may not know it you have been using this kit throughout chapter. Fields, Field types, and Widgets are all products of CCK, now known simply as part of Drupal. The difference in naming is because CCK was developed before Drupal 7 and wasn't fully incorporated into Drupal until this version. Prior to Drupal 7 CCK was a contributed module that had to be added to Drupal separately.

The CCK contributed module is still alive and very active. The latest features go into the contributed module before they are allowed in core so if you like the custom content types so far you'll love the CCK module. The module can be found at `http://drupal.org/project/cck`.

Check out the CCK modules category of find new field types, widgets, and more. `http://drupal.org/taxonomy/term/88`.

VIEWS

Now considered to be an essential piece of Drupal, Views is an incredibly powerful contributed module. Views can be downloaded at `http://drupal.org/project/views`. At its core, Views is nothing more that a query builder to pull nodes from the database and display them as you see fit. For example, you may choose to display the following:

➤ A list of all blog entries sorted by author instead of the date (Drupal's default)

➤ The frontpage showing only content that is (a) promoted to the frontpage, (b) written by certain authors, and (c) for this month only

➤ The top content determined by the number of views

➤ The top content determined by the number of comments

If the data is in Drupal and you can dream it up, Views can probably display it. Views is covered in Chapter 11, "Views."

ADMINISTERING NODES

To review all of the content on your website click either Content in the top administration bar, Find content in your shortcuts, or navigate to Administer ⇨ Content. This interface, shown in Figure 6-34 displays all nodes and provides you with a basic filtering mechanism to narrow down the list of nodes shown. You can perform the following operations en masse on the nodes listed: publish, unpublish, promote to the frontpage, remove from front page, make sticky, remove stickiness, or delete.

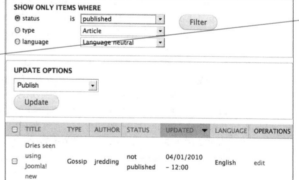

Users need the Administer nodes permission in order to use this interface.

FIGURE 6-34

Although the default administration interface gets the job done, it does have some limitations. For example, what if you want to update the status of 1,000 nodes or make a change such as disabling comments on all nodes? For these operations check out the contributed module Views bulk operations.

➤ **Views bulk operations** (`http://drupal.org/project/views_bulk_operations`) — This is an advanced bulk operation module that can change just about anything on a node, including adding and deleting taxonomy terms (tags), changing status, modifying ownership, and so on. Utilizing the Views module makes it incredibly flexible and powerful, but also complex. This module is not for the uninitiated but a wonderful module after you get your site up and running.

CONTENT MODERATION

Due to the complexity of moderation and no single moderation standard, Drupal does not provide a moderation system out of the box. This should not be seen as a fault but rather a testament to Drupal's flexibility. Moderation can be done in several ways; here are just a few.

➤ **Triggers and actions** — Covered in Chapter 10, triggers and actions can send your moderator an e-mail when new content is posted alerting them to review the content. A simple default unpublished state that the moderator flips to published can provide basic moderation.

➤ **Workflow** — Also covered in Chapter 10, the Workflow module can provide for a comprehensive moderation strategy and is a piece of content that must flow between multiple parties before being approved for publishing on the site.

➤ **Views + Views bulk operations** — Defaulting your content to the unpublished state and then setting it to publish can provide a very simple, and easy, moderation system. Views can build custom lists of content and Views bulk operation can operate on them en masse.

➤ **Modr8** — An out-of-the-box proper moderation system for Drupal that adds a moderate status to your content types. Find it at `http://drupal.org/project/modr8`.

Quick and Easy Moderation

If your site receives only a few bits of content at a time and requires a pre-approval method of moderation then you can use Drupal's built-in tools to provide moderation. In the first exercise you created the Gossip content with the default Published state unchecked. This unpublished state can be used to flag the content for moderation. The only item left to do is to navigate to Administer ➪ Content and filter for unpublished Gossip content types as shown in Figure 6-35.

You can then use the Update options to publish multiple nodes at the same time.

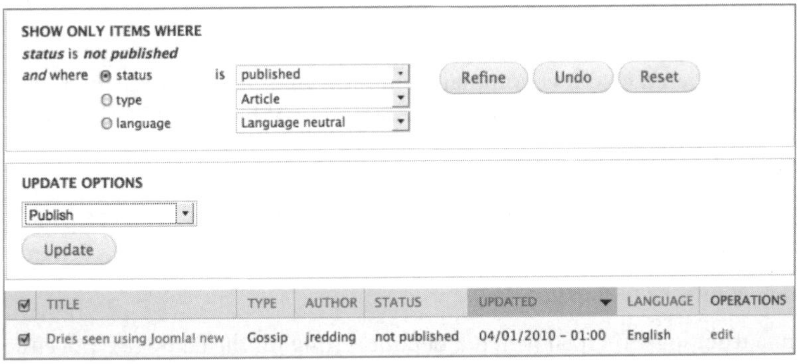

FIGURE 6-35

NODES IN A NUTSHELL

At this point in the chapter you've covered a broad range of the node system. The node system is powerful because of the items that can attach themselves to the node thus extending it. You saw this when adding and configuring the new fields.

In review, the node system in Drupal provides:

➤ Ability to create numerous custom content types.

➤ Each content type can contain numerous custom fields such as a file upload field, image field, drop-down selection, checkboxes, additional text areas, and more.

➤ Each content type automatically receives five permissions; Create, Edit own, Edit all, Delete own, Delete all.

➤ Revisions to nodes are tracked whenever the Create new revision box is checked. Check this box in the content type's default settings to automatically track all revisions.

The Drupal community has extended the node system by providing numerous contributed modules freely available on drupal.org. You can find more modules that work with nodes, provide custom node types, or simply add new content at, `http://drupal.org/taxonomy/term/57`.

All of this power can come with a performance price, however, as high flexibility requires a bit of extra processing power. This performance price is one reason why you will come across contributed modules that do not use the node system but rather store their data separately. When choosing new contributed modules or deciding to build your own module or custom content type consider the advantages (comments, revisions, custom fields, etc.) and disadvantages of the node system.

The following section switches focus over to the second most important piece of content on your site, comments.

COMMENTS

Comments can breathe life into your website by providing a method for users to respond to your site's content. Enabled by default, the Comment module not only allows commenting on nodes but also provides an administrative and moderation interface. As you saw in Chapter 3 comments are by default enabled for the Article content type but not for the page content type. This can be easily changed by modifying the content type's default settings.

The earlier parts of this chapter covered enabling comments on individual nodes. A recap might help to ensure that you have all the rights bits in place. The quick steps to enabling commenting are:

➤ Enable the comment module (done by default).

➤ Users need the Post comments permission. If you'd like them to immediately bypass moderation also grant the Post comments without approval permission.

➤ Users need the Access comment permission to view comments.

➤ Set the node's comment settings to Open (often a default setting on the content type) either on the individual node or by setting a default for all newly created nodes (Administer ⇨ Structure ⇨ Content types, then edit the appropriate content type).

That's it! Read on to review the comment administration and moderation settings as well as more detailed information on the individual pieces.

PERMISSIONS

Before users can post or see comments you will need to grant them permission. Figure 6-36 shows the four comments permissions.

➤ **Administer comments** — Users may add, edit, or delete comments. This permission is required for comment moderators.

➤ **Access comments** — Typically granted to anonymous users to allow them to see the commentary.

➤ **Post comments** — Users with permission can submit a comment but it will not appear on the site until a comment moderator has approved the comment.

➤ **Post comments without approval** — Users bypass the moderation process and have their comments posted immediately.

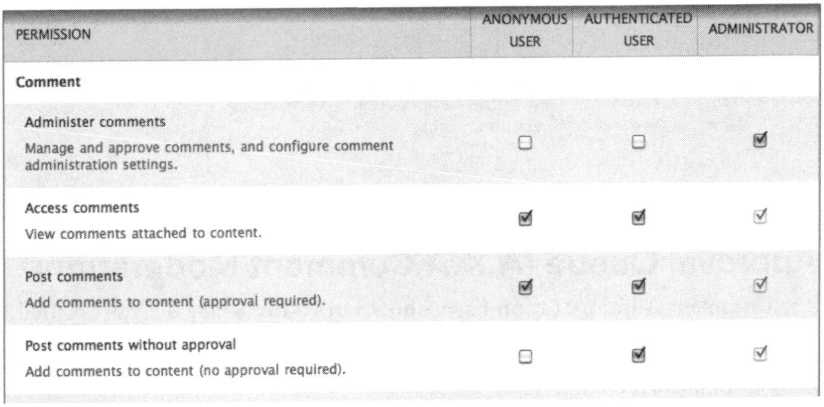

PERMISSION	ANONYMOUS USER	AUTHENTICATED USER	ADMINISTRATOR
Comment			
Administer comments Manage and approve comments, and configure comment administration settings.	☐	☐	☑
Access comments View comments attached to content.	☑	☑	☑
Post comments Add comments to content (approval required).	☑	☑	☑
Post comments without approval Add comments to content (no approval required).	☐	☑	☑

FIGURE 6-36

Comment Administration

Users with the Administer comments have two options for managing comments. They can choose to navigate to the individual nodes where all comments will be shown (published or unpublished) or use the site wide comment administration page. Typically the site wide administration page is the most useful. Figure 6-37 shows a typical comment for those with the Administer comments permission.

Comments

First comment

My first comment, ain't it cute?

delete   edit   reply

FIGURE 6-37

As you might expect, the delete, edit, and reply buttons do exactly what they say. Users with the Administer comments permission can change the published status, submission date, author of a comment as well as modify the subject and comment. This permission is site wide. Needless to say this is an immense amount of power.

Comment Administration Page

Comments are administered and moderated similarly to nodes. Users with the Administer comments permissions can click over to Administer ➪ Content ➪ Comments to view your site's comments, as shown in Figure 6-38. This page lists all published comments currently visible on the website and provides an option to Unpublish or Delete them. If you hover over the comment subject a tooltip will show the first few lines of the comment. Unpublished comments are placed in the Approval queue accessed at the top of the page.

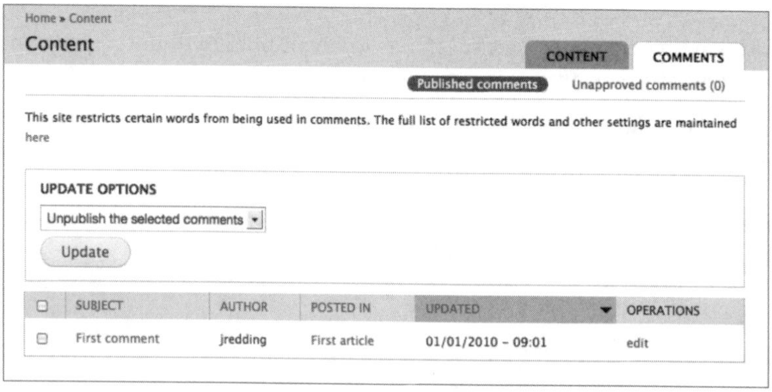

FIGURE 6-38

Comment Approval Queue (A.K.A Comment Moderation)

At the top of the Comment Administration Page, shown in Figure 6-38, is a tab entitled Unapproved comments. Comments appear on this tab via two methods:

➤ Manually unpublished comments.

➤ Comments left by users who have the Post Comments permission and do not have the Post Comments Without Approval permission.

TRY IT OUT Enabling Comment Moderation

In this exercise, you will implement moderated comments on the Gossip content type for all anonymous users, but authenticated users will be able to post without moderation. Follow these steps:

1. Ensure the Comment module is enabled at Administer ➪ Modules.

2. Assign the following permissions, as shown in Figure 6-39, by navigating to Administer ➪ Configuration ➪ Permissions Post Comments to the Anonymous User role. Post Comments and Post comments Without Approval to the Authenticated User role.

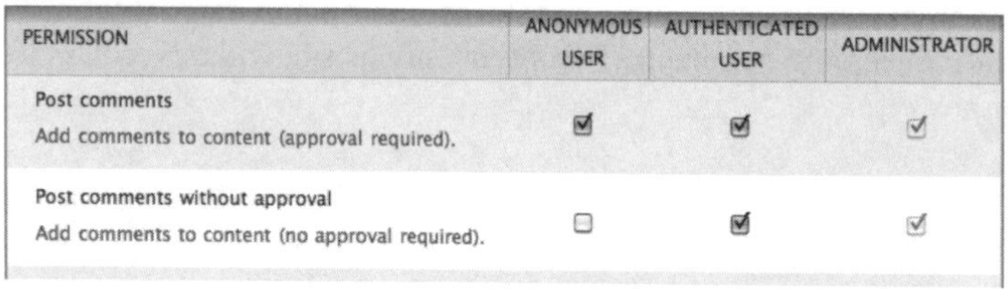

FIGURE 6-39

3. Ensure that commenting is enabled for the Gossip Content Type. Navigate to Administer ⇨ Structure ⇨ Content types, then click edit to the far right of the Gossip content type. Under comment settings ensure that Open is selected as shown in Figure 6-40.

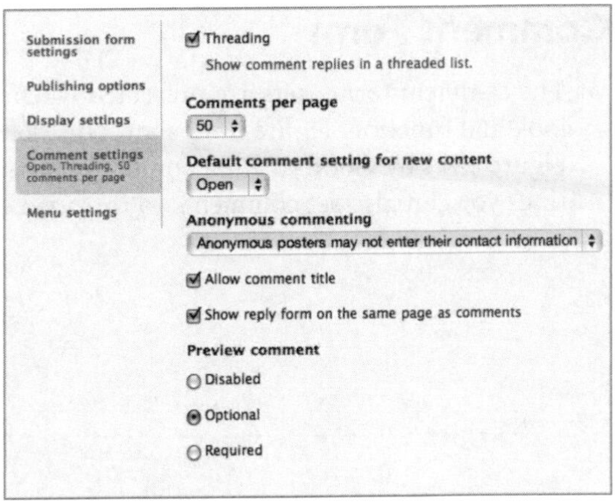

At this point the configuration is complete continue to ensure that everything is working as expected.

4. Create a new Gossip node by clicking Add content in the Navigation menu then Gossip in the content type list.

5. Add a comment on the newly created node by clicking Add New Comment at the bottom of the node, shown in Figure 6-41.

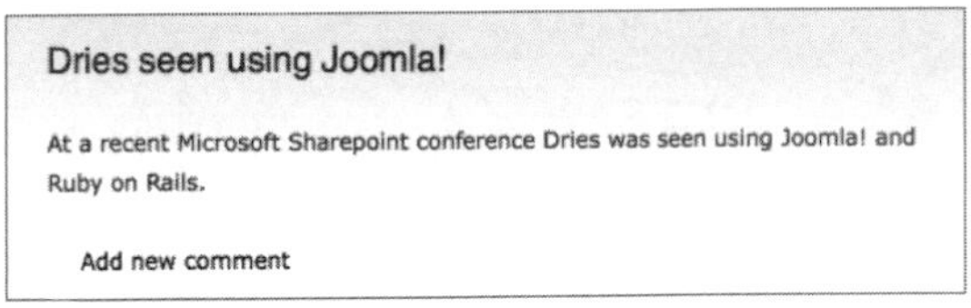

The comment should appear immediately on the website as your user account is granted the Post comments without approval permission. If it does not appear immediately review the permissions from step 2.

FIGURE 6-40

FIGURE 6-41

Add a comment as an anonymous user to ensure everything is setup correctly.

6. Log out and navigate back to the node you just created.

7. Add a new comment to the page.

The comment will not appear on the page as the anonymous user was granted the Post comments permission. Continue on to approve the comment.

8. Log in as an administrator and navigate to Administer ⇨ Content ⇨ Comments.

9. Click the Approval queue tab (see Figure 6-38).

10. Check the box next to the newly created comment then choose `Published Selected Comments` from the dropdown and click Update.

Alternatively you can click the approve link located underneath the comments, shown in Figure 6-42.

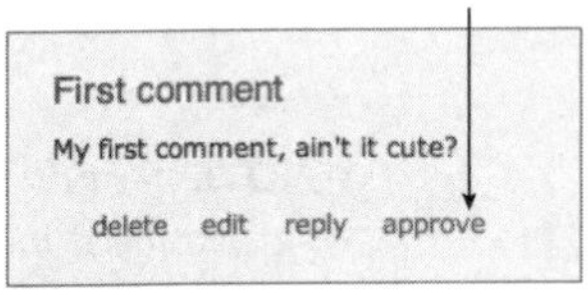

FIGURE 6-42

How It Works

Drupal's comment moderation is based upon the permission the users have. Comments left by users with only the `Post comments` permission won't be available on the site until they are approved by a user with the `Administer comments` permission. Users that also have the `Post comments without approval` permission can bypass moderation.

Users with the Administer comments permission must approve comments left by users with only the Post Comments permission. Users with the Post Comment Without Approval permission, obviously, bypass the approval (i.e., moderation) process.

Comment Form

The comment form users are presented when leaving a comment has a few options to modify its look and function. Figure 6-43 shows the default form. Configure the comment form to look like Figure 6-44 by modifying the content type settings, shown in Figure 6-45. Within content type settings you can also set comments to threaded or flat and limit the number of comments per page.

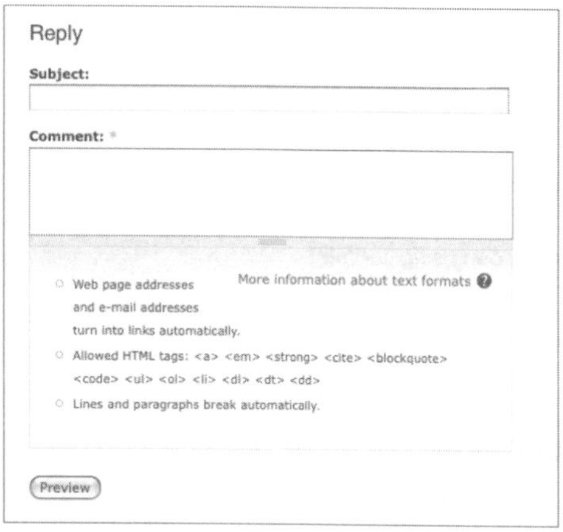

FIGURE 6-43

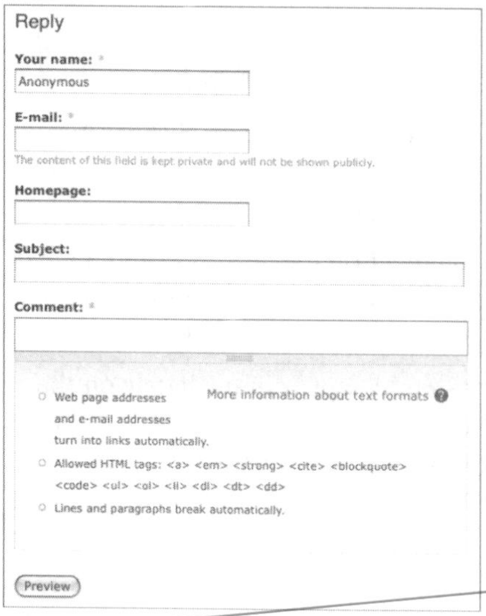

FIGURE 6-44

FIGURE 6-45

> **NOTE** Modify the name of the Anonymous user as Administer ➪ Configuration ➪ Account settings (under People and Permissions)

Allowing Rich Text Comments

Comments are initially constrained to a small set of HTML through the use of a Text format, by default this is set to filtered HTML as discussed in Chapter 4. You can allow more HTML by simply modifying the filtered HMTL text format or assigning a new default text format at Administer ➪ Configuration ➪ Text formats (under Content Authoring).

You can enable wiki-code, BBCode or other syntax easily by installing the appropriate text format module. Find these and other similar modules here: `http://drupal.org/taxonomy/term/63`

> **NOTE** *Never allow un-trusted users the ability to post Full (unfiltered) HTML. Doing so will open your site to malicious code such as a cross-site scripting attack or fake password forms.*

WYSIWYG

Available for content, comments, and nearly every multi-line text area on your Drupal site a What You See Is What You Get (WYSIWYG) editor, like the CKEditor shown in Figure 6-46, can make it easy for users to create rich text pages or comments. Find out more out at `http://drupal.org/project/wysiwyg`.

SPAM

Despite predictions that by the mid 2000s spam would be eliminated, it is still a problem today. Any website running without spam protection will quickly be overrun by dummy comments, nodes, or user accounts created by spam robots. Moderation will help to protect your website from displaying these spam nodes or comments but will overwhelm your moderators with tedious deletion. Spam must to be stopped before it reaches moderation or your website. Here are a few ways you can stop spam before it hits your website:

➤ **Mollom** (`http://drupal.org/project/mollom`) — An adaptive service that filters nodes and comments as they are submitted. If the text matches existing known spam, they are rejected outright; if there is question about their authenticity, a *captcha* is presented to the user so they can prove they are human. If spam does slip through you can report it to Mollom to help it learn how to spot spam.

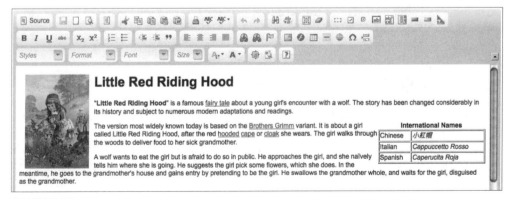

FIGURE 6-46

Mollom requires both a module and an account at http://mollom.com.

➤ **Captcha** (http://drupal.org/project/captcha) — A *captcha* is the funny little image of numbers and letters that you see on forms throughout the Web, shown in Figure 6-47. The words and letters are contorted so that a computer cannot read them but a human can. This module will place a captcha image on the comment form, hopefully ensuring that an actual person is submitting the comment.

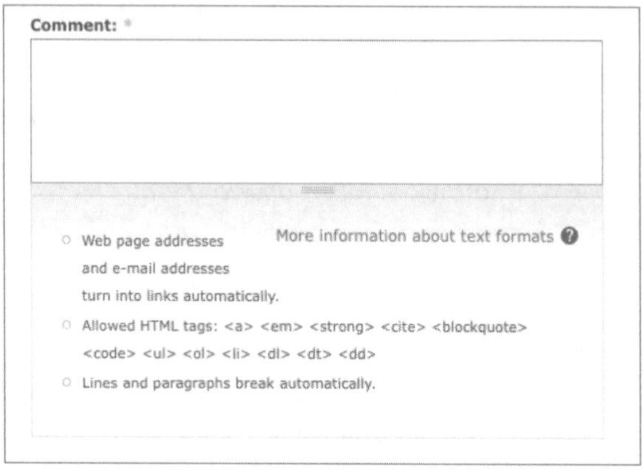

FIGURE 6-47

The captcha module also works with a unique module that not only helps to fight spam but also to digitize books; reCAPTCHA. From the reCAPTCHA website (http://recaptcha.net): "reCAPTCHA improves the process of digitizing books by sending words that cannot be read by computers to the Web in the form of CAPTCHAs for humans to decipher". By using reCAPTCHA you'll not only protect your site from spam but also help to digitize books that were written before the era of the computer.

➤ **IP Blocking** — Sometimes spammers continually attack your site from a single computer or IP address. You may be alerted to this from a system administrator, Drupal's reports, or from the server's system logs. If you know the IP address you can block it directly by entering it in the IP Address Blocking section (Administer ➪ Configuration ➪ IP Address Blocking (under People and permissions). IP Addresses blocked here will be stopped before Drupal has a chance to load, which can free up significant resources previously consumed by a ruthless spammer.

NOTE Enable Mollom or CAPTCHA to protect user registrations as many spam bots are designed to create a user account first and then use that account to post spam comments.

RSS AGGREGATION

The Aggregator module included with Drupal's core allows you to pull in content from other sites for display on your own. This is a great way to curate content for your visitors and site members. Planet Drupal (http://drupal.org/planet) is an excellent example of aggregation. The Planet pulls Drupal related news from over 350 sources displaying them in a single page and providing a single combined RSS feed.

Follow the next two exercises to create your own custom Planet. Before you begin be sure the Aggregator module is enabled by visiting Modules.

TRY IT OUT   Import an RSS Feed

In this exercise you will import the Wall Street Journal's top news stories for display on your site.

1. With the Aggregator module enabled navigate to Configuration ⇨ Web services — Feed aggregator.

2. Begin by adding a feed. First click Add feed as shown in Figure 6-48 then enter the following information as shown in Figure 6-49.

➤ Title: WSJ

➤ URL: `http://online.wsj.com/xml/rss/3_7011.xml`

➤ Update interval: 6 hours

➤ News items in block: 3

3. Click Save.

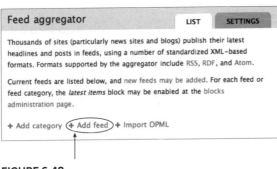

FIGURE 6-48

FIGURE 6-49

4. The Aggregator configuration page you should name contains something similar to Figure 6-50. Click update items to retrieve the latest headlines from the RSS feed. Drupal will automatically update the headlines every six hours as indicated by the Update interval.

Feed overview

TITLE	ITEMS	LAST UPDATE	NEXT UPDATE	OPERATIONS		
WSJ	0 items	never	never	edit	remove items	update items

FIGURE 6-50

How It Works

Based on the Update interval set per feed, Drupal will retrieve the latest headlines from these headlines. Automatic updates depend upon Cron running correctly. Cron is covered in Chapter 3, "Your First Drupal Website."

Displaying the Feed

To display the content retrieved from the RSS feed Drupal creates both a page and a block. The page is accessible by clicking the feed's title (Figure 6-50) and will have the URL structure `http://local-host/aggregator/source/X` where x is the ID of the feed. A great tip is to clean up this URL by adding a URL alias at Configuration ➪ Search and metadata ➪ URL aliases as shown in Figure 6-51.

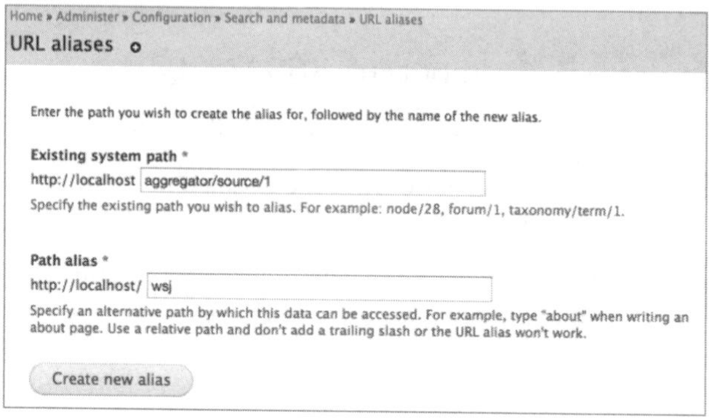

Blocks are available with all other blocks at Structure ➪ Blocks and named after the feed title as shown in Figure 6-52. You must assign them to a region before they are visible on your site. The number of items that appear in a block is set in each individual feed's configuration.

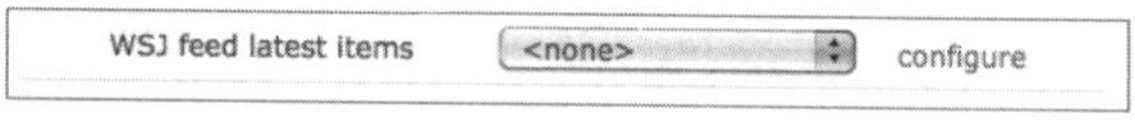

Home » Administer » Configuration » Search and metadata » URL aliases

URL aliases ○

Enter the path you wish to create the alias for, followed by the name of the new alias.

Existing system path *
http://localhost `aggregator/source/1`
Specify the existing path you wish to alias. For example: node/28, forum/1, taxonomy/term/1.

Path alias *
http://localhost/ `wsj`
Specify an alternative path by which this data can be accessed. For example, type "about" when writing an about page. Use a relative path and don't add a trailing slash or the URL alias won't work.

Create new alias

FIGURE 6-51

| WSJ feed latest items | <none> | ⬍ | configure |

FIGURE 6-52

TRY IT OUT   **Aggregate Multiple RSS Feeds to a Single Page and RSS Feed**

In this exercise you will combine two RSS feeds that will be displayed on a single page and can be viewed through a single RSS feed.

1. Navigate to the Aggregator module's configuration page at Configuration ➪ Web Services ➪ Feed Aggregator.

2. Add a new category with the following information as shown in Figure 6-53:

➤ **Title:** External News Sites

➤ **Description:** A combination of several important news feeds.

Title *
External News Sites

Description
A combination of several important news feeds

Save

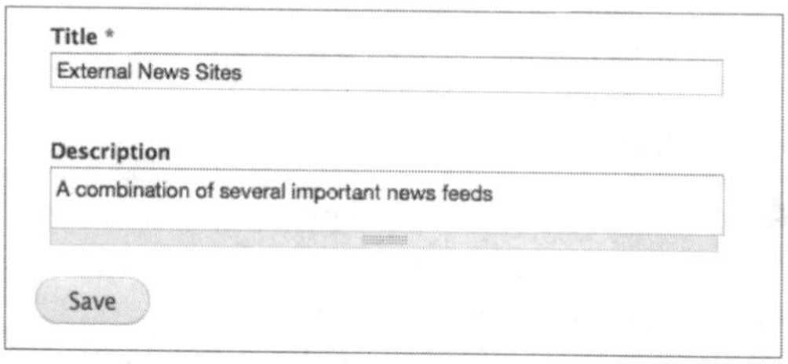

FIGURE 6-53

3. Click Save on the List at the top of the page to return to the main configuration page.

4. Following the instructions introduced in the previous exercise, add a second feed for the New York Times: `http://www.nytimes.com/services/xml/rss/nyt/GlobalHome.xml`.

Categorize this feed as part of External News Sites by checking the box near the Save button as shown in Figure 6-54.

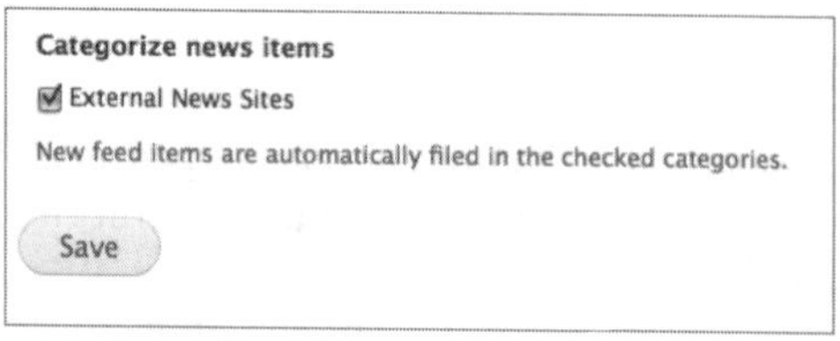

Categorize news items
☑ External News Sites
New feed items are automatically filed in the checked categories.

Save

5. Click Save.

FIGURE 6-54

6. Return to the front configuration page and edit the WSJ feed to add it to External News Sites category. When finished your summary should appear as in Figure 6-55.

Feed overview						
TITLE	ITEMS	LAST UPDATE	NEXT UPDATE	OPERATIONS		
NY Times	11 items	1 sec ago	5 hours 59 min left	edit	remove items	update items
WSJ	21 items	34 min 28 sec ago	5 hours 25 min left	edit	remove items	update items

FIGURE 6-55

How It Works

Aggregator categories combine multiple feeds into a single page, block, and RSS feed. Access the page by clicking on the category title. The block is available in the usual place (Structure ⇨ Blocks) and the number of items displayed are configured within the block's configuration. Find the RSS feed by navigating to the category's page and scrolling to the bottom or to `http://localhost/aggregator/rss/X` where X is the ID number of the category.

Configuring the Aggregation Settings

Drupal's defaults are sane if you will be aggregating only a few RSS feeds but should be adjusted if you aggregate a significant number. Click on Settings at the top of the Feed Aggregator main page to adjust the defaults shown in Figure 6-56. The most important setting on this page is Discard items older than. When Drupal retrieves data it is placed within your site's database. The more feeds and content you aggregate combined with the length of time you keep them will increase the size of your database. Adjust these settings based upon the relevancy of having the data available on your site.

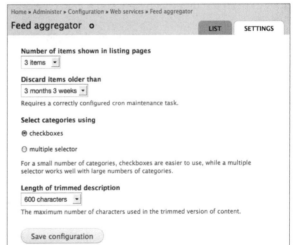

FIGURE 6-56

The first setting, Items shown in source and categories pages, refers to the URLS:

```
http://localhost/aggregator/sources
http://localhost/aggregator/categories
```

> **NOTE** *Need more features? Want to aggregate a non-RSS enabled site? Check out the FeedAPI available at* `http://drupal.org/project/feedapi`. *When combined with views this aggregator is extremely powerful.*

SUMMARY

This chapter covered quite a bit of material. After completing this chapter you should have a basic understanding of Drupal's node system, particularly what a node is and why it sets Drupal apart from other systems. You also learned how to create new nodes types, use the CCK system to extend your nodes, as well as how to administer nodes and assign appropriate permissions. The comment system was also discussed including how to add, edit, and delete comments, enable comment moderation, modify the comment form and fight spam. Spam not only affects comments but also your site as a whole, it is important to protect every user input against potential spam.

In the next chapter you'll explore the User management section and learn how to add users, manage roles, permissions, and other user settings.

EXERCISES

1. What are nodes and how does Drupal use them?

2. What is a Content type field?

3. Explain the difference between a field type and field widget.

4. How many images can be uploaded using a single image field?

5. What is an Image style?

6. When adding a field with multiple allowed values what is the purpose of using the following syntax?

   1 | Option A

   2 | Option B

   3 | Option C

Answers to the Exercises can be found in the Appendix.

▶ **WHAT YOU LEARNED IN THIS CHAPTER**

➤   Nodes are one of the building blocks for content in Drupal.

➤   All nodes have versioning, can have comments and can be extended by node-related modules.

➤   The Content Construction Kit (CCK) allows you to add new fields to existing nodes. Contributed modules extend CCK by offering custom field types.

➤   CCK field types constrain the input to a particular format (for example: address, phone number, numeric, etc.)

➤   Widgets are used to display CCK fields allowing you to customize how you request data from the user (for example: drop-down menu, checkbox, text field, etc.)

➤   Comments can be enabled for any node by simply editing the comment settings on the node.

➤   The content type settings can be used to set defaults for comment settings or other items when a node is created.

➤   When allowing comments or nodes from anonymous users be sure to download and install a spam module.

User Management

➤ Creating user accounts

➤ Using OpenID

➤ Creating roles and permissions

➤ Setting up user account e-mails (new account, password reset, and so on)

➤ Creating custom user profiles

➤ What happens when a user cancels their account

➤ Moderating new user accounts

➤ Managing sessions

Unless you plan to be an extremely busy person, you'll most likely want to recruit a few people to help manage your site. You'll also probably want to allow your site visitors to create an account on your site. Like most websites, a user account provides a visitor with a personal profile and allows them to track their content, and you can grant them permissions. As you saw in Chapter 3, "Your First Drupal Site," creating a members-only website is as easy as removing the permission from the Anonymous User role.

In this chapter, you dig deeper into user account management to explore the settings that control what notification e-mails are sent to the user (such as password requests, new accounts, and so on), what happens when a user account is canceled (is their data kept or removed?), and the important permissions to watch out for. You'll also create custom user profiles and explore the OpenID module to encourage users who are registered on external sites to register on your site.

CREATING USER ACCOUNTS

With your Drupal website, you can choose what your visitors can do with or without a user account. For example, a default Drupal website allows all site visitors to view published content but does not allow them to post comments. You can allow all site visitors to post comments by simply granting them the permission. First, here's a bit of terminology.

Site visitors that are not logged in are *anonymous users*, once they create an account and log into it they become an *authenticated user*. The purpose of creating an account in Drupal is to uniquely assign content or permissions to a user. Similar to a government ID number, Drupal assigns each user a unique ID, which is used to link their comments, content, votes, profiles, and other data to them. Without this ID, Drupal cannot track the user. Drupal will create a local account for the user even if they log in with an external username and password (as is the case with OpenID).

People

Your users are known as *people* on your site, and their accounts can be accessed through the People link in the top Administration menu. From this section, you can also block, unblock, cancel accounts, or add and remove users to and from roles, as shown in Figure 7-1.

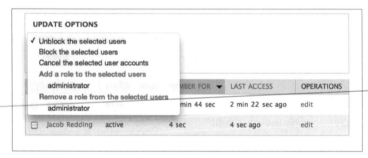

FIGURE 7-1

Anonymous Users

An anonymous user is any site visitor who does not log into an account. The name you use for anonymous users is configured at Administer ➪ Configuration ➪ Account Settings (under People and Permissions). You are free to call these anonymous folks anything you'd like (such as "Anonymous Coward" for the Slashdot crowd or "Lone Thespian" for the drama club). Once configured, the name is modified for all previous and future anonymous postings.

CREATING ACCOUNTS

You can specify who can and who cannot create user accounts on your site. By default, Drupal allows all visitors to create a user account provided that they can verify their e-mail address by clicking a verification link sent to them. This is configured at Administer ➪ Configuration ➪ Account Settings (People and Permissions), as shown in Figure 7-2.

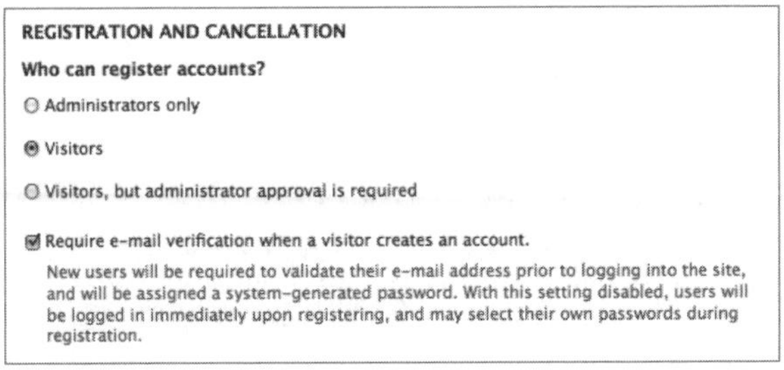

REGISTRATION AND CANCELLATION

Who can register accounts?

◯ Administrators only

◉ Visitors

◯ Visitors, but administrator approval is required

☑ Require e-mail verification when a visitor creates an account.

New users will be required to validate their e-mail address prior to logging into the site, and will be assigned a system-generated password. With this setting disabled, users will be logged in immediately upon registering, and may select their own passwords during registration.

FIGURE 7-2

Note that by default the Require E-mail Verification box is checked. This will cause Drupal to send out a "Welcome (awaiting approval)" e-mail to the user (configured lower in the page). The user must then click a link within the e-mail to verify their e-mail address.

Follow the next exercise to enable user account moderation, forcing new user accounts to be manually verified before they can be used on the site.

TRY IT OUT   **Enabling User Account Moderation**

Follow these steps to enable moderation on new user accounts:

1. In the top navigation bar, choose Configuration ⇨ Account Settings, as shown in Figure 7-3.

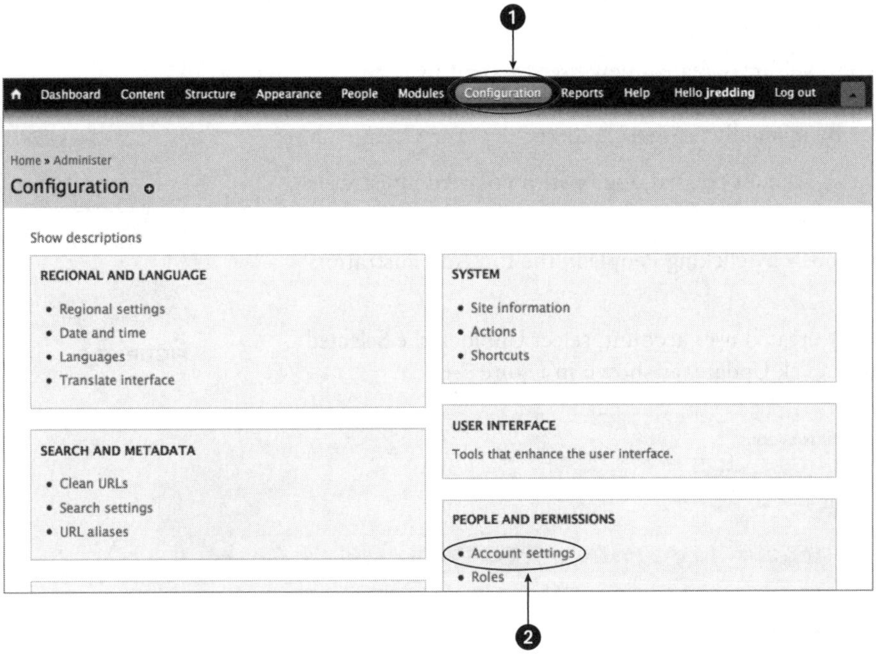

FIGURE 7-3

2. In the Registration and Cancellation section, select Visitors, But Administrator Approval Is Required, as shown in Figure 7-4.

3. Click the Save Configuration button at the bottom of the page.

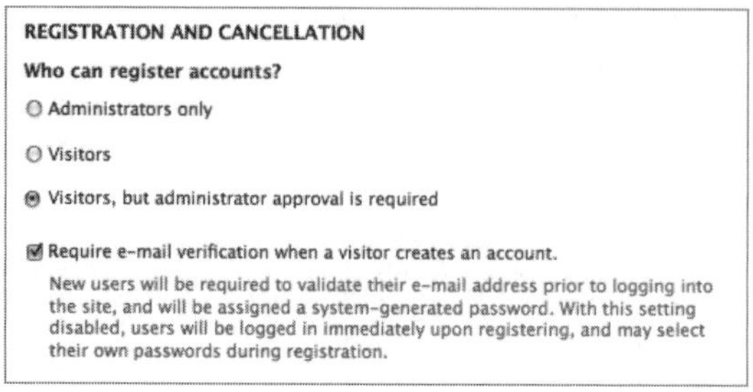

How It Works

The account settings define how Drupal handles accounts created by site visitors. In this exercise, you are forcing administrator approval for all user accounts.

REGISTRATION AND CANCELLATION

Who can register accounts?

○ Administrators only

○ Visitors

◉ Visitors, but administrator approval is required

☑ Require e-mail verification when a visitor creates an account.

New users will be required to validate their e-mail address prior to logging into the site, and will be assigned a system-generated password. With this setting disabled, users will be logged in immediately upon registering, and may select their own passwords during registration.

FIGURE 7-4

Approving Accounts in Moderation

When administrator approval is required for user accounts, Drupal sets the newly created user account to blocked status. You will have to manually unblock the account. Follow the next exercise to learn how to do this.

TRY IT OUT   **Unblocking New User Accounts**

In this exercise, you unblock newly created user accounts. (Please complete the previous exercise before continuing, if you have not already done so.)

1. Log out of your website. Create a new user account by clicking Create New Account under the User Login block as shown in Figure 7-5, or by manually navigating to `http://localhost/user`.

2. With a new user account created, log in with your Administrator account.

3. Navigate to `People` by clicking People in the top Administration menu.

4. Select the newly created user account, select Unblock the Selected Users, and then click Update, as shown in Figure 7-6.

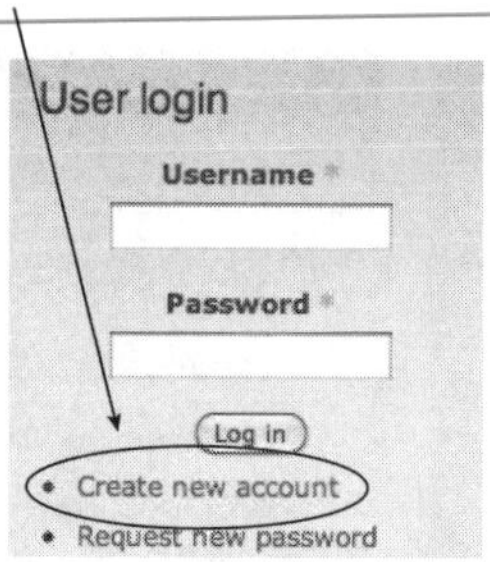

User login

Username *

Password *

Log in

• Create new account
• Request new password

FIGURE 7-5

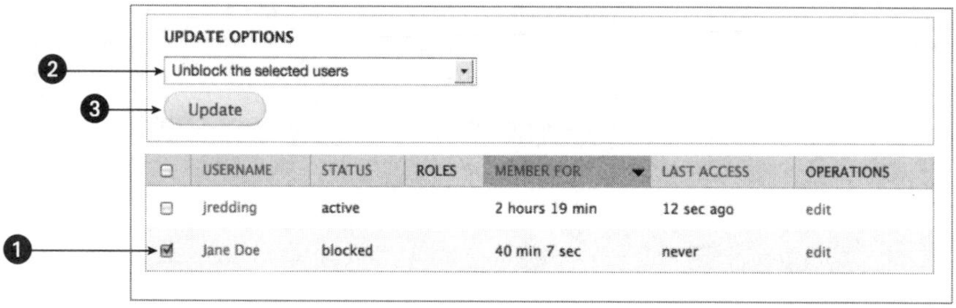

UPDATE OPTIONS

 Unblock the selected users ▼

③ → Update

	USERNAME	STATUS	ROLES	MEMBER FOR ▼	LAST ACCESS	OPERATIONS
☐	jredding	active		2 hours 19 min	12 sec ago	edit
☑	Jane Doe	blocked		40 min 7 sec	never	edit

FIGURE 7-6

How It Works

Accounts in moderation are set as blocked and require manual unblocking before the account can be used. If you also have e-mail verification enabled, the user must verify their e-mail address in order to update their password. As an Administrator, you can manually set the user's password to bypass the e-mail verification process.

Setting a Password During Registration

You probably noticed that when creating a new user account, you are not prompted to choose a password. This is the behavior when the Require E-mail Verification When a Visitor Creates An Account box is checked. To allow users to specify their own password during registration, simply uncheck this box within Account Settings.

CANCELING ACCOUNTS

When a user decides to leave your community or you decide to delete their account, you (or they) have a decision to make. What do you do with their account and the content they have created? Here are your options:

➤   The content can be deleted with the user.

➤   The user's account can be disabled and its content associated with the now defunct account.

➤   The content can remain but be reassigned to the anonymous user.

You choose the desired option on the Account Settings page, as shown in Figure 7-7.

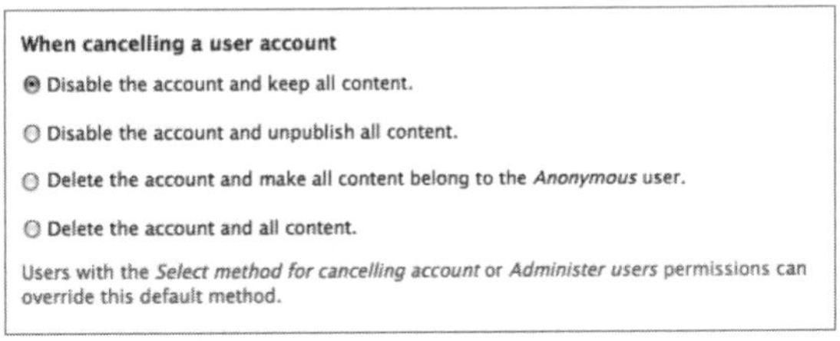

A user can cancel their own account only if you grant them the Cancel Account permission. If the user has this permission, you may also grant them the Select Method for Cancelling Own Account per-

> **When cancelling a user account**
> ⊖ Disable the account and keep all content.
> ○ Disable the account and unpublish all content.
> ○ Delete the account and make all content belong to the *Anonymous* user.
> ○ Delete the account and all content.
> Users with the *Select method for cancelling account* or *Administer users* permissions can override this default method.

FIGURE 7-7

mission to allow them to override the site-wide default, as stated at the bottom of Figure 7-7.

SETTING UP ACCOUNT E-MAILS

When a new user registers on your site, Drupal will send them a Welcome e-mail. When a user requests a password reset, an e-mail is sent with the details. E-mails are sent for various account-related activities. You can configure these e-mails on the Account Settings page as shown in Figure 7-8.

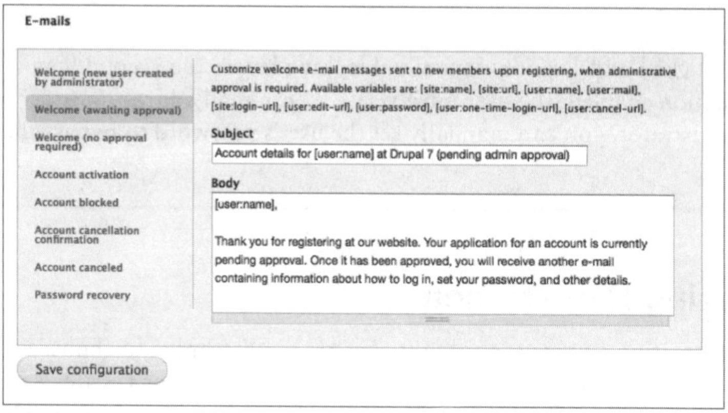

FIGURE 7-8

Follow the next exercise to create a customized Welcome e-mail.

TRY IT OUT   Customizing Your Welcome E-mail

In this exercise, you create a customized Welcome e-mail that will be sent to each new user.

1.   Navigate to Configuration ⇨ Account Settings.

2.   At the bottom of the page under Emails, select Welcome (No Approval Required).

3.   Type in the following information:

```
Hey there [user:name], and welcome to our community. Please click the link below to verify
your e-mail address and enable your account. We look forward to seeing you around the
community.
[user:one-time-login-url]

For security reasons, this URL can only be used once. Once you have logged in, you can
modify your password and other account settings at [user:edit-url].

See you around the community!
```

4.   Click the Save Configuration button at the bottom of the page.

How It Works

As you saw in the exercise, Drupal sends out several e-mails for various account activities. Each of these e-mails has a number of variables that can be used to create a personal touch to your site's e-mails.

USING OPENID

Have you ever asked yourself why you have to create a new username and password on every site? The hassle of trying to remember a new username and password has quickly become an Internet annoyance nearly on par with spam. Your site visitors are probably feeling this Internet pain and may decide to not sign up on your site because they don't want yet another username and password. OpenID to the rescue!

OpenID allows users to login to an OpenID-enabled site by using their centralized OpenID. An example of OpenID is using a Flickr username and password to log into your Drupal website. Users can set up an OpenID with any OpenID provider. OpenID providers include Google, Yahoo!, LiveJournal, Blogger, MySpace, AOL, Flickr, Orange, Hyves, and Wordpress.com. With OpenID, users can use a username and password from any of these providers to log into their account on your website.

Users who log into your site with an OpenID have an account on your site, but the OpenID provider handles the authentication of their username and password. Your site also does not store their password so if they changed their password the account still works. Follow along with the next exercise to enable OpenID for your site visitors and to log into your account with an OpenID from one of the many OpenID providers.

 NOTE *Learn more about OpenID at* `http://openid.net`*.*

TRY IT OUT   **Logging in Using an OpenID**

In this exercise, you explore OpenID by using your existing Google, Yahoo!, Flickr, MySpace, or other OpenID provider account.

1. Log in with your Administrator account.

2. Enable the OpenID module at Configuration ⇨ Modules.

3. Navigate to your user account page, and then click OpenID Identities as shown in Figure 7-9.

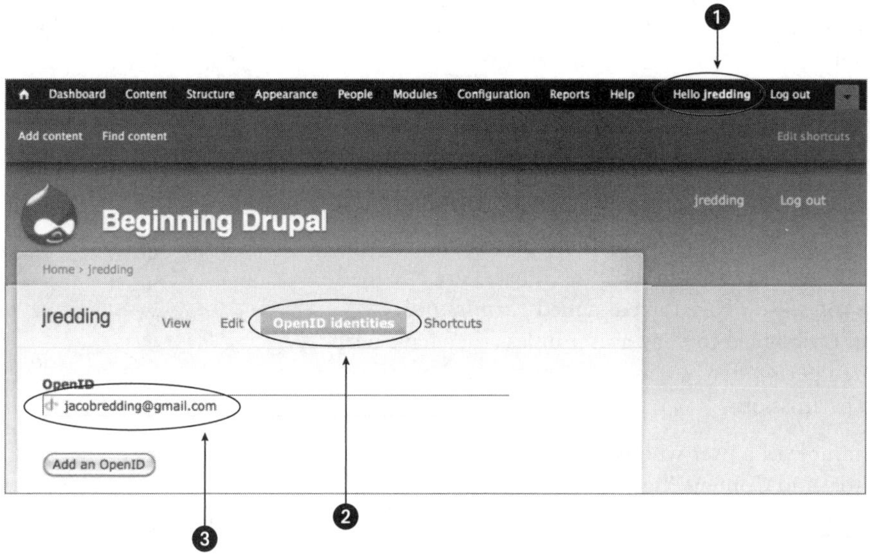

FIGURE 7-9

4.   Add your OpenID. Here are a few examples:

```
your-email@gmail.com
flickr.com/username
openid.aol.com/screenname
myspace.com/your-username
blogname.blogspot.com
```

You can find more examples at http://openid.net/get-an-openid/.

FIGURE 7-10

5.   Once your OpenID has been verified, log out and test your new OpenID-enabled login by clicking Log In Using OpenID, as shown in Figure 7-10.

How It Works

OpenID maps a user account on your site with an external OpenID provider for the purposes of authenticating the user. OpenID is not a substitute for a user account but instead is a method for a web-centralized username and password. You still retain the ability to block or cancel a user's account at any time.

What If a User Doesn't Have an Account?

Users who attempt to log into your site by using an OpenID that is not associated with a preexisting user account will be prompted to create an account on your site. OpenID is a method of authentication that adheres to your site's account creation policies.

What If Your Users Don't Have OpenIDs?

Users without an OpenID can continue to use a created username and password. If they later obtain an OpenID, they can associate it with their existing Drupal account as you did in the last exercise. The only difference between an OpenID-enabled account and a non-OpenID account is the method of authentication.

CREATING ROLES AND PERMISSIONS

A site without activity can be rather boring. Let your users roam free on your site by providing them with the permission to be creative on your site. As discussed in Chapter 3, users are assigned to one or more *roles*. Roles are then assigned *permissions*. Because Drupal is designed to deny a user unless they have been explicitly granted permission, a user will receive a culmination of their roles and permissions.

Consider an example of a user who has three roles: Authenticated User, Web Editor, and Content Manager, as illustrated in Figure 7-11. Review the permissions laid out in Figure 7-12.

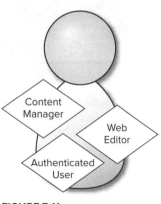

FIGURE 7-11

PERMISSION	ANONYMOUS USER	AUTHENTICATED USER	ADMINISTRATOR	CONTENT MANAGER	WEB EDITOR
Create *Article* content	☐	☑	☑	☑	☑
Edit own *Article* content	☐	☐	☑	☑	☐
Edit any *Article* content	☐	☐	☑	☐	☑
Delete own *Article* content	☐	☐	☑	☐	☐
Delete any *Article* content	☐	☐	☑	☐	☑

FIGURE 7-12

Can this user delete their Article content? Will they be able to delete Articles they did not create?

The answer to both of these questions is yes. Every user that logs into your site becomes a member of the *Authenticated User* role and therefore has the *Create Article content* permission. As a Content Manager, they receive the permission to edit their own Articles. Finally, as a Web Editor, they are granted additional permissions that includes the ability to edit and delete any Article content. Note that if the user is only a Web Editor and not a Content Manager, they would only have the ability to edit Article content and not to create Articles.

In the next two exercises, you create a new Web Editor role that provides users with the ability to edit all Articles on your site.

TRY IT OUT Creating a New Role

Follow these steps to create a Web Editor role:

1. Log in with your Administrator account and navigate to Configuration ⇨ Roles (under People and Permissions).

2. Enter `Web Editor` in the text box at the bottom of the screen and then click the Add Role button, as shown in Figure 7-13.

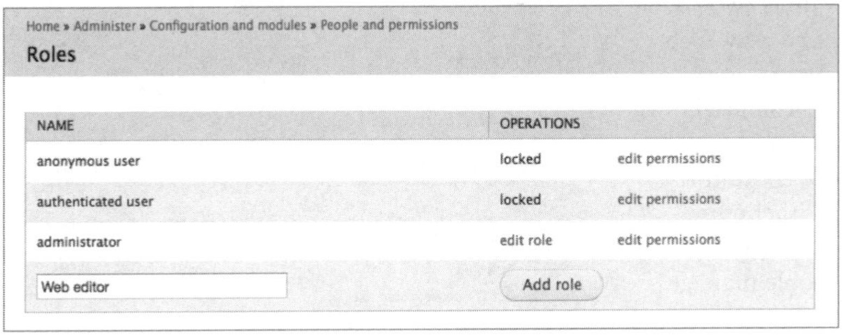

Home » Administer » Configuration and modules » People and permissions

Roles

NAME		OPERATIONS	
anonymous user		locked	edit permissions
authenticated user		locked	edit permissions
administrator		edit role	edit permissions
Web editor		Add role	

FIGURE 7-13

How It Works

In Drupal, a role is nothing more than a name. It serves as a way to map users to a set of permissions.

In the next exercise, you assign permissions to this newly created role.

TRY IT OUT **Assigning Permissions to a Role**

Follow these steps to assign permissions to the Web Editor role:

1. Navigate to the permissions page with one of the following two methods:

   ➤ Choose Configuration ➪ Permissions.

   ➤ On the Roles page, click Edit Permissions to the right of the role.

   Note that using the Roles ➪ Permissions method de-clutters the Permission page by showing only a single role, as demonstrated in Figure 7-14.

2. On the Permission page, assign the Create Article Content and Edit Any Article Content permissions to the Web Editor role, as shown in Figure 7-14.

3. Click the Save Permissions button at the bottom of the page.

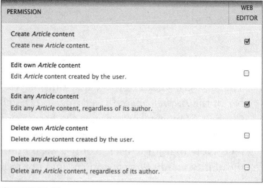

FIGURE 7-14

How It Works

Permissions are assigned to roles. Because permissions are granting and never denying, a user will be given the highest access permission in any of the roles they are assigned to. In this example, you will assign the Edit Any Article permission to the Web editor so they can edit their own articles, even though they were not explicitly granted the permission under their username.

After completing the previous two exercises, you are left with a new Web Editor role that has the permission to edit all Article content. You need to complete the circle by assigning one or more users to the Web Editor role. To do this, you can either edit their account directly as shown in Figure 7-15, or use the People management page as shown in Figure 7-16.

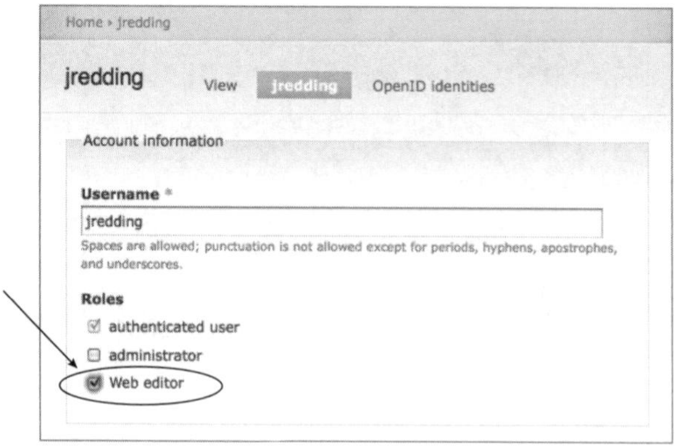

FIGURE 7-15

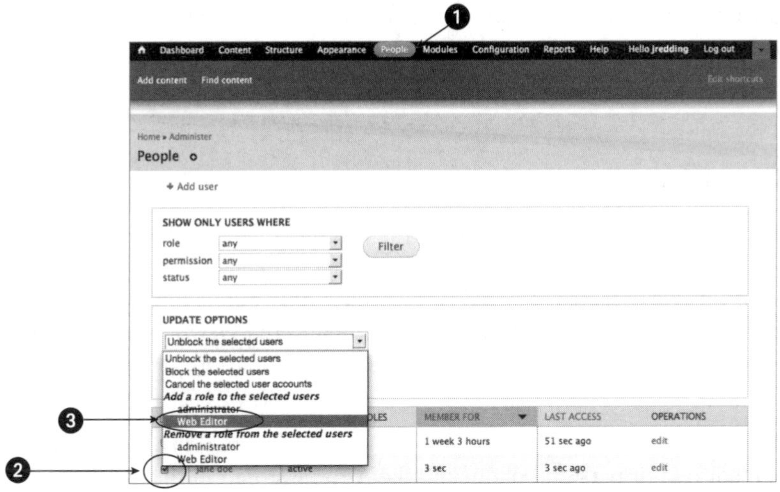

FIGURE 7-16

Administrator Role

You've probably noticed that the Administrator role is automatically granted every permission. There isn't anything special about this role, except that it is preset within the Account Settings to automatically be assigned new permissions, as shown in Figure 7-17. You are free to set this to any available role.

ADMINISTRATOR ROLE

Administrator role

administrator

This role will be automatically assigned new permissions whenever a module is enabled. Changing this setting will not affect existing permissions.

FIGURE 7-17

CREATING CUSTOM USER PROFILES

Profiles help to connect your community members by allowing them to describe themselves and their interests. A profile may include where the member went to school, where they work, their favorite foods, or their favorite sports. Members can then browse profiles to find others with similar interests or you could group users by their profile information, such as all members interested in football or basketball.

Profiles in Drupal 7

The Drupal community did something truly amazing with profiles in Drupal 7. They extended the use of Fields, the ones you learned about in Chapter 6, "Content," to user profiles. The ability to use your site's Fields on user profiles allows you to create highly customized profiles and take advantage of the numerous contributed field types available on Drupal.org.

Unfortunately this new functionality came at a small price, your confusion. Drupal 7's core ships with two different methods to create user profiles. The first is the old method, using the built-in and aptly named Profile module. The new and preferable method is to use Fields. This chapter will discuss both methods.

User Profiles vs. User Fields

You may be asking yourself what the difference is between the Profile module and user fields. This is the confusing part; on the surface the two methods are nearly identical. They both allow you to capture additional information from the user. If your goal is to capture only public information (that is, information added by the user and available to all site visitors) the differences won't seem significant (if there are any.) However, if you are capturing private and hidden information, the differences are quite significant.

The core Profile module provides both private and hidden items out of the box. Private information such as a member's physical address or personal phone number can be stored in the user's profile but visible only by the user and not by the general public. Hidden fields allow you to store administrative information, such as the user's account manager. Hidden fields are not accessible by the user but are directly associated with their account. These two bits of functionality are not available with Fields but can be added with contributed modules such as the Profile 2 module (`http://drupal .org/project/profile2`).

A more in-depth answer lies in Drupal's roadmap. The Content Construction Kit (CCK) module introduced Fields several years ago as a contributed module to Drupal 5. Drupal 6 integrated partial functionality of configurable fields from CCK, but only for content types. Beginning with Drupal 7, fields were fully integrated and extended to other parts of the system, including taxonomy and users. Due to their complexity, user profiles have not been fully ported to fields. For example, private and hidden fields are not available with fields; neither is the ability to provide hidden storage fields for use by modules or themes. It is highly likely that this functionality will be available in Drupal 8, at which time the Profile module will become obsolete and a migration from it to fields will be provided.

Give It to Me Straight

If you are new to Drupal 7 and are not upgrading from a Drupal 6 site then you should use fields and ignore the Profile module. Fields will provide you more flexibility and you can take advantage of hundreds of modules on Drupal.org. If you are upgrading from Drupal 6 (or any other version of Drupal) look into migrating your profiles over to fields using a contributed module such as Profile migrate (`http://drupal.org/project/profile_migrate`). If you cannot migrate your profiles, continuing to use the core Profile module will not introduce any problems. In fact it is extremely stable. When you upgrade to Drupal 8, you can migrate to fields at that time. Remember that the Profile module is at the end of its life.

Using Fields for Profiles

One of the many advantages of using Fields to create a custom user profile is that you already know how to use it. That is if you have read Chapter 6. Unlike the Profile module, the field types here are the same Content Construction Kit (CCK) field types used throughout your system. All of the

Drupal 7 CCK modules work for user accounts in the same way as they do for content or taxonomy terms. Because using fields has already been covered in Chapter 6, this chapter doesn't provide any exercises on using Fields. If you have questions, flip back to Chapter 6 and review the Digging Deeper into Fields section.

Fields are added via Configuration ⇨ Account Settings, as shown in Figure 7-18.

Home » Administer » Configuration and modules » People and permissions » Account settings

Account settings ⚙

SETTINGS | MANAGE FIELDS | MANAGE DISPLAY

This form lets administrators add, edit, and arrange fields for storing user data.

Configure block

LABEL	NAME	FIELD	WIDGET	OPERATIONS
⊹ User name and password	account	User module account form elements		
⊹ History	summary	User module history view element.		
⊹ Timezone	timezone	User module timezone form element.		
⊹ **Add new field**				
	field_	- Select a field type - ▾	- Select a widget - ▾	
Label	Field name (a–z, 0–9, _)	Type of data to store.	Form element to edit the data.	

Save

FIGURE 7-18

Using the Core Profile Module

You may find that you need to use the core Profile module. This may be because your site was upgraded from Drupal 6 or because your profile is very simple, won't be expanded, and you need private or hidden fields and don't want to use contributed modules. In the following three exercises, you will explore how to create user profiles with Drupal's core Profile module. You start by creating a profile that contains public and private fields. Next, you allow site visitors to view user profiles and a page that displays all members interested in a particular sport. Finally, you explore what a hidden field is and how you can use it within your organization.

At the end of this first exercise, you will have a profile like the one shown in Figure 7-19. Each user can fill out their profile within their account profile as shown in Figure 7-20, or during account registration as shown in Figure 7-21. Note that you control which fields appear on the user registration page. For example, the Favorite Sport field appears on the profile page (Figure 7-20) but not on the account creation page (Figure 7-21).

Drupal 7

jredding   Log out

Home

jredding   View   jredding   OpenID Identities   Shortcuts

General information

First name   Jacob

Last name   Redding

Favorite sport   Swimming

History

Member for   5 days 5 hours

FIGURE 7-19

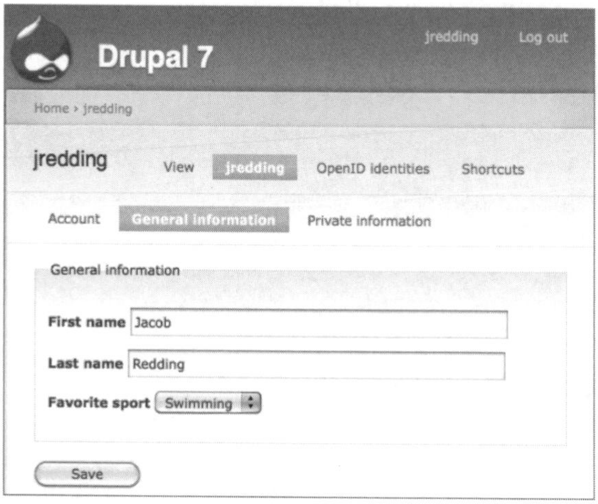

FIGURE 7-20

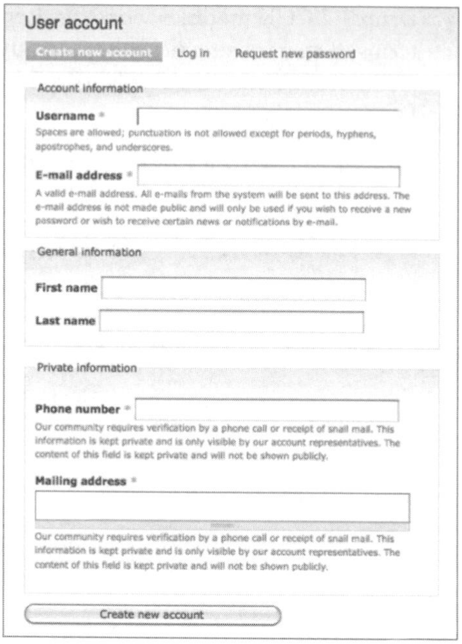

FIGURE 7-21

TRY IT OUT   Defining a User Profile

In this exercise, you define a user profile with fields for a user's first name, last name, and favorite sport. You also add private fields for the user's personal phone number and mailing address, which will only be accessible by the user and site administrators.

1. Enable the Profile module by navigating to Modules.

2. Navigate to Configuration ⇨ Profiles (under People and Permissions).

3. Create the First Name field by clicking the Single-Line Textfield option at the bottom of the Profiles page and entering the following information:

    ➤ Category: **General information**

    ➤ Title: `First name`

    ➤ Form Name: `profile_first_name`

    ➤ Visibility: Select Public Field, content shown on profile page but not used on member list pages.

    ➤ Visible In User Registration Form: Check this box

Click the Save Field button when you're done, Figure 7-22 displays the completed form.

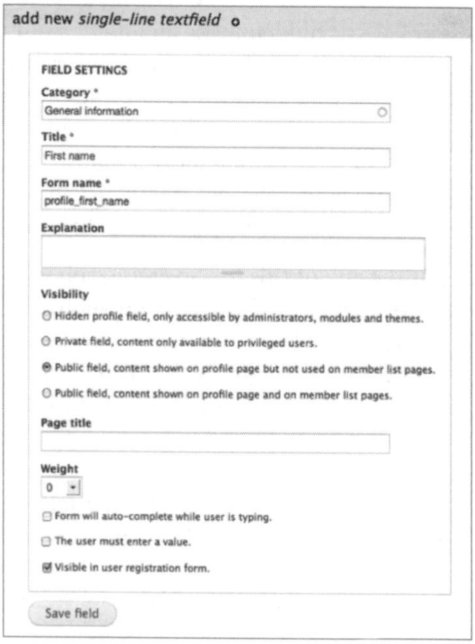

FIGURE 7-22

4. Create the Last Name field by clicking the Single-Line Textfield option at the bottom of the Profiles page and enter the following information:

➤ Category: **General information**

➤ Title: **Last name**

➤ Form name: **profile_last_name**

➤ Visibility: Select Public field, content shown on profile page but not used on member list pages.

➤ Visible In User Registration Form: Check this box.

Click the Save Field button when you're done.

5. Create the Favorite Sport field by clicking List Selection at the bottom of the Profiles page and enter the following information:

➤ Category: **General information**

➤ Title: **Favorite sport**

➤ Form Name: **profile_favorite_sport**

➤ Selection Options:

> **Football**
> **Baseball**
> **Basketball**
> **Swimming**

➤ Visibility: Select Public Field, content shown on profile page but not used on member list pages.

➤ Page Title: **Members that enjoy the sport: %value**

Click the Save Field button when you're done.

6. Create the Phone Number field by clicking the Single-Line Textfield option at the bottom of the Profiles page and entering the following information:

➤ Category: **Private information**

➤ Title: **Phone number**

➤ Form Name: **profile_phone_number**

➤ Visibility: Select Public Field, content only available to privileged users.

➤ The User Must Enter A Value: Check this box.

➤ Visible In User Registration Form: Check this box.

Click the Save Field button when you're done.

7. Create the Mailing Address field by clicking the Single-Line Textfield option at the bottom of the Profiles page and entering the following information:

➤ Category: **Private information**

➤ Title: **Mailing address**

➤ Form name: `profile_mailing_address`

➤ Visibility: Select Private Field, content only available to privileged users.

➤ The User Must Enter A Value: Check this box.

➤ Visible In User Registration Form: Check this box.

Click the Save Field button when you're done.

8. Once the fields have been added reorder them on the profile creation page such that they appear like the completed profile shown in Figure 7-23. Click Save Configuration when you are done.

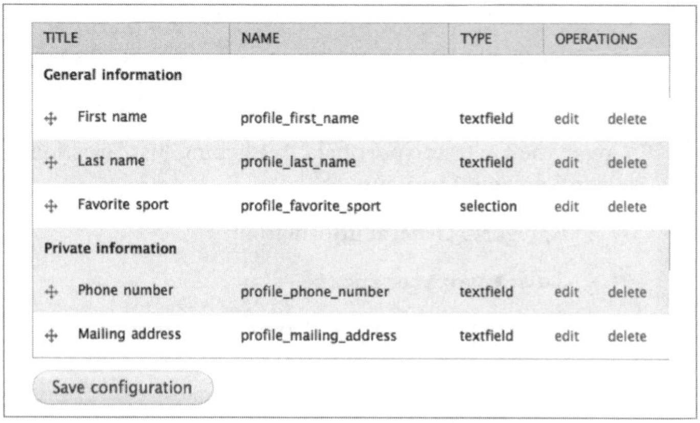

9. Verify the new fields by navigating to your user account. It should look similar to what was shown previously in Figure 7-20.

TITLE	NAME	TYPE	OPERATIONS	
General information				
⊹ First name	profile_first_name	textfield	edit	delete
⊹ Last name	profile_last_name	textfield	edit	delete
⊹ Favorite sport	profile_favorite_sport	selection	edit	delete
Private information				
⊹ Phone number	profile_phone_number	textfield	edit	delete
⊹ Mailing address	profile_mailing_address	textfield	edit	delete

 Save configuration

10. Verify that the new fields appear in the account creation

FIGURE 7-23

page by logging out and then clicking Create New Account. The registration page should look similar to what was shown previously in Figure 7-21.

How It Works

A user profile, created by the core Profile module, is a collection of profile fields grouped into categories. Categories appear as separate tabs on the user's account page and within individual Fieldsets on the account creation page (Figures 7-20 and 7-21). You can choose which of the fields are available to the public and required during account registration, such as names and favorite sports, and which fields are private fields available to only the user and site administrators, such as contact information.

Controlling Access to User Profiles

In order to view the public fields of your member's profiles, the viewing user must have the View User Profiles permission. By default this is only granted to Administrators; your visitors are unable to view the profiles although they can fill out their own personal profiles. Follow the next exercise to grant and to view the page created for all members interested in a particular sport.

TRY IT OUT   **Enabling Access to Your Users' Profiles**

In this exercise, you grant anonymous users the ability to view user profiles and the Members that enjoy the sport: %value page.

1.   Log in with your Administrator account. Grant the Access User Profiles permission to the Anonymous User role by navigating to Configuration ➪ Permissions (under People and Permissions).

2.   Create a few new user accounts and select Swimming in the Favorite Sport profile field for each.

> **NOTE**   *The Devel module (*`http://drupal.org/project/devel`*) can be used to autogenerate users for testing and development purposes.*

3.   With a few new accounts created, navigate to a user's profile and click the Swimming link in Favorite Sports as shown in Figure 7-24. If their favorite sport is not a link, verify that the Page Title was set correctly in the Favorite Sport profile field (step 5 of the previous exercise).

In the figure, the URL for the field is `http://localhost/profile/ profile_favorite_sport/ Swimming,` where `profile_favorite_sport` is the Form Name set on the user profile and Swimming is one of the field's values.

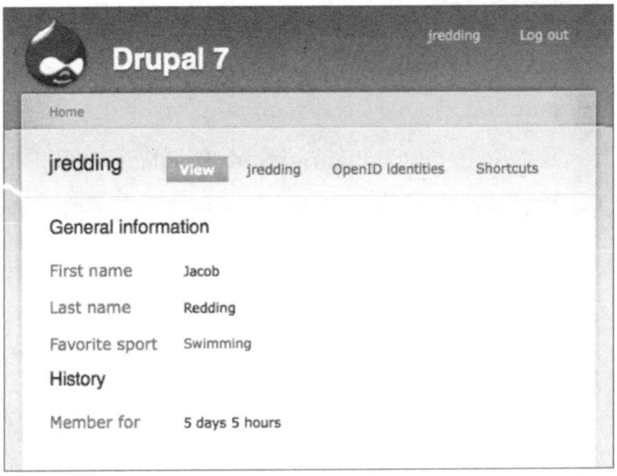

FIGURE 7-24

> **NOTE**   *Add a URL alias, as discussed in Chapter 6, to make the profile available at a friendlier URL such as* `http://localhost/swimming-members.`

How It Works

Users must have the Access User Profiles permission in order to see the public fields of other users' profiles. Public fields with a Page Title are converted into links that lead to a listing of all users with the same Fieldsetting. In this example, because Swimming was selected, all members interested in swimming were displayed.

Hidden Fields

In the previous exercises, you explored public and private fields. The user who is creating the profile enters these two fields. Public fields are available for all site visitors to view, but only site administrators can see private fields. By contrast, *hidden fields* are available only to administrators for both input and viewing. The user of the profile cannot view the hidden fields on their profile.

Hidden fields are useful when you need to store information about a user, but you don't want them to see or modify the data. For example, a hidden field can be used to set the name of the user's account manager or include administrative notes about the user.

In the next exercise, you'll work on a site that requires manual verification and approval of all user accounts and allow this verification to happen with a phone call, receipt of a piece of snail mail, or a credit check. You then add a hidden field to the user's profile to capture how the verification happened.

TRY IT OUT   **Adding a Hidden Field to a User Profile**

In this exercise, you add a hidden field to your profiles to capture information on a user's account manager and how the user was manually verified.

1. Navigate to Configuration ⇨ Profiles.

2. Create the Account Manager field by clicking the Single-Line Textfield option at the bottom of the Profiles page and entering the following information:

➤ Category: **Account information**

➤ Title: **Account manager**

➤ Form name: **profile_account_manager**

➤ Visibility: Select Hidden Profile Field, only accessible by administrators, modules and themes.

Click the Save Field button when you're done, Figure 7-25 displays the completed form.

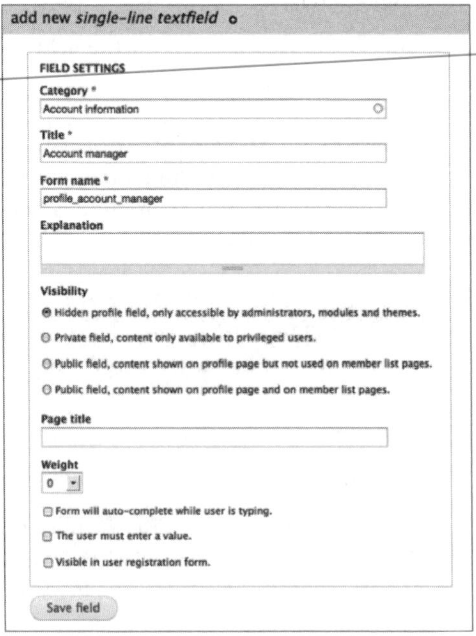

3. Create the Verification Method field by clicking List Selection at the bottom of the Profiles page and entering the following information:

➤ Category: **Account information**

➤ Title: **Verification method**

➤ Form name: **profile_verification_method**

FIGURE 7-25

➤   Selection Options:

```
Over the phone
Mailing address
Credit check
```

➤   Visibility: Select Hidden Profile Field, only accessible by administrators, modules and themes.

Click the Save Field button when you're done.

4.   Navigate to a user account that is not part of the Administrator role. Fill out the Account Manager field and select a verification method.

5.   Log out and navigate to the user account modified in step 4. Verify that the fields created are not visible.

6.   Log in as the user whose profile you modified in step 4. Verify that you cannot modify the two fields created in this exercise.

How It Works

Hidden fields are available only to users who have the Administer Users permission. In this exercise you created two new fields under a new category none of which are accessible to the user. These fields are used for storing administrative data about the user directly on their account.

Visibility Options Summarized

The following is a summary of the visibility options you will encounter.

Public fields — Entered by the user creating the profile and viewable by all users who have the Access User Profiles permission. Select available on member list pages if you want other members to be able to browse profiles by the field.

Private fields — Entered by the user creating the profile but viewable only by administrators who have the Administer Users permission. Examples include a personal address or phone number field.

Hidden fields — Entered by and available only to administrators who have the Administer Users permission.

TRACKING USER ACTIVITY

What is the most active thread on your website?

Is there a particular blog post generating a lot of comments?

What is the most recent activity for the user Sally or John?

If you have questions such as these, the Tracker module is what you want. The Tracker module provides a method to stay on top of your site's activity and provides users a way to stay on top of their personal activity. Simply enable the Tracker module, and you're off and running. A Track tab will appear on each user's account page as shown in Figure 7-26.

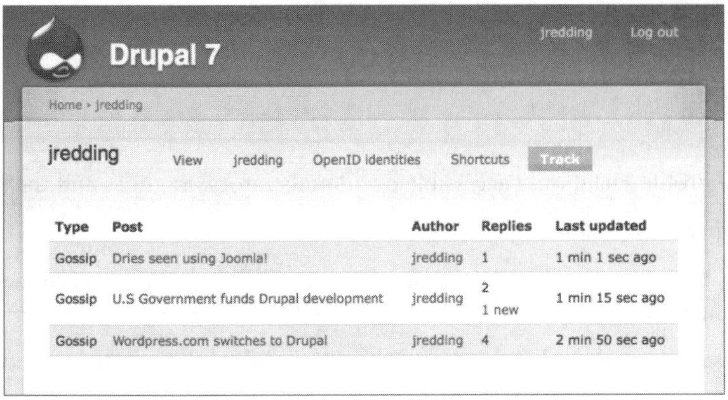

FIGURE 7-26

The Tracker module also provides the following URLs:

`http://localhost/tracker`: Logged-in user's most recent activity

`http://localhost/tracker/all`: Recent site-wide activity

`http://localhost/tracker/`*uid*: Recent activity for the user with the uid specified (for example, `http://localhost/tracker/1`)

Using Views to Create Custom Tracking Pages and Blocks

The Tracker is a great feature of Drupal that allows users to see their posted content and the comment activity on it. Tracker does this in a fast and efficient manner, providing little reason to not use it. However, Tracker does not contain many options — for example, it doesn't provide a block showing the logged-in user's most recent comments or a quick-access block with the user's most recent content. The Views module can extend the Tracker module's reports to add new fields or blocks, or to broaden or narrow its scope.

Although a bit premature in this book, Views is an important contributed module to know about and is discussed in detail in Chapter 11, "Views." But the following two Try It Out exercises can help you get started in providing a more positive user experience on your site. If you have not yet used Views, flip over to Chapter 11, download the Views module from `http://drupal.org/project/views` and install it, and return here after you have read and finished the exercises in that chapter. Keep in mind that Views is a very powerful module and you can accidentally provide users access to content they would not normally be privy to.

> **WARNING** *At the time of this writing, the Views module was not fully upgraded to Drupal 7; thus, the following two exercises were written on a very early beta version of Views. However, the information should be similar if not identical to the final released version.*

TRY IT OUT **Modifying the Tracker View**

In this exercise, you use the Views module to modify the default reports used by the Tracker module. To follow this exercise, you need to have the Tracker and Views module enabled. Views is a contributed module that must be downloaded and installed separately from Drupal. You can download Views from `http://drupal.org/project/views`.

1. Navigate to Views at Structure ⇨ Views.

2. Enable the built-in Tracker view as shown in Figure 7-27.

> Default Node view: **tracker** (default)   Enable
>
> Title: Recent posts   Shows all new activity on system.
> Path: tracker
> Page

FIGURE 7-27

3. Add a new Block display to the Tracker view by selecting Block from the far-left drop-down box and clicking Add Display, as shown in Figure 7-28.

4. Modify the new Block Display to show only the last five items. To do this, click Items Per Page in the Basic Settings list with the Block Display selected, as shown in Figure 7-28. Click the Override button to set these changes only for the Block display and not the Page display, as shown in Figure 7-29. Once the field has been overridden, change the value from 25 to 5 and click the Update button. (Note that if the button title is Update Default Display, the field has *not* been overridden. Be sure you have clicked the Override button.)

5. In the Block display override the User Posted Or Commented argument. To do this, select Node: User Posted or Commented under Arguments, and then click the Override button, as shown in Figure 7-30. Important: Be sure that the Block display is selected in the drop-down menu on the left side of the screen.

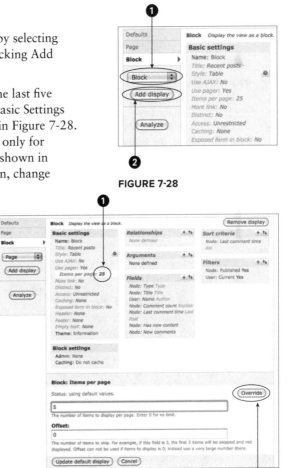

FIGURE 7-28

FIGURE 7-29

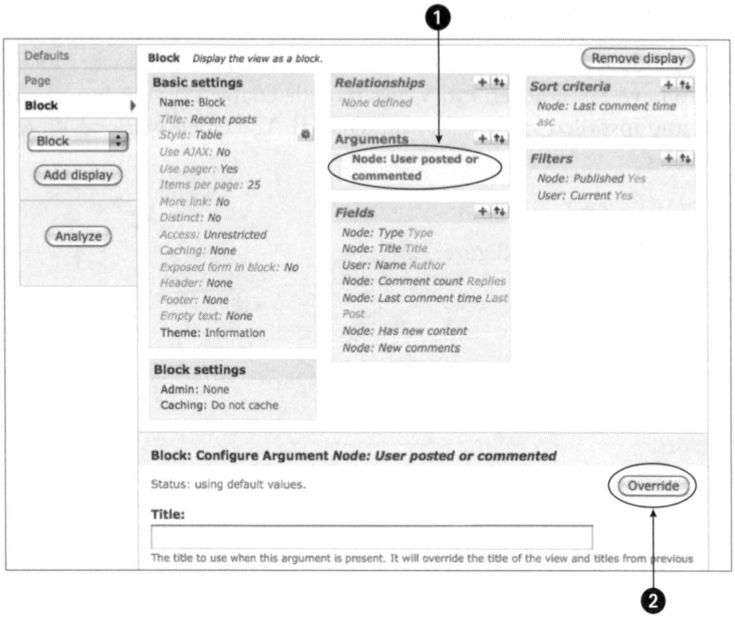

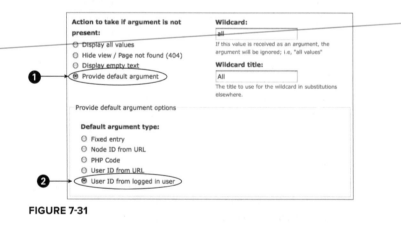

FIGURE 7-30

6. In the settings of the *over-ridden* Node: User Posted or Commented argument, select the following options as shown in Figure 7-31:

   ➤ Action To Take If Argument Is Not Present: Select the Provide Default Argument option.

   ➤ Default Argument Type: Select the User ID From Logged In User option.

FIGURE 7-31

7. Save the view and then set your new block on the Block Administration page at Structure ➪ Block. The block title will be Tracker: Block.

How It Works

The Views module can be used to extend the reports of existing modules such as the Tracker module. In this exercise, you added a new Block display and limited the number of items for that block to five. You were careful to use the **override** option so that the default Page display (http://localhost/tracker) was not modified.

You also overrode and modified the argument for the block so that it uses the User ID of the currently logged in user. Arguments are the pieces of the URL that come after the view's location. For example, in the URL `http://localhost/tracker/5`, the number 5 is the argument for User ID 5. Because a block is not located at a specific URL, but instead is part of many pages and URLs, you need to provide a default argument.

Follow along in the next exercise to create a new view that displays all of the latest Articles that the user has posted, regardless of the status of the posts. This block will provide the user with quick access to their most-recently published or soon-to-be-published content.

TRY IT OUT Using Views to Create a Custom Activity Block

In this exercise, you create a custom block that displays the currently logged-in user's recent Articles, published or not. Figure 7-42 at the end of this exercise shows the completed block.

1. Navigate to views at Structure ⇨ Views.

2. Click Add at the top of the Views page, and then enter the following information as shown in Figure 7-32:

➤ View Name: `recent_articles`

➤ View Description: `Recent Articles by user`

➤ View Tag: `articles, user`

➤ View Type: Select the Node option

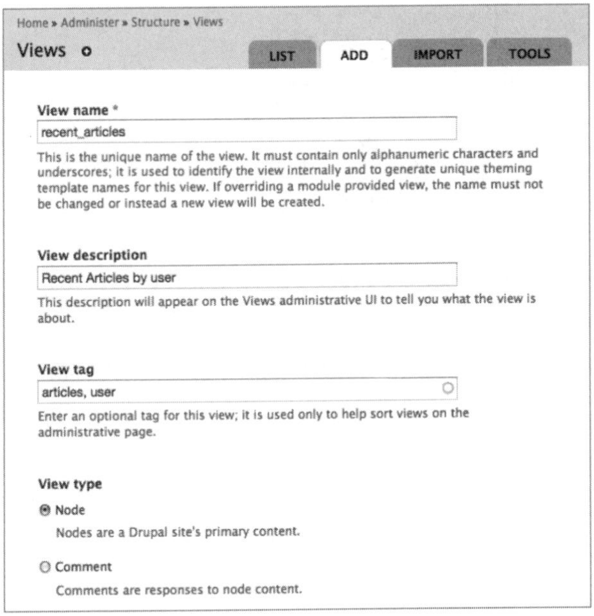

FIGURE 7-32

3. Under Style settings set the Row Style to Fields as shown in Figure 7-33.

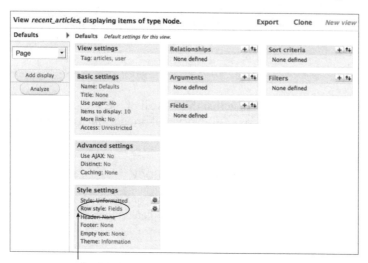

FIGURE 7-33

4. On the far right of the create View page, add a new filter by clicking the + button next to Filters, as shown in Figure 7-34.

5. Scroll down to view the filters. Select the Node option from the Groups drop-down list and then select Node: Type, as shown in Figure 7-35.

6. Click the Add button then select Article under the Node Type as shown in Figure 7-36.

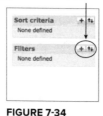

FIGURE 7-34

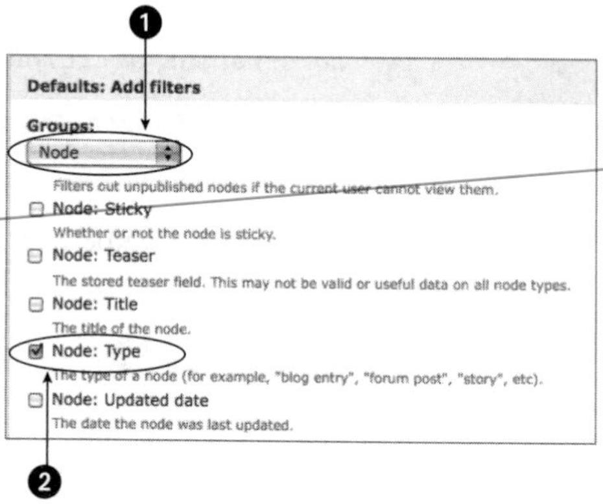

FIGURE 7-35

7. Add the User: Current filter to limit the results to only the content posted by the currently logged in user, as shown in Figure 7-37.

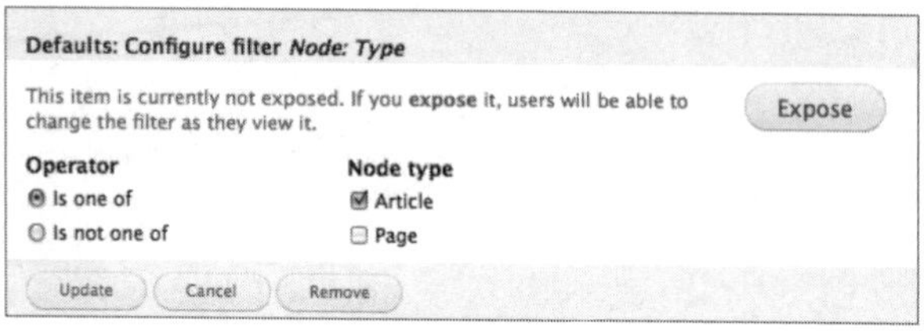

FIGURE 7-36

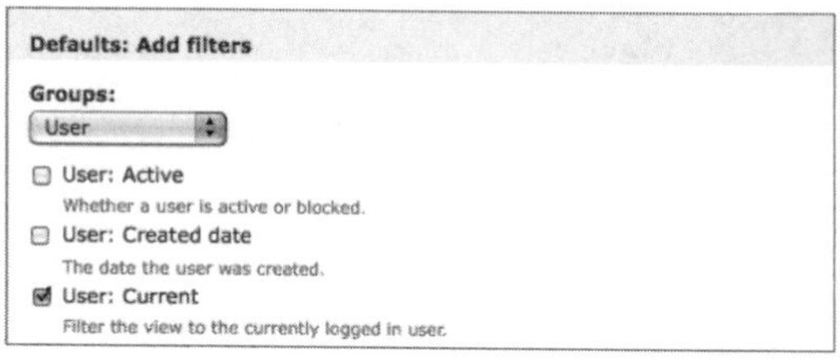

FIGURE 7-37

8. Add the Node: Title, Node: Published, and Node: Edit Link fields by clicking + next to the Fields box, as shown in Figure 7-38.

9. Within Fields click **Node: Title** to access the Node: Title fieldsettings, and check the **Link This Field To Its Node** box as shown in Figure 7-39.

10. Click the + button next to Sort Criteria and select Node: Updated Date – Descending.

11. Add a Block display by selecting Block on the far left and then clicking the Add Display button, as shown in Figure 7-40.

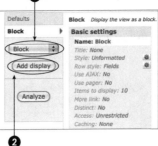

FIGURE 7-38

FIGURE 7-39

FIGURE 7-40

12. Change the Block display style to a Table. To do this, within Style settings click the word Unformatted next to Style, then select Table from the settings below the view, as shown in Figure 7-41.

13. Verify that you have entered and selected the following criteria, as shown in Figure 7-42:

> **Style Settings**
>> Style: Table
>> Row Style: Fields

> **Fields**
>> Node: Title (link this field to its node)
>> Node: Published
>> Node: Edit Link

> **Sort Criteria**
>> Node: Updated Date – Descending

> **Filters**
>> Node: Type – Is one of Article
>> User: Current Yes

> **Displays**
>> Block

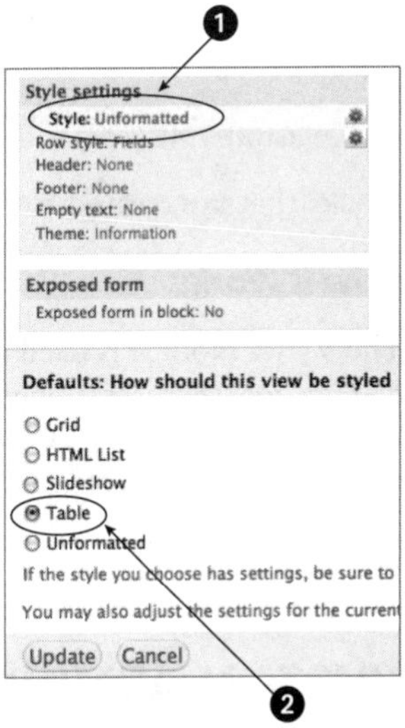

FIGURE 7-41

The fully configured view is shown in Figure 7-42, and the resulting block is shown in Figure 7-43.

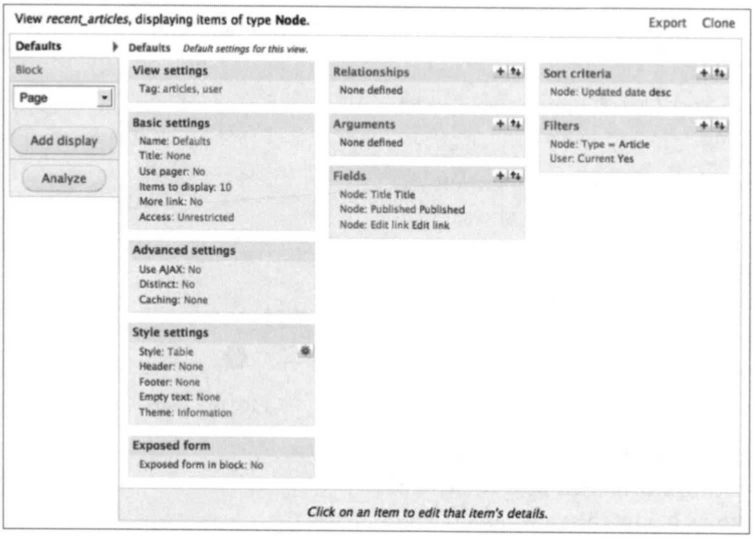

FIGURE 7-42

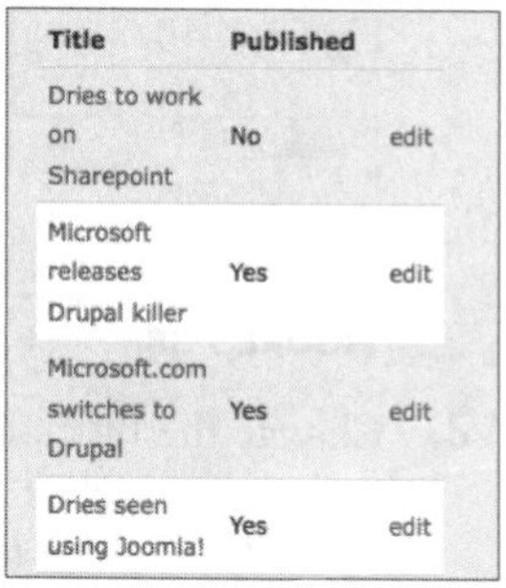

FIGURE 7-43

Blocks that are created from views are controlled like all other site blocks at Structure ⇨ Blocks.

How It Works

The Views module is used to pull data out of your Drupal database and display it on your site. Each display, whether it is a page or a block, can display sets of fields with the results narrowed down by the view's filters. In this exercise, you used the User: Current filter, which will create a unique set of results for each logged-in user.

CUSTOM ADMINISTRATION PAGES WITH VIEWS

When your site begins to grow and you find yourself with thousands, tens of thousands or, lucky you, hundreds of thousands of users, you might find that the built-in user management interface does not provide you with enough options. For example, you may want a page that displays the users that have logged in within the past X days, or a listing of all users with an e-mail address from a certain domain. The marketing department may want an up-to-date report on the number of users within a certain age range (based up a profile field) or users who speak a particular language.

Whatever the requirements are, you can more than likely get what you need from Views. Views can create custom pages that not only display a listing of users, but also provide a dynamically configurable user interface such as the one shown in Figure 7-44, which allows you to search for users by their e-mail address, the time their account was created, and/or the last time they accessed the site. Each of these can be set independently of the other.

FIGURE 7-44

In the following exercise, you create the user administration screen shown in Figure 7-44. This exercise is presented only as a Views recipe — if you have not yet created a view or completed the exercises earlier in this chapter, you should do so before attempting this.

TRY IT OUT   Creating a User Administration Screen

In this exercise, you create a user administration screen that allows you to filter users by their e-mail address, the date their account was created, and/or the last time they accessed the site (as shown previously in Figure 7-40).

1. Navigate to the Views administration page. Create a new user view by selecting User under the View Type as shown in Figure 7-45.

2. Configure the view according to the following settings:

    ➤ **Style Settings**

    Style: Table

    ➤ **Fields**

    User: Name

    User: Last access

    User: Edit link

    ➤ **Filters**

    User: E-mail

    User: Created date

    User: Last access

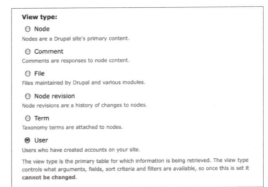

FIGURE 7-45

3.   Create the top filter bar shown in Figure 7-46 by exposing each filter. First click the filter name, and then click Expose within its settings, as shown in Figure 7-47.

User: E-mail	User: Created date	User: Last access
Contains ⬍	Is greater than ⬍	Is greater than ⬍
gmail.com	1 week ago	1 day

(Apply)

FIGURE 7-46

① ②

Basic settings
Name: Defaults
Title: None
Style: Table
Use AJAX: No
Use pager: No
Items to display: 10
More link: No
Distinct: No
Access: Unrestricted
Caching: None
Exposed form in block: No
Header: None
Footer: None
Empty text: None
Theme: Information

Arguments   + ↑↓
None defined

Fields   + ↑↓
User: Name **Name**
User: Last access **Last access**
User: Edit link **Edit link**

Filters   + ↑↓
User: E-mail **contains**
User: Created date =
User: Last access =

Defaults: Configure filter *User: E-mail*

This item is currently not exposed. If you **expose** it, users will be able to change the filter as they view it.   (Expose)

Operator: **Value:**
○ Is equal to
⊖ Is not equal to
⦿ Contains

FIGURE 7-47

4.   When exposing the filter, check the Unlock Operator box to allow modification of the equal to, greater than, less than, and so on operators.

5.   Add a Page display and a tab to the People Management page by performing the following steps:

  a.   Add a page display.

  b.   Under Page settings set the Path to / admin/people/users-by-email).

  c.   Set the Type to Menu Tab and enter **Users by email/date** as the Title, as shown in Figure 7-48.

FIGURE 7-48

How It Works

By using Views, you can create highly customizable administration pages. Exposed filters allow users to dynamically modify a report to narrow the result set, and an edit link field provides convenient access to a user account. In this exercise, you constructed the view and then added it to the standard People Management interface by using two settings. First, the Path was set within the same URL as the existing User Management interface with an additional level, example `http://localhost/admin/people/users-by-email`. Second, the menu type was set as Menu Tab. The combination of these two automatically places a new tab on the existing People Management page.

> **NOTE** The Views Bulk Operations contributed module (`http://drupal.org/project/views_bulk_operations`) is a great addition to administration pages created with Views. It enables you to bulk-update the results of the view, be it content or users.

USER SESSIONS

If you've used online banking, then you are aware of a session. Most banks expire your session and automatically log you out after 10 minutes. They fear that you would walk away from your computer or, heaven forbid, your laptop would get stolen, leaving your bank account open to anyone sitting at the computer. You've probably noticed that Drupal works the exact opposite way. By default, Drupal allows a session to stay open for an entire month without any activity before it is ended.

So how does this work?

When a user logs into your website, a session is created for them, a record is made in the database, and a cookie is set on the user's browser. This session remembers what the user has done on your site as well as the fact that they are logged in. If the user navigates away from your website, the session does not end. This allows them to return in the future and still maintain their logged-in status as well as site state.

When a user returns to your site, their browser presents Drupal with a session cookie. Drupal takes this cookie and compares it to a Session table within the database to ensure that it is valid, as demonstrated in Figure 7-49. If the session is valid, Drupal restores the session, picking up where the user last left off. If the session is not valid, Drupal requires the user to log back in and create a new session. This entire process happens in less than a second and is transparent to the user.

FIGURE 7-49

Forcing Sessions to Expire

Although the default behavior of Drupal is to let a session last quite a long time, it can be desirable to override this behavior and force a session to expire earlier. You may choose to do this because you are running a secure application that must verify your user's identities or because of server limitations when dealing with millions of users and their associated sessions. Each session is stored in the Drupal's database session table, and a million sessions on a slow database server can cause some issues.

The Short Answer

You can use the Auto Logout contributed module (`http://drupal.org/project/autologout`) to automatically expire sessions.

The Longer and More Detailed Answer

Drupal uses PHP's built-in session handling system and controls it within `settings.php`. Specifically, the following two lines control how long a session should last before PHP expires it:

```
ini_set('session.cookie_lifetime',  2000000);
ini_set('session.gc_maxlifetime',   200000);
```

`session.cookie_lifetime` tells the client's browser that their cookie should last only 2,000,000 seconds (roughly 23 days).

`session.gc_maxlifetime` is PHP's garbage collection. This says that sessions older than 200,000 seconds (roughly 2.3 days) should be automatically expired, provided that garbage collection is actually running (as explained in the following paragraphs).

To expire sessions earlier than these defaults, you can reduce these numbers in `settings.php` to expire cookies earlier and run the garbage collection more often. By default, PHP runs garbage collection, meaning cleaning up old sessions, on 1 percent of page requests. You can modify this by putting the following lines within `settings.php`:

```
ini_set('session.gc_probability', 1);
ini_set('session.gc_divisor', 100);
```

These settings indicate that garbage collection will run 1 out of 100 times. A few systems disable this or set the probability to 0. Why? Performance.

Even if garbage collection is run on only 1 percent of the page requests, this means that 1 percent of your visitors will experience a slowdown as PHP locates the old sessions and expires them. The length of this slowdown is determined by how many sessions and how many expired sessions you have. A site with little traffic and nearly zero sessions won't notice a slowdown, but a site with millions of logged in users and thus millions of sessions may notice a considerable slowdown.

If you have a need for speed, then disabling PHP's garbage collection and doing manual cleanup is preferable. You can use the Session Expire module (`http://drupal.org/project/session_expire`) to manually remove old sessions from the database on a schedule that you set.

SUMMARY

Users are the life of any website, and managing your users is key to the success of your site. In this chapter, you learned how to add users to a role and how to assign permissions to roles. Because permissions are cumulative, users that are members of multiple roles will receive all the permissions of their roles. Profiles allow your users to connect by learning about each other. Remember to set a Page Title on profile fields that can be browsed so that users can quickly identify other people with similar interests.

This chapter introduced Views to show you how easy it is to create customized blocks to help your users interact on your site. You also learned how to use Views to create customized administration pages.

Finally, you learned about the OpenID module, which allows your users to use a web-centralized username and password to log into your site. The acceptance of OpenID is growing rapidly, and we are getting closer to building an Internet wherein a single username and password can be used across all websites. The realization of this dream, however, is in your hands and the hands of every web developer and site administrator. Help this dream become a reality by enabling the OpenID module and encouraging its use on your site.

EXERCISES

1. What is OpenID and how is it used in Drupal?

2. What is the purpose of a role?

3. How does a private profile field differ from a hidden profile field?

4. What happens when a user cancels their account?

Answers to these Exercises can be found in the Appendix.

▶ WHAT YOU LEARNED IN THIS CHAPTER

➤ OpenID is a web-centralized method of authentication that allows all Internet users to use a single username and password across all OpenID enabled websites.

➤ Permissions are assigned to roles and users can be added to one or more roles.

➤ The Profile module is used to create customized user profiles.

➤ The Tracker module provides a per-user page showing their latest activity and recent threads.

➤ Views can create customized blocks for showing a user's latest posts or comments.

8

Taxonomy

Newcomers to Drupal have found the taxonomy system to be one of the most intimidating and mysterious areas of Drupal. The word *taxonomy* was thought to be so confusing that it was renamed *category* in Drupal 5, but it was renamed back to taxonomy in Drupal 6 (and Drupal 7) because the mixture of words taxonomy and category was found to be even more confusing. Fortunately, this area is only intimidating because of its title and is neither complex nor confusing. If you've found yourself intimidated or confused by this area of Drupal in the past, take a deep breath, sit back, relax, and read this short chapter.

This chapter reviews Drupal's taxonomy system and provides examples of how you can make the most of this system to organize and categorize your site's content.

IN SIMPLE TERMS

In simple terms taxonomy is used to categorize your content. For example if you were writing a food related blog you could categorize a blog post with terms (tags) such as Middle Eastern, hummus, and pita, or Asian, noodles, and Peking-duck. Using terms will allow your site visitors to select all content relating to Middle Eastern food or for you to create an Asian food section.

TERMINOLOGY

Before diving into taxonomy, here are some words and their definitions:

➤ **Taxonomy** — The common definition of *taxonomy* is the practice and science of classification, and Drupal uses the term to describe exactly this activity. Taxonomy is used to describe the overall system in Drupal that categorizes content. The taxonomy system uses *vocabularies* and *terms*.

➤ **Vocabulary** — This refers to a collection or bin of terms. For example, you may have a vocabulary for Neighborhood, Food Type, or Department.

➤ **Term** — An individual word within a vocabulary used to categorize a set of content. A term is specific to a single Vocabulary but can be used on multiple pieces of content.

➤ **Parent** — A term may be the child of one or more parent terms. A geographic classification is a good example of this hierarchy. In the following example, Miami is a child of Florida, which is a child of the United States, which is a child of North America:

```
North America
--United States
---Florida
----Miami
```

VOCABULARIES

Vocabularies are the collection of terms used to categorize content. You might have already used a vocabulary without knowing it. For example, when freetagging content as shown in Figure 8-1, each tag entered

FIGURE 8-1

becomes a term in the Tags vocabulary. You could even consider the vocabulary a bucket of terms.

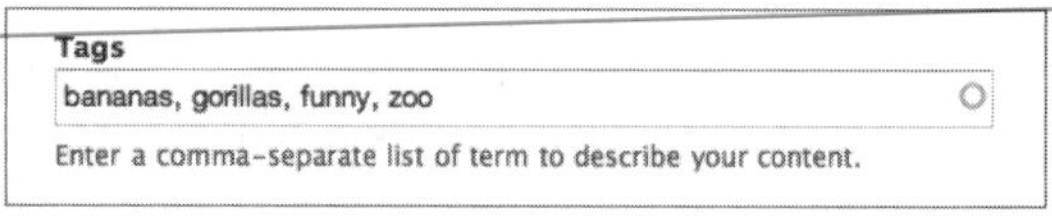

Managing or creating new vocabularies is performed at Administer ⇨ Structure ⇨ Taxonomy. The first screen, shown in Figure 8-2, displays all current vocabularies.

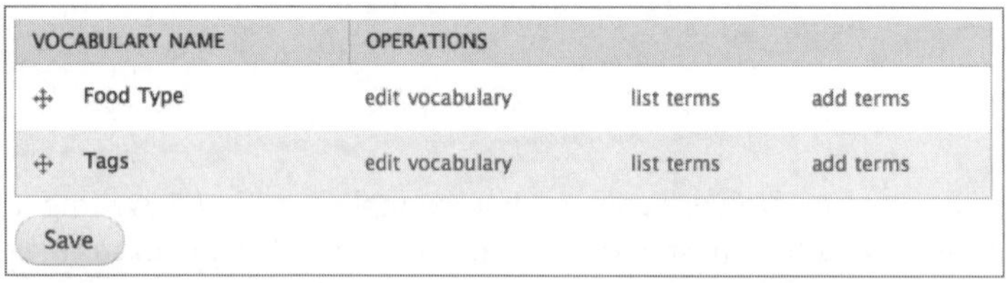

FIGURE 8-2

A vocabulary is a holding container for terms and as such you give it a name and a brief description. Within the settings of each vocabulary you can also manage the fields of a term similarly to the fields on a content type. Fields will be discussed later.

TERMS

Terms are the individual classifiers used within a vocabulary. For example, if the name of the vocabulary is Food Type, the terms might be Middle Eastern, Chinese, Japanese, American, German, and so on. At their most basic level, terms include a name and description but can also contain a URL alias as shown in Figure 8-3. Setting a URL alias automatically provides a list of content categorized with this term. For example, Figure 8-3 will make all content categorized as Middle Eastern available at `http://localhost/blog/category/ middle-eastern`.

▾ IDENTIFICATION

Term name *

Middle Eastern

URL alias

blog/category/middle-eastern

Optionally specify an alternative URL by which this term can be accessed. Use a relative path and don't add a trailing slash or the URL alias won't work.

Description

All of my blog posts relating to the glorious foods from the middle east.

A description of the term. To be displayed on taxonomy/term pages and RSS feeds.

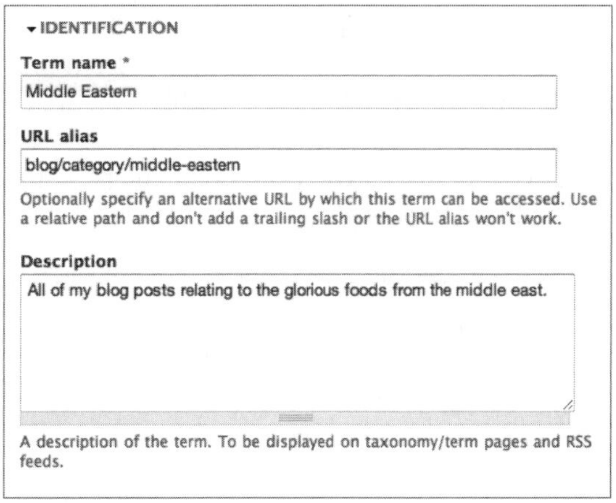

FIGURE 8-3

Note that the description will be presented to your site visitors when they view this term's URL and its corresponding RSS feed, available by clicking the RSS icon at the bottom of the term's URL.

Advanced Options

Hidden just below the name and description is where you specify a term's parent(s) (i.e., hierarchy). For example, as shown in Figure 8-4, Jordanian food can be a child of Middle Eastern. Select `<root>` to specify a new top-level parent.

▾ IDENTIFICATION

Term name *

Jordanian

URL alias

blog/category/middle-eastern/jordanian

Optionally specify an alternative URL by which this term can be accessed. Use a relative path and don't add a trailing slash or the URL alias won't work.

Description

Jordan, a land of scrumptious sweets and fabulous grilled meats. All of my posts related to Jordan are contained here, stayed tuned as I write more about this country's delicious foods.

A description of the term. To be displayed on taxonomy/term pages and RSS feeds.

▾ ADVANCED OPTIONS

Parent terms

<root>
Asian
Middle Eastern

Weight *

0

Terms are displayed in ascending order by weight.

Save

FIGURE 8-4

Weight

Immediately below the parent is a term's weight (Figure 8-4). The *weight* is the order in which the terms appear. A term that is weighted 3 is "lighter" than a term that is weighted 5, so it will appear higher in a list. Terms are always ordered first by weight and then alphabetically. Note that the weights are set automatically when you drag and drop them on the List Terms page of the vocabulary, which usually leads one to leave the weight at 0 and set drag it to its correct position on the List Terms page. You can also define parent and child term relationship using drag and drop on the List Terms page.

> **NOTE** The drag and drop interface on the List Terms vocabulary page requires JavaScript. If the interface doesn't appear or work for you check your JavaScript settings.

USING TERMS ON YOUR CONTENT

With an understanding of vocabularies and terms under your belt follow the next exercise to add the Food type category to your Article content type.

TRY IT OUT Adding Taxonomy to Your Content

In this exercise you will add a Food Type category to your Article content type allowing you to categorize the article as about Asian or Middle Eastern food. This exercise will walk you through three basic steps; (1) adding a vocabulary, (2) adding terms to the vocabulary, (3) adding a taxonomy field to the Article content type.

Step 1 – Adding a Food Type Vocabulary

1. Navigate to Taxonomy by clicking Structure in the top administration bar then Taxonomy.

2. Click Add Vocabulary at the top of the page, as shown in Figure 8-5.

3. Enter the following

Name: Food Type

Description: Categorize Articles according to the food written about.

4. Click Save.

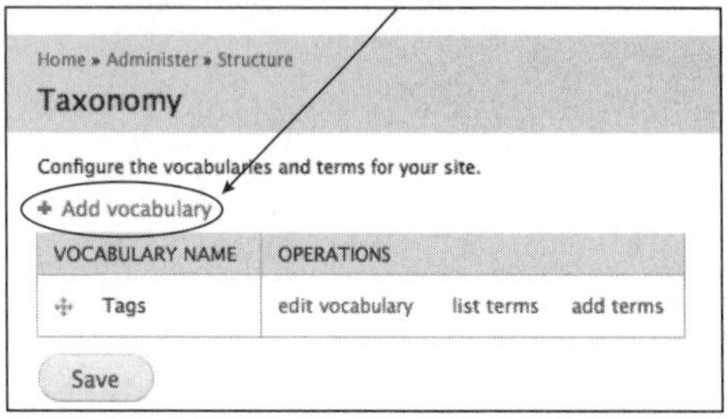

FIGURE 8-5

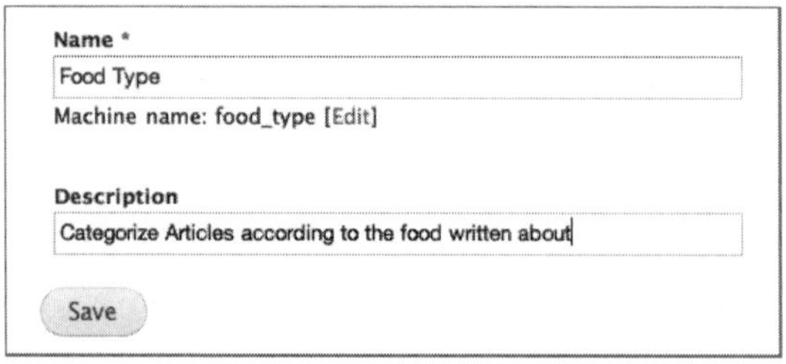

FIGURE 8-6

Step 2 – Add Terms to the Vocabulary

1. At the main taxonomy page click Add term to the far right of the Food Type vocabulary, as shown in Figure 8-7.

FIGURE 8-7

2. Enter the following:

> **Name:** Middle Eastern
>
> **URL alias:** articles/categories/food-type/middle-eastern
>
> **Description:** Articles relating to Middle Eastern food

3. Click Save.

4. Continue to add terms until your terms page looks like that shown in Figure 8-8.

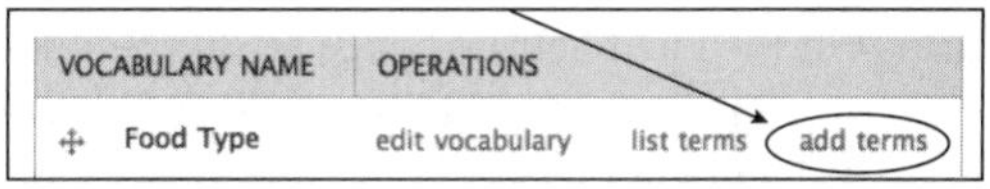

FIGURE 8-8

Step 3 – Add a Vocabulary Field to Your Article Content Type

1. Navigate to your content type administration page at Structure ➪ Content types.

2. Click edit to the far right of the Article content type.

3. Click Manage fields as shown in Figure 8-9.

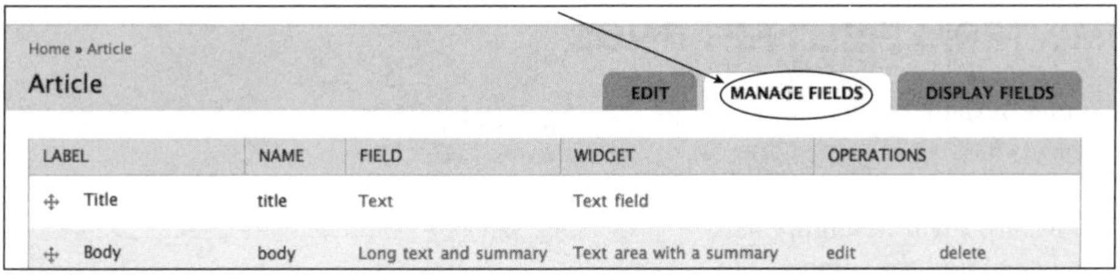

Home » Article				
Article		EDIT	MANAGE FIELDS	DISPLAY FIELDS
LABEL	NAME	FIELD	WIDGET	OPERATIONS
⊹ Title	title	Text	Text field	
⊹ Body	body	Long text and summary	Text area with a summary	edit delete

FIGURE 8-9

4. Near the bottom of the Manage fields page type in and select the following information under Add new field, as shown in Figure 8-10.

> **Label:** Food Type
>
> **Field name:** food_type
>
> **Type of data to store:** Taxonomy term
>
> **Form element to edit the data:** Select list

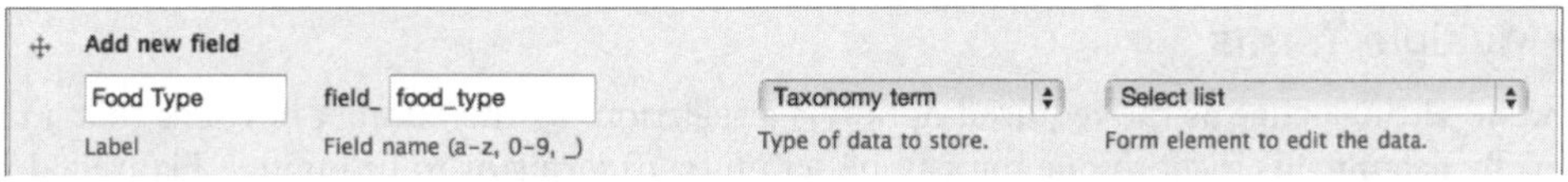

⊹ **Add new field**			
Food Type	field_ food_type	Taxonomy term ⬍	Select list ⬍
Label	Field name (a–z, 0–9, _)	Type of data to store.	Form element to edit the data.

FIGURE 8-10

5. On the Field Settings page select the Food Type vocabulary and click Save field settings, as shown in Figure 8-11.

If all went well when you navigate to Add content ⇨ Article you should now see a Food Type select list as shown in Figure 8-12.

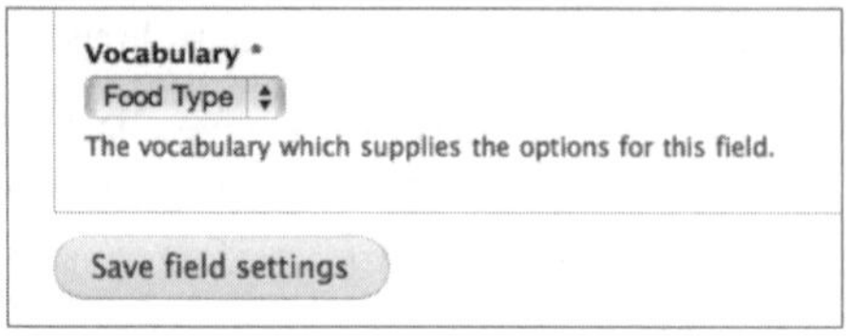

FIGURE 8-11

FIGURE 8-12

How It Works

As you've seen, a vocabulary is a container for terms. Terms have a simple descriptor and a URL where the categorized content can be accessed. If you haven't already added an Article, selecting one of the Food Type terms then navigate to that term's corresponding URL. For example, `http://localhost/articles/categories/food-type/middle-eastern`.

Note that when adding a vocabulary selection to a content type it is done in the same manner as other content type fields, as demonstrated in Chapter 6, "Content." This provides immense flexibility as the Widget selection can be modified to a single select list, multiple select list, checkboxes, radio buttons, or a free-tagging form. Additionally the field settings (accessed by clicking Edit on the field) allow you to set the field to required as well as setting the number of terms a user can use to categorize the content.

TAXONOMY TERM FIELD SETTINGS

As demonstrated in the last exercise a vocabulary selection is added to a content type by adding a taxonomy term field. This allows for great flexibility as well as the ability to add the same vocabulary twice. For example, as shown in Figure 8-13, one field provides a drop-down selection and the other allows the user to type in a new term.

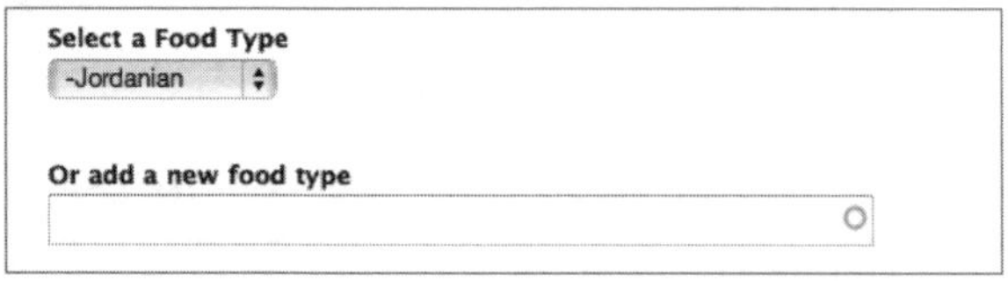

FIGURE 8-13

Below are a few common settings on a taxonomy field and how to accomplish them.

Requiring a Term to be Selected

To require your users to select at least one term, click to the far right of the field and on the settings form select the required checkbox, see Figure 8-14.

Allowing Multiple Terms

On the same settings page as the required option is a selection for the number of terms that a user can enter. By default this is set to one but can be set up to 10 terms or to unlimited. Figure 8-15 demonstrates how to configure the number of allowed terms.

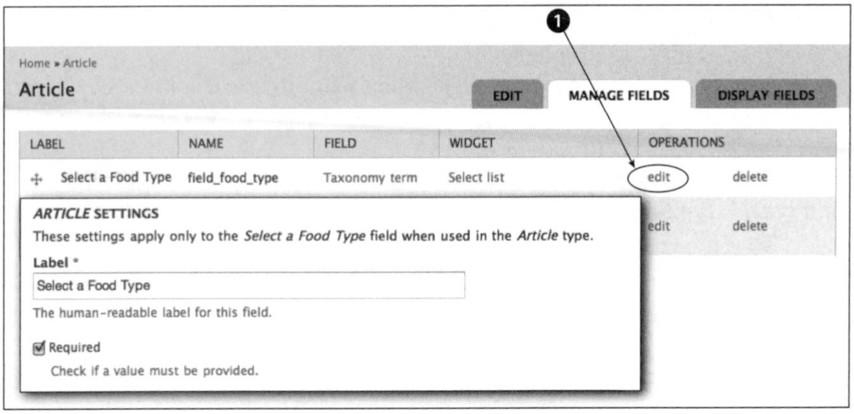

FIGURE 8-14

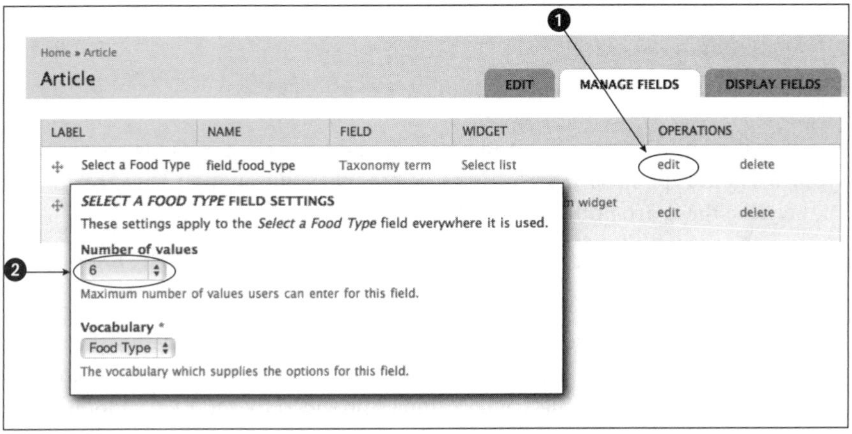

FIGURE 8-15

Allowing Users to Freely Add Terms (freetagging)

To allow users to freely add terms you simply modify the Widget to a form that presents the users with a textbox, as demonstrated in Figure 8-13. Note that you change the widget by clicking the Widgets title to the left of the edit link, as shown in Figure 8-16.

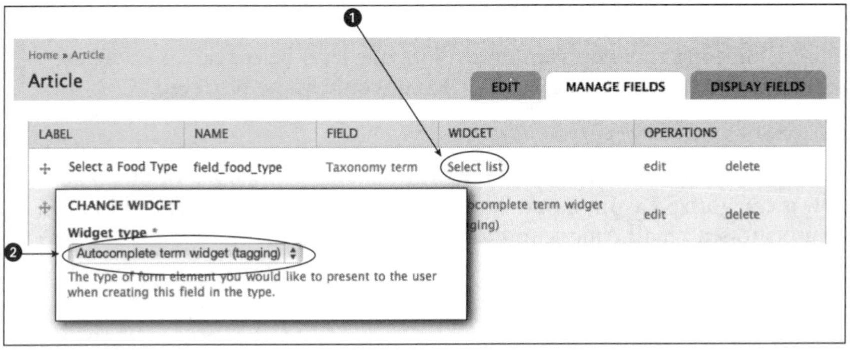

FIGURE 8-16

A TERM'S PARENT/CHILD RELATIONSHIP

Each term may be the child of one or more parents, which allows you to create a hierarchy of terms. Consider the following example.

> ✎ **NOTE** *Note that (x) is the term id.*

```
American (4)
--Burgers (10)
----McDonalds (11)
----In 'n Out (12)
----Burger King (13)
--Chicken (14)
----Popeye's (15)
----Church's (16)
----McDonalds (11)
```

As you can see, In 'n Out is a child of Burgers and a grandchild of American. This parent-child relationship allows your users to type in or search for **In n Out** without having to also relate it to Burgers or American, because these are both implied in the relationship hierarchy.

A child may also have more than one parent. In the preceding example, McDonalds is both a child of both Burgers and Chicken.

Now how does this work in practice? Unfortunately, Drupal doesn't provide a point-and-click method to use this out of the box. Contributed modules, such as Views, can utilize this structure. Using the preceding term hierarchy, consider the following URL examples provided by the Views module:

➤ http://*localhost*/taxonomy/term/11

   This URL will retrieve all items categorized under McDonalds.

➤ http://localhost/taxonomy/term/10

   This URL will retrieve all items tagged as Burgers but will *not* retrieve McDonalds, In 'n Out, or Burger King. To do this, you would add a *depth* to the URL like this:

   http://localhost/taxonomy/term/10/1

   The addition of 1 indicates that you want to explore one level below Burgers. Thus, Burgers, McDonalds, In 'n Out, and Burger King would all be retrieved.

➤ http://localhost/taxonomy/term/4/1

   This URL retrieves all content categorized as American and as *Burgers* or Chicken but no content that was categorized as In 'n out. The depth isn't deep enough thus adding a 2 or 3 would allow users to search all American food.

   http://localhost/taxonomy/term/4/2.

Note that all of the above URLs are based upon the Views module, which is discussed in Chapter 11, "Internationalization." Views also allows you to construct pages based upon multiple required or options terms. Consider the following examples:

➤ `http://localhost/taxonomy/term/11+13` for all McDonald's *or* Burger King categorized content.

➤ `http://localhost/taxonomy/term/10,14` for all Burgers *and* Chicken categorized content. Adding a depth to this would grab the respective restaurants, `http://localhost/taxonomy/term/10,14/1`

RSS FeedsEach term provides an RSS feed of all content categorized with the term. The feeds are accessible at `http://localhost/taxonomy/term/<term-id>/feed`. You can retrieve the term id by looking at the URL on the taxonomy administration page or by navigating to the term's URL alias and clicking the RSS icon at the lower right corner of the page.

USING VIEWS TO DISPLAY TERM PAGES

Views is a highly configurable module that allows you to create a large variety of custom pages, blocks, RSS feeds, and other content listings. This module is a perfect complement to taxonomy as it allows you or your users to pinpoint the content they would like based upon selected terms or a term's hierarchy (i.e., Select burgers to find McDonalds, In 'n Out, and Burger King).

Chapter 11 covers the installation and configuration of this module so it is worth a pause here to skip to Chapter 11 and run through the exercises. Once you are familiar with view return to this portion of the chapter to learn how to use Views specifically for taxonomy pages.

> *NOTE* At the time of writing the Views module was not updated to Drupal 7. The following exercises and screenshots are from Drupal 6.

The Views module is aware of taxonomy's vocabularies and terms including the terms dynamically added by users. In the following exercise you will explore Views' built-in taxonomy/term page and modify the default depth to display all child terms.

TRY IT OUT   Modifying the Default Taxonomy Depth

In this exercise you explore the Views module default taxonomy/term page and modify the depth to display all child terms.

1. Download and install the Views module from `http://drupal.org/project/views`.

2. Once installed, navigate to Administer ➪ Site building ➪ Views (Drupal 6). Drupal 7 should place it at Administer ➪ Structure ➪ Views or provide an option in the top Administration bar.

3. The main page of Views displays a listing of every available view. A view may be a URL path, a block, an RSS feed, or a combination of these. Scroll to the bottom of the page and find the view labeled `taxonomy_term`, as shown in Figure 8-17.

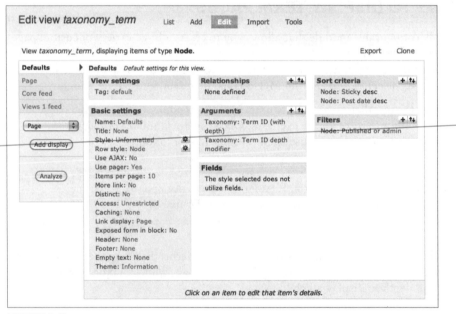

Default Node view: **taxonomy_term** (default)		Enable
Path: taxonomy/term/% Feed, Page	A view to emulate Drupal core's handling of taxonomy/term; it also emulates Views 1's handling by having two possible feeds.	
Default Node view: **tracker** (default)		Enable
Title: Recent posts Path: tracker Page	Shows all new activity on system.	

FIGURE 8-17

Note that this view provides both a Feed (RSS) and a Page as indicated directly underneath the path of taxonomy/term/%. Also note that the view is currently disabled evident by the Enable link to the far right. This indicates that Drupal's core is handing the URL path /taxonomy/term/% but once Enabled Views manages this URL, it will allow you to customize the listings.

4. Click the Enable link on the far right of the view (shown in Figure 8-17).

5. Once enabled, click the edit link to view the details of the view, shown in Figure 8-18.

FIGURE 8-18

6. In the middle of this page is the meat of the view within the Arguments section shown in Figure 8-19. Click the link Taxonomy: Term ID (with depth).

7. Displayed below the view settings, often requiring you to scroll down, is a listing of options for the argument. Near the Update button you will see an option for Depth, shown in Figure 8-20. By default this is set to 0, meaning that no child terms will be displayed.
Set the Depth to 10 then click Update.

Relationships	+ ↑↓
None defined	

Arguments	+ ↑↓
Taxonomy: Term ID (with depth)	
Taxonomy: Term ID depth modifier	

Fields	
The style selected does not utilize fields.	

FIGURE 8-19

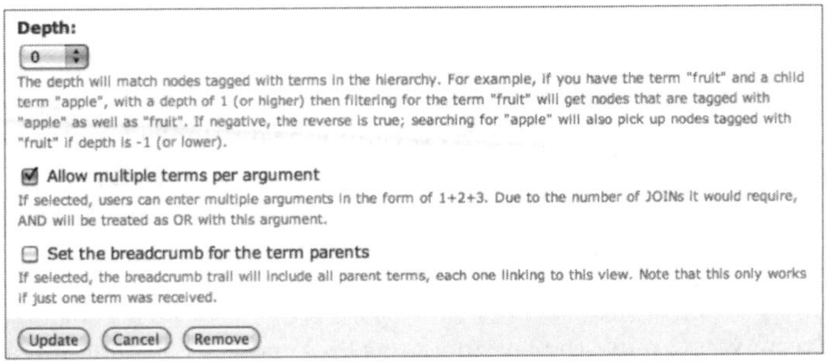

Depth:

`0`

The depth will match nodes tagged with terms in the hierarchy. For example, if you have the term "fruit" and a child term "apple", with a depth of 1 (or higher) then filtering for the term "fruit" will get nodes that are tagged with "apple" as well as "fruit". If negative, the reverse is true; searching for "apple" will also pick up nodes tagged with "fruit" if depth is -1 (or lower).

☑ **Allow multiple terms per argument**

If selected, users can enter multiple arguments in the form of 1+2+3. Due to the number of JOINs it would require, AND will be treated as OR with this argument.

☐ **Set the breadcrumb for the term parents**

If selected, the breadcrumb trail will include all parent terms, each one linking to this view. Note that this only works if just one term was received.

(Update) (Cancel) (Remove)

FIGURE 8-20

8. Explore your new settings by navigating to a top-level parent term. For example, Middle Eastern food available at `http://localhost/taxonomy/term/1`.

How It Works

The Views module works by taking over the URL path `/taxonomy/term/<term-id>` thus overriding the default behavior. Once this view has been enabled you are free to modify the view to display your content how you see fit. Flip to Chapter 11 for more information on how to use Views.

Display Multiple Terms on a Single Page

You may be wondering how you can create pages or feeds that display content that is categorized within a set of terms. For example, Articles categorized as Middle Eastern OR Japanese.

This is accomplished by using the Views module and also occurs within the Argument options you saw in the previous exercise. Return to Step 6 of the previous exercise and the options of the `Taxonomy: Term ID` argument. (view: taxonomy_term ⇨ Arguments, click on the `Term ID` argument).

Setting the `Argument type` setting to `Term IDs separated by , or +` allows a URL to accept multiple term IDs, as shown in Figure 8-21.

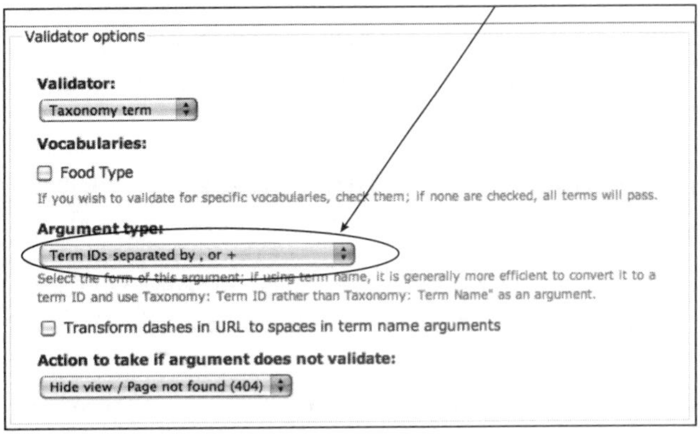

For example, consider that term Middle Eastern has an id of 1 and Japanese has an id of 2. You could use the following URL to retrieve both content categorized as Middle Eastern or Japanese.

`http://localhost/taxonomy/term/1+2`

Validator options

Validator:

`Taxonomy term`

Vocabularies:

☐ Food Type

If you wish to validate for specific vocabularies, check them; if none are checked, all terms will pass.

Argument type:

`Term IDs separated by , or +`

Select the form of this argument; if using term name, it is generally more efficient to convert it to a term ID and use Taxonomy: Term ID rather than Taxonomy: Term Name as an argument.

☐ Transform dashes in URL to spaces in term name arguments

Action to take if argument does not validate:

`Hide view / Page not found (404)`

FIGURE 8-21

API

Although an advanced topic that will be discussed in Chapter 15, "Custom Modules," later in this book, the taxonomy Application Programming Interface (API) cannot be overlooked in this chapter. When you're writing custom modules or using custom PHP code, you can take advantage of this API to save time and code. This section gives you a few examples to get you started, and then in later chapters you can really dig into custom module development. Don't worry if any of this seems confusing right now — simply skip over it and return after you have read Chapter 15.

To find all nodes with a specific term you can use the `taxonomy_select_nodes` API function as follows:

```php
<?php
  $term_id = 1;
  $node_ids = taxonomy_select_nodes($term_id);
  $nodes = nodes_load_multiple($node_ids);
  foreach($nodes as $nid => $node) {
    print "Found: $node->title  <br/>";
  }
?>
```

Read more at: `http://api.drupal.org/api/function/taxonomy_select_nodes/7`.

If you are unsure of the term's ID but know its name, you can use the following API, which attempts to match a name (string) to a term:

```
taxonomy_get_term_by_name($name)
```

The API can also help you find all child terms or parent (ancestor) terms with these respective functions.

```
taxonomy_get_children($tid, $vid = 0, $key = 'tid')
```

and

```
taxonomy_get_parents_all($tid)
```

These are just a few API functions — there are over a dozen more. You can find the full list of API functions at `http://api.drupal.org` by searching for the word **taxonomy**.

THEMING CONSIDERATIONS

Taxonomy, like all pieces of Drupal, can be molded and customized to fit your site's unique personality. You'll learn more about custom theming in Chapter 13, "Theming," but to get you started here is some specific information about customizing the look of your taxonomy pages.

Customizing Each Section

A common complaint of using a taxonomy approach is that each Section doesn't have its own unique identity. However, this couldn't be further from the truth. There are several methods you can use to create separate identities for each Section, so that the pages on Middle Eastern food look different than the pages on Japanese food. Here are a few methods.

Fields

Similarly to adding images to content, discussed in Chapter 6, an image field can be added to a vocabularies terms. Using custom fields you could, for example, display a mouth-watering picture of a Shawarma on the taxonomy pages showing Middle Eastern food blogs.

Individually Themed Landing Pages

Chapter 13 discusses theming in detail but here is a jump-start. Drupal provides the ability to theme individual pages by using a non-aliased path. For example, if you want to theme the Middle Eastern term page (term id 1), you could use the following template file: `page-taxonomy-term-1.tpl.php`. To theme the page on Japanese food (term id 2) differently, use the template file `page-taxonomy-term-2.tpl.php`.

When implemented in a custom theme (as discussed in Chapter 13), these templates give you full control over the look and feel of the individual landing pages.

Views

Each individual View and View display can be individually themed. Using Views you can create custom pages that not only display subsections of your categorized content but also do so in a uniquely themed manner.

USEFUL CONTRIBUTED MODULES

> **NOTE** At the time of writing many of these modules had not been upgraded to Drupal 7.

Taxonomy is one of the most powerful modules in Drupal, but the power comes more from its design than from its interface. Fortunately, the Drupal community has added to the functionality of taxonomy by contributing modules. These modules can be found at `http://drupal.org/project` under the Taxonomy category (`http://drupal.org/taxonomy/term/71`). To help you with your search, the following sections describe some useful modules. (Also be sure to check `Drupal.org` for the latest modules.)

Menus from Taxonomy

While reading this chapter you may have wondered if there was a way to create menus out of your taxonomy terms. There is! The appropriately named Taxonomy Menu module creates a menu for each designated vocabulary. When the vocabulary is modified, the menu is as well, making the management of your site's content even easier. The Taxonomy Menu is available at `http://drupal.org/project/taxonomy_menu`.

Interface

Taxonomy Browser (http://drupal.org/project/taxonomy_browser) provides a nice and simple interface for browsing a site's content by its categories. This module is particularly useful if your site contains a large number of taxonomy terms.

Faceted Search (http://drupal.org/project/faceted_search) is one of the more exciting modules for Drupal. This module utilizes taxonomy as well as other modules to help your users find data on your site fast. A simple example of this module is a classifieds website that allows users to continuously filter their requirements. When searching for a house, a user may click the term For Sale, then the term 3+ Bedrooms, and then the term Downtown to narrow their search results down. The standard Drupal interface does not provide this ability, even though under the surface the functionality is available — Faceted Search adds this missing interface.

Administration

Once you discover the power of the taxonomy system and categorization, you and your users will soon start adding terms to everything. Unfortunately, at about this time, you'll also discover that the default interface is missing quite a bit of functionality when working on a large number of terms.

Taxonomy Manager (http://drupal.org/project/taxonomy_manager) module provides an interface for the mass adding, deleting, and editing of terms; merging of terms; and moving terms under new parents/children; as well as an export interface. This is a must-have module for any site with a large number of terms.

SUMMARY

As you've seen in this chapter, the Taxonomy module provides a lot more than just simple categorization. Aggregation pages show all nodes under one or more categories, RSS feeds are provided for individual or combined categories, and a robust API makes the Taxonomy module one of the most powerful features of Drupal. Although the name sounds complex, the management and use of it is anything but.

Now that you have an understanding of taxonomy, the next chapter will prepare you to launch your website.

EXERCISES

1. What is taxonomy and how is it used in Drupal?

2. Give an example of parent and child terms.

3. Why is the taxonomy system so popular and important in Drupal?

4. How does the weight system work in Drupal?

5. What is the advantage of the API (Application Programming Interface)?

Answers to the Exercises can be found in the Appendix.

▶ **WHAT YOU LEARNED IN THIS CHAPTER**

➤ Taxonomy is used to describe the overall system in Drupal that categorizes content. The taxonomy system uses vocabularies, which are the collection of terms used to categorize nodes.

➤ Drupal automatically creates a page dedicated to displaying content categorized with the term. Each one of these pages also has a corresponding RSS feed.

➤ You can create a hierarchy of terms, with each child being able to have more than one parent term. These terms can be sorted alphabetically and by weight.

➤ When you're writing custom modules or using custom PHP code, you can take advantage of API (Application Programming Interface) to save time and code.

9

Search, Performance, Statistics, and Reporting

WHAT YOU WILL LEARN IN THIS CHAPTER:

➤ Enabling and configuring your search engine

➤ Extending the search capabilities on your site

➤ Speeding up your site by enabling caching

➤ Optimizing your CSS and JavaScript files

➤ Taking your site offline by using maintenance mode

➤ Reviewing your site's status report

➤ Finding important information in your site's logs

➤ Enabling and configuring the statistics module

Thus far, you have added user accounts, created and managed your content, and explored many of your site's configuration settings. In this chapter, you explore two of the most important aspects of creating a robust website. The first is enabling and configuring your search engine to provide a way for your visitors to dig through your site's content. The second is performance, or perhaps better said, how to make your site fast. In this chapter, you explore Drupal's caching options and other site optimization techniques.

Before getting too deep into your site, you'll also want to take the time to learn how to read your site's reports in order to determine the health and status of your site. Drupal reports can alert you to possible hacking attempts and errors with module code, and even show you the latest updated content. Using these reports, you can stay on top of the activity on your site and rest assured that your site is working properly.

SEARCH

Your site may have the most thought-provoking and informative articles on the Web, but if people can't find them, your message won't be heard. With just a tad bit of configuration, you can get a search engine up and running on your site in no time at all. Drupal's core search modules automatically index your site's content types (Articles, Pages, and so on) and your users, making them all available to search queries. You can selectively exclude content types from the search as well as users. The Search module also includes a block that can be displayed within any region or a special form.

Follow along in the first exercise to enable search on your site.

TRY IT OUT   Enabling Search on Your Site

In this exercise, you enable the Search module, enable the Search block, and set search permissions.

1. Log in as an Administrator and navigate to Modules.

2. Enable the core Search module.

3. Navigate to Structure ⇨ Blocks, and drag the Search Form block from the Disabled section to one of your theme's available regions, such as the Left Sidebar. Click the Save Blocks button.

4. Navigate to Configuration ⇨ Permissions (under People and Permissions), and set the following permissions as shown in Figure 9-1:

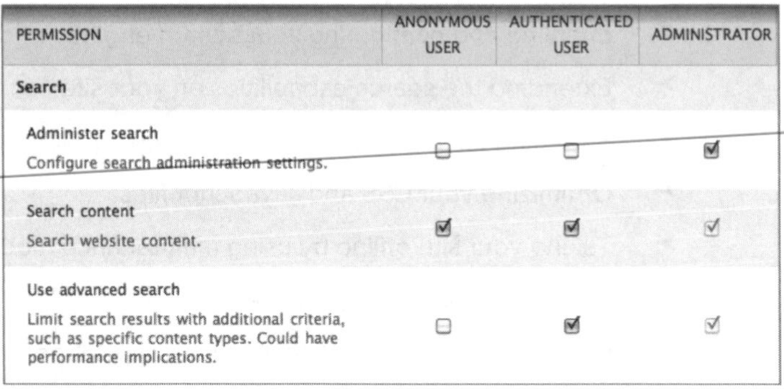

PERMISSION	ANONYMOUS USER	AUTHENTICATED USER	ADMINISTRATOR
Search			
Administer search Configure search administration settings.	☐	☐	☑
Search content Search website content.	☑	☑	☑
Use advanced search Limit search results with additional criteria, such as specific content types. Could have performance implications.	☐	☑	☑

FIGURE 9-1

- ➤ Search Content: Check the Anonymous User and Authenticated User boxes.
- ➤ Use Advanced Search: Check the Authenticated User box.

5. Click the Save Configuration button.

6. Navigate to your new search engine page at `http://localhost/search`.

How It Works

Once enabled, the Search module provides a search form block for use throughout your site and a dedicated search page at `http://localhost/search`. Granting users the Search Content permission allows them to use the Search block form and the dedicated Search page at `http://localhost/search`.

Indexing Your Content

Indexing your content could also be called making your site's search engine work. If you perform a search after completing the previous exercise, you won't get any results — this is because your site has not been indexed yet. Indexing occurs automatically when your site runs cron (discussed in Chapter 3, "Your First Drupal Website"). You can see the status of your site's index, as shown in Figure 9-2, by navigating to Configuration ⇨ Search Settings.

INDEXING STATUS
0% of the site has been indexed. There are 512 items left to index.
Re-index site

FIGURE 9-2

You can either wait for your site to run cron, or run cron manually by navigating to Reports ⇨ Status Report and clicking the Run Cron Manually link shown in Figure 9-3.

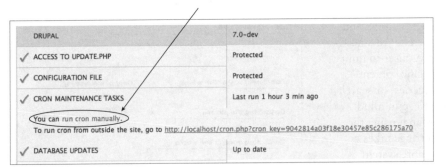

DRUPAL	7.0-dev
✓ ACCESS TO UPDATE.PHP	Protected
✓ CONFIGURATION FILE	Protected
✓ CRON MAINTENANCE TASKS	Last run 1 hour 3 min ago
You can run cron manually. To run cron from outside the site, go to http://localhost/cron.php?cron_key=9042814a03f18e30457e85c286175a70	
✓ DATABASE UPDATES	Up to date

FIGURE 9-3

During each cron run, Drupal indexes as much content as possible, up to the limit imposed by the indexing throttle or your server's capacity. The larger the length of a typical node, comment, or piece of content, the more memory and resources Drupal will need to analyze it. If your server runs out of memory or cannot process the data within the time allotted by your server, a timeout will occur and Drupal won't properly index your site. Throttling helps by limiting Drupal to a set number of items per indexing cycle, as shown in Figure 9-4.

INDEXING THROTTLE

Number of items to index per cron run
100

The maximum number of items indexed in each pass of a cron maintenance task. If necessary, reduce the number of items to prevent timeouts and memory errors while indexing.

FIGURE 9-4

If a limit is set at 100, and your site contains 512 pieces of content, cron will need to run at least six times before your site's content will be fully searchable. To find out how quickly your server can index content, you simply manually run cron and check your index status between each run. Then compare the time needed to the amount of content on your site to determine a reasonable limit.

> **NOTE** *For testing purposes, you can use the Devel module (*http://drupal.org/project/devel*) to generate large amounts of dummy content.*

Once a piece of content has been indexed by Drupal, it is not indexed again unless the content has been edited or updated. If you think that Drupal has not indexed your content properly, or if your index is corrupt (possibly due to timeout or memory issues from an overly large throttle), you can force Drupal to re-index all of your content by clicking the Re-index Site button (shown previously in Figure 9-2). This will cause Drupal to wipe your entire search index and start from scratch. Be aware, however, that this could lead to a slow and unresponsive website until the index has been rebuilt.

Advanced Search Settings

During the first Try It Out exercise, you set a permission that allowed authenticated users to use the Advanced Search features available at `http://localhost/search` and shown in Figure 9-5. The Advanced Search options allow a user to limit their search to a specific content type, use negative queries, or search for whole phrases. Keep in mind that conducting a search using the Advanced Search settings takes longer and utilizes more system resources, which is why you did not grant the permission to anonymous users.

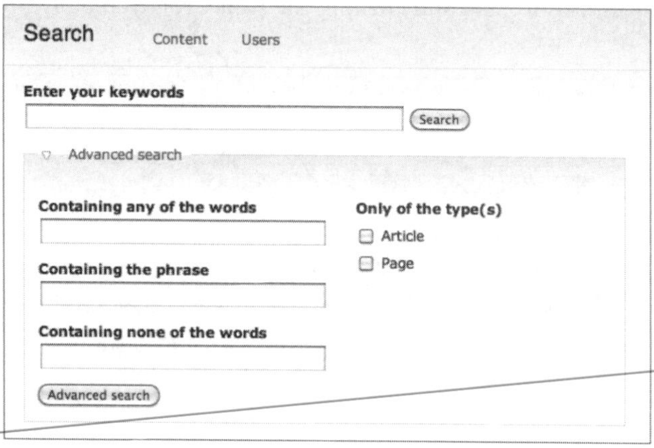

FIGURE 9-5

Indexing Settings

A search index is somewhat similar to the index of a book. Individual words are discovered in the text, and a pointer (i.e., a link) to where each of these words can be found is stored in the database. When a user performs a search on your site they look at the search index in the database. Drupal uses the minimum word length to determine what is or is not a word.

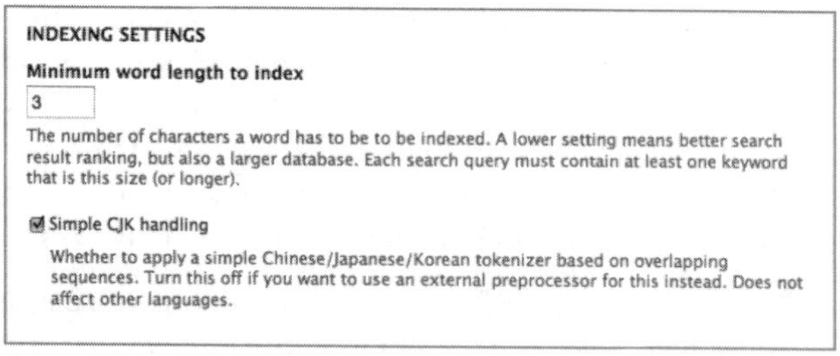

FIGURE 9-6

The default settings, shown in Figure 9-6, define a word as being at least three characters in length. This means that the words *at*, *be*, *do*, *no*, and *we* would not be indexed. This might be reasonable in the English language, but consider character-based languages such as Chinese. The two-character words 鸡肉, 番茄, 拉面, and 上海 (chicken meat, tomato, pulled noodles, and Shanghai) wouldn't be indexed with a three-character word limit. In this case, the word length should be set to 1.

Modifying the minimum word length will require (and force) your site to be re-indexed. Cron will then need to be run enough times to re-index your site.

CJK Handling

Simple CJK handling helps Drupal index Chinese, Japanese, and Korean content by splitting a string of characters into distinguishable and searchable individual characters. This feature has no impact on performance and is best left checked unless you have installed a module (external preprocessor) that will assist Drupal in indexing CJK content.

> **WARNING** *Drupal's built-in CJK handler, also known as a tokenizer, is a very basic handler, and although it works great for occasional C/J/K language postings, it is not recommended for a site that primarily uses a character-based language. Although not updated to Drupal 7 at the time of this writing, the Chinese Word Splitter module (*`http://drupal.org/project/csplitter`*) can dramatically improve search relevancy for Chinese character-based websites.*

Content Ranking

A better title for this section might be "How to Define What's Relevant to Your Users." Content ranking allows you to modify the order in which results are returned during a search process, and help direct Drupal to what is relevant to your users. Opposite of most ordering in Drupal, a higher number means higher relevancy. The example shown in Figure 9-7 would cause content promoted to the frontpage to be returned higher in the search results than other content with a high number of user comments, even though content that has been commented on would still appear higher than content that only contains the keyword.

CONTENT RANKING	
FACTOR	WEIGHT
Number of comments	4
Keyword relevance	1
Content is sticky at top of lists	2
Content is promoted to the front page	10
Recently posted	0
Number of views	2

FIGURE 9-7

Note that modules can add additional content ranking factors allowing you to fine tune your search results. For example, the core Statistics module adds a ranking item for the number of views.

Set this order to what you believe is relevant for the search patterns on your website. Modifying the content ranking will not require re-indexing.

Faceted Search

Users often resort to a search engine after they become frustrated at the inability to find the information they were searching for. The Faceted Search module (`http://drupal.org/project/faceted_search`) lets users drill down through your site's content to narrow down the results and hone in on what they want. With this module enabled, users can filter content by multiple sets of taxonomy terms, search phrases, or a combination of the two. This is commonly done by adding a block with a set of top-level links that users start from to drill down into your site's content.

Outsourcing Search

Drupal's built-in search engine is great for small sites that don't have much content, but as your content grows and your users expect more relevant search results, you'll start to see signs of stress on your site. (After all, Google, Microsoft, and Yahoo! wouldn't be in an all out slugfest if search were easy.) Consider outsourcing your search results with one of the following modules:

➤ **Acquia Search** (`http://acquia.com/products-services/acquia-search`) — Based on the extremely powerful and complex Apache Lucene and Apache Solr (the same technologies that power the search on `http://drupal.org`), Acquia Search provides you all the power with none of the complexity. This quick drop-in replacement for Drupal's Search engine will provide you with faster searches, more relevant results, and a host of other features.

➤ **Google Custom Search** — This customizable Google search engine can provide all of the power of Google with none of the work. Read more about Google Custom Search at `http://www.google.com/cse/`, and then add it to your site at `http://drupal.org/project/google_appliance`, if it meets your needs.

If You Don't Want to Outsource

If you are running an intranet, have privacy concerns, or simply don't want a third party crawling through your content, there are other options. The Apache Solr and Lucene open source search engines are extremely powerful, highly flexible, and freely available. Better yet, they have been integrated with Drupal.

You can learn more about the Apache Solr Drupal module at `http://drupal.org/project/apachesolr`, and read more about Lucene at `http://lucene.apache.org`.

Be warned that although these search engines are incredibly powerful, they are also very complex. Entire books are dedicated to their installation and configuration. If this is your first introduction to Drupal or a content management system (CMS), you should leave this until a bit later in your Drupal journey.

PERFORMANCE

A fast site is a happy site. Before going live with your site, visit the performance settings to dramatically increase the performance of your website. Drupal enables you to enhance your site's performance in two ways. The first is to increase the speed on your server by serving cached (pre-rendered) pages. The second is to increase the speed on the client's computer by reducing the number of requests to the server, thus allowing the browser to display the web page faster.

Navigate to Configuration ➪ Performance (under Development) and adjust the settings as described in the next few pages.

Caching

Like a pirate who stows away his treasure in order to retrieve it later, *caching* is the act of taking something that is pre-made and storing it for later use. Drupal uses caching extensively to enhance performance. A single Drupal page may require hundreds of database queries and possibly thousands of calls to module functions. All of this processing makes it possible for you to create a highly dynamic and flexible website that responds with up-to-the-second information. However, this can also slow your site down, particularly when you have thousands of users accessing your site at the same time and exponentially increasing the number of database queries and module function calls.

Drupal renders a page or block in its entirety and stores the results in a cache. Subsequent calls to the page or block are retrieved from that cache instead of rebuilding the page or block from scratch. This dramatically increases the speed of a site with no side effects, leaving you with little reason to not turn it on. Read on to learn how this works.

Cache Blocks

Although the Cache Blocks feature is just a simple checkbox, as shown in Figure 9-8, it is incredibly powerful. When this is enabled, Drupal pre-renders the cache blocks on your site and hands them out to both anonymous and authenticated users. However, blocks that must be dynamic, such as user-specific blocks, will bypass this caching mechanism. This setting should always be enabled.

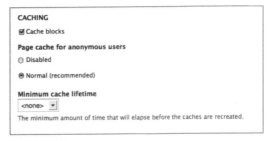

FIGURE 9-8

Page Cache for Anonymous Users

The Page Cache for Anonymous Users setting can dramatically increase the speed of your site for anonymous users, while decreasing the load on your server. This is a win-win setting and should always be enabled on a production site.

When this is set to Normal, Drupal will send anonymous users a page from the cache instead of building one from scratch, dramatically increasing performance. However, when you're developing a site, you may not immediately see the changes you make to settings, themes, or modules; thus disabling Page Cache is preferable during development. Don't forget to re-enable this setting before you go live with your site.

Minimum Cache Lifetime

A cached page is updated whenever an event occurs that would modify the page, such as updates to the content or comments posted to the content. The caching system may be defeated on high-traffic sites, because Drupal will be continually updating the cache. In this situation, adjusting the Minimum Cache Lifetime setting forces Drupal to wait until a specified time period has passed before refreshing the cache. This setting will reduce the load on the server and keep your site responding quickly; but it may give your users outdated and stale information. So unless you have an incredibly high-traffic site, you should leave this setting at <none> as shown previously in Figure 9-8.

Bandwidth Optimization

A default installation of Drupal sends approximately nine separate Cascading Style Sheets (CSS) files to the client. When combined with JavaScript files, this number can grow to over 14. Every visitor to your site has to retrieve each one of these files, causing their browser to work harder and causing the overall experience of your website to be slower. Microsoft's Internet explorer web browser also imposes a 31 Style Sheet limit, often resulting in a broken website; a site with numerous modules will quickly add more than this amount.

A quick and easy way to speed up client-side performance (and to fix IE) is to reduce the number of files sent to the client by aggregating your CSS and JavaScript files as shown in Figure 9-9. When Drupal is enabled, it combines all CSS files into a single file and all JavaScript files into a single file. This reduces the number of requests to only two (one for CSS and one for JavaScript), increasing the speed of your website.

BANDWIDTH OPTIMIZATION

External resources can be optimized automatically, which can reduce both the size and number of requests made to your website.

☑ Aggregate and compress CSS files into one file.

☑ Aggregate JavaScript files into one file.

FIGURE 9-9

The following code listings demonstrate the difference in CSS file links before and after CSS file optimization.

Available for download on Wrox.com

BEFORE OPTIMIZATION

```
<link type="text/css" rel="stylesheet" media="all" href="/modules/node/node.css" />
<link type="text/css" rel="stylesheet" media="all" href="/modules/system/system.css" />
<link type="text/css" rel="stylesheet" media="all" href="/modules/user/user.css" />
<link type="text/css" rel="stylesheet" media="all" href="/themes/garland/style.css" />
```

Available for download on Wrox.com

AFTER OPTIMIZATION

```
<link type="text/css" rel="stylesheet" media="all" href="/sites/default/files/css/
ee520a854c13fcca38c5ea37330101cf.css" />
```

Drupal takes this CSS optimization one step further by reducing bandwidth consumption and client processing time by removing white space and comments from the CSS files. CSS and JavaScript files are combined into new files leaving the originals unmodified.

Clearing Cached Data

If your site is experiencing issues with module changes, theme changes, or new data not appearing, then clearing the cache might help to solve the problem. However, keep in mind that the Clear Cache button shown above in Figure 9-8 clears all of Drupal's cached data. The more data your site has, the longer it will take to rebuild the cache. While the cache is being rebuilt, your site may respond slower than average.

The Need for Speed

If you find that your site needs better performance than Drupal's core provides, look into using one of the following modules.

➤ **Boost** (`http://drupal.org/project/boost`)—Sites with large numbers of anonymous users can see a very significant performance boost with this module. The module is simple to install and easy to configure.

➤ **Memcache** (`http://drupal.org/project/memcache`)—Sites with large numbers of logged-in authenticated users can increase performance by caching the requests made to the database through the use of a third-party caching mechanism called *memcached*. The Memcache module enables Drupal to use memcached. This is an advanced module and requires access to the server as well as a bit of Linux/Unix expertise to install and configure it.

➤ **CacheRouter** (`http://drupal.org/project/cacherouter`)—Taking the best from all caching worlds, this module routes requests to the most appropriate caching technology. Very significant performance increases have been seen with this module, and, depending on its use, the installation and configuration can be relatively straightforward.

TRY IT OUT Increasing Your Site's Performance with Caching

In this exercise, you increase your site's performance by enabling block and page caching. You also increase client-side performance by aggregating your CSS and JavaScript files.

1. Log in as an Administrator and navigate to Configuration ➪ Performance (under Development).

2. Check the Cache Blocks box.

3. Click the Normal (Recommended) radio button under Page Cache for Anonymous Users.

4. Under Bandwidth Optimization, select both the option to aggregate and compress CSS files and the option to aggregate JavaScript files.

Figure 9-10 shows the final settings.

```
CACHING
☑ Cache blocks

Page cache for anonymous users
○ Disabled

◉ Normal (recommended)

Minimum cache lifetime
<none>  ▾
The minimum amount of time that will elapse before the caches are
recreated.
```

```
BANDWIDTH OPTIMIZATION
External resources can be optimized automatically, which can reduce
both the size and number of requests made to your website.
☑ Aggregate and compress CSS files into one file.

☑ Aggregate JavaScript files into one file.
```

FIGURE 9-10

How It Works

Caching is an essential part of any live website. Enabling block caching frees up server resources and provides a faster experience for all users. Serving pre-built cached pages to anonymous users significantly increases the performance of your website and reduces the burden on your server resources. Finally, aggregating your site's CSS and JavaScript files speeds up client-side performance.

These basic and easy-to-use settings not only reduce the load on your server but also provide a much faster experience on your site. These are the bare-minimum settings for any live site.

REPORTING

This is definitely the least fun, exciting, or sexy portion of administering a Drupal website, but it's undeniably one of the most important. Periodic review of your reports can alert you to security updates, hack attempts, database errors, application issues, or other items that could bring your site offline. You can also glean valuable information from these reports, such as where your traffic is coming from or what people are searching for. Enabled modules can also add their own custom reports (for example, the Statistics module adds the Top Visitors report). This is an area that simply cannot be overlooked.

The Reports page, shown in Figure 9-11, is accessed by clicking Reports in the top Administration menu or by choosing Reports in the Administer page.

Many of the reports are straightforward and require no further explanation. For example, Top 'Page Not Found' Errors, Top 'Access Denied' Errors, and Available Updates reports provide exactly what their titles state. The reports that are available to you depend on the modules you have enabled, because modules may provide their own reports. Table 9-1 lists the reports provided by the core, Statistics, and Search modules.

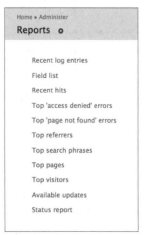

FIGURE 9-11

TABLE 9-1

DRUPAL CORE	STATISTICS MODULE	SEARCH MODULE
Recent Log Entries		
Field List		
Top 'Access Denied' Errors		
Top 'Page Not Found' Errors		
Available Updates		
Status Report	Recent Hits	
Top Referrers		
Top Pages		
Top Visitors	Top Search Phrases	

One of the first reports you should view is the same report that Drupal will point you to should it detect a potential problem with your site: the Status Report.

Status Report

The Status Report provides a one-stop shop for information on your site's configuration, including the web server type and version, PHP version, common PHP configuration settings, and notices about any potential problems with your site. If you seek help with your site from Internet Relay Chat (IRC) channels, drupal.org's forum, or Drupal professionals, the information on this page will assist them in troubleshooting your issues.

Drupal sets one of three statuses on each of the messages: OK, Warning, or Error. If an error is reported, as shown in Figure 9-12, then Drupal will notify you of this by placing a banner above the Administer page as shown in Figure 9-13.

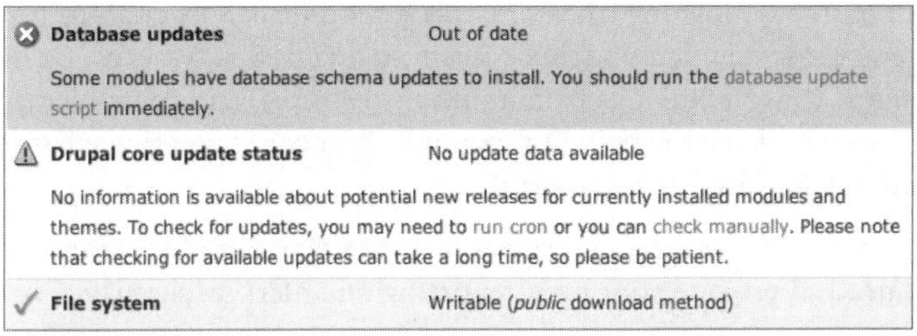

⊗ **Database updates**	Out of date
Some modules have database schema updates to install. You should run the database update script immediately.	
⚠ **Drupal core update status**	No update data available
No information is available about potential new releases for currently installed modules and themes. To check for updates, you may need to run cron or you can check manually. Please note that checking for available updates can take a long time, so please be patient.	
✓ **File system**	Writable (*public* download method)

FIGURE 9-12

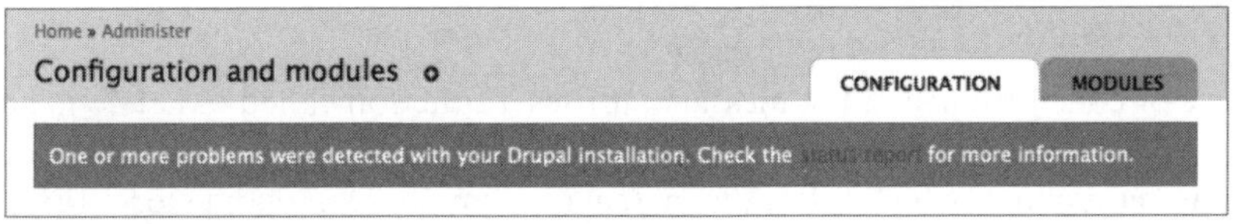

Home » Administer
Configuration and modules o

CONFIGURATION   MODULES

One or more problems were detected with your Drupal installation. Check the status report for more information.

FIGURE 9-13

Errors should be addressed immediately to prevent any serious problems with your site and to keep it running optimally.

Recent Log Entries

Every site will generate database and system messages that range from simple notifications such as "Session opened for Joe Smith" (meaning that he logged in) to critical system errors that require immediate attention. Drupal stores these messages and retains them accordingly to your site's set-ting at Configuration ⇨ Development ⇨ Logging and Errors. At first glance, the Recent Log Entries page may be intimidating and filled with too much noise to be useful. However, you can use the Filter Log Messages information, shown in Figure 9-14, to craft specialty reports that show the most relevant information. For

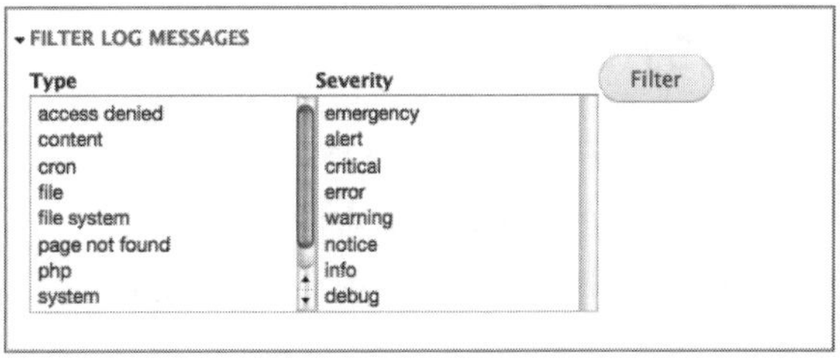

▾ FILTER LOG MESSAGES

Type	Severity		Filter
access denied	emergency		
content	alert		
cron	critical		
file	error		
file system	warning		
page not found	notice		
php	info		
system	debug		

FIGURE 9-14

example, you can create a report that notifies you of new user accounts, which includes information about who created the account and a link to the new user's account, as shown in Figure 9-15.

TYPE	DATE	▼	MESSAGE	USER	OPERATIONS
user	01/02/2010 – 23:20		New user: *John Doe* (*jhon@localhost*).	jredding	edit
user	01/01/2010 – 11:23		New user: *jane doe* (*jan@localhost*).	Anonymous (not verified)	edit

FIGURE 9-15

Syslog

In addition to, or as a substitute for, database logging, the core Syslog module can be enabled to route messages to your server's operating system logging mechanism. Using Syslog, you can tie in with your existing monitoring systems, consolidate logs from multiple websites, and route messages to different log files (and possibly different departments). For example, you could create a separate log for Access Denied messages and one for User Account notifications.

A Syslog server is separate from Drupal, and the messages travel only one way out of Drupal. If you decide to use only Syslog, you will need to provide your own reporting and alert mechanisms.

Using Syslog for Database Logging

Database logging is an intensive process, and using Syslog can dramatically reduce database activity, thus increasing site performance.

When a module or a piece of code produces a log message, it uses a function called `watchdog`. The `watchdog` function collects and passes log messages to a storage mechanism. By default, Drupal enables the Database Logging module, which takes the messages from `watchdog` and stores them in the database. On large sites, this can introduce heavy database activity that can slow down your site performance. To improve performance, use the Syslog module to store the messages on a Syslog server — preferably one that is separate from your Drupal server.

> **NOTE** The contributed Logging and Alerts module (`http://drupal.org/proj-ect/logging_alerts`) offers a number of features that can help you manage your logs.

STATISTICS

What's your most popular content?

What blog post is getting the most views?

Where are you site visitors coming from?

If you would like the answers to these questions then the core module Statistic is what you want. The Statistics module logs site visits and increments a view counter for your content. Get started by first enabling the Statistic module (included with Drupal) then navigating to Configuration ⇨ Statistics to enable the access log, the content views counter, or both, as shown in Figure 9-16.

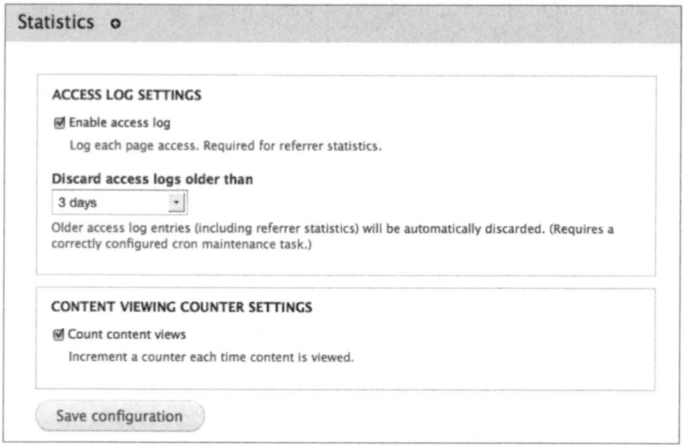

FIGURE 9-16

Access Log

When a user visits your site and for every page they view a log entry will be made recording the event. This log is created in real time keeping your site statistics up to date. After the access log has been enabled at Configuration ⇨ Statistics navigate to Reports to view the following reports:

➤ Recent hits

➤ Top referrers

➤ Top pages

➤ Top visitors

Content Views

Enable the Count content views option to add a counter at the bottom of each post displaying the number of views the content has. You also need to enable this option if you will be creating a page or block showing the most popular content. Although a "most popular" block or page view is not provided by the Statistics module, you can easily create them using the Views module (Chapter 11, "Views").

Performance Considerations

The Statistics module adds a log entry for each access to your website. The Statistics log is kept within you site's database thus this module creates a lot of additional database activity on your site, which can have a negative performance impact. This module is a great and necessary if you want to display your site's statistics externally to your visitors. For example, display a sentence such as "This blog post has received 5,600 views!"

If you do not need to show the data publicly consider using Google Analytics (covered in Chapter 19, "Preflight Checklist") instead of the Statistics module. The analysis is more in depth, features more robust and, best of all, the performance is significantly faster.

SUMMARY

A site's search engine can be its most valuable asset, because it provides visitors the ability to find your site's content. It can also be the site's worst enemy because of the amount of server resources it requires, particularly when the advanced search features are used. As you learned in this chapter, you can free up system resources and increase the speed of your site by ensuring that your block and page caching are turned on and that you are aggregating your CSS and JavaScript files. The settings you worked with in this chapter's exercises are truly the bare minimum of what every site needs for optimal performance.

Once your site has outgrown these built-in caching methods, you can turn to Boost, CacheRouter, Memcache, and a host of other performance-enhancing modules. Drupal also supports multiple front-end servers, reverse proxies, and back-end databases to help a website scale up from tens of thousands of hits to hundreds of millions.

In the next chapter, you continue your journey through Drupal by visiting its automation robots, triggers, and actions.

EXERCISES

1. What is a search index and when is it created?

2. Why is there a separate permission for the advanced search?

3. What is a cache?

4. How does block cache differ from page cache?

5. Why is CSS aggregation important?

Answers to these Exercises can be found in the Appendix.

▶ **WHAT YOU LEARNED IN THIS CHAPTER**

➤ The Search module provides a search block and a dedicated page at `http://localhost/search`.

➤ Allow people to search your site by granting them the Search content permissions.

➤ Your content must be indexed before the search engine can return results.

➤ Block caching speeds up your site for all users.

➤ Page caching is used only for anonymous users.

➤ Turn on CSS and JavaScript aggregation to increase your site performance for all users.

➤ Check your reports often to avoid any potential issues with your site.

10

Triggers, Actions, Workflow, and Rules

WHAT YOU WILL LEARN IN THIS CHAPTER:

➤   Use triggers and actions in such a way that you are notified when a new user signs up on the site

➤   Create an editorial review and approval workflow for your site's content

➤   Automatically promote content to the frontpage when a select group of users create or comment on it

➤   Automatically demote content from the frontpage after a set amount of time has passed

> ⊗   **WARNING** *At the time of writing Workflow and Rules were not updated to Drupal 7. This chapter was written against Drupal 6. The concepts and exercise should still remain valid with minor changes when the Drupal 7 versions are released.*

Bring out the robots! In this chapter, you'll learn how to automate the administration and upkeep of your website. Imagine being notified every time a user signs up, when new content is added, or when a post is promoted to the frontpage. The core Trigger module and actions (affectionately referred to as Drupal's robots) can do this for you and much more. The contributed module Workflow then utilizes these robots to walk your content through a series of stages. For example, a story can be tracked from its initial creation through peer review and editorial review until it is published. Each step is logged and documented, so you're never left wondering who did the review and publishing.

This chapter also introduces the ultimate Mr. Roboto: Rules. The contributed Rules module unleashes intelligent robots that can automate nearly any task on your website. You can automatically publish and promote to the frontpage content written by a select group of users on your site, and then schedule that same content to be demoted (or swapped) after a set amount of time has passed (a favorite of many newspaper websites). Just like a real robot, Rules can be a little tricky to understand, but after you get control of it, it's there to do your bidding.

TRIGGERS AND ACTIONS

Although introduced much earlier, *actions* became a part of the core beginning with Drupal 6. Actions introduced the first robots into Drupal as a way of segmenting tasks so that they could be automated. Some of the actions included with Drupal's core include publishing and un-publishing a node, promoting and demoting a page to the frontpage, sending an e-mail, and many others. It is often a user who performs these activities, but because technically speaking, these activities are actions, they could be performed by nearly anything, including other modules. An example of a module that can perform actions is the Trigger module.

The Trigger module, also included with Drupal core, operates on events such as a post being saved, a comment added, or a new user registration. When an event occurs, the Trigger module can fire off an action (or actions). For example, when a new user registers (an event), the Trigger module can cause an e-mail to be sent to you (an action). When triggers are combined with actions, automation robots are created.

Working with Actions

Actions are a core and central part of Drupal; therefore, they are always available for use. You can view the complete set of actions or create new actions at Administer ➪ Configuration ➪ System ➪ Actions. Figure 10-1 shows the default actions available. Note that each action has a type shown on the left — this is typically the name of the module that performs the action. All modules have the ability to provide custom actions, so your site may contain additional actions not listed here.

At the bottom of the Actions page (located at Administer ➪ Configuration ➪ System ➪ Actions), you have the option of adding new actions, known as *advanced* actions. Figure 10-2 shows the core actions that you can customize.

Here are a few examples of how you could use these core actions:

➤ **Send E-mail** — Create a customized e-mail to be sent to you when a new user registers or new content is posted to the site.

➤ **Unpublish Comment Containing Keyword(s)** — Automatically remove comments containing foul language or the URLs of your competitors.

➤ **Redirect to URL** — Send new users to a special welcome page or return users to a "What's new" page.

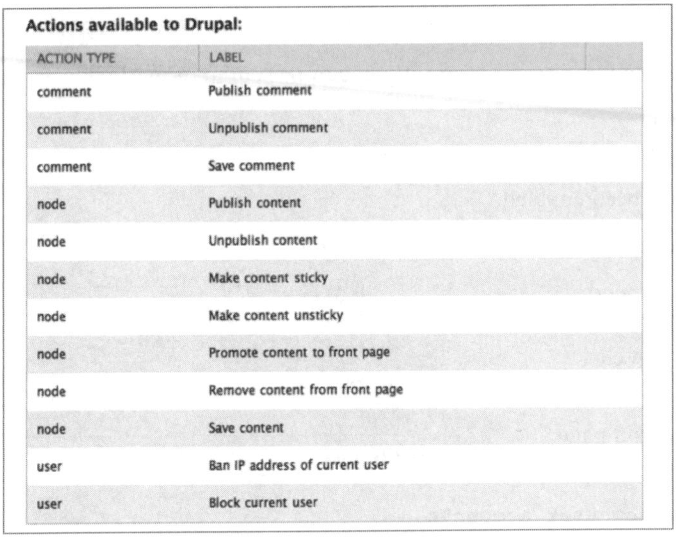

Actions available to Drupal:

ACTION TYPE	LABEL
comment	Publish comment
comment	Unpublish comment
comment	Save comment
node	Publish content
node	Unpublish content
node	Make content sticky
node	Make content unsticky
node	Promote content to front page
node	Remove content from front page
node	Save content
user	Ban IP address of current user
user	Block current user

FIGURE 10-1

An action by itself does nothing. Actions must be triggered by custom PHP code or a module, such as the Trigger module. For example, if you just add a new Unpublish Comment Containing Keyword(s) action, no comments will be unpublished — ever. The action must be triggered. In this example, you could use the Trigger module's After Saving a New Comment trigger to fire the Unpublish Comment Containing Keyword(s) action.

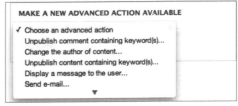

MAKE A NEW ADVANCED ACTION AVAILABLE

✓ Choose an advanced action
Unpublish comment containing keyword(s)...
Change the author of content...
Unpublish content containing keyword(s)...
Display a message to the user...
Send e-mail...

FIGURE 10-2

Working with Triggers

Not every site will require custom triggers, so the Trigger module is disabled by default. When this module is enabled, triggers can be found at Administer ➪ Structure ➪ Triggers. Triggers are arranged by broad categories: Comment, Node, System, Taxonomy, and User by default. Under each category is a set of triggers, and each trigger can have one or more actions assigned to it. A few examples of triggers include After Saving a New Comment, After Saving a New Post, and After a New User Has Been Created.

In general, you assign an action to a trigger by selecting it under the trigger for which you'd like it be used. However, actions may be trigger-specific, so you will not see every action available for each trigger. For example, the Promote Node to Front Page action won't be available for the User Has Logged In trigger, because the two items are unrelated.

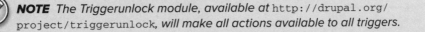

NOTE The Triggerunlock module, available at http://drupal.org/project/triggerunlock, will make all actions available to all triggers.

TRY IT OUT   Sending an E-mail to an Administrator When a New User Registers

In this exercise, you will create a new action and trigger so that you can be sent an e-mail whenever a new user registers on your website.

First, create a Send E-mail action as follows:

1.   Ensure that the Trigger module has been enabled.

2.   Navigate to Administer ⇨ Configuration ⇨ Actions (Under System).

3.   At the bottom of the screen, choose Send E-mail under Make a New Advanced Action Available (see Figure 10-3), and then click Create.

> MAKE A NEW ADVANCED ACTION AVAILABLE
>
> Send e-mail...   ⬦
>
> Create

FIGURE 10-3

4.   On the Configure an Advanced Action page, type in the following information:

➤   Label — `Notify admin of new user accounts`

➤   Recipient — Your e-mail address

➤   Subject — `A new user has registered`

➤   Message — `A new user with the name [user:name] has registered.`

5.   Click the Save button.

Now add this action to the appropriate trigger as follows:

1.   Navigate to Administer ⇨ Structure ⇨ Triggers.

2.   Click the Users tab at the top of the screen, as shown in Figure 10-4.

3.   Under the Trigger: After Creating a New User Account line, add the trigger Notify Admin of New User Accounts. The result should look like Figure 10-5.

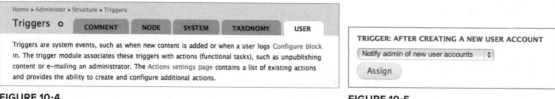

Home » Administer » Structure » Triggers

Triggers ⚙ | COMMENT | NODE | SYSTEM | TAXONOMY | USER |

Triggers are system events, such as when new content is added or when a user logs Configure block in. The trigger module associates these triggers with actions (functional tasks), such as unpublishing content or e-mailing an administrator. The Actions settings page contains a list of existing actions and provides the ability to create and configure additional actions.

FIGURE 10-4

TRIGGER: AFTER CREATING A NEW USER ACCOUNT

Notify admin of new user accounts ⬦

Assign

FIGURE 10-5

4.   Test the new trigger by logging out and creating a new user account.

How It Works

In this exercise, you first created an action — in other words, you told Drupal what to do. Next you told Drupal when to do it by assigning that action to a trigger. This combination activated a little robot that automatically sends you an e-mail whenever a new user account is created.

Next Steps

Much of the power of triggers and actions is not in what you see, but in what you don't see. Triggers and actions provide powerful hooks that other modules can utilize to extend their functionality while also providing you, the site's administrator, with an immense amount of control over your website. One of the contributed modules that utilizes triggers and actions is the Workflow module.

WORKFLOW

The Workflow module hooks into and utilizes triggers and actions to create a configurable workflow for your nodes. A *workflow* is a series of states that a node passes through or between. For example, story nodes may have a workflow with four states: Draft, Peer Review, Editor Review, and Approved/Published. When an author writes a story, it enters the Draft state. The author may then pass the story to the Peer Review state. The peer reviewers may either return it to the Draft state or pass it up to Editor Review state. Depending on how you configure the workflow, a node may be forced to pass through the states in succession or may jump around the states. For example, if an editor writes a story, he or she may immediately approve it, skipping the Peer Review and Editor Review states.

Along with each state change, the Workflow module tracks who, how, and/or when the change was initiated, and allows commentary on the state change. If you combine the Workflow module with revision control (a core feature of Drupal), you immediately have a powerful editorial review system that can show you every modification to a node along with the crucial details of who, what, and when.

The Workflow module is tightly integrated with triggers and actions. A state change can be initiated by a user or through an action. For example, commenting on a node could trigger an action that progresses the node in the workflow. State changes are also triggers; thus, when a node enters a new state, an action could be performed. For example, moving from Draft to Peer Review state could trigger a Send E-mail action to alert the peer reviewer.

The following example is lengthy due to the complexity involved with using workflow, triggers, and actions, but it will help you truly understand how these are all tied together. Over the next several pages, you will create an editorial workflow with three states: Draft, Editor Review, and Approved/Published. The workflow is as follows:

1. Authors create stories that are placed into Draft state.
2. Authors submit their drafts for editorial review.
3. Editors receive an e-mail notifying them of a draft pending review.
4. Editors may approve or reject the story.
5. Authors are notified of rejected posts, and they can read comments from the editors, revise their work, and resubmit it to the editorial queue.
6. Approved posts are published on the website.

The Workflow module is not part of Drupal core, so it must be downloaded separately. You can find it at http://drupal.org/project/workflow.

TRY IT OUT   Creating an Editorial Review Workflow

Follow these steps to create an editorial review workflow with Draft, Editor Review, and Approved/
Published states. Please note that at the time of writing the workflow module was not updated for
Drupal 7. This chapter describes the process for Drupal 6, which should be similar to that for Drupal 7.

1. Ensure that the Trigger module is enabled.

2. Download, install, and enable the Workflow module (`http://drupal.org/project/workflow`).

3. Create two new roles: `Writers` and `Editors`.

4. Create two user accounts: `Writer` and `Editor`.

5. Add the Editor account into the Editors role and the Writer account into the Writers role.

6. Assign the following permissions to the Editors role:

   ➤ Node: `Access content`

   ➤ Node: `Administer nodes`

   ➤ Node: `Edit any story content`

   ➤ Workflow: `Access workflow summary views`

   ➤ Workflow: `Schedule workflow transitions`

7. Assign the following permissions to the Writers role:

   ➤ Node: `Create story nodes`

   ➤ Node: `Edit own story nodes`

   ➤ Workflow: `Access workflow summary views`

   ➤ Workflow: `Schedule workflow transitions`

Create the Actions

Before you create the workflow, you need to create the actions that will be used within the workflow.
In this example, you will be sending e-mails to the authors and editors to notify them of a new post, a
rejected post, and an approved post. Follow these steps to create the new Send E-mail actions:

1. Navigate to Administer ➪ Site Configuration ➪ Actions.

2. Create a new Send E-mail action with the following information, as shown in Figure 10-6:

   ➤ Description: `Notify editor of a story pending review`

   ➤ Recipient: Your e-mail address

   ➤ Subject: `Story awaiting review`

   ➤ Message:

   ```
   Greetings Editor,

       %username has submitted a story for your review.

   -Happy Web Team
   ```

Description:

Notify editor of a story pending review

A unique description for this advanced action. This description will be displayed in the interface of modules that integrate with actions, such as Trigger module.

Recipient:

editor@example.com

The email address to which the message should be sent OR enter %author if you would like to send an e-mail to the author of the original post.

Subject:

Story awaiting review

The subject of the message.

Message:

Greetings Editor,
    %username has submitted a story for your review.

-Happy Web Team

The message that should be sent. You may include the following variables: %site_name, %username, %node_url, %node_type, %title, %teaser, %body. Not all variables will be available in all contexts.

(Save)

FIGURE 10-6

3. Create a new Send E-mail action with the following information:

➤ Description: `Notify author of return to Draft status`

➤ Recipient: `%author`

➤ Subject: `Additional work required for your story`

➤ Message:

```
Greetings %username,

   Your story entitled %title has been reviewed but not yet approved.
Please review the editor comments, revise your story, and resubmit it
for editor review. We look forward to seeing your completed work.

Thank you for your contribution,

-Happy Web Team
```

4. Create a new Send E-mail action with the following information:

➤ Description: `Notify author of story approval`

➤ Recipient: `%author`

➤ Subject: `Your story has been approved`

➤ Message:

```
Greetings %username,

   Congratulations, your story entitled %title has been approved.

Thank you for your contribution,

-Happy Web Team
```

> **NOTE** *The Token module (*`http://drupal.org/project/token`*) can provide additional variables for use in the automated e-mails sent by an action.*

Create the Workflow

With the three Send E-mail actions set up, you are ready to create the Workflow. Ensure that the Workflow module is installed and enabled, and then follow these steps:

1. Navigate to Administer ➪ Site Building ➪ Workflow.

2. Click Add Workflow and name it **Review Process,** as shown in Figure 10-7.

In the next steps you will add multiple states to this workflow. The result is shown in Figure 10-8.

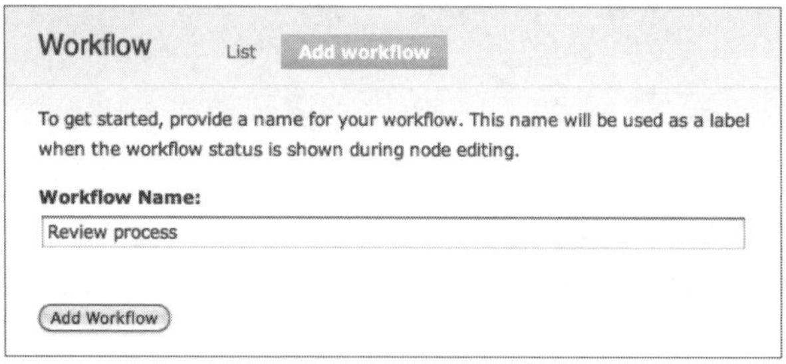

FIGURE 10-7

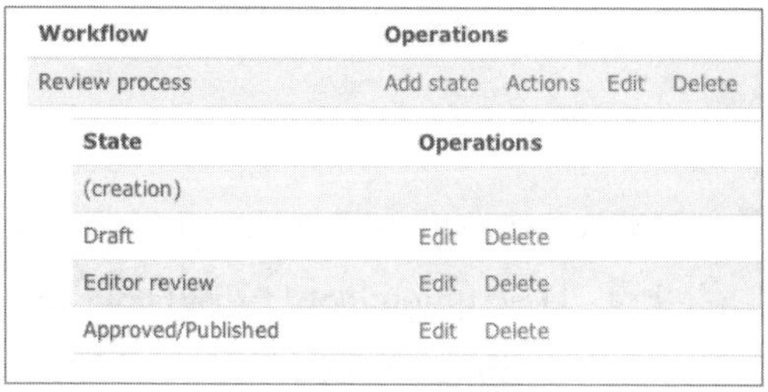

FIGURE 10-8

3. Click Add State to the right of the newly created workflow and enter the following, as shown in Figure 10-9:

➤ State name: `Draft`

➤ Weight: `0`

> **NOTE** *The weight of a state is important, because states are processed in order of their weights.*

4. Click Add State to the right of the newly created workflow and enter the following:

➤ State name: `Editor review`

➤ Weight: `1`

5. Click Add State to the right of the newly created workflow and enter the following:

➤ State name: `Approved/Published`

➤ Weight: `2`

6. At the bottom of the Workflow page, set the workflow of the Story content type to Review Process, as shown in Figure 10-10. Click the Save Workflow Mapping button.

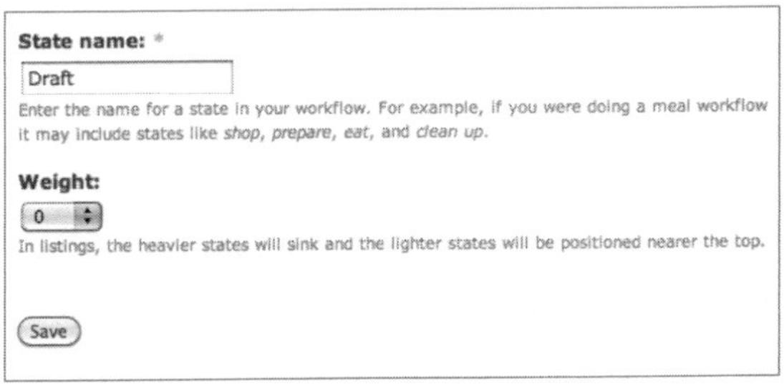

Each content type may have a separate workflow. The form for changing workflow state can be displayed when editing a node, editing a comment for a node, or both.

Content Type	Workflow	Display Workflow Form for:
Article	`<None>`	☑ Post ☐ Comment
Blog entry	`<None>`	☑ Post ☐ Comment
Story	`Review process`	☑ Post ☐ Comment

(Save workflow mapping)

State name: *

`Draft`

Enter the name for a state in your workflow. For example, if you were doing a meal workflow it may include states like *shop, prepare, eat,* and *clean up.*

Weight:

`0`

In listings, the heavier states will sink and the lighter states will be positioned nearer the top.

(Save)

FIGURE 10-9

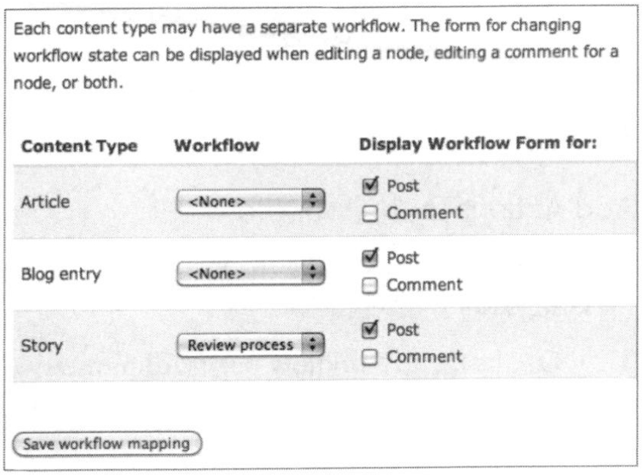

FIGURE 10-10

7. Back on the main Workflow page click the Edit link to the right of the Review Process workflow to configure the state mapping.

8. On the Edit screen of the Review Process workflow, select the following checkboxes:

➤ (creation) ⇨ Draft: Author

➤ Draft ⇨ Editor Review: Author

➤ Editor Review ⇨ Draft: Editors

➤ Editor Review ⇨ Approved/Published: Editors

➤ Approved/Published: None

Figure 10-11 shows the completed Review Process permission set.

From / To →	Draft	Editor review	Approved/Published
(creation)	☑ author ☐ anonymous user ☐ authenticated user ☐ Editors	☐ author ☐ anonymous user ☐ authenticated user ☐ Editors	☐ author ☐ anonymous user ☐ authenticated user ☐ Editors
Draft		☑ author ☐ anonymous user ☐ authenticated user ☐ Editors	☐ author ☐ anonymous user ☐ authenticated user ☐ Editors
Editor review	☐ author ☐ anonymous user ☐ authenticated user ☑ Editors		☐ author ☐ anonymous user ☐ authenticated user ☑ Editors
Approved/Published	☐ author ☐ anonymous user ☐ authenticated user ☐ Editors	☐ author ☐ anonymous user ☐ authenticated user ☐ Editors	

FIGURE 10-11

9. While still on the Edit screen of the Review Process workflow, check Author and Editors under Workflow Tab Permissions, as shown in Figure 10-12.

10. Click the Save button.

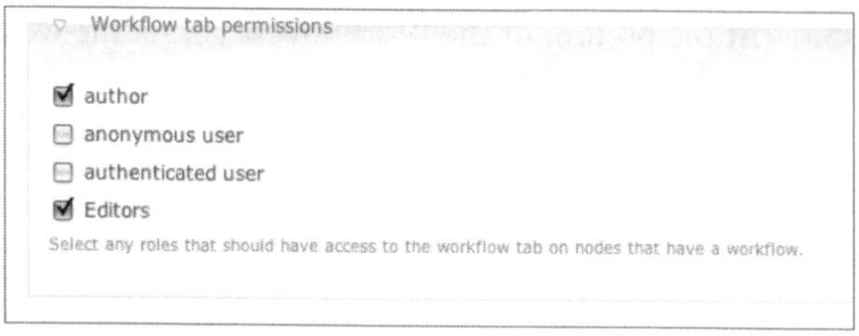

FIGURE 10-12

Add Actions to the Workflow

Next, you need to associate the Send E-mail actions with their respective state change triggers. Follow these steps:

1. On the main Workflow page (Administer ⇨ Site Building ⇨ Workflow), click Actions to the right of the Review Process workflow. This will bring you to the Workflow tab of the Trigger module configuration screen.

2. Associate the Send E-mail actions under the corresponding triggers, as shown in Figure 10-13.

Trigger	Action
When *page* moves from *Review process: (creation)* to *Review process: Draft*	Unpublish post Save post
When *page* moves from *Review process: Draft* to *Review process: Editor Review*	Notify editor of story pending review
When *page* moves from *Review process: Editor Review* to *Review process: Draft*	Notify author of return to draft status
When *page* moves from *Review process: Editor Review* to *Review process: Approved/Published*	Notify author of story approval Publish post Save post

FIGURE 10-13

Test!

After a multitude of steps, you are finally done with the workflow creation process. At this point, when writers create a story, it will immediately be placed in the Draft state. They can then use the Workflow tab to send the draft to the editor for review. Editors may approve the story (place it in the Approved/Published state) or reject the story (place it back in the Draft state). After a story is in the Approved/Published state, neither the writer nor the editor can modify its state. To test this, follow these steps:

1. Log out and login as **Writer**.

2. Create a new story node using any text for a title and body.

3. Save the story node you just created, and note the new Workflow tab at the top of the screen, as shown in Figure 10-14. Click this new tab.

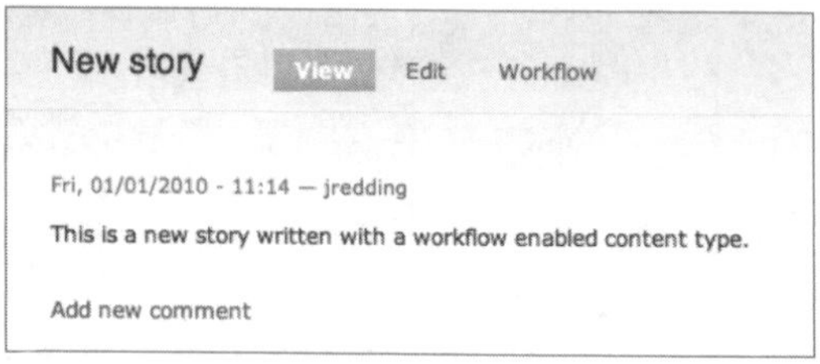

New story   View   Edit   Workflow

Fri, 01/01/2010 - 11:14 — jredding

This is a new story written with a workflow enabled content type.

Add new comment

FIGURE 10-14

4. Choose the Editor Review option, enter a comment, and click Submit. Refer to Figure 10-15 for an example.

5. Note the URL of the node you are editing.

6. Log out and log back in as `Editor`.

7. Navigate to the URL from step 5.

> **NOTE** *The Workflow module integrates with the Views modules, allowing you to create a custom list of nodes within a specified state.*

8. Choose the Approved/Published option, add a comment, and click Submit. Figure 10-16 demonstrates how this should appear.

Current state: **Draft**

Change *Review process* state:
- ○ Draft
- ◉ Editor review

Schedule:
- ◉ Immediately
- ○ Schedule for state change at:

[Jan ▼] [26 ▼] [2009 ▼]

Please enter a time in 24 hour (eg. HH:MM) format. If no time is included, the defa current time is: Mon, 01/26/2009 - 13:31

Comment:

Please consider this article for the front page

A comment to put in the workflow log.

(Submit)

Current state: **Editor review**

Change *Review process* state:
- ◉ Draft
- ○ Editor review
- ○ Approved/Published

Schedule:
- ◉ Immediately
- ○ Schedule for state change at:

[Jan ▼] [26 ▼] [2009 ▼]

Please enter a time in 24 hour (eg. HH:MM) format. If no time is included, the default will 01/26/2009 - 22:32

Comment:

A comment to put in the workflow log.

(Submit)

FIGURE 10-15    **FIGURE 10-16**

You're done! Now that you have walked through each step of a workflow, take a few minutes to bounce a node around the states of a workflow. You will have to do this on a new node, however, because the permissions set during the exercise do not allow a node to change state after it reaches the Approved/Published state. A nice feature of the Workflow module is the work log that manages to track each state change along with the details of the state change. Figure 10-17 shows a sample work log.

How It Works

If you take a step back and look at the exercise from a high level, you should notice that the Workflow module is really acting like a type of glue between triggers and actions. Although it's a powerful module in its own right, the reliance on triggers and actions to fire off events and perform operations (such as sending e-mails) is what provides you with ultimate configurability. A birds-eye view of this exercise shows you the following:

Old State	New State	By	Comment
Approved/Published	**Approved/Published**	Editor	Thank you for the revisions. Approved!
Editor review	Approved/Published	Editor	Thank you for the revisions. Approved!
Draft	Editor review	Writer	
Editor review	Draft	Editor	Please rewrite the introductory paragraph and add a few more examples to the text. Thank you
Draft	Editor review	Writer	Please consider this article for the front page
(creation)	Draft	Writer	

FIGURE 10-17

➤ Stories have three states provided by the Workflow module: Draft, Editor Review, and Approved/Published.

➤ Each state change causes a trigger event.

➤ Each trigger event fires off an action (sends an e-mail or publishes the story).

➤ After the Approved/Published state is reached, the story is published and the states can no longer be changed.

The Workflow module is a great example of what can be accomplished by combining Drupal's core functionality with additional contributed code. However, triggers and actions do have a few gaps in their functionality — in other words, the robots they create can lack a bit of brainpower. To add some intelligence back to the automation front, the contributed Rules module was created. That is the topic of the next section.

RULES

The Rules module is a replacement for the core Trigger module. In many respects, these two modules overlap in functionality, offering a nearly identical feature set. The Rules module, however, adds a great deal of new functionality and flexibility. For example, with Rules, you can create a trigger that automatically promotes stories to the frontpage, but only if the story was authored by an editor. The ability to trigger actions based upon a set of criteria being met is not available in core Drupal.

If you're asking yourself why this feature set wasn't simply built into Drupal's core triggers and actions, remember that the core is designed to not only be powerful, flexible, and configurable but also lightweight. Not every site will require the robustness of the Rules module. This is, however, why Drupal provides a great foundation and framework for contributed modules to build upon. You can plug in the functionality you need and leave out what you don't.

The Rules module can be downloaded at `http://drupal.org/project/rules`.

FEATURES OF THE RULES MODULE

The Rules module is similar to the Trigger module, but differs in the following four main areas:

- ➤ **Conditions** — Before an action is fired, a set of criteria must be met. These criteria are known, in the programming world as *IF statements*. For example, *if* the node author is within a certain role, then promote their node to the frontpage; or *if* the node is of a certain type *and* the author is a certain role, then promote the node. The default Trigger module only provides an ability to promote without condition.

- ➤ **Rule sets** — Multiple rules can be grouped together in such a way that they run in a specific order. Rule sets also allow for easy triggering of rules from custom code or other modules. An example of a rule set might be a batch of rules that control the promotion and demotion of content from the frontpage.

- ➤ **Scheduling** — Rule sets can be scheduled to run at a specific date/time or after a set amount of time has passed. For example, you could create a rule that automatically promotes a node to the frontpage and then schedules it to be demoted after four hours.

- ➤ **Input evaluators and token integration** — The Rules module integrates with the Token module (`http://drupal.org/project/token`) as well as Drupal's core PHP filter. The combination of these two integrations provides nearly limitless possibilities when writing conditions or actions. A few examples include firing actions only on nodes that have a certain taxonomy term, are written by users that have been registered for at least 60 days, or are written by users with the name Jacob.

The Rules module is a complex module, but after you unravel its complexity, you'll quickly see how powerful it can be. After completing the next two examples, you should have an idea of the power that lies within this module.

TRY IT OUT   **Robotically Promote Content to the Frontpage**

Using the Rules module, you will create a rule that automatically promotes a node to the frontpage when a member of the Editors role posts a comment on the node.

Prerequisites

The following prerequisite steps were performed in the exercises earlier in this chapter:

- ➤ Create a new role named Editors.

- ➤ Create a user account named Editor and add this account to the Editors role.

    Before proceeding download, install, and enable the Rules module, which also includes the Rules administration UI module. You can download Rules from (`http://drupal.org/project/rules`).

Create the Rule

Follow these steps to create the rule:

1. Navigate to Administer ➪ Rules.

2. Click the Triggered Rules link.

3. Click the Add New Rule tab, and then enter or select the following information and save the changes:

➤ **Label:** Promote content to the frontpage

➤ **Event:** After publishing a comment

➤ **This rule is active and should be evaluated when the associated event occurs:** Check this box

➤ **Weight:** 0

Figure 10-18 displays the Rule information.

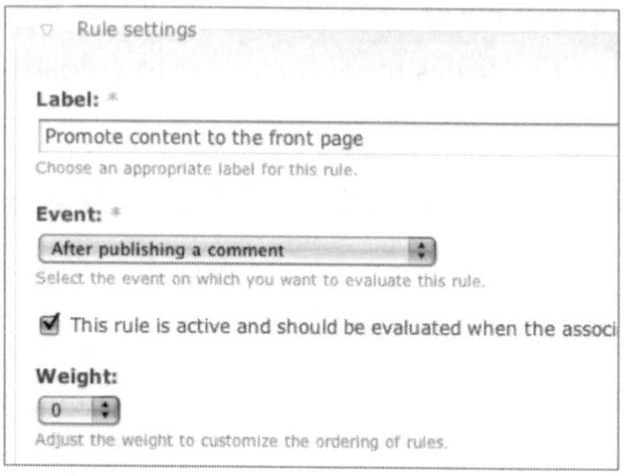

4. Under the Rule Elements, click Add a Condition. Then select User as Role(s) as shown in Figure 10-19.

5. Select the following settings (if they are not already selected), and then save your changes:

➤ **Label:** User has role(s)

➤ **Arguments configuration, User:** published comment author

➤ **Negate:** unchecked

➤ **Select role(s):** Editors

➤ **Match against any or all of the selected roles:** any

➤ Weight: 0

Figure 10-20 displays the completed condition.

6. Back on the Rule's page under Rule Elements, click Add an Action. Then select Promote Content to Front Page, as shown in Figure 10-21.

7. Select the following settings (if they are not already selected), and then save your changes:

➤ **Label:** Promote content to frontpage

➤ **Arguments configuration:** commented content

➤ **Permanently apply changes:** Check this box

➤ Weight: 0

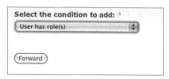

FIGURE 10-18

FIGURE 10-19

FIGURE 10-20

After saving your changes, the completed rule with conditions and actions should look like Figure 10-22.

How It Works

The Rules module, like the Trigger module, operates on an initial event. In this example, the triggering event is the publishing of a comment as established when the trigger was created. When a comment is published, the Rules module runs the triggered rule first, checking that the comment author is in the Editors role. If so, the action is then performed and the story is promoted to the frontpage.

Of course, you still have to deal with the inflated egos of the editors if they know that a single comment from them can immediately promote a post to the frontpage.

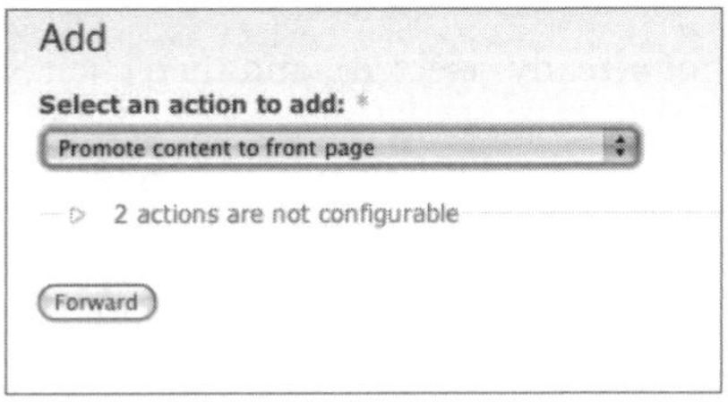

FIGURE 10-21

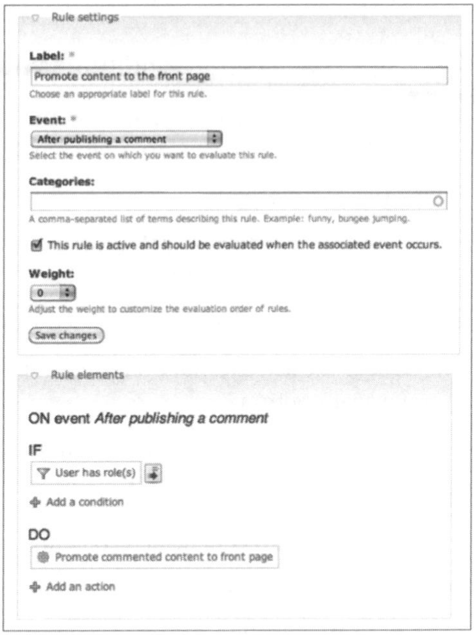

FIGURE 10-22

CONDITIONS

A single condition already makes the Rules module much more powerful than the built-in triggers, but Rules goes even further than that. Rules can evaluate multiple conditions either in succession or in groups. When Rules evaluates multiple conditions, they are ORed or ANDed together. ANDed conditions require every condition to be true in order for the action to be triggered. ORed conditions require only a single condition. Rules refers to OR or AND as the logical operation.

Consider the rule from the first example but with an additional condition as follows:

➤ **Triggering event** — After publishing a comment

➤ **Condition 1** — User leaving a comment is in the Editors role

➤ **Condition 2** — Content type containing the comment is of type story

➤ **Action** — Promote commented content to the frontpage

If the logical operation is OR, either condition can be met as follows:

➤ Any comment on a story node will cause the story to be immediately promoted to the frontpage.

➤ Any comment left by an editor regardless of content type (page, story, forum post, and so on) will cause the content to be promoted to the frontpage.

If the logical operation is AND, then both conditions must be met. The commenter must be in the Editors role *and* the node must be of type Story for it to be promoted to the frontpage.

TRY IT OUT   Using Conditions within Rules

In this exercise, you will expand upon the previous rule by adding a second condition as well as a logical operation. You will need to have completed the previous exercise before continuing.

Follow these steps:

1. Navigate to Administer ⇨ Rules and click to edit the rule you created in the previous exercise, Promote Content to the Front Page.

2. Under the Rule Elements, click Add a Condition.

3. Under the Select Condition to Add line, choose Node: Content Has Type, and then click the Forward button.

4. Select the following settings (if they are not already selected), and then click Save:

➤ **Label:** Content has type

➤ **Content:** commented content

➤ **Content types:** Story

➤ **Weight:** 0

How It Works

All subsequent conditions added are automatically used with an AND logical operator. At this point, the two conditions must be met in order for the action to be performed, so the commenter must be a member of the Editors role and the node must be of type Story.

Conditions gain a lot of power from the ability to be grouped together and set to a logical OR or AND setting. This means that you can have a group of conditions that all must be met or just a few of them met. You can even have groups of conditions that are dependent on other groups of conditions. For example, one comment from an Editor OR at least 5 comments from non-editors will promote the content to the frontpage.

TRY IT OUT   Explore OR type Conditions

In this exercise, you will convert the AND logical operation created in the previous example to an OR logical operation. Follow these steps:

1. Navigate to Administer ⇨ Rules and click to edit the rule Promote Content to the Front Page (created in the previous exercise).

2. Under the Rule Elements, you should have two rules with an AND logical operation, as shown in Figure 10-23.

Conditions

👤 User has role(s) ▸▤

AND

👤 Commented content is Story ▸▤

➕ Add a condition

FIGURE 10-23

OR logical operations can be utilized only within a condition group, thus you will need to create a conditional group.

3. To the right of the Commented Content Is Story condition, click the small Indent button. This will create a new condition group, place the condition within it, and set the logical operation to OR. The result should look like Figure 10-24.

At this point, the overall logical operation is still AND because the User Has Role(s) condition is outside the condition group and is being ANDed to the group. The logical operation OR is being used only within the group. The User Has Role(s) condition needs to be created within the condition group.

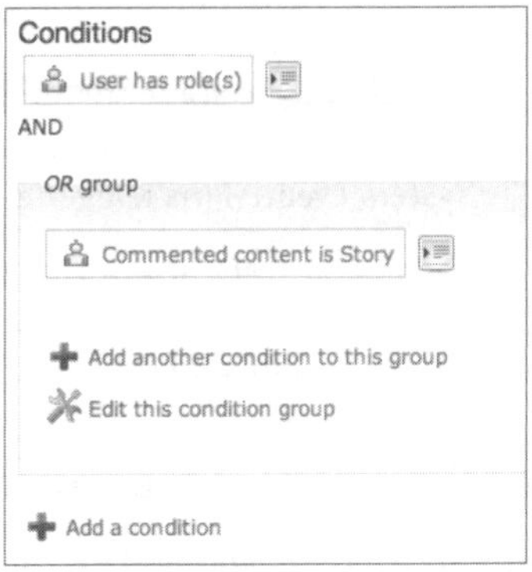

FIGURE 10-24

4. Create a new condition within the condition group by clicking Add Another Condition to this Group and choosing User: User has Role(s). Then click Forward.

5. Select the following settings (if they are not already selected), and then click Save:

➤ **Label:** User has role(s)

➤ **Arguments configuration,** User: published comment author

➤ **Negate:** unchecked

➤ **Select role(s):** Editors

➤ **Match against any or all of the selected roles:** any

➤ **Weight:** 0

6. Remove the previous User Has Role(s) condition by clicking Edit the Condition and choosing Delete.

Figure 10-25 demonstrates how your conditions should look.

FIGURE 10-25

How It Works

Condition groups can choose between an OR or AND logical operation. All conditions within a condition group receive the same logical operation. In this exercise, both the User has Role(s) and Comment Content is Story conditions will be ORed together, because that is the logical operation of the group. The original User Has Role(s) condition had to be removed because it was outside the group; therefore, it had to be ANDed to the group.

One of the nice things about condition groups is that the logical operation can be changed without modifying the conditions within it. If you are unsure as to which logical operation you want to use, you can save time by creating all of your conditions within a group.

As you might have seen (or assumed), a rule may have multiple condition groups, and each of those groups may have multiple conditions and/or condition groups. Although this provides a lot of flexibility, it could also lead to quite a bit of confusion if too many conditions or groups are involved. Remember that at the core of conditions are simple truth statements. The rule is simply trying to evaluate if something is true.

SCHEDULER AND RULE SETS

The Rule Scheduler module straightforwardly schedules rules. However, it doesn't schedule the rules that you have been working with in this chapter. Those rules are known as *triggered rules*, meaning that they have some sort of trigger event. The Rule Scheduler module schedules rule sets, which have no trigger event. A *rule set* is a collection of rules that will be triggered by something other than a system event. This trigger could be custom PHP code or a schedule.

To demonstrate how a rule set and the Rule Scheduler operate, the following exercise walks you through two main operations: creating a rule set, and scheduling the rule set by using the previously created triggered rule.

TRY IT OUT   Automatically Demote Content from the Frontpage

In this exercise, you will expand upon the previous example and schedule automatically promoted content to be removed from the frontpage after four hours. You will need to have completed the previous two exercises.

Create the Rule Set

You need to first create a rule set that demotes a node (content) from the frontpage. Follow these steps:

1.   Navigate to Administer ⇨ Rules.

2.   Click Rule Sets and then Add a New Rule Set.

3.   Enter the following information, as shown in Figure 10-26, then click Save:

➤   Label: `Demote content from the frontpage`

➤   Machine Readable Name: `demote_content_frontpage` (The machine readable name is used by custom PHP code.)

Arguments

➤   Data Type: `Content`

➤   Label: Content

➤   Machine readable name: content

4.   On the main Rule Set screen, click the title of the recently created rule set.

5.   Click Add a New Rule at the top of the screen, and then type in the following, as shown in Figure 10-27:

➤   Label: Demote content from the frontpage

➤   Rule set: Demote content from the frontpage

FIGURE 10-26

➤ **This rule is active and should be evaluated when the associated event occurs:** Check this box

➤ **Weight:** 0

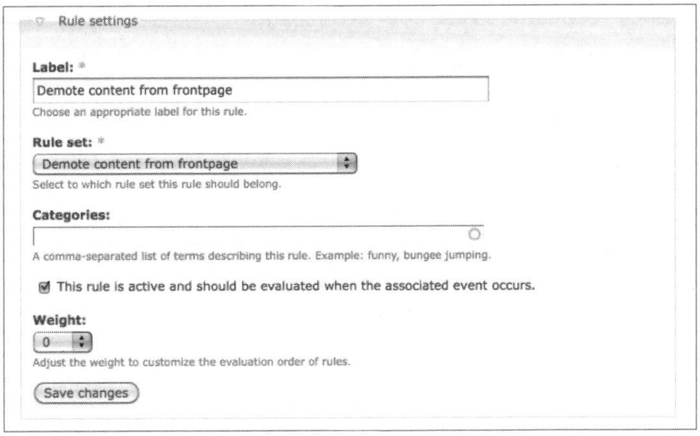

FIGURE 10-27

6. Within the recently created rule, add an action with the following details:

➤ **Action to add:** Remove content from the frontpage

> **NOTE** *If you do not see the "Remove content from the front page" action, verify that rule set created in Step 3 has an argument of "Content".*

➤ **Arguments configuration, Content:** Content

➤ **Permanently apply changes:** Check this box

➤ **Weight:** 0

7. Click Save. The rule set is complete.

Trigger the Rule Set

With a rule set that will demote from the frontpage any node that is passed to it (known as an *argument*), you only need to trigger the rule set. Follow these steps to use the triggered rule created in the previous exercise and the Rule Scheduler to trigger the rule set:

1. Enable the Rule Scheduler module that is included with the rules module.

2. Navigate to Administer ➩ Rules, click Triggered Rules, and then select Promote Content to the Frontpage.

3. Add an action to this rule with the following details, as shown in Figure 10-28:

➤ Action: `Rule Scheduler: Schedule Demote Content from the frontpage`

➤ Label: `Schedule Demote Content from the frontpage`

➤ Arguments Configuration, Content: `Commented Content`

➤ Identifier: Remove content from frontpage

➤ Scheduled Evaluation Date: `+4 hours`

> ✎ **NOTE** *You can also use strings such as +1 day, +1 week, and so on.*

➤ Weight: `0`

4. Click the Save button.

How It Works

Remember that only rule sets can be scheduled. In this example, you first created a rule set that contained a rule with an action to demote items from the frontpage. Because a rule set is not triggered by a system event, it must be told what to expect from the triggering event (the scheduler). This *expectation* is the argument to the rule set, which in this example was content (node). You then scheduled the rule set.

The basic flow is as follows:

Editing action *Schedule Demote content from frontpage*

Label: *

Schedule Demote content from frontpage

Customize the label for this action.

Arguments configuration

Content:

commented content

Identifier: *

Remove content from frontpage

User provided string to identify the task. Existing tasks for this rule set with the same identifier will be replaced

Scheduled evaluation date: *

+4 hours

Weight:

0

Adjust the weight to customize the ordering of actions.

Save

FIGURE 10-28

1. Comment is published.

2. The triggered rule runs on the published comment.

3. The triggered rule discovers the node that the comment is attached to.

4. The triggered rule schedules the rule set, passing the node as an argument.

5. Cron runs, triggering the scheduled rule set at the defined time.

6. The rule set runs the conditions and actions within each rule, passing the node as an argument to each one.

7. The Demote action demotes the content from the frontpage.

INPUT EVALUATORS

This is an advanced option that can take some time to understand for the uninitiated, particularly for those that have never programmed before. The Rules module will evaluate the input you give it every time the action is run. The two forms of input evaluation are PHP code and Tokens, provided by the Token module (`http://drupal.org/project/token`). You can use these in conditions or actions. For example, an action can dynamically modify the title of a post by adding the author's name to it, or a condition can be written that checks to make sure the user has been a member for at least 60 days.

The following exercise will introduce you to the concept of input evaluators by using a small snippet of PHP code.

TRY IT OUT   **Promote Content with Five or More Comments**

In this exercise, you will create a triggered rule that promotes content to the frontpage if the post receives five or more comments. Follow these steps:

1.   Ensure that the PHP Filter module is enabled.

2.   Navigate to Administer ➪ Rules ➪ Triggered Rules.

3.   Click the Add New Rule tab, and then enter or select the following information and save the changes:

➤   Label: `Front page promotion for five or more comments`

➤   Event: `After publishing a comment`

➤   This rule is active and should be evaluated when the associated event occurs: Check this box

➤   Weight: `0`

4.   Under the Rule Elements, click Add a Condition and then select PHP: Execute Custom PHP Code. (If you do not see this option, make sure the PHP Filter module is enabled.)

5.   Enter the following PHP code (do not enter <?php ?>), and then click Save:

```
if ($node->comment_count >= 5 ) {
  return TRUE;
}
else {
  return FALSE;
}
```

6.   Add the Promote Content to Front Page action.

7.   Save and then test this new action by creating a node and adding at least five comments to it. When testing, be sure to disable all previous Promote to Front Page rules.

How It Works

The condition uses custom PHP code, which is evaluated at run time. Drupal provides the variable $node->comment_count that contains the current number of comments on a node. The PHP code in the example tells Rules that the condition is true (return TRUE) if the number of comments is above or equal to five; otherwise, it tells Rules that the condition is false (return FALSE). True means that the Condition passes and that the action should be ran.

SUMMARY

This chapter covered a number of different ways in which you can automate tasks on your websites. Triggers and actions built into Drupal's core are great ways of automating simple tedious tasks such as sending e-mails, promoting items, and so on. The contributed Workflow module extends the trigger and action functionality to walk nodes through a series of states known as a workflow. You saw how to create workflow that progresses a node from draft to editor review and then on to final approval and publishing. Finally, you looked at how the contributed Rules module adds intelligence and increased flexibility to triggers and actions.

This chapter demonstrated only a tiny fraction of what is available through the Trigger, Actions, Workflow, and Rules modules. The combination of these modules truly puts you into the driver's seat of your own Mr. Roboto. Soon you will find yourself saying, "Domo arigato, Mr. Roboto."

In the next chapter, you'll look at using the Views module to display your content throughout your site in creative and flexible ways.

EXERCISES

1. What is the core Trigger module and how can you use it?

2. Where can you find the Trigger module?

3. What does the Workflow module do?

4. What is special about the Rules module?

5. What does the Rule Scheduler do?

Answers to the Exercises can be found in the Appendix.

▶ **WHAT YOU LEARNED IN THIS CHAPTER**

➤ Monitor new user registrations by having an e-mail sent to you.

➤ Create a content editorial workflow from a draft stage and review through final approval while maintaining a log history, as well as review comments.

➤ Automatically promote content to the frontpage if a certain class of users comment on the content.

➤ Automatically promote content to the frontpage if it receives more than five comments.

➤ Schedule content to be automatically demoted from the frontpage after a set amount of time has passed.

11

Views

➤ Exploring and modifying default views, including Drupal's default frontpage

➤ Unraveling fields, filters, and sort criteria

➤ Creating a photo gallery using views

➤ Understanding Views arguments

➤ Using exposed filters

➤ Creating custom administrative pages and reports using Views

➤ Understanding relationships in Views

The brainchild of Earl Miles and made possible by a great community of developers, the contributed module Views has quickly become a necessity for almost all Drupal websites. Views is a query builder that reaches into your database and pulls out your data, and then sorts it, filters it, rearranges it, and molds it into whatever form you want. It is a highly customizable module that creates lists, tables, pages, blocks, RSS feeds, and more in order to showcase your site's content, users, files, images, and nearly anything else you have on your site. No programming is required.

This chapter starts with a high-level overview and then unpeels the layers of views through a series of exercises. You should complete the exercises in succession, because each one builds upon the work of the others. At the end of this chapter, you'll walk away understanding how Views works and how you can make it do what you want.

ADVANCED HELP

Earl and the developers of Views have gone beyond the call of duty by heavily documenting the use of the module. The Advanced Help module adds pages of free documentation right into the Views interface to help guide you along as you build your views. You can download the Advanced Help module from `http://drupal.org/project/advanced_help`.

OVERVIEW OF VIEWS

Pardon the pun, but the best place to begin is with an overview. Start by going to `http://drupal.org/project/views` and downloading the latest version of Views. After Views is installed and enabled, navigate to Structure ➪ Views. You should see a screen similar to the one shown in Figure 11-1.

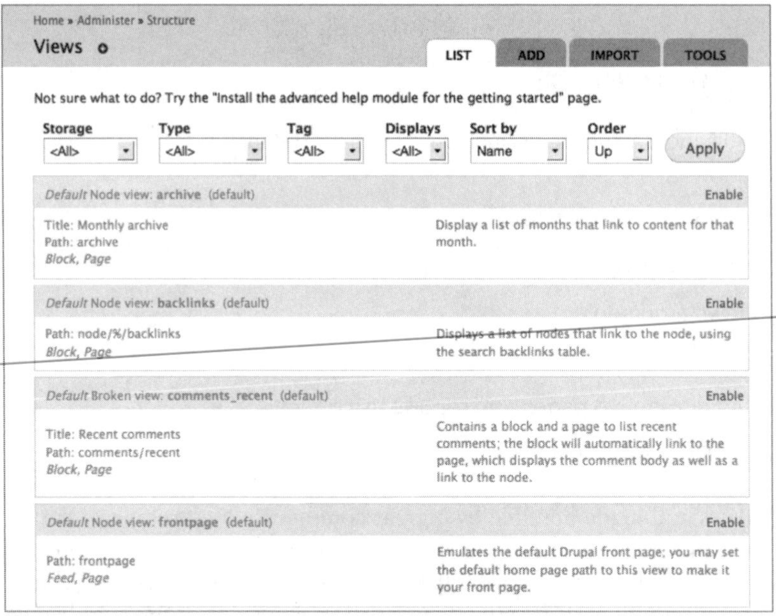

Home » Administer » Structure

Views ○

| LIST | ADD | IMPORT | TOOLS |

Not sure what to do? Try the "Install the advanced help module for the getting started" page.

| Storage | Type | Tag | Displays | Sort by | Order | |
| <All> | <All> | <All> | <All> | Name | Up | Apply |

Default Node view: **archive** (default)   Enable

Title: Monthly archive
Path: archive
Block, Page

Display a list of months that link to content for that month.

Default Node view: **backlinks** (default)   Enable

Path: node/%/backlinks
Block, Page

Displays a list of nodes that link to the node, using the search backlinks table.

Default Broken view: **comments_recent** (default)   Enable

Title: Recent comments
Path: comments/recent
Block, Page

Contains a block and a page to list recent comments; the block will automatically link to the page, which displays the comment body as well as a link to the node.

Default Node view: **frontpage** (default)   Enable

Path: frontpage
Feed, Page

Emulates the default Drupal front page; you may set the default home page path to this view to make it your front page.

FIGURE 11-1

> ⊗ **WARNING** *At the time of this writing, Views had not been fully ported to Drupal 7. The information here is relevant to the released version, but the screenshots may vary slightly.*

This screen lists all available views on your site. This includes views you created, views added by modules you installed, and default views provided by modules or from Views itself. Looking at Figure 11-1, you can see that four views are available: Archive, Backlinks, Comments_Recent, and Frontpage. If you're following along on your site, you'll notice many more. Each default view has an

Enable button to the far right, indicating that the view is currently disabled and thus not functioning on your site.

The disabled views listed in Figure 11-1 are defaults that provide either new functionality or emulate existing pages, providing you with a foundation to begin your customization. Although you'll spend most of your time in this chapter building new views, you'll begin by exploring the default Frontpage view.

THE FRONTPAGE VIEW

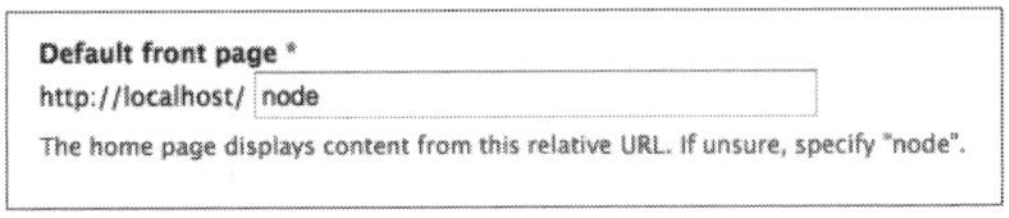

Views includes a default view entitled Frontpage that directly emulates the functionality of Drupal's default frontpage, which is displayed when the default frontpage is set to `node` at Configuration ➪ Site Information, as shown in

FIGURE 11-2

Figure 11-2. Of course, you do not need to use this view to modify your frontpage — it is just provided for convenience. Drupal's default frontpage (Figure 11-2) can be set to any available path on your site.

Explore the Frontpage View

Enable the Frontpage view by clicking the Enable link to the far right of the view. The Frontpage view will then float to the top of the list, because enabled views are always listed before disabled views. Click the Edit link on the far right of the view. You should see a screen like the one shown in Figure 11-3.

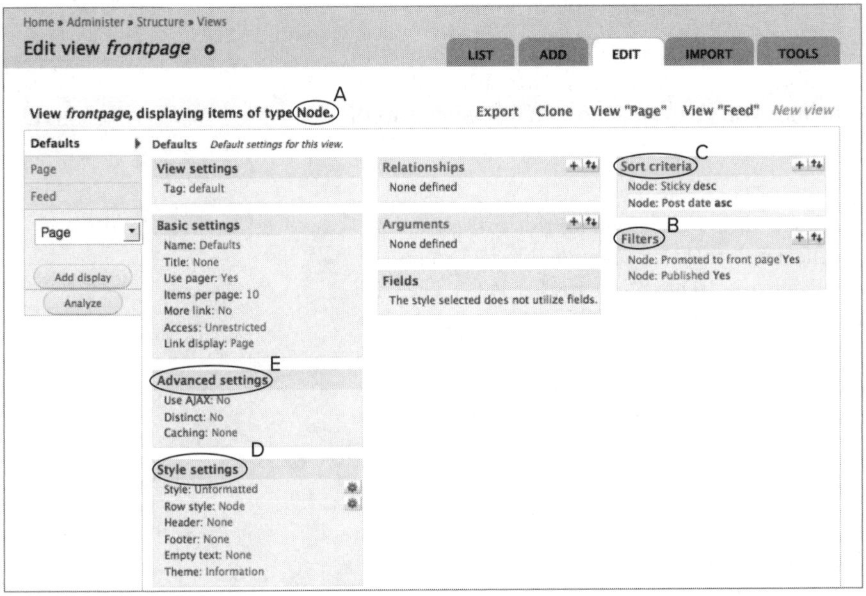

FIGURE 11-3

At first glance, a view can be incredibly intimidating because of the large amount of information presented on a single screen. If you dissect it slowly, you'll unravel it in no time. When I see a view for the first time, my eyes follow the letter pattern shown in Figure 11-3, first checking the type of items displayed and then unraveling it from right to left, bottom to top. After completing this chapter, you may decide to use a similar method or concoct your own methodology to dissect a view.

Using the letter pattern in Figure 11-3, you can unravel the view as follows:

➤ **A: View Type** — Each view displays certain objects on your site, such as nodes, users, comments, files, and so on. This view is displaying Node items, as shown in Figure 11-4.

> View *frontpage,* displaying items of type Node.

FIGURE 11-4

➤ **B: Filters** — From A, you know that this view is retrieving nodes from the database. The filters here narrow down the list of nodes retrieved. In this view, only nodes that have been promoted to the frontpage and published are retrieved, as shown in Figure 11-5.

> Filters
> Node: Promoted to front page Yes
> Node: Published Yes

FIGURE 11-5

➤ **C: Sort Criteria** — After the results have been narrowed down, the Sort Criteria arranges them into the order you desire. This view sorts by the posted date and places sticky posts on the top of the list, as shown in Figure 11-6.

> Sort criteria
> Node: Sticky desc
> Node: Post date asc

FIGURE 11-6

➤ **D: Row Style** — This view sets the style to Node (shown in Figure 11-7), meaning that each piece of content (node) will be displayed as it normally appears on the site (as a teaser with a Read More link). The Views module will not control the appearance of the node. You'll learn later that this setting could also be Fields, which would allow you to precisely control the output.

> Style settings
> Style: Unformatted
> Row style: Node
> Header: None
> Footer: None
> Empty text: None
> Theme: Information

FIGURE 11-7

➤ **E: Basic Settings** — In these settings, note that Use Pager is enabled and that Items Per Page is set to 10, as shown in Figure 11-8. If you've posted more than 10 items to the frontpage, you've probably seen this pager at the bottom of the page.

To configure the Views settings for an item (in this case, a node), you can click either the item's title (for example, Node: Promoted To Frontpage) or its value (the 10 next to Items Per Page) The trick of Views is that all items are configured in the same area, which is located below the View's configuration settings and usually hidden below the viewable area of the page. For example, if you want to change the number of items per page, you would first click 10, and then scroll down and modify the number, then click the Update button, as shown in Figure 11-9.

Follow along in the next exercise to change your site's frontpage to this new view and to modify the view so it shows only the latest three articles, leaving out any pages or other content types.

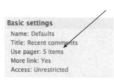

Basic settings
Name: Defaults
Title: Recent comments
Use pager: 5 items
More link: Yes
Access: Unrestricted

FIGURE 11-8

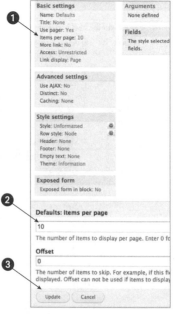

FIGURE 11-9

TRY IT OUT   Using a View for Your Frontpage

In this exercise, you will set your site's frontpage to the Frontpage view and then modify the Frontpage view to display only the latest three Articles.

1. Navigate to Structure ⇨ Views. If you are within the Frontpage view, navigate back to the list of views by clicking the List tab at the top of the page. If you have not yet enabled the Frontpage view do so by clicking the Enable button to the far right of the view.

Default Node view: **frontpage** (default)   Edit | Export | Clone | Disable

Path: frontpage   Emulates the default Drupal front page;
Feed, Page   you may set the default home page path
                         to this view to make it your front page.

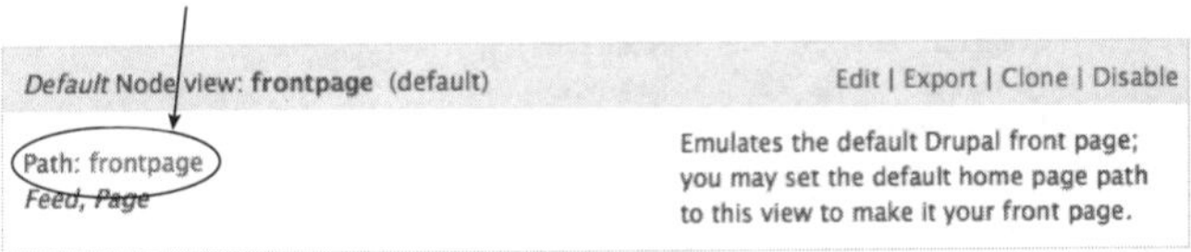

FIGURE 11-10

2. Note the path of the view as shown in Figure 11-10.

Default front page *

http://localhost/ frontpage

The home page displays content from this relative URL. If unsure, specify "node".

3. Navigate to Configuration ⇨ Site Information, and set the frontpage to the path of the view as shown in Figure 11-11.

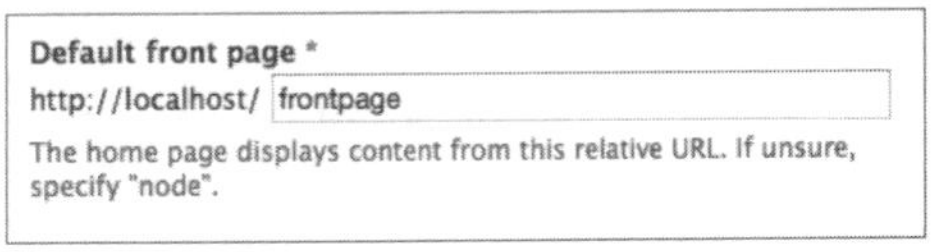

FIGURE 11-11

4. Navigate back to Views at Structure ⇨ Views, and then click to edit the Frontpage view.

5. Change the number of items to display as follows:

a. Click the number 10 located to the right of Items Per Page.

b. Scroll down under the view's settings (possibly below your visible area) and set the number to 3, leaving the offset at 0.

c. Click Update.

6. Add a new filter to display only Articles as follows:

Filters   +
Node: Promoted to front page Yes
Node: Published Yes

a. On the far right of the view under Filters, click the + button, as shown in Figure 11-12.

FIGURE 11-12

b. In the edit area (below all the settings), select Node under Groups, select Node: Type, and then click Add as shown in Figure 11-13.

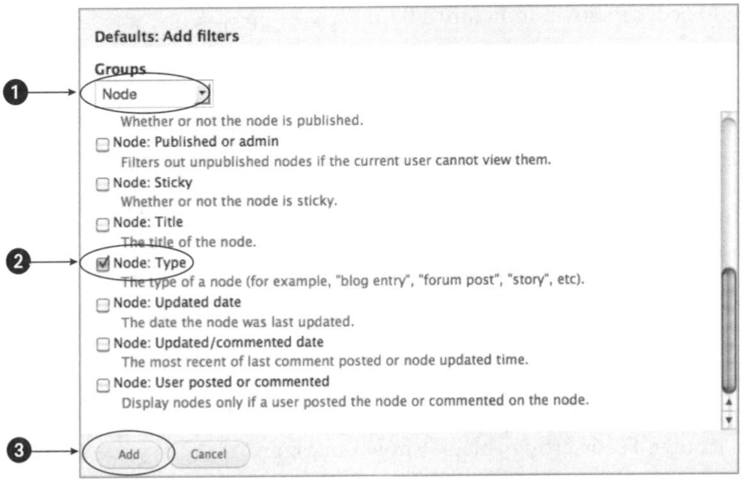

Defaults: Add filters

Groups

❶ → Node

  Whether or not the node is published.
☐ Node: Published or admin
  Filters out unpublished nodes if the current user cannot view them.
☐ Node: Sticky
  Whether or not the node is sticky.
☐ Node: Title
  The title of the node.
❷ → ☑ Node: Type
  The type of a node (for example, "blog entry", "forum post", "story", etc.).
☐ Node: Updated date
  The date the node was last updated.
☐ Node: Updated/commented date
  The most recent of last comment posted or node updated time.
☐ Node: User posted or commented
  Display nodes only if a user posted the node or commented on the node.

❸ → Add   Cancel

FIGURE 11-13

c. Select Is One Of as the Operator, check Article as the Node Type, and then click Update, as shown in Figure 11-14.

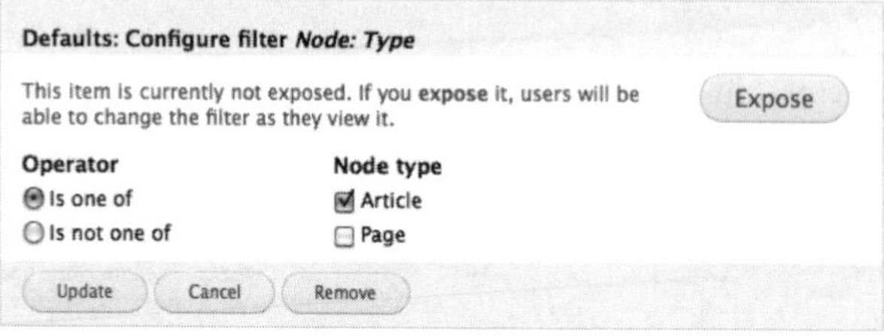

Defaults: Configure filter *Node: Type*

This item is currently not exposed. If you **expose** it, users will be
able to change the filter as they view it.

Expose

Operator
- Is one of
- Is not one of

Node type
- Article
- Page

Update   Cancel   Remove

FIGURE 11-14

7. Click Save at the bottom of the view.

How It Works

A view's Filters narrow down the results retrieved, and the Items Per Page limits the results. When you have finished configuring a view, you have to save it to make the changes permanent. Clicking the Update button on a view's settings page does not save the changes, you must also click the view's Save button.

DISPLAYS

View *frontpage*, displaying items of type **Node**.

Defaults ▶ Defaults *Default settings for this view.*

Page
Feed

Page ▾

Add display
Analyze

You may be wondering how the Frontpage view had a path of /frontpage. The answer lies on the left side of the view in what is known as a *display*. A view pulls the data and sorts, filters, limits, and manipulates it. A display is how the data will be shown (displayed) to your site visitors. Each view may have one or more displays that take the output of a view and make it available in different ways. The Frontpage view has two added displays: Page and Feed, as shown in Figure 11-15.

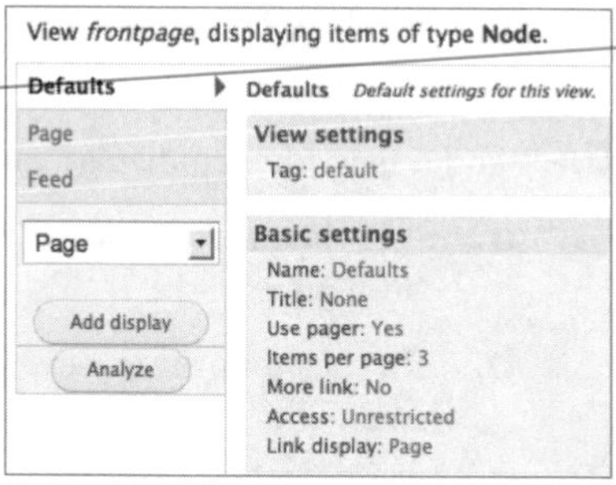

View settings
Tag: default

Basic settings
Name: Defaults
Title: None
Use pager: Yes
Items per page: 3
More link: No
Access: Unrestricted
Link display: Page

FIGURE 11-15

Page Display

A Page display is used to show the output of a view at a URL path on your site; for example, http://localhost/frontpage. Click the Page display on the left of the Frontpage view (shown previously in Figure 11-15). Everything looks pretty much the same; but if you have a keen eye, you will notice a new Page Settings block (shown in Figure 11-16) under the Style Settings.

Page settings
Path: frontpage
Menu: No menu

FIGURE 11-16

Here you can set the URL path of the display and, optionally, add it to one of your site menus.

Feed Display

Feed displays are used to provide RSS feeds for your views. Similar to the Page display, a Feed display adds its own Feed settings block (shown in Figure 11-17) underneath Style Settings.

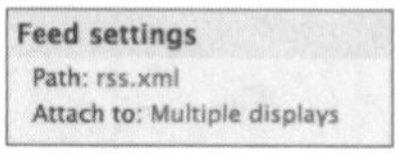

Feed settings
Path: rss.xml
Attach to: Multiple displays

FIGURE 11-17

The Path is the URL where the RSS feed will be available.

Attach To is an interesting and wonderful option that allows you to easily attach this RSS feed to any of the other displays. When an RSS feed is attached to another display, the RSS icon 🔊 will appear in the lower-right corner of the attached-to display.

Why All Displays Are the Same

You're probably wondering why each display has a complete set of configuration options that appear to mimic the original ones. If you look back at the list of displays shown in Figure 11-15, you'll see that the very top display is named Defaults. Whenever you add a new view or edit an existing view, you always start with the Defaults display. The configuration of Defaults is pushed to all of the view's displays, but each display can override the default settings.

Overrides

Overriding allows you to create a very complex view within Defaults to serve as a base view. You can then override pieces of the base view to meet the needs of a specific display. For example, a Block display may need to be limited to only five items, but an RSS feed can display the last 50 items, even though both are retrieving the same content. You could also add more than one of the same display type. For example, you could add a second Page display to the Frontpage view to provide a different sort or filter the results down even further. By using the Defaults display, which pushes to all of the other displays, you can create consistency between your various methods of display.

In the next exercise, you explore defaults and overrides by creating a new Block display that shows the latest five entries in a list style. You'll also dig into the next area of Views, using Filters.

TRY IT OUT   **Adding a New Block Display**

In this exercise, you add a new Block display to your Frontpage view. This block will display the latest five articles instead of the three shown on the Frontpage.

1.   Navigate to the Views administration page, find the Frontpage view, and then click edit to the far right of the view.

2.   Add a new Block display by choosing Block from the drop-down menu on the left (shown in Figure 11-18) and clicking Add Display.

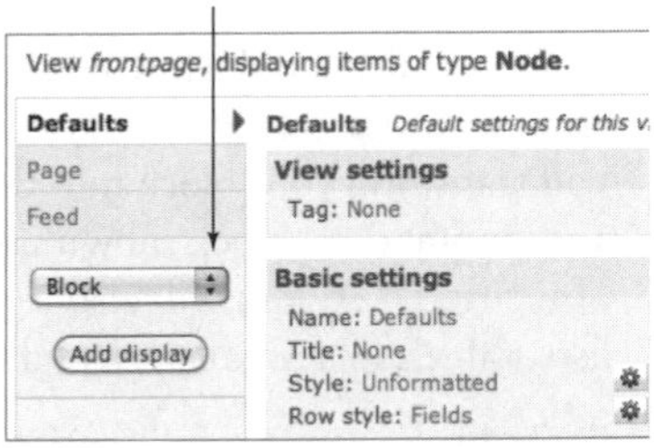

3.   With the new Block display selected as shown in Figure 11-19, click the number 3, change the value to 5, and then click the Override button as shown in Figure 11-20.

When you click the Override button, the lower button changes its title from Update Default Display to simply Update. This indicates that you are overriding a default setting within this display.

4.   Save the view.

FIGURE 11-18

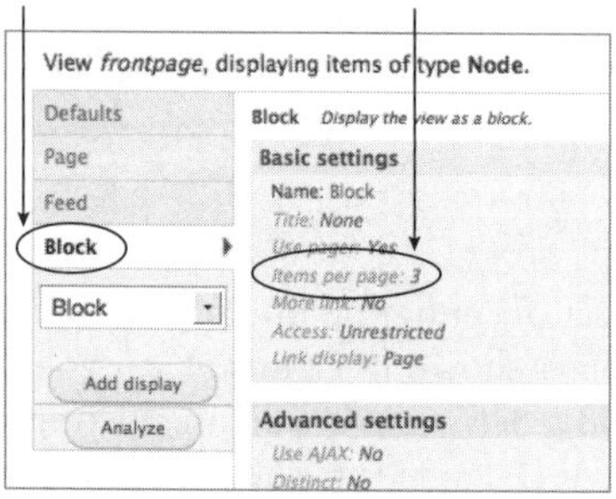

FIGURE 11-19

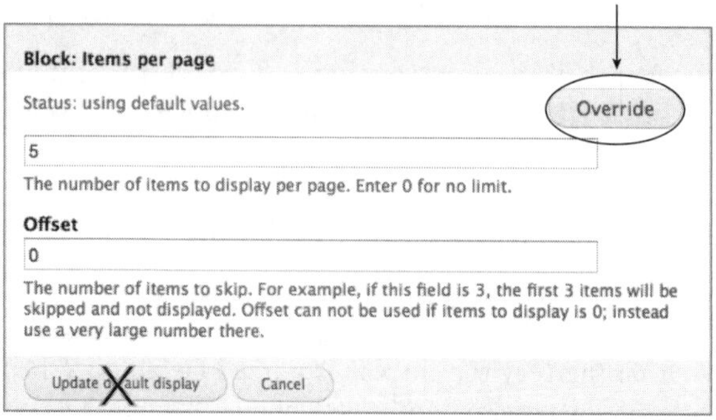

FIGURE 11-20

5. Set your new block (named after the view name: Frontpage) at Structure ⇨ Blocks in the same manner as other blocks.

How It Works

Displays are used to output the same list of retrieved content in different formats. A Block display creates a new site block that can be used alongside and in the same manner as other site blocks at Structure ⇨ Blocks. Each view can override the settings passed down to it from the Defaults display as you did in this exercise by overriding the number of items displayed.

STYLE SETTINGS

After completing the preceding exercise, you most likely discovered an ugly block that looked like your site's frontpage crammed into the left sidebar, which was probably not what you were expecting. The left side of Figure 11-21 shows what your default block would look like if left as is. This section introduces Style Settings, which will transform your block into the much cleaner and summarized block shown on the right side of Figure 11-21. You will also learn how to create lists, tables, image galleries, and more.

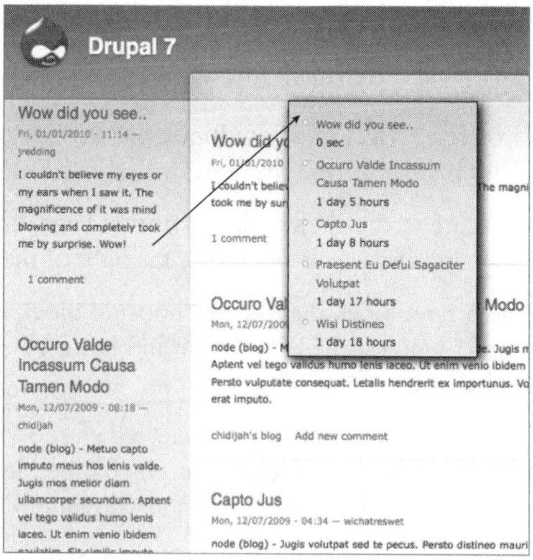

Each display can either inherit the Default display settings or override them. Some of the Style Settings, shown in Figure 11-22, are straightforward. Header is for text to be displayed above the view, and footer is for text to be displayed below it. Empty text is shown only if the view returns no results (for example,

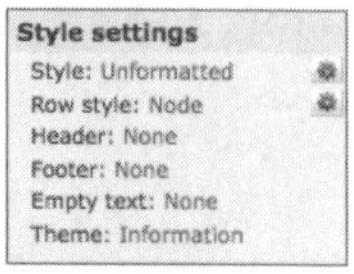

FIGURE 11-21

FIGURE 11-22

if you return all nodes with more than 10 comments). Row Style and Style are the interesting settings here.

Row Style

Each item retrieved from the database is placed into a logical row. If your view displays three nodes, then you have three rows. The Row Style determines how each row (item) is styled. Figure 11-23 shows the Frontpage view's default, Node. This means that each node will be styled according to the site's node theming (node.tpl.php, covered in Chapter 13) and run through the standard Node system (hook_nodes, covered in Chapter 16 and Chapter 17). This is a great style if you want to create blog pages, news roles, and so on. Clicking the gear to the right of the Row Style under the Style Settings (shown previously in Figure 11-22) allows you to select options for the respective system such as displaying the teaser or full node.

Changing the Row Style to Fields will bypass your site's Node system, allowing you to explicitly determine what is to be retrieved from the database and how it will be displayed. After you set this to Fields, you can then define the individual fields you want to display in your view as shown in Figure 11-24.

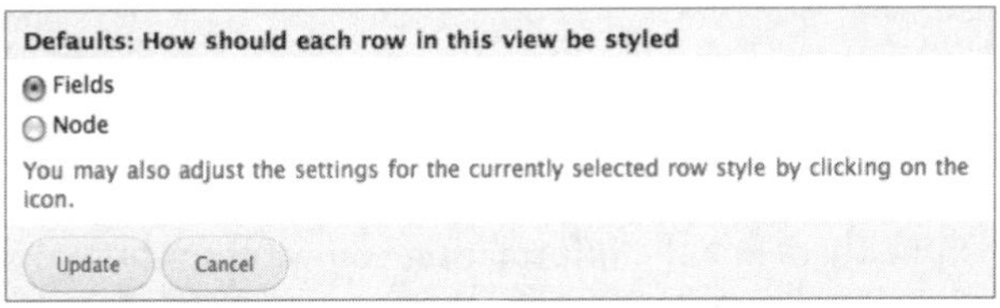

FIGURE 11-23

FIGURE 11-24

Style

Located directly above the Row Style in the Style Settings is the overall Style of the display (as shown previously in Figure 11-22). Figure 11-25 shows the default values available, which include the ability to create a grid, an HTML listing, or a table, or simply leave the result unformatted. Unformatted lists work well if you are implementing a custom design. In the next exercise, you'll modify your Frontpage block to display as a list (as shown in previously in Figure 11-21) and then move on to creating an Image gallery using Style Settings.

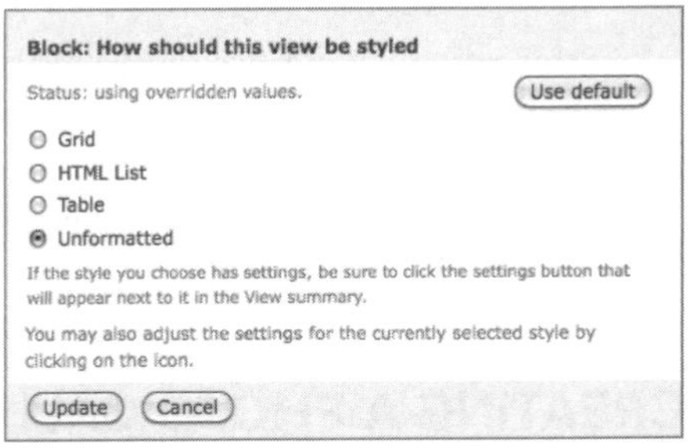

FIGURE 11-25

TRY IT OUT   Using Fields

In this exercise, you modify your Frontpage block and switch the Row Style from Node to Fields. You'll also add in fields and configure the style of the block.

1. Navigate to the edit page of your Frontpage view.

2.   With the Block display selected, click Node as the Row Style under Style Settings. In the upper-right corner of the Row Style box, click Override to confine this setting to the block. Do *not* click Update Default Display. Set the default style to Fields, as shown in Figure 11-23. After clicking Update you will be presented with a new screen, Row Style Options. Leave the Row Style options at the defaults.

3.   Directly above the Row Style, set the Style to HTML List. Be sure to click the Override button to confine this setting to the block.

4.   Within the Fields box, add the following fields by clicking the + button:

☑ Link this field to its node
This will override any other link you have set.

(Update) (Cancel) (Remove)

FIGURE 11-26

➤   Node: Title

➤   Node: Post Date

➤   After clicking Update to add these fields you will be presented with a configuration screen for each of the fields. They will appear one after another. Leave all configuration settings at the defaults except for the Link This Field To Its Node option for the Node:Title field, enable this option as shown in Figure 11-26.

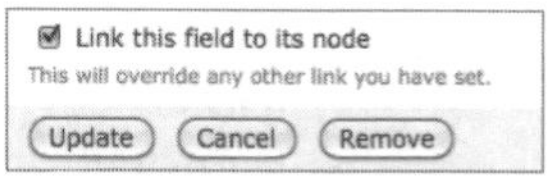

5.   Within the Basic Settings, set More Link to No. Be sure to set this to Override to confine this setting to the block.

6.   Save your view.

How It Works

Setting the Row Style to Fields allows you to explicitly define the information you want to showcase. In this example, only the node's title and post date were shown. Other options were modified on a per-display basis, such as removing the More link and changing the Style setting to an HTML list.

At this point, you have explored nearly every part of the Frontpage view. You could continue adding new displays and exploring the more complex parts of views, but it is probably best to start creating your own views. The exercises that follow are condensed yet more complex. If you have trouble locating a setting or configuration, refer to the images in the earlier exercises. New settings are explained before they are used in an exercise.

CREATING A PHOTO GALLERY

Adding images in Drupal gets easier with every new Drupal release, and Drupal 7 makes it positively child's play. Image styles, introduced in Chapter 6, "Content," automatically create thumbnail, preview, and large versions of uploaded images. Views can then pull these images and display them in a 3x3 grid, 4x4 grid, vertically, horizontally, or in nearly any manner you can dream of.

Follow along in the next two exercises to create a photo gallery like the one shown in Figure 11-27. In the first exercise, you create a new content type: Photo. Creating content types is covered in Chapter 6, so this exercise provides only the high-level steps. In the second exercise, you create your gallery.

FIGURE 11-27

TRY IT OUT Creating a New Photo Content Type

In this exercise, you create a new content type named Photo and add an Image field to it so that users can upload photos.

1. Navigate to Structure ⇨ Content Types and click Add Content Type.

2. Enter or set the following information and then click Save Content Type:

Submission Form Settings

➤ Name: `Photo`

➤ Title Field Label: `Photo caption`

➤ Body Field Label: Leave this field blank

➤ Preview Before Submitting: Disabled

Publishing Options

➤ Published

➤ Leave all other options unchecked

3. Add a new Image field to the Photo content type, as shown in Figure 11-28. Accept the field's default settings.

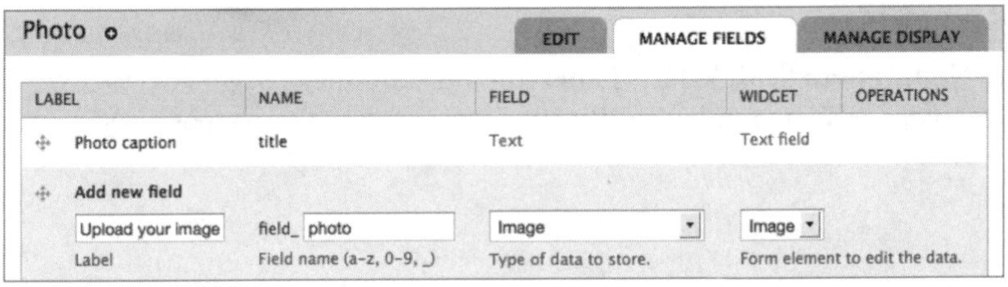

Photo ○			EDIT	MANAGE FIELDS	MANAGE DISPLAY

LABEL	NAME	FIELD	WIDGET	OPERATIONS
⊹ Photo caption	title	Text	Text field	
⊹ **Add new field**				
Upload your image	field_ photo	Image ▾	Image ▾	
Label	Field name (a–z, 0–9, _)	Type of data to store.	Form element to edit the data.	

FIGURE 11-28

How It Works

The base foundation of any photo gallery is a photo, and an image field provides the ability to get images into Drupal. Creating a new content type specifically for photos allows you to expand upon the fields of the photo to add items such as photo credit, categorization tags, exit data, and so on.

Now that you have a new content type for photos, take a few minutes to upload some photos before moving on to creating the photo gallery in the next exercise.

TRY IT OUT   Creating the Photo Gallery

In this exercise, you create a view to display the image fields of your Photo content type in a 4x4 grid.

1.   Navigate to Structure ⇨ Views, click Add at the top of the page, and type in the following information:

➤   View Name: `photo_gallery`

➤   View Description: `My wonderful photos`

➤   View Tag: `photos, gallery`

➤   View Type: Node

2.   Click Next and add the following filters:

➤   Node: Type: `One of Photos`

➤   Node: Published: Yes

3.   Add the following sort criteria:

➤   Global: `Random`

4.   Set the following Style Settings:

➤   Row Style: Fields

➤   Style: Grid

➤   Set the Number Of Columns to **4** and the Alignment to Horizontal as shown in Figure 11-29.

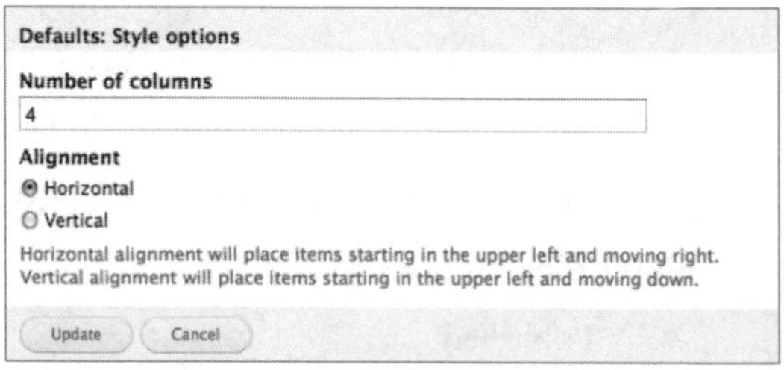

Defaults: Style options

Number of columns

4

Alignment

◉ Horizontal

○ Vertical

Horizontal alignment will place items starting in the upper left and moving right. Vertical alignment will place items starting in the upper left and moving down.

(Update)   (Cancel)

FIGURE 11-29

5.   Under Basic Settings, set the following:

➤   Items To Display: **16** (4 across and 4 down is 16)

➤   Use Pager: Full pager

6.   Under Fields, add the Node: Photo field. Set the Label to None and the Format to `thumbnail image` as shown in Figure 11-30.

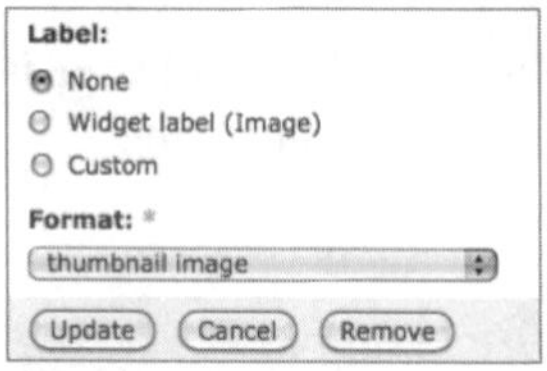

Label:

◉ None

○ Widget label (Image)

○ Custom

Format: *

[thumbnail image ▼]

(Update) (Cancel) (Remove)

FIGURE 11-30

7. Add a Page display, and then with the Page display selected, set the Path to /gallery as shown in Figure 11-31.

8. Save your view.

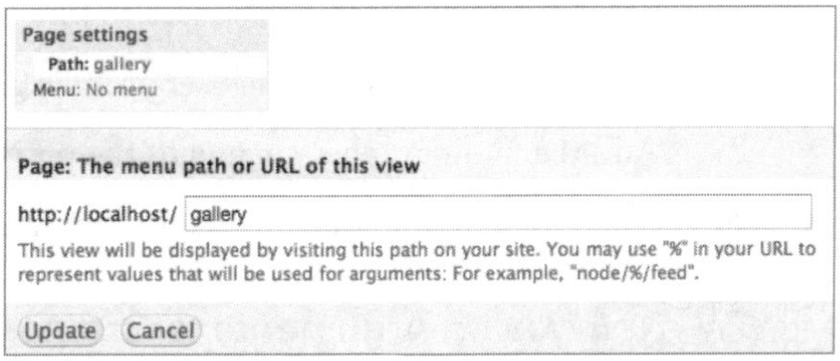

How It Works

The magic of this view lies in just three settings: the Row Style set to Fields, the Style set to Grid,

Page settings
    Path: gallery
   Menu: No menu

Page: The menu path or URL of this view

http://localhost/   gallery

This view will be displayed by visiting this path on your site. You may use "%" in your URL to represent values that will be used for arguments: For example, "node/%/feed".

Update   Cancel

FIGURE 11-31

and the Photo Fieldset to use an Image style. Drupal 7's built-in Image styles automatically resize the images, allowing you to quickly create a gallery that matches your website.

> **NOTE** *The Lightbox2 contributed module (*http://drupal.org/project/lightbox2*) provides a very nice pop-up enlargement of an image. After you install and enable this module, you can revisit the Photo field's options and direct views to use Lightbox for the enlarged view.*

The Style Settings of a view are quite powerful and allow you to format your site's output in numerous ways. Contributed modules can also extend views by adding in new Styles. The Views Slideshow contributed module (http://drupal.org/project/views_slideshow) is an example of this. It provides a method to create a slideshow out of your photos. In fact, you could add it to your Gallery view to create a nice automatically rotating slideshow of your photos.

Your journey through views is just getting started. The next section teaches you how to leverage arguments so you can extend your photo gallery to provide per-user photo galleries.

ARGUMENTS

Arguments are a powerful and often underutilized part of Views. An argument is a variable that alters the results returned by a view; in other words, it is a dynamically configured filter. For example, Figure 11-32 shows the argument jredding being used with the gallery URL (the view). This argument will filter the results so that only photos from jredding are shown.

Photos by jredding | Beginning Drupal

http://localhost/gallery/jredding

View   argument

FIGURE 11-32

In this section, you'll modify your gallery so that the photographer's name appears below their photo, as shown in Figure 11-33. When a user clicks that photographer's name, the gallery displays only that photographer's photos. You'll also give each user their own private photo gallery at: http://localhost/gallery/<username>.

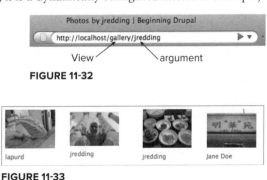

lapurd   jredding   jredding   Jane Doe

FIGURE 11-33

You'll create this setup in three exercises as follows:

1. Add an argument to create user-specific galleries.

2. Add the photographer's name to the photo.

3. Add a link on the user's name to point to their private gallery.

TRY IT OUT **Using Arguments to Create User Photo Galleries**

In this exercise, you add an argument to your Gallery view to create a unique photo gallery for every user on your site.

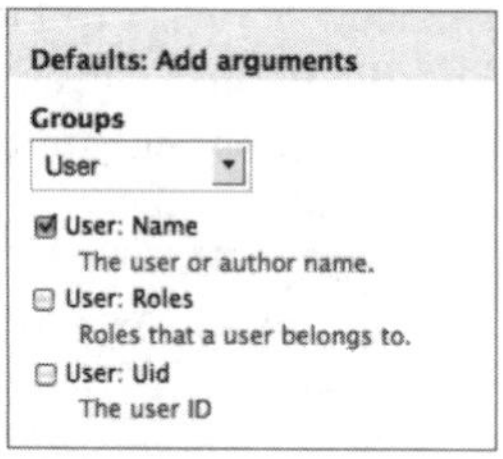

1. Within your Gallery view, select the Defaults display. Add a new argument by clicking the + in the upper-right corner of the Arguments box, and then select User: Name as shown in Figure 11-34.

2. Set the following User: Name options, leaving all other options at the defaults, as shown in Figure 11-35.

> Title: `Photos by %1`

> Breadcrumb: `All photos`

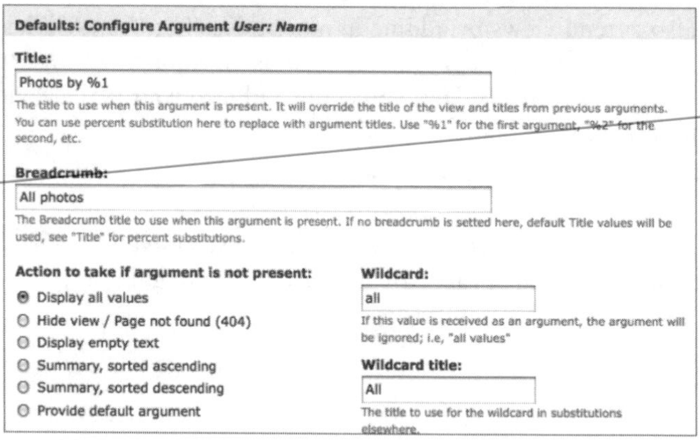

Defaults: Add arguments

Groups

User

☑ User: Name
   The user or author name.
☐ User: Roles
   Roles that a user belongs to.
☐ User: Uid
   The user ID

FIGURE 11-34

Defaults: Configure Argument *User: Name*

Title:

Photos by %1

The title to use when this argument is present. It will override the title of the view and titles from previous arguments. You can use percent substitution here to replace with argument titles. Use "%1" for the first argument, "%2" for the second, etc.

Breadcrumb:

All photos

The Breadcrumb title to use when this argument is present. If no breadcrumb is setted here, default Title values will be used, see "Title" for percent substitutions.

Action to take if argument is not present: **Wildcard:**

⦿ Display all values   all
○ Hide view / Page not found (404)   If this value is received as an argument, the argument will
○ Display empty text   be ignored; i.e, "all values"
○ Summary, sorted ascending   **Wildcard title:**
○ Summary, sorted descending   All
○ Provide default argument   The title to use for the wildcard in substitutions
                                                        elsewhere.

FIGURE 11-35

3. Click the Update button.

4. Save your view.

How It Works

An argument works by taking the variable placed after the view's URL. In this exercise, the argument would be used by manually typing in the URL `http://localhost/gallery/<your-username>`. When using an argument, you can dynamically set the Page's title and breadcrumb as demonstrated in

Figure 11-36. Note that you can choose what happens if an argument is not present. The defaults show all values (according to the view's filters), but another popular choice is Hide view /Page not found (404), which would eliminate the All Users photo gallery and create only user-specific galleries.

FIGURE 11-36

With your argument in place, the next step is to add the user's name to the bottom of the photo.

TRY IT OUT **Adding the Photographer's Name to the Photo**

In this exercise, you add the name of the photo's author (the photographer) to the bottom of the photo.

1. Using the Default display within your View, add the User: Name field.

2. Keep the default Fields options as they are. Your Fields box should look similar to Figure 11-37.

FIGURE 11-37

How It Works

As you learned in earlier exercises, you can easily add a field by using the Fields row style. Because the view is using a horizontal Grid style, each field is aligned vertically within the column. Fields appear in the way they are arranged within the view, but you can rearrange them by clicking the double-arrow button in the upper-right corner of the Fields box.

Link the User's Name to Their Photo Gallery

The User: Name field defaults to linking back to the user's account, which doesn't provide the correct results. You want the URL to link back to your gallery and append the user's name to the end of the URL. Fortunately, Views allows you to override nearly everything, including the URLs it automatically creates. Follow the next exercise to do exactly this.

TRY IT OUT Linking to the User's Photo Gallery

In this exercise, you modify the user's link to point to their personal photo gallery.

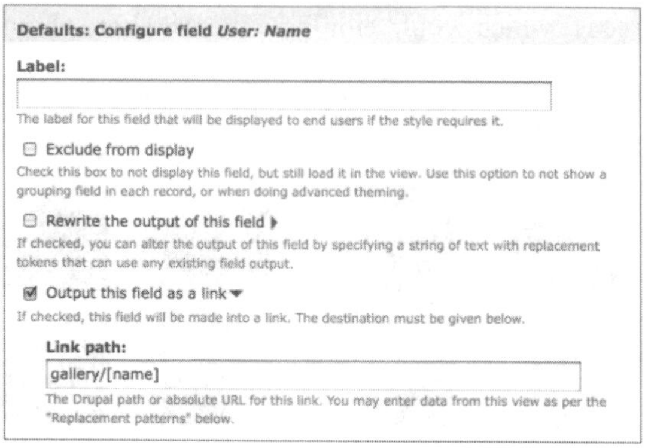

1. Open the options of the User: Name field by clicking the words User: Name.

2. Set the following options, as shown in Figure 11-38.

➤ Leave the Label field blank.

➤ Select the Output This field As A Link option.

➤ Enter `gallery/[name]` in the Link Path field.

Defaults: Configure field *User: Name*

Label:

The label for this field that will be displayed to end users if the style requires it.

☐ Exclude from display
Check this box to not display this field, but still load it in the view. Use this option to not show a grouping field in each record, or when doing advanced theming.

☐ Rewrite the output of this field ▶
If checked, you can alter the output of this field by specifying a string of text with replacement tokens that can use any existing field output.

☑ Output this field as a link ▼
If checked, this field will be made into a link. The destination must be given below.

Link path:
gallery/[name]
The Drupal path or absolute URL for this link. You may enter data from this view as per the "Replacement patterns" below.

FIGURE 11-38

3. Uncheck the Link This Field To Its User option as shown in Figure 11-39, and then click Update.

4. Save your view.

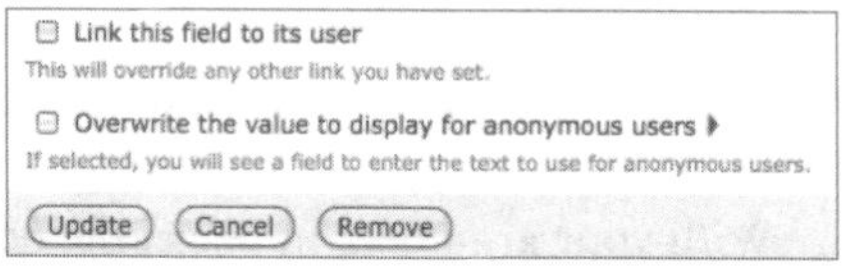

How It Works

☐ Link this field to its user
This will override any other link you have set.

☐ Overwrite the value to display for anonymous users ▶
If selected, you will see a field to enter the text to use for anonymous users.

(Update) (Cancel) (Remove)

FIGURE 11-39

Each field that Views outputs can be uniquely customized within each view or display, allowing you to create a very unique and custom website. The [name] portion of the Link path is a replacement variable that will create custom links to each user's individual gallery. Replacement variables come from other fields on the view or from the contributed Token module (`http://drupal.org/project/token`).

Using an argument is a powerful method to take a single view and extend it to provide customized pages for a nearly unlimited number of uses. A great method not demonstrated in this chapter is the use of Glossary Mode as an option on the argument. Glossary Mode enables you to display pages according to specific criteria, such as all photos by users that begin with the letter *J* or the letters *Jac*.

Another way to create a highly customized page is by using an exposed filter, as described in the next section.

> ⊗ **WARNING** *When using an argument with variables that may contain spaces or non-standard characters (such as ñ, é, ü, and so on), try to find a numeric alternative. For example, instead of using the username, you can use the user id. Spaces and other non-standard characters in arguments can sometimes wreak havoc on a view. Numeric arguments provide more consistent results.*

EXPOSED FILTERS

An *exposed filter* is a Views filter that can be modified by the user in real time without the user modifying the underlying view. Consider Figure 11-40, which shows an example of a custom Comment Moderation page. The filters at the top of the page are modifiable by any user with permission to see the view.

FIGURE 11-40

Exposed filters are a great way to create custom administration pages such as the Comment page shown in Figure 11-40. In the next few exercises, you'll explore exposed filters, relationships, and menu settings by creating a robust Comment administration page.

> **WARNING** *A view bypasses all site permissions and can provide access to data that would normally be inaccessible by a user. Please read the Permissions section before placing a view such as this on your site.*

TRY IT OUT Creating a Custom Comment Review Page

In this exercise, you create a new Comment administration page.

1. Create a new view with the following information:

   ➤ View Name: `comment_review`

   ➤ View Description: `A robust comment administration page`

   ➤ View Tag: `comment, administration`

   ➤ View Type: Comment

2. Configure your new Comment-based view with the following settings, leaving all other options at their defaults:

   Basic Settings

   ➤ Items To Display: `20`

   ➤ Use Pager: Full pager

   Style Settings

   ➤ Style: Table

Fields

➤ Comment: Title

➤ Comment: Post date

➤ Comment: Author

Filters

➤ Comment: Author

➤ Comment: Post date

➤ Comment: In moderation

Sort Criteria

➤ Comment: Post date – desc

3. Expose the filters by clicking Expose button on the configuration page on each of the filters. For example to expose the Comment:Author filter first click Comment:Author then click the expose button in the upper right corner, as shown in Figure 11-41.

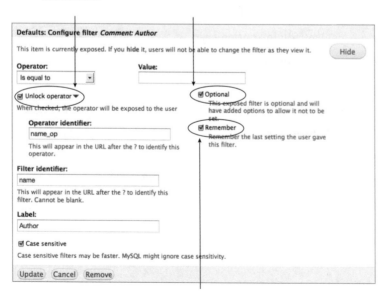

Defaults: Configure filter *Comment: Author*

This item is currently not exposed. If you **expose** it, users will be able to change the filter as they view it.

Expose

Operator:
Is equal to

Value:

☑ Case sensitive

Case sensitive filters may be faster. MySQL might ignore case sensitivity.

Update Cancel Remove

FIGURE 11-41

4. When you click Expose, several new options are available to you. Select the following options as shown in Figure 11-42.

➤ Unlock Operator

➤ Optional

➤ Remember

Defaults: Configure filter *Comment: Author*

This item is currently exposed. If you **hide** it, users will not be able to change the filter as they view it.

Hide

Operator:
Is equal to

Value:

☑ Unlock operator ▼
When checked, the operator will be exposed to the user

Operator identifier:
name_op
This will appear in the URL after the ? to identify this operator.

☑ Optional
This exposed filter is optional and will have added options to allow it not to be set.

☑ Remember
Remember the last setting the user gave this filter.

Filter identifier:
name
This will appear in the URL after the ? to identify this filter. Cannot be blank.

Label:
Author

☑ Case sensitive
Case sensitive filters may be faster. MySQL might ignore case sensitivity.

Update Cancel Remove

FIGURE 11-42

5. Expose the Comment: Post Date and Comment: In Moderation filters with the same options as those used for Comment: Author.

6. Add a new Page display and set the path to **/admin/content/comment/review**.

7. Save your view which should look similar to Figure 11-43.

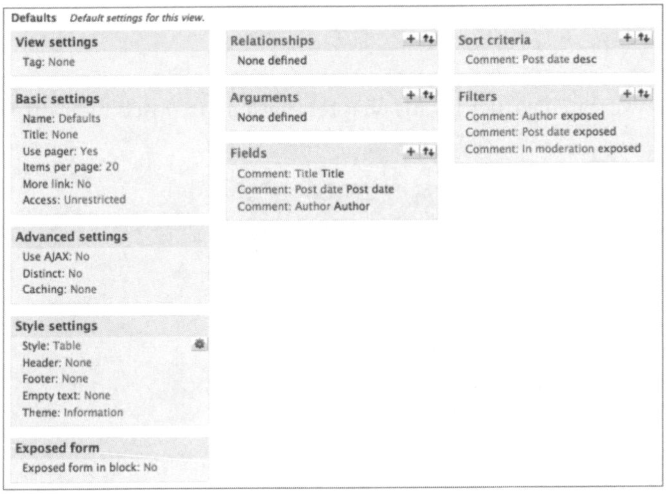

FIGURE 11-43

How It Works

Each filter within a view can be hidden or exposed. The default is to hide the filters, allowing configuration only within the view. Exposing a filter allows anyone with access to the view to modify the results and create a custom report.

After completing this exercise, you should be left with a view that is similar to the one shown previously in Figure 11-40. You can access the view by manually navigating to `http://localhost/admin/content/comment/review`. You can easily create administration pages such as this Comment Review page by using exposed filters. To help make your life easy, Views has a few more tricks up its sleeve, as you'll discover in the next few sections.

Exposed Items in a Block

Placing the exposed filters at the top of your view is not always optimal. Thankfully, Views allows you to take these exposed filters and place them in a block. To do this, simply set Exposed Form In Block to Yes, as shown in Figure 11-44.

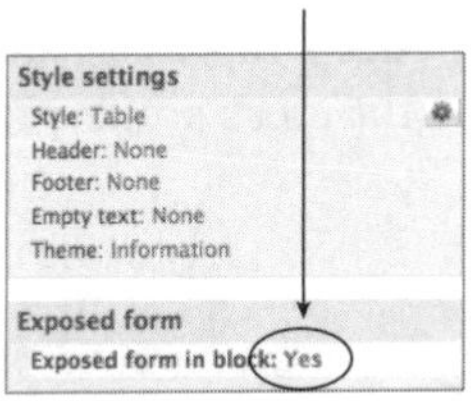

FIGURE 11-44

New blocks named after the view and the display for which they are relevant are available at Structure ➪ Blocks, as shown in Figure 11-45.

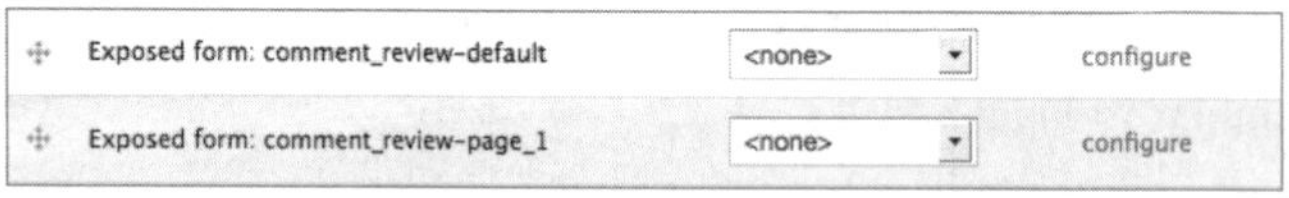

✛	Exposed form: comment_review–default	<none> ▾	configure
✛	Exposed form: comment_review–page_1	<none> ▾	configure

FIGURE 11-45

Figure 11-46 shows the Gallery view created earlier in this chapter, with an exposed filter displayed as a block in the left sidebar.

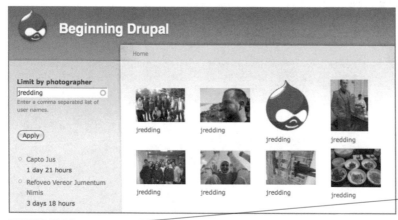

FIGURE 11-46

> ✎ **NOTE** To create an administration page that can perform mass edits or updates on all content retrieved by a view, use the Views Bulk Operations (VBO) contributed module available at `http://drupal.org/project/views_bulk_operations`.

Making Your View Accessible via a Tab

A great trick when using Views is to place your custom view alongside existing tab or menu structures. Take a look at Figure 11-47 and notice that the selection Comment Review selection is available alongside Drupal's default administration pages. Also consider Figure 11-48, which shows a custom tab on the user's profile page that links them to a custom view with a listing of all of their comments.

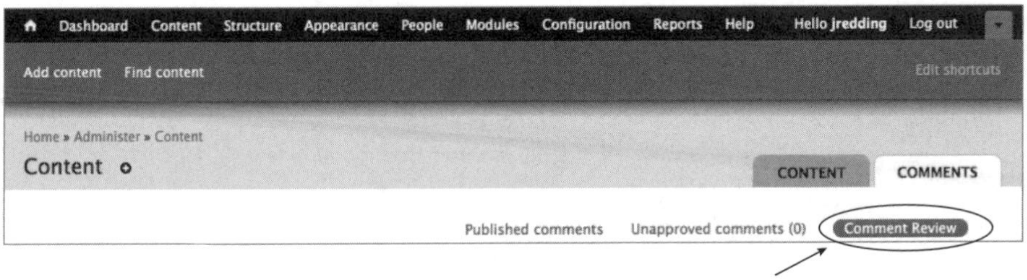

FIGURE 11-47

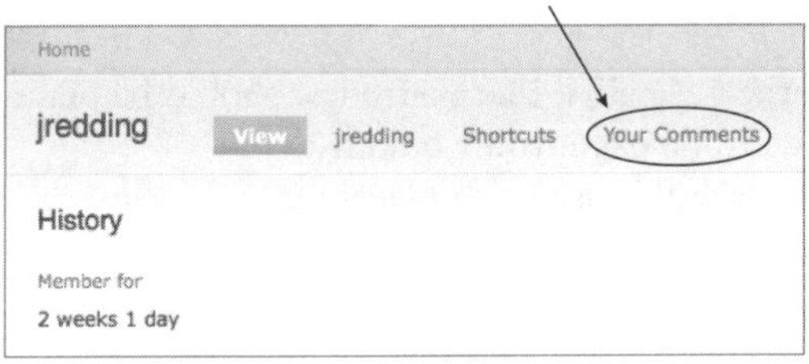

FIGURE 11-48

Follow the next exercise to place your custom Comment Review page alongside Drupal's default administration pages.

TRY IT OUT Extending Drupal's Administration Pages

In this exercise you'll add a tab with your custom administration page alongside Drupal's default administration pages, as shown in Figure 11-47.

1. Within the Comment Review view, select the Page display.

2. Under Page Settings set the Path to **admin/ content/comment/review**.

3. Edit the menu settings by entering the following information as shown in Figure 11-49:

   ➤ Type: Menu tab

   ➤ Title: **Comment review**

   ➤ Weight: **10**

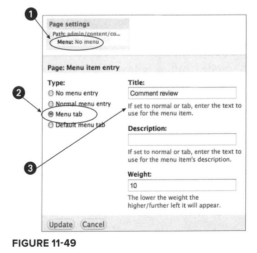

FIGURE 11-49

How It Works

This is a very simple setting that really helps your site shine. Drupal's menus work on URL paths. If you navigate to `http://localhost/admin/content/comment`, you'll notice that Unapproved Comments is located at `/admin/content/comment/approval`, which is underneath `/admin/content/comment`.

When you set your view's path to `/admin/content/comment/review` and then set it to a Menu tab, Drupal automatically adds a tab on the `/admin/content/comment` administration page. Figure 11-50 helps to illustrate this process.

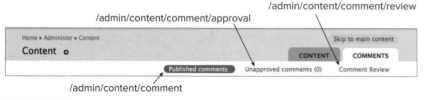

FIGURE 11-50

The only tricky part when adding a tab is determining the base URL that your view should be placed underneath. For example, to add a view tab to the User Profile page, you would use `/user/%/view-name` (as in `/user/%/comments`). The `%` symbol is used as a placeholder for the user-id. If you add a new tab to the Node edit screen, the path would be `node/%/edit/view-name`.

RELATIONSHIPS

If you tried clicking around on your new Comment Review page, you might have noticed that none of the fields that are available in a comment-type view relate to the node that the comment was in reply to. Information such as the node's title and author is missing. So how do you find the most popular content on your site ranked by frequency of comments? The answer lies in *relationships*.

A relationship connects two pieces of content. For example a comment is related to a node, so a relationship establishes this connection. When one connection is established, relationships can be made to other related items. For example, if a comment is related to a node, it can then be related to the node's author or taxonomy terms. You could then use this double-connection to find all comments posted to nodes tagged with a certain category. In SQL terms, a relationship is known as a *join*.

In the next exercise, you add a relationship to the node the comments were made on in order to add the node's title and its published date on your Comment Review page, as shown in Figure 11-51.

Comment: Author	Comment: Post date	Moderated		
	Is greater than	<Any>	Apply	
	5 weeks ago			

Title	Post date	Author	Node Title	Node date
Lobortis	7 weeks 6 days ago	Iapurd	Microsoft.com switches to Drupal	37 weeks 2 days ago
Cogo Magna Fere Blandit	11 weeks 56 min ago	Iapurd	Joomla! merges with Wordpress	39 weeks 14 hours ago
Abdo Vereor Abdo Saepius	11 weeks 6 days ago	LovemesomeDrupal	Microsoft.com switches to Drupal	37 weeks 2 days ago
Imputo	12 weeks 3 days ago	Jane Doe	Microsoft releases Drupal killer	48 weeks 4 min ago
Acsi Pala Cogo Populus	12 weeks 5 days ago	John Doe	Microsoft.com switches to Drupal	37 weeks 2 days ago

FIGURE 11-51

TRY IT OUT Adding a Relationship

In this exercise, you add a relationship to your Comment Review view in order to pull more information about the node the comment was posted on.

1. Within the comment_review view add the following relationship by clicking + in the upper-right corner of the Relationships box, as shown in Figure 11-52.

2. Add the Comment: Node relationship, as shown in Figure 11-53. Accept the default options.

3. With a relationship established, add the following two filters so that your Fields box looks like Figure 11-54:

➤ (Node) Node: Title — `Node Title`

➤ (Node) Node: Post date — `Node date`

4. Save your view.

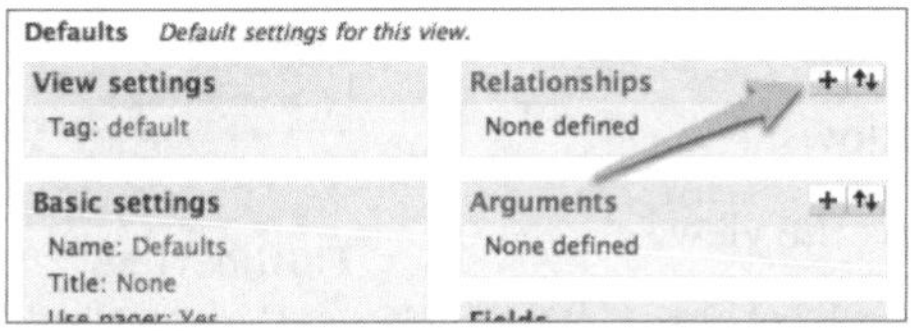

FIGURE 11-52

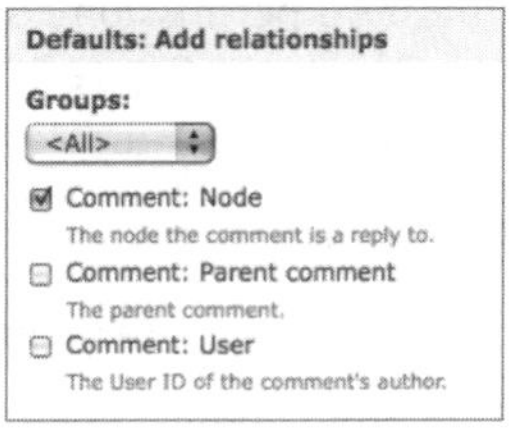

FIGURE 11-53

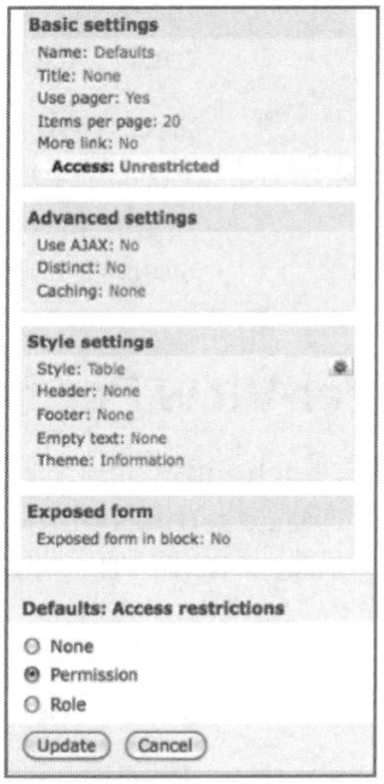

FIGURE 11-54

How It Works

A relationship creates a connection between two pieces of content on your site. For performance reasons, a view does not automatically add relationships, because each relationship can have a downward impact on performance.

After completing this exercise, revisit the Add Relationships screen and note that you can add more relationships such as Taxonomy and Node Revision. When one relationship has been established, Views can follow it to make connections with other items within your system. Keep in mind that the deeper your relationship is, the slower the view will perform. You can mitigate part of this performance slowdown by enabling caching as discussed in the next section.

PERMISSIONS

Views is an extremely powerful module and can retrieve nearly everything in your database. In fact, it is so powerful that it can retrieve anything regardless of any permission or other content restrictions on the data. For this reason, it is important to manage the permission on your views carefully.

Views maintains two types of permissions: all-views permissions and per-view permissions.

All-Views Permissions

These permissions control access to all views. You can configure the following all-views permissions at Configuration ➪ Permissions:

➤ **Administer Views** — This permission grants access to create, edit, and delete every view on the system. Needless to say, this is a very sensitive permission and should only be granted to trusted users.

➤ **Access All Views** — The name of this permission is slightly misleading. It allows users to *bypass* per-view permissions in order to see every view unrestricted. This permission should not be given to authenticated users or anonymous users; instead, use the per-view permissions to control access.

Per-View Permissions

Each individual view maintains a permission control setting set within the Basic settings of the view, as shown in Figure 11-55. Like all of settings displays within the view can override it per-display.

Access can be set either by permission or by role as follows:

FIGURE 11-55

➤ **Role** — Select one or more roles that can access the view.

➤ **Permission** — This setting allows you to select an existing site permission. Users with this permission will be able to access this view. Commonly this is set to the permission, View Published Content.

CACHING (AKA PERFORMANCE)

Views can be highly complex and can pull data from every nook and cranny in your database for easy viewing by your site visitors. Unfortunately, all of this power can come at a cost of performance. Typically, the more complex and advanced your views become, the slower they are. Fortunately, Views has ways to fight back against the slowdown demon.

Caching

After you have completed constructing your View and before you make it available for the world to see, turn on the individual view's cache under Advanced Settings, as shown in Figure 11-56. Next set caching to time-based caching and select how long to cache the query results and rendered output, as shown in Figure 11-57.

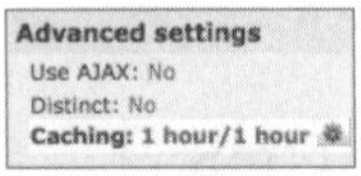

Each view has two methods of caching, described below. You will need to select the appropriate time to cache each option based upon the relevancy for your data. For example, if data does not change often but the way it is displayed does, then caching query

Advanced settings
Use AJAX: No
Distinct: No
Caching: 1 hour/1 hour ⚙

FIGURE 11-56

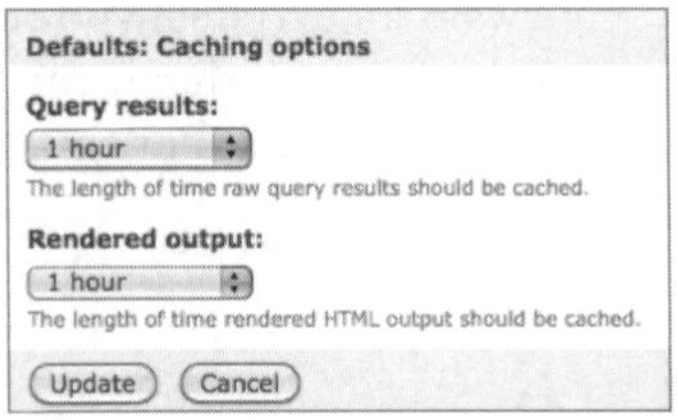

Defaults: Caching options

Query results:
[1 hour ＄]
The length of time raw query results should be cached.

Rendered output:
[1 hour ＄]
The length of time rendered HTML output should be cached.

(Update) (Cancel)

FIGURE 11-57

results longer than the rendered output is appropriate. If you are unsure set both of them to the same time.

> **Query Results** — A view creates an SQL query that is sent to the database. If a view contains several relationships or fields, this query can take a significant amount of time. This setting will remember the results pulled from the data for a set amount of time, thus reducing database activity and increasing the speed of your website.

> **Rendered Output** — After data has been retrieved from the database, it is run through your site's theming process to turn it into the HTML shown as a block, page, or RSS feed. This setting defines the amount of time before the view will recreate the HTML. A long setting will increase performance at the cost of stale data.

Block Caching

Block displays have additional cache settings. This is because blocks are typically unique to the page, user, or user's role. For example, you wouldn't want to use Cache Once for Everything if the block displayed different results for each user. This setting would cause the block to fail by displaying the same results to every user. Figure 11-58 shows the block caching options that you can set under Block Settings on the Block display of a view.

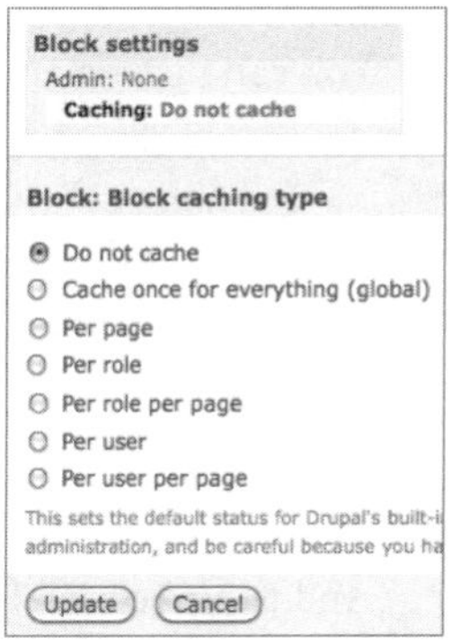

Best Practices

To get the best performance out of your views, keep the following in mind:

> Row styles of type Fields are faster than rows of type Node.

> Keep relationships to a minimum.

> Numeric argument variables are faster than text-based arguments (for example, user-id (their ID number) is faster than username).

> Filters or arguments that allow for case-sensitive queries are generally faster than those that perform case-insensitive queries.

> Keep the Items Per Page to a reasonable number. The higher the number, the slower the query.

> The Distinct setting under Basic Settings can eliminate duplication in your views, but it comes at a significant performance hit. If your view has significant duplication, rethink your view's plan.

FIGURE 11-58

This book does not cover SQL performance tuning, but be aware that Views is a SQL query builder — thus, most SQL and database performance techniques will speed up your views' pages, blocks, and RSS feeds. If you run into performance issues, don't be afraid to call up your local MySQL expert. Of course, you can always jump into the #drupal-support IRC channel or ask for assistance on Drupal.org's forums.

ADVANCED VIEWS

This chapter covers Views' immense and complex Graphical User Interface (GUI). But Views also contains an even more powerful Application Programming Interface (API) that allows module developers to extend and enhance views. Because it is an advanced developer topic, this book does not cover the API. You can learn more about the API on the Views project page at http:// drupal.org/project/views.

There is one topic, however, that even non-developers use from time to time: embedding a view. Embedding a view is using a small bit of PHP code to include a view within an existing page or block. You may do this to add a view to the bottom of a manually created page or to group multiple views together. This process is relatively simple and requires little PHP knowledge. The basic syntax is as follows:

```
views_embed_view($view_name, $display)
```

You can include any view's arguments within an array as the third argument, like this:

```
views_embed_view($view_name, $display, $arguments )
```

So to embed the Comment Review view you created in this chapter, you would use the following syntax:

```php
<?php
views_embed_view('comment_review', 'page')
?>
```

And to embed the Photo Gallery view from the first part of this chapter with the photographer's name as the argument, you would use the following syntax:

```php
<?php
views_embed_view('photo_gallery', 'page'), array('jredding'));
?>
```

> **NOTE** You can use the Panels module (http://drupal.org/project/panels) to group multiple views together on the same page and configure other complex groupings via a GUI (no programming required).

SUMMARY

Views' flexibility and power has caused it to become a mainstay in the toolbox of nearly every Drupal developer. Although this chapter covered the major aspects of Views and walked you through the details of multiple different views, it has only scratched the surface of Views' complexity. Like many things in Drupal, Views is an intense first experience, and it takes a while to get comfortable using it. Fortunately, because of its wide use, you'll get plenty of practice while building your site, and help is never more than an IRC channel away (try #drupal-support).

When you feel a bit more comfortable with Views, particularly with how filters and fields work, you can skip over to the Views modules category on Drupal.org (`http://drupal.org/taxonomy/term/89`) to find modules that will add new styles, row styles, filters, and more. I'm a fan of the Views Slideshow module (`http://drupal.org/project/views_slideshow`), which creates Image slideshows from a view, and the Views Bulk Operations (VBO) module (`http://drupal.org/project/views_bulk_operations`), which performs modifications en masse on a view's result set, making site administration a breeze. There are nearly 300 modules that have extended Views, so there is a good chance that you'll find the right combination of modules needed to customize your site exactly the way you want it.

EXERCISES

1. What is the Advanced Help module?

2. What is the difference between a filter and an exposed filter?

3. What permission would you assign a user to allow them to use exposed filters?

4. What permissions are available for Views?

5. What is the easiest way to increase the performance of your view?

6. What is the difference between an exposed filter and an argument?

7. What is a relationship?

8. What is the difference between a Style and Row Style?

Answers to these Exercises can be found in the Appendix.

▶ **WHAT YOU LEARNED IN THIS CHAPTER**

> ➤ The Advanced Help module provides extensive documentation directly on the Views UI.

> ➤ You can use a view to retrieve data from your database and mold and manipulate it via View Displays to create pages, blocks, or RSS feeds.

> ➤ Displays should be consistent with the defaults. However, you can override them only as necessary to properly format the data.

> ➤ Arguments are used to create dynamic customized pages based upon a URL path. For example `http://localhost/gallery/jredding` would create a photo gallery for the user `jredding`.

> ➤ Exposed filters can create custom search or reporting pages by using URL variables; for example, `http://localhost/comments?uid=1&post_date=today`.

> ➤ A relationship connects an object to another object, such as a node to its author. For performance reasons, relationships are not automatic.

> ➤ You can assign access permissions to your view using existing site permissions or by providing access based on user roles.

> ➤ Before going live with a view, be sure to turn on caching.

12

Internationalization

WHAT YOU WILL LEARN IN THIS CHAPTER:

➤ Localizing your website

➤ Changing your site's default language

➤ Add multilingual support to your site

➤ Using the L10N client module

➤ Translating your site's content

➤ Using the I18N module

Hola, Bonjour, Guten Tag, 你好, 今日は! Our planet holds billions of people spread across thousands of miles, but the Internet has connected all of us with the click of a mouse — it truly is a small world after all. In this chapter, you'll learn how to translate your website to reach your audience through the most effective form of communication: language. This may be through creating a monolingual site with content only in Spanish, French, or Chinese. Or you can create a multilingual site with content in German, Ukrainian, Japanese, and English. Whatever language your visitors use, Drupal can speak it.

A BIT OF TERMINOLOGY

The term *internationalization* is often used as a very broad and ambiguous term referring to numerous actions, all of which relate to modifying Drupal's core language (English) and its settings. Internationalization generally relates to two activities: localizing and translating. Here are a few terms to help you decipher the lingo of internationalization:

➤ **Localizing** — Refers to the modification of the user interface to the local standards. This may include translating the text used for menus, buttons, links, and administrative screens, or changing the format of dates, times, currency, and so on.

➤ **Locale** — The name of Drupal's core module used for localizing your site.

➤ **Translation** — Translating your site's Articles, Pages, and other added content to a language other than your site's default.

➤ **Content translation** — The name of Drupal's core module that allows you to translate your site's content.

➤ **i18n** — Abbreviation of *internationalization*, based on the fact that there are 18 letters between the first letter (*i*) and the last letter (*n*) of the word. In this book, i18n refers to the contributed module available at `http://drupal.org/project/i18n`.

➤ **l10n** — Abbreviation of *localization*, because of the fact that there are 10 letters between the first letter (*l*) and the last letter (*n*) of the word.

The most important distinction in terminology is that of localizing versus translating. Localizing is the act of translating the interfaces provided by Drupal or contributed modules. Translating is the act of translating content that you have added to your site.

LOCALIZING

To ease communication within a highly international and worldwide developer base, the Drupal community settled on using English as a base language. This means that Drupal's core, contributed modules, and themes are written in English and ship with an English interface. However, they are all written in a manner that allows the text to be easily translated into your local language, and enables you to easily modify the format of items such as the date, time, time zones, and the like.

If you change your site's default language or add a second language, you'll want to localize the interface to match the locale or language used.

This section covers localizing your site's interface. It starts with a few of the base settings and then quickly moves on to show you how to modify your default language or add a second language.

Regional Settings

The first step to preparing your site for a multilingual or multinational audience is to set your site's default regional settings. You access these settings at Configuration ➪ Regional Settings. You can configure your site's default country, day of the week (used for calendar displays), and time zones as shown in Figure 12-1. There is also an option to enable your users to set their own time zone, which would modify all dates and times to reflect the user's selected time zone. A user's timezone is effective only for their personal use of the site.

Regional settings ○

LOCALE

Default country

United States

First day of week

Sunday

TIME ZONES

Default time zone

America/Los Angeles: Saturday, December 12, 2009 - 23:02 -0800

☑ Users may set their own time zone.

☐ Remind users at login if their time zone is not set.
Only applied if users may set their own time zone.

Time zone for new users

◉ Default time zone.

○ Empty time zone.

○ Users may set their own time zone at registration.

Only applied if users may set their own time zone.

FIGURE 12-1

Date and Time

Do you write your dates in the format mm/dd/yyy (as in 12/31/2010), dd/mm/yyy (as in 31/12/2010), or [month] [date], [year] (as in December 31, 2010)?

However you present date and times, Drupal can display them according to your local language, cultural, or personal preferences. Set them at Configuration ⇨ Date and Time, as shown in Figure 12-2. Without additional configuration, Drupal uses three date types: Long, Medium, and Short. Medium is the default type used for most date and times, including the byline information shown on Articles.

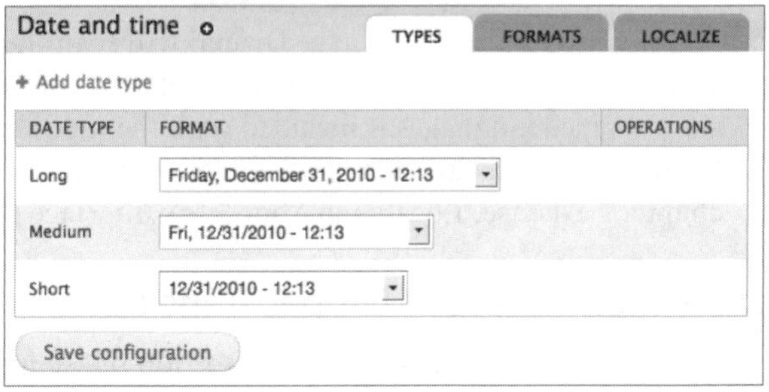

FIGURE 12-2

When you add a second language to your site (discussed later), you use the Localize tab to configure each format per language. For example, you could configure the Medium format to appear as 12/31/2010 for the English language and as 31/12/2010 when the site is viewed in Spanish.

> **NOTE** *Module or theme developers use* `format_date(timestamp, type)`, *to properly display date and times, which allows for local translation. Read more at* `http://api.drupal.org/api/function/format_date/7`.

Localizing Your Site's Interface

You can localize (translate) the interface to a single language or to multiple languages. The basic steps to localizing your interface are as follows:

1. Enable the Locale module.

2. Add a new language at Configuration ⇨ Languages.

3. Upload an existing translation or create one yourself.

A translation is added to Drupal through one or more Portable Object (.po) file. If these are already present on your site they will be automatically imported when a new language is added thus eliminating step three. Before jumping to the exercises on adding a translation take a few minutes to learn about these important .po files.

Portable Object (.po) Files

Portable Object (.po) files are web standard files used to translate a set of strings from a base language to a second language in what is known as the Gettext Portable Object Template format. These files are language-specific and relate to a specific set of strings. Each contributed module or theme you download may include a translations folder that contains language-specific .po files for translating the strings used by the module or theme.

For example the Spanish translation for the core Node module contains the following string and translation:

```
msgid "Read more"
msgstr "Leer más"
```

When you add a new language Drupal will scan the directories searching for .po files and copy the strings and translations into a Strings table in your database. If a .po file corresponding to one of your site's enabled languages is included with the module, it will be automatically imported. If you enable a language after installing a module, you will have to manually add the .po files, demonstrated in this chapter's exercise, Localizing Your Site's Interface using `http://localize.drupal.org`.

The Current State of Drupal Translation

Translations in Drupal are in a transition phase moving from a static translation to a more dynamic, up-to-date, and community managed translation system. In the past a single team of translators would collaborate to create a translation of Drupal, releasing their work on drupal.org. Problems arose when the team couldn't keep up with the rapid pace of Drupal development or the translation of thousands of Drupal modules. A new approach was taken.

In the new approach the team model shifted to a distributed model, enlisting every translated Drupal site. The L10N Client and Server modules were developed, which allow site owners (like you) to submit translations to a central server. When you translate your own site you can also contribute to the translation of other Drupal sites, without having to do extra work. When these modules are fully developed they will also download translations to your site, making the process of translating your site easier.

This chapter will start by guiding you through the current method of adding a translation, then in a second exercise introduce you to the new method of adding a translation. The method you will use is dependent on the language of your site. For example, the Spanish translation has already transitioned to the new method. Many other languages have not yet made the transition

You are encouraged to do both exercises to familiarize yourself with how Drupal is translated. Performing both exercises will cause no harm to your website because Drupal simply ignores string translations that have already been imported.

Follow along in this first exercise to learn how to use the translations available at http://drupal.org/project/Translations. The Ukrainian translation is used for this example but you may choose any other available language.

TRY IT OUT   **Localizing Your Site's Interface using** `drupal.org/project/Translations`

In this exercise, you add the Ukrainian translation to your site.

1.   Enable the Locale module.

2.   Navigate to `http://drupal.org/project/Translations` then find the Ukrainian Language project page. Languages are listed alphabetically.
Alternatively you can navigate directly to the project's page at `http://drupal.org/project/uk`.

3. Download the Drupal 7 translation and place the downloaded .tar.gz file in your site's root directory, as shown in Figure 12-3. Note the additional uk-7.x-1.1.tar.gz file in the lower right corner.

FIGURE 12-3

4. From a command line, navigate to your Drupal directory and type in the following command:

```
tar zxvf uk-7.x-1.1.tar.gz
```

> **NOTE** Replace uk-7.x.1.1.tar.gz with the downloaded file name. This will place numerous .po files throughout your Drupal install.

5. Navigate to Configuration ➪ Languages (under Regional and Language), and then click Add Language at the top of the page as shown in Figure 12-4.

Home » Administer » Configuration » Regional and language

Languages ⚙

| | | LIST | DETECTION AND SELECTION |

With multiple languages enabled, interface text can be translated, registered users may select their preferred language, and authors can assign a specific language to content. Download contributed translations from Drupal.org.

➔ **✛ Add language**

ENGLISH NAME	NATIVE NAME	CODE	DIRECTION	ENABLED	DEFAULT	OPERATIONS
✛ English	English	en	Left to right	☑	◉	edit

Save configuration

FIGURE 12-4

6. Select Ukrainian from the predefined languages list, select Add language, as shown in Figure 12-5. Drupal will import the string translations from the .po files you added in this exercise.

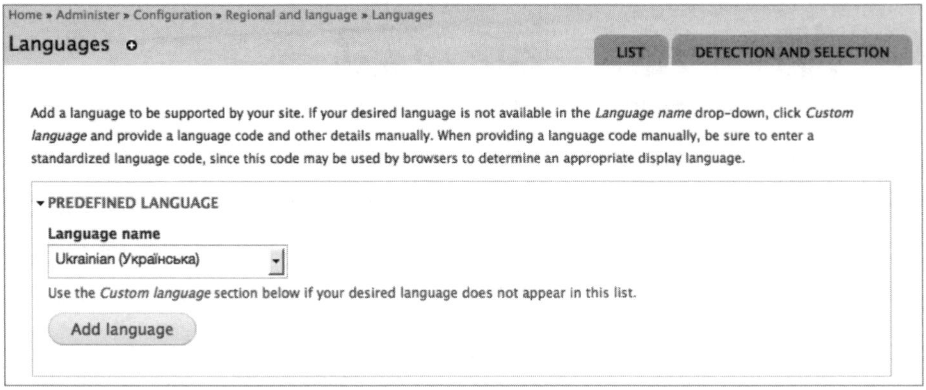

Home » Administer » Configuration » Regional and language » Languages

Languages ⚙   LIST   DETECTION AND SELECTION

Add a language to be supported by your site. If your desired language is not available in the *Language name* drop-down, click *Custom language* and provide a language code and other details manually. When providing a language code manually, be sure to enter a standardized language code, since this code may be used by browsers to determine an appropriate display language.

▼ PREDEFINED LANGUAGE

Language name

Ukrainian (Українська) ▾

Use the *Custom language* section below if your desired language does not appear in this list.

(Add language)

FIGURE 12-5

How It Works

Drupal can simultaneously provide its interface and content in multiple languages. Before it can do so, it needs to know the languages to be offered and how those languages are identified (their RFC 4646 identifiers), and it must create a repository for the language. You did all of this by simply selecting the predefined Ukrainian language. Whenever possible, you should use Drupal's predefined languages, because they are based on RFC standards.

When a new language is added, Drupal searches all directories for .po files. In this exercise you downloaded the files from `http://drupal.org/project/Translations` and added them to your Drupal directory with the `tar zxvf` command. Later, when you update Drupal you will not need to repeat this exercise, as the translation is already available. The .po files are only required for the initial import.

The previous exercise demonstrated the much more ubiquitous but deprecated method of adding a new language. The next exercise demonstrates the newer method that at the time of writing was still under development. This method works with the new centralized translation server at `http://localize.drupal.org`, where you can find the most up to date information and translations. It is also designed to compliment the localization client, available at `http://drupal.org/project/l10n_client` and discussed later in this chapter.

TRY IT OUT   **Localizing Your Site's Interface using** `http://localize.drupal.org`

In this exercise, you add the Spanish translation to your site using `http://localize.drupal.org`.

1. Navigate to Configuration ➪ Languages (under Regional and Language), then click Add Language at the top of the page.

2. Select Spanish from the Predefined Language list, then click Add Language. Note that no strings will be imported because Drupal does not have .po files to import. You will retrieve these from `http://localize.drupal.org`.

3. Navigate to `http://localize.drupal.org` and login with your Drupal.org username and password. Create an account on drupal.org if you do not have one.

4. Select the Spanish language from the frontpage, then click the Choose button, as shown in Figure 12-6.

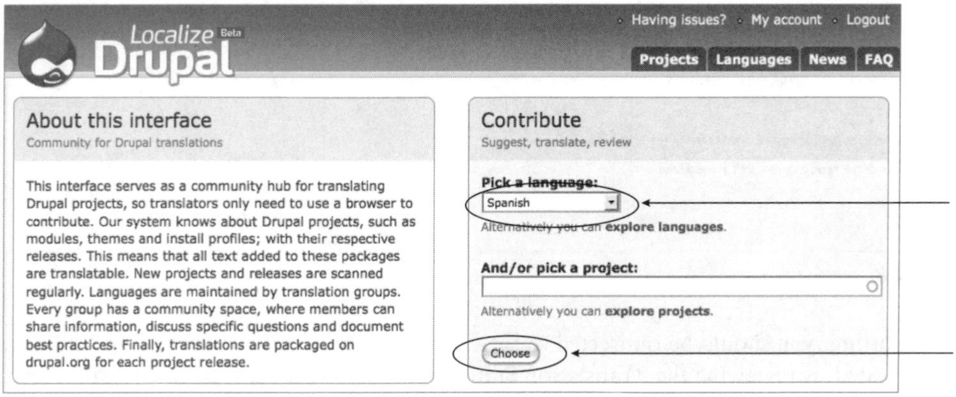

FIGURE 12-6

5. Join the Spanish group by clicking the Join link on the project's home page.

6. Click the Export tab and select the following options as shown in Figure 12-7:

➤ **Project:** Drupal

➤ **Release:** Drupal 7 (Drupal 6 is also acceptable)

➤ **Type:** Include both English original and translations

➤ **Packaging:** All in one file

➤ **Verbosity:** Compact file optimized for size, not desktop editing

Click the Export button and save the resulting file to your local disk.

7. On your Drupal site, navigate to Configuration ⇨ Translate Interface (under Regional and Language), and click Import. On the Import Translation page, add the Spanish translation file you downloaded in step 1 as shown in Figure 12-8.

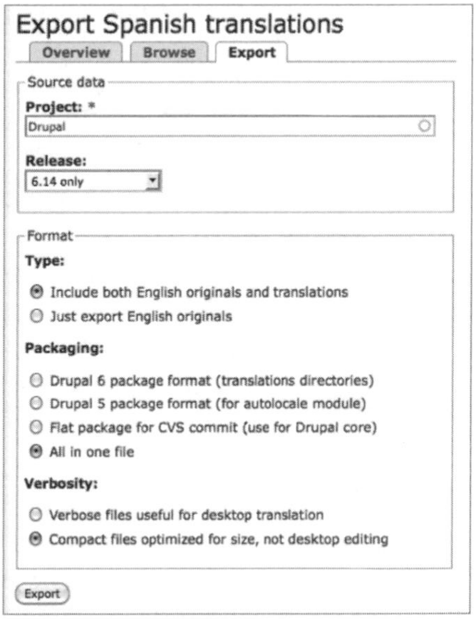

FIGURE 12-7

FIGURE 12-8

8. After importing, you should be redirected to the Overview page. Verify that the translation was properly added by reviewing the Translation Status column on this page, as shown in Figure 12-9.

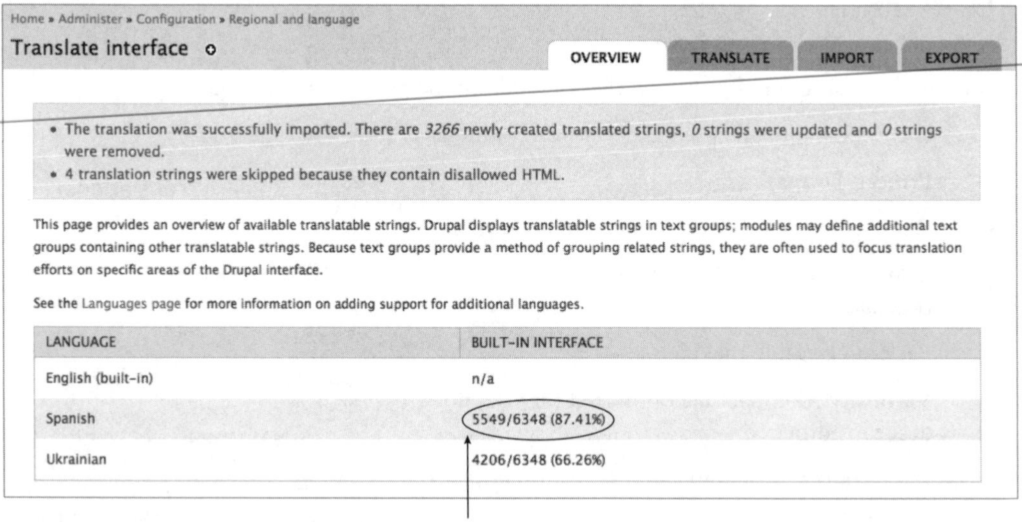

FIGURE 12-9

How It Works

Self-organized community groups located all over the world maintain translations of Drupal. Beginning in late 2009, these groups began to use the centralized website `http://localize.drupal.org` to collaborate on and to share their translations. (Previously, these groups collaborated at `http://drupal.org/proj-ect/Translations`, and although translations still exist at that site, it's best to use `localize.drupal.org` instead.) In this exercise, you downloaded the latest translation of the Drupal project. Note that you could have just as easily downloaded a translation of any contributed module or theme available on Drupal.org.

The translations are graciously donated and worked on by groups of community volunteers. This centralized worldwide collaboration often leads to translations being more readily available in more languages and for more projects. However, this also means that a translation may not be 100-percent complete, as shown in Figure 12-9. At the time of this writing, the Spanish translation was only 87-percent complete. The untranslated portions are output in English.

Your Site's Primary Language

Now that you have added three different languages to your website you may be wondering why your website is still displayed in English. This is because your default language is English. Change this at Configuration ➪ Language by selecting the Default radio button next to the language you want your site's primary language to be.

At this point, your site may not be fully translated, and a bit later in this chapter, you'll learn how to complete your site's localization so that you have a fully translated site. But before doing that, you'll take a step back and learn how Drupal determines when a user will receive an English, Ukrainian, or Spanish site. More specifically, you'll learn the answers to the following questions:

➤ Will the user have to manually click a Spanish link?

➤ Should Drupal use the user's browser information?

➤ What about the URL they used to access your site?

Accessing Your Localized Site

You might be wondering how your site visitors flip to the other languages of your site. You can direct Drupal to automatically select your site's language based on the visitor's information, allow users to manually select a new language, or you can choose to do a combination of both. Unfortunately, none of these options are automatically configured thus your users will be unable to select a different language until you enable one or more options.

The first step to allow your users to change your site's language is to enable and configure one or more language negotiation methods. After a negotiation method is set, you can use one of the two Language Switcher blocks (Structure ➪ Blocks). One block is used to change the site's language, and the other is used to change only the language of the content.

Language Negotiation

Language negotiation is set at Configuration ➪ Languages ➪ Configure, as shown in Figure 12-10. Drupal provides numerous ways to either automatically detect a user's language or to provide them a method to manually change the language used. Note that the detection methods are set for both your site's content language and your site's interface, although these are commonly configured to the same set of detection methods. Drag and drop these detection methods in a preferred order of use. Drupal will begin detection with the first enabled method and continue through the ordered list until a language is found.

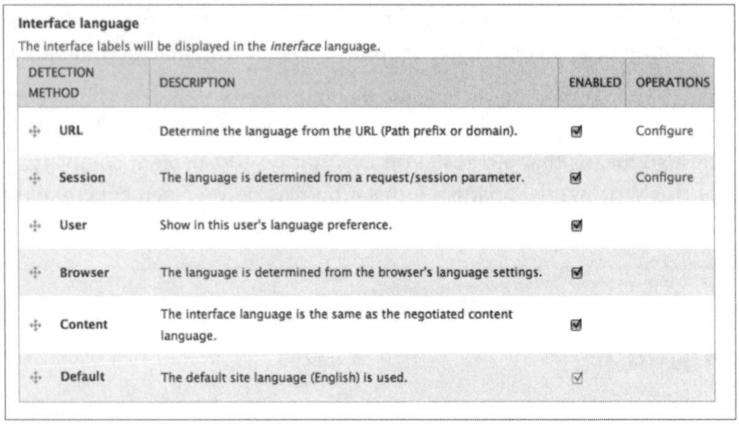

Interface language

The interface labels will be displayed in the *interface* language.

DETECTION METHOD	DESCRIPTION	ENABLED	OPERATIONS
⊹ URL	Determine the language from the URL (Path prefix or domain).	☑	Configure
⊹ Session	The language is determined from a request/session parameter.	☑	Configure
⊹ User	Show in this user's language preference.	☑	
⊹ Browser	The language is determined from the browser's language settings.	☑	
⊹ Content	The interface language is the same as the negotiated content language.	☑	
⊹ Default	The default site language (English) is used.	☑	

FIGURE 12-10

The available negotiation methods are described in the following subsections.

URL

When this detection method is used the site's language is determined by either an additional path on your URL or by your domain name. Here are some examples:

Path prefix

English: `http://example.com/en`

Spanish: `http://example.com/es`

Domain

English: `http://en.example.com`

Spanish: `http://es.example.com`

Spanish: `http://example.es`

> ⊗ **WARNING** *If you choose to use the domain method you must ensure that your web server and DNS is configured to respond to the domain names chosen.*

When you have decided on the URL or domain name that will be used for a language, configure it with the respective language (e.g., Configuration ➪ Languages ➪ Spanish (Edit)). For example, Figure 12-11 displays the settings for the Spanish language that can be accessed at `http://example.es`. A more common method, and Drupal's default, is to use a Path Prefix of `es`. This is the method used throughout this chapter.

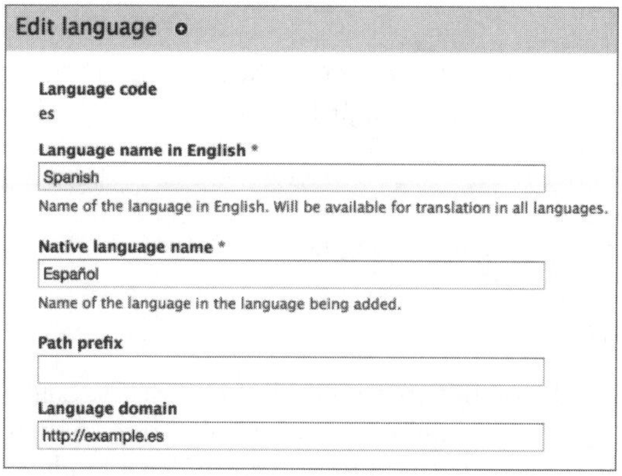

FIGURE 12-11

Session

The Session detection method uses a URL variable to determine the site's language. This is useful if you are migrating from another content management and would like to maintain the same URL structure.

If you decide to use the Session method then your URLs would look similar to the following:

```
http://localhost/about-us?language=es
```

This URL would display the About Us page in Spanish.

```
http://localhost/about-us?language=en
```

This URL would display the About Us page in English.

In the configuration of this detection method you can configure the name used for the variable. For example, you can change `?language=es` to `?idioma=es`.

User

If this detection method is used the users of your site can select the site's language within their user account's preferences.

Browser

A common annoyance to tourists vacationing in foreign lands, this detection method will use the language of the visitor's web browser to select the site's language. For example, if your site is available in Spanish and the user visiting your site is using a computer that has Spanish set as its default language then your site will automatically select the Spanish translation. This detection method does not use geography as a determination, only the language set within the visitor's browser.

Content

This detection method uses the language of your site's content to determine the language of your site. For example, you can write an About Us page in Spanish and English. When the Spanish About Us page is accessed then the site's language will switch to Spanish. This might include the navigation menu, header, logo, and so on.

Later in this chapter you will learn how to add content in multiple languages.

Completing Your Site's Localization

As mentioned previously, Drupal's core and contributed modules are standardized to use the English language. This means that a module's menu items, hyperlinks, administrative settings, information messages, and so on will be displayed in English unless they have been translated. When a module needs to output a link, menu item, message, or other text-based item — which are referred to as *strings* — it will use the Drupal function t(). This function places the string, which is in English, into your database's Strings table. When a translation is used, the English string is matched to a translation, and the translated version used. If no translation exists, the original English version is used.

If you find this confusing, follow along with this example workflow:

1. Module X needs to tell a site administrator that an unspecified error has occurred. The module uses the following code:

```
drupal_set_message(t('Unspecified error'));
```

2. The string is then placed into the Strings table, accessible at Configuration ⇨ Translate Interface ⇨ Translate, as shown in Figure 12-12.

3. You can then provide a translation for the string by clicking the edit link to the right of the string. Figure 12-13 shows two translations for the original Unspecified error text. Translations are always based on the original English text, even if your site's default language is not English. Note that strings that are missing a translation will display a crossed-out language name, as shown previously in the second string in Figure 12-12.

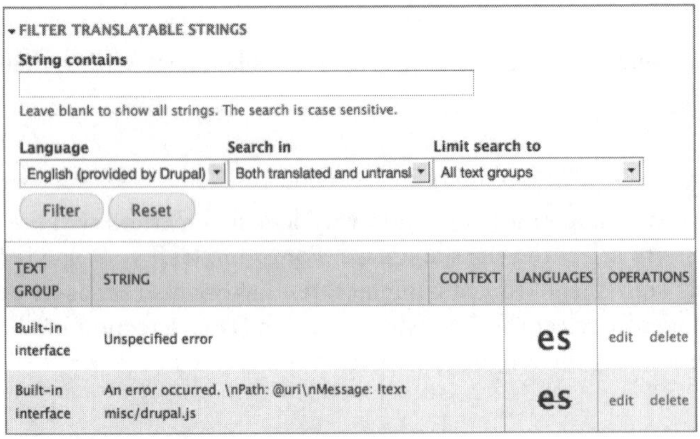

FIGURE 12-12

FIGURE 12-13

Notes on String Translation

Translating strings such as the one shown in Figure 12-13 is pretty straightforward. But you will frequently run into more complex strings such as the following (the second string in Figure 12-12):

```
An error occurred. \nPath: @uri\nMessage: !text
```

This string contains two \n (new line) characters, a @uri variable, and a !text variable. When displayed on your site, this string might look like what's shown in Figure 12-14.

To translate this message simply copy the string as is, paste it into the appropriate language translation of the string, and translate the English portion. Keep the variables @url and !text as is. For example:

FIGURE 12-14

```
Un error ha ocurrido. \nRuta: @uri\nMensaje: !text
```

To learn more about the variables used in the original strings, read the documentation for the t() function at http://api.drupal.org/api/function/t/7.

Making Translation Easy with the L10N Client

The latest, greatest, and easiest way to translate your site's interface is with the Localization (L10N) client. Drupal's built-in translation interface places every string on a single page, which works well to help you discover what is left to be translated but doesn't help you understand the context of the translation. The L10N client provides an on-page editor that allows translators to simply click the untranslated string and immediately translate it. Even better, the L10N client can be configured to send your translation directly to http://localize.drupal.org, making your local translation team part of a global translation team.

Follow the next exercise to begin using the localization client.

> **TRY IT OUT** Using the Localization Client

The L10N client can make interface translation easy and allow you to easily share your translations. In this exercise you will use the L10N Client to translate your site's interface.

1. Download, install, and enable the L10N client from http://drupal.org/project/l10n_client.

2. Allow your translators to use the client by assigning them permission, as shown in Figure 12-15.

PERMISSION	ANONYMOUS USER	AUTHENTICATED USER	ADMINISTRATOR
Localization client			
Use on-page translation Makes it possible to translate the Drupal interface on-page.	☐	☐	☑
Submit translations to localization server Allows users to submit translations to a remote localization server.	☐	☐	☑

FIGURE 12-15

3. With permissions set, navigate to any page on your site and click the Translate Text button in the lower-right corner of the page, as shown in Figure 12-16.

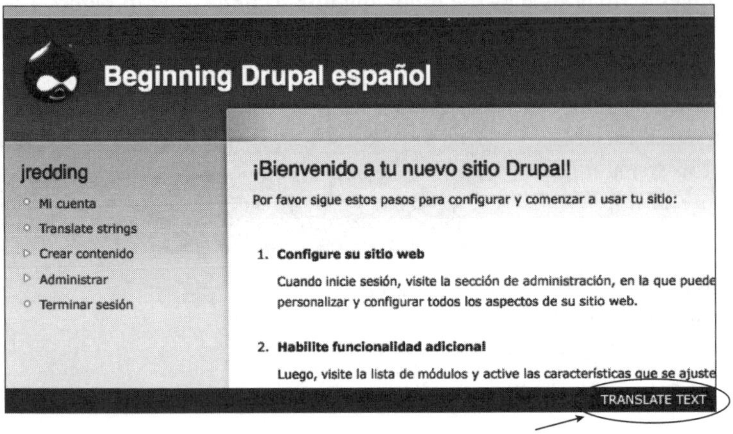

FIGURE 12-16

4. All translatable strings found on the page will appear on the far-left side of the pop-up window. Translated strings are displayed in green and missing translations are displayed in white. Add your translation in the far-right window and click Save Translation, as shown in Figure 12-17.

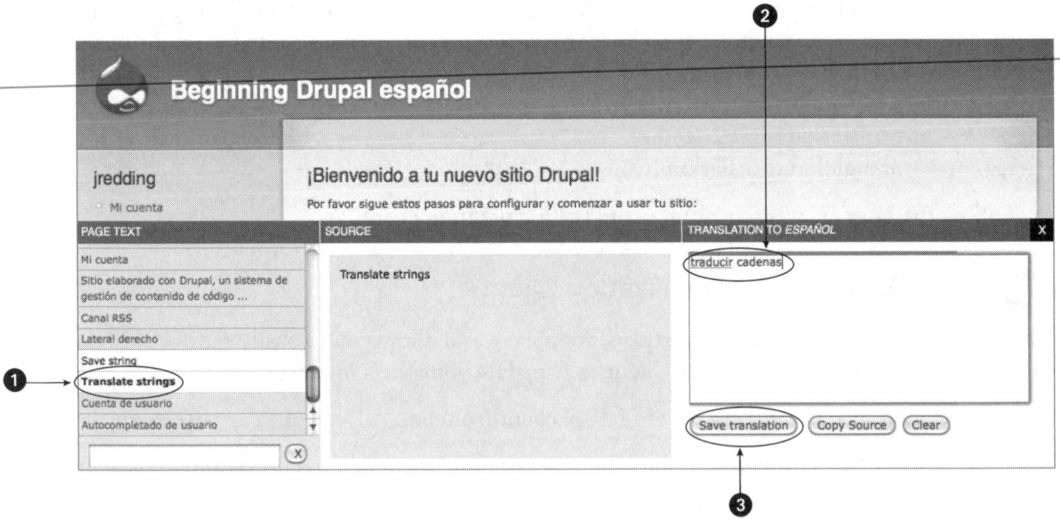

FIGURE 12-17

How It Works

The L10N client serves as a compliment to Drupal's built-in string translation interface. It displays all translatable strings on a page, making it easy to navigate to any page and ensure it has been properly and fully localized.

As mentioned previously, Drupal's translations are created by and maintained by an active community of translators. Becoming a part of this community requires nothing more than a few minutes of your time. The L10Nclient can submit your translated strings to `http://localize.drupal.org`, helping to complete the translation of Drupal's core and contributed modules. Follow the next exercise to learn how to participate on `localize.drupal.org`.

> **NOTE** *You can add users to your translation team by granting them the* `Translate interface texts` *permission.*

TRY IT OUT   **Getting Involved and Sharing Your Translations**

In this exercise, you configure the L10N client to share your translations with `http://localize.drupal.org` in order to get involved with the translation of Drupal and its contributed modules.

1. Use your drupal.org account to login to and join a translation group at `http://localize.drupal.org`.

2. On your site, configure the L10N client to use `http://localize.drupal.org` as follows:

a. Navigate to Configuration ➪ Languages ➪ Sharing.

b. Check the Enable Sharing Translations With Server option.

c. Type **http://localize.drupal.org** in the Address of Localization Server to Use box.

If everything is successful, you will receive a positive verification message as shown in Figure 12-18.

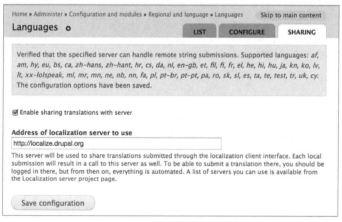

FIGURE 12-18

3. Using the same browser, open two tabs. In one tab, navigate to `http://localize.drupal.org` to verify that you are logged in and a member of the group that you will be submitting translated strings to. In the second tab, navigate to your Drupal site and begin translating.

How It Works

When the L10N client is configured to use `localize.drupal.org`, it will simultaneously save your translations to your local site and submit them to http://localize.drupal.org. The L10N client uses the credentials stored within your browser when submitting the strings, so you need to be logged into `localize.drupal.org` before you begin submitting strings.

Each translation group on `localize.drupal.org` maintains a moderation method to provide quality control on all translations. When you begin submitting translations, take a few minutes to get involved with the translation group and help with moderation.

You are now on your way to localizing your site's interface to all enabled languages. In this next section you'll learn how to translate your site's content. If you are running a monolingual site and don't need to translate your content (because you wrote it in your site's language) you can skip this section.

In the last exercise in this section, you create a language-specific distribution of Drupal. This exercise is tucked away at the end of the section due to a new feature on Drupal.org called Packaged Drupal Distributions (aka: Install Profiles), which may provide language-specific Drupal distributions by the end of 2010. Be sure to check `http://drupal.org` and the L10N Install profile at `http://drupal.org/project/l10n_install` to see if these distributions are available before you create your own — you may save yourself a lot of time.

TRY IT OUT Installing Drupal with a Language other than English

In this exercise, you create a version of Drupal that installs with the Spanish language.

1. Download a fresh copy of Drupal 7 from `http://drupal.org`. Uncompress the download file to create a Drupal directory. This is done in the same manner as a standard installation of Drupal.

2. Navigate to `http://localize.drupal.org` and select the Spanish group. Click the Export tab and select the following options, as shown in Figure 12-19:

  ➤ **Project:** Drupal

  ➤ **Release:** 7 (Drupal 6 will also work)

  ➤ **Type:** Include both English original and translations

  ➤ **Packaging:** Drupal 6 package format (translations directories)

  ➤ **Verbosity:** Compact files optimized for size, not desktop editing

3. Click the Export button at the bottom of the page, and save the resulting compressed `.tgz` file.

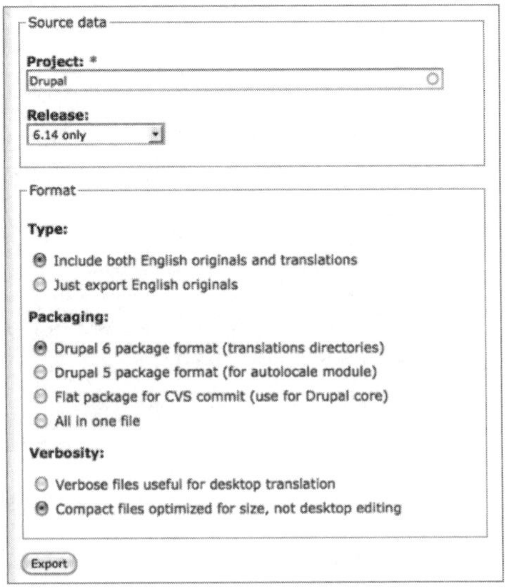

FIGURE 12-19

4. Copy the newly downloaded translations file to the fresh download of Drupal 7, as demonstrated in Figure 12-20.

5. Uncompress the translations file within the Drupal 7 directory without creating new directories. You can do this from a command line with the following command.

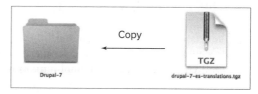

FIGURE 12-20

```
tar zxvf drupal-7-es-translations.tgz
```

6. Install Drupal. During the installation process, select the new language as shown in Figure 12-21.

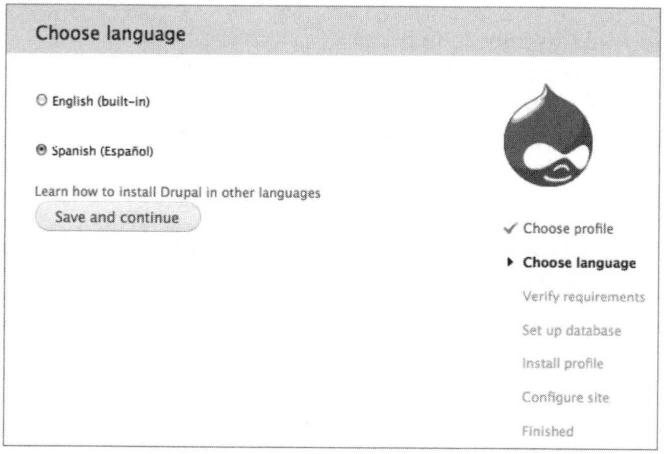

FIGURE 12-21

How It Works

The compressed translations file you downloaded from `http://localize.drupal.org` contains a folder hierarchy that mimics Drupal's folder hierarchy. When the file is uncompressed, it places new `.po` files into the respective folders of each module in Drupal and in Drupal's translations folder.

If you use an application such as WinZip to decompress the file, be sure that it does not create a new folder structure (a default setting). For example, the compressed translations file contains the following file:

```
modules/user/translations/modules-upload.es.po
```

This file must be placed in the following Drupal folder:

```
modules/user/translations
```

Drupal will find these new `.po` files and prompt you to select a language during installation.

TRANSLATING YOUR CONTENT

The second half of creating a multilingual site is to translate your site's content — the Articles and Pages you have added to the site. If you will be a running a monolingual site, there is no reason to add content translation, because you can simply submit all of your information in that language. You translate your site's content using Drupal's core Content Translation module. This module provides a method to translate your site's content and a method to link a piece of content to multiple translations of it, such as an About Us page that is written in English and then translated and linked to Spanish and French versions, as shown in Figure 12-22.

Linking content, as shown in Figure 12-22, is important because Drupal can use the link to display the appropriate content based

FIGURE 12-22

upon the requested language. For example, if a user is navigating the site in English and reading the About Us page, if they click the Spanish link to view a Spanish translation of the site, Drupal will also find the linked Spanish version of the About Us page and display it. If content is not linked then the user will see a Spanish website with an English version of the About Us page.

The Content Translation module not only facilitates the translation and the linkage, it also provides several interfaces for managing your translations and tracking your site's translation status.

You added the Spanish language to your site earlier in this chapter, so you are ready to dig right in and begin translating your content. Follow along in the next exercise to learn how to use the Content Translation module.

TRY IT OUT **Using the Content Translation Module**

In the exercise, you enable content translation to add an About Us page with both an English and a Spanish translation. If you have not yet added the Spanish language to your site, please follow the exercises earlier in this chapter to do so.

1. Enable the Content Translation module at Modules.

2. Configure the Page content type to allow for translation by navigating to Structure ⇨ Content Types ⇨ Page (Edit) and then under Publishing Options select Enabled, With Translation under Multilingual Support as shown in Figure 12-23. Click Save.

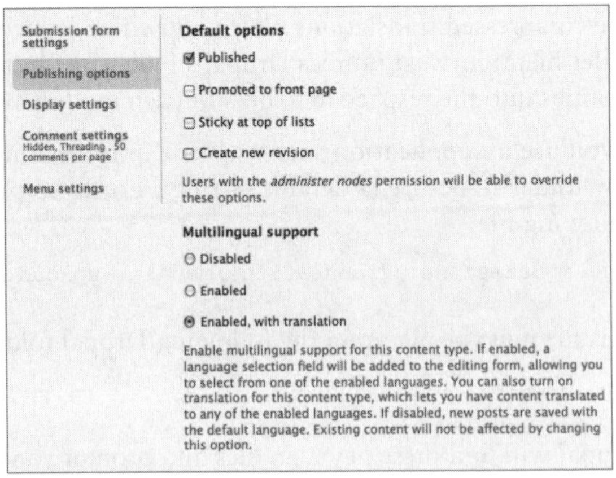

FIGURE 12-23

3. Create a new Page (Create Content ⇨ Page) using the following information, as shown in Figure 12-24:

➤ Title: **About us**

➤ Body: **Thank you for taking the time to look at our new site.**

➤ Language: Select English from the drop-down list (if it is not already selected)

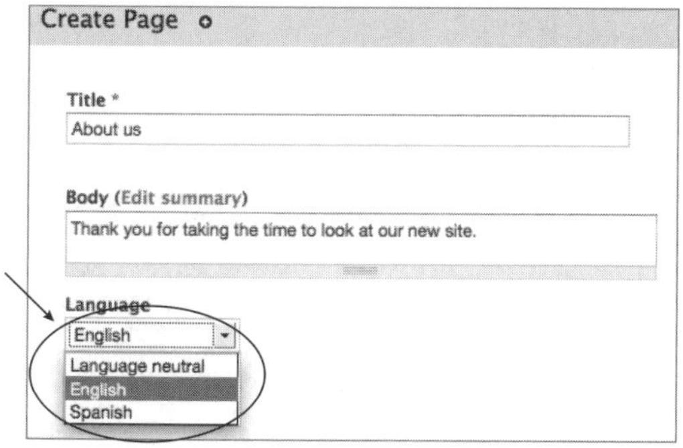

Create Page ⊙

Title *
About us

Body (Edit summary)
Thank you for taking the time to look at our new site.

Language
English
Language neutral
English
Spanish

FIGURE 12-24

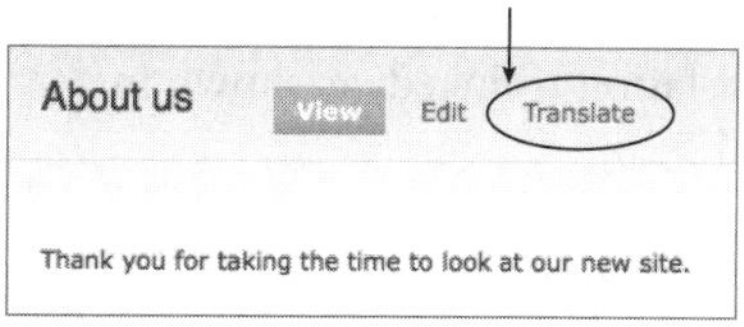

About us   View   Edit   Translate

Thank you for taking the time to look at our new site.

FIGURE 12-25

> **NOTE** *Use the Language Select module (*`http://drupal.org/project/language_select`*) to automatically select a language and/or force a language to be selected.*

4. Click the Translate tab on the newly created content, as shown in Figure 12-25.

> **NOTE** *Users must have the Translate Content permission in order to submit translations of existing content.*

5. On the Translate tab, click the **add translation** link on the far-right of the Spanish language row as shown in Figure 12-26.

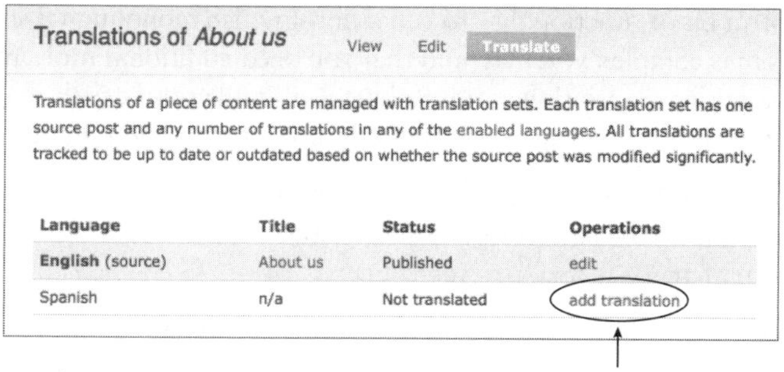

Translations of *About us*   View   Edit   Translate

Translations of a piece of content are managed with translation sets. Each translation set has one source post and any number of translations in any of the enabled languages. All translations are tracked to be up to date or outdated based on whether the source post was modified significantly.

Language	Title	Status	Operations
English (source)	About us	Published	edit
Spanish	n/a	Not translated	add translation

FIGURE 12-26

6. Type in the following information for the new page as shown in Figure 12-27, and then click Save:

➤ Title: `Acerca de nosotros`

➤ Body: `Gracias por tomar el tiempo de ver nuestro nuevo de sítio web!`

➤ Language: Spanish (this should not be editable)

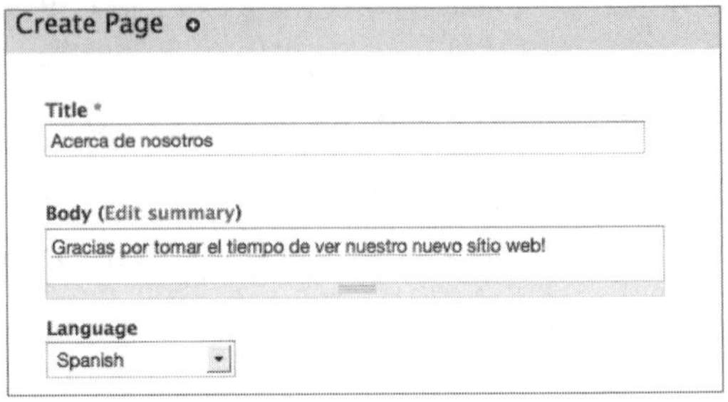

Create Page ⊙

Title *

Acerca de nosotros

Body (Edit summary)

Gracias por tomar el tiempo de ver nuestro nuevo sítio web!

Language

Spanish ▾

FIGURE 12-27

7. After you have saved the translation from the previous step, navigate back to the Translate tab to verify that the translation is linked, as shown in Figure 12-28.

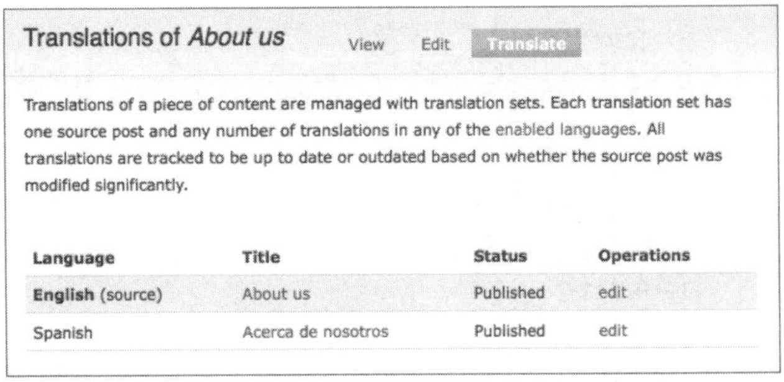

How It Works

The Content Translation module provides a method for you to create and link a translation of an existing node. Note that each translation of a node is an independent node and maintains its own settings, but they are linked to each other. This link is a critical element that allows users to easily navigate to different translations of a piece of content and to be automatically shown content in their requested language (with a fallback to the original language if no translation exists).

Figure 12-29 demonstrates how this automatic link works.

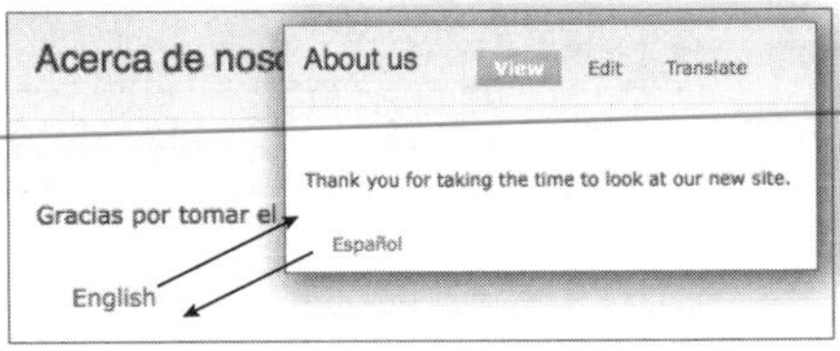

Translations of *About us*   View   Edit   Translate

Translations of a piece of content are managed with translation sets. Each translation set has one source post and any number of translations in any of the enabled languages. All translations are tracked to be up to date or outdated based on whether the source post was modified significantly.

Language	Title	Status	Operations
English (source)	About us	Published	edit
Spanish	Acerca de nosotros	Published	edit

FIGURE 12-28

Acerca de nos⊙ About us   View   Edit   Translate

Thank you for taking the time to look at our new site.

Gracias por tomar el⊿   Español

English

FIGURE 12-29

BEYOND THE BASICS

Drupal's core download provides quite a bit of functionality to run a non-English monolingual site and even a multilingual site. If your site is complex you may find that you need additional tools and functionality, particularly if you work with a translation team. Robust tools and reports such as those that show your site's overall translation status, are available with the Internationalization modules.

Internationalization, known as *i18n*, is a collection of modules that enhances the built-in translation functionality by adding new interfaces, new translation functionality, and robust reporting. You can download the i18n module from `http://drupal.org/project/i18n`.

There are numerous online resources for translating sites from or to nearly every language. The online handbook on Drupal.org is a great place to start if you are looking for specific translation features. This handbook is available at `http://drupal.org/node/133977`.

Finally, translation and localization in Drupal were made possible by people like you participating at http://localize.drupal.org and within Drupal forums, and contributing patches to Drupal's core. Connect with other site administrators and translators at http://groups.drupal.org/internationalization to learn the latest tips and tricks for creating robust multi-lingual sites.

SUMMARY

Drupal's community is a worldwide collage of language and culture backgrounds. These folks work together to build Drupal sites all over the world for audiences who speak nearly every language. Drupal 7 has a unique ability to translate not only its own interface, but also the interface of other modules you add over time. The built-in Locale module provides this interface translation. If you couple the Locale module with the contributed Localization module and visit http://localize.drupal.org, you'll be up and running with a fully translated website in no time while also participating in a worldwide community of users who speak your language.

Drupal is fully UTF-8 compliant, meaning that you can submit your content in any language without worrying that Drupal will mangle your content. Of course, you can also choose to turn on the Content Translation module, submit your content in multiple languages, and have Drupal manage the links between each of the translations. Lastly, don't forget to configure your language and the language negotiation methods so that Drupal can present the right language to your site visitors.

Adios, Au revoir, Auf Wiedersehen, 再见 さようなら!

EXERCISES

1. How does localization differ from translation?

2. What are the basic steps to translating your content?

3. What does i18n stand for?

Answers to the Exercises can be found in the Appendix.

► **WHAT YOU LEARNED IN THIS CHAPTER**

➤ Localizing refers to translating your site's interface. Use the Locale module.

➤ Translation refers to offering your content in more than one language. Use the Content Translation module.

➤ Drupal's interface consists of numerous pieces of translatable text known as *strings*. Strings are translated per language at Configuration ➪ Languages.

➤ Use `http://localize.drupal.org` to find the latest translation of Drupal and its contributed modules.

➤ Localization is a great way to finish your site's translation and contribute your translation back to the community, further enhancing Drupal's internationalization (`http://drupal.org/project/l10n`).

➤ Your site's language is changed based on the negotiation method(s) enabled at Configuration ➪ Languages ➪ Configure.

Theming

WHAT YOU WILL LEARN IN THIS CHAPTER:

➤ Theme configuration and settings

➤ Installing new themes

➤ Creating your own custom theme

➤ Adding or overriding CSS and JavaScript files

➤ Modifying Drupal's HTML structure with .tpl.php files

➤ The Theme developer module

➤ Sub-themes

➤ Template.php, template suggestions and function overrides

There comes a time in every web development project when you take a step back from your work and stare in awe at the functionality. It does everything that you, or your client, asked for and more. Your site has the power to connect people and/or convey information in a way that is completely unique. But your site has one major flaw. It looks just like every other Drupal site.

The common criticism of using a standardized web development platform is that it will look like every other site. With Drupal, nothing could be further from the truth.

Theming is the term used to describe the act of modifying a site's layout, color scheme and, possibly, its HTML structure. Drupal has been written in such a way that the core functionality and modules (the gears) of a site and its output are separated. Some have referred to Drupal's architecture as a Model-View-Controller (MVC), while others have said it is a Presentation-Abstraction-Control (PAC). Regardless of how it is described, what should be understood is that Drupal separates the handling of data from the presentation of data.

One way to visualize this separation is to think of a chocolate factory. On one end of the factory, you have those wonderful ingredients cacao beans, sugar, milk, and vanilla. On the other end, you have molds and wrappers. Drupal's core and contributed modules are like the machinery that takes the cacao beans and other ingredients and mixes them into a fine chocolate. As the chocolate makes it way down the factory line, it is eventually put into a mold, placed in a wrapper, and shipped to the customer. Drupal's theming process is the mold and wrapper. The theme is what changes how the customer sees the chocolate.

This chapter begins by exploring the front-end interface and then slowly peels away the layers of a theme to explore its inner workings.

At the end of this chapter you will be armed with the information to fully customize your own unique place on the web.

ADMINISTERING THEMES

Before you create your own custom theme take a few minutes to review the next several pages that explore how themes are installed, configured, and administered. These pages expand on the topics introduced in Chapter 5, "Administration — Blocks, Menus, and Themes."

Installing New Themes

A site can have an unlimited number of themes installed, enabled, and working at the same time. You may not have noticed but Drupal uses two themes in its default installation. When first installed Garland is your site's main theme and Seven is your administration theme, this is why you experience a flip in the look of your site when you are viewing your site's administration pages or creating or editing content. Contributed modules could also change your site's theme amongst all installed and enabled themes. For example, changing the theme can be based upon the content type being viewed, the page requested, a user's preference, or even the time of day.

A large and growing community of theme developers posts their themes, freely available under the GPL license, at `http://drupal.org/project/Themes`. When browsing for a new theme keep in mind that Drupal themes are written to a version of the Drupal core and are not backward- or forward-compatible. This means that if you are using Drupal 7, you will need a Drupal 7 theme — Drupal 5 and Drupal 6 themes will not work.

When you find a theme you like install it by placing its uncompressed folder within the Themes folder under your site's directory (for example: `/sites/example.com/themes`) or within `/sites/all/themes` to make the theme available to all sites in a multi-site setup. The Themes directory might not exist by default so if it doesn't just create it.

> **WARNING** *An in-depth guide to theme installation can be found at* `http://drupal.org/node/176045`.

TRY IT OUT | **Install a New Theme**

In this exercise you will install the Painted Drupal 7 theme to change your site's look and feel.

1. Download the Painted theme from `http://drupal.org/project/painted`.

2. Uncompress the files and place the `painted` folder within `sites/all/themes`. The result should look like Figure 13-1.

3. Within the theme installed log in as an Administrator and click Appearance in the top administration bar.

4. Enable the new Painted theme and set it as the default, as shown in Figure 13-2.

5. Navigate to your site's home page to see the changes.

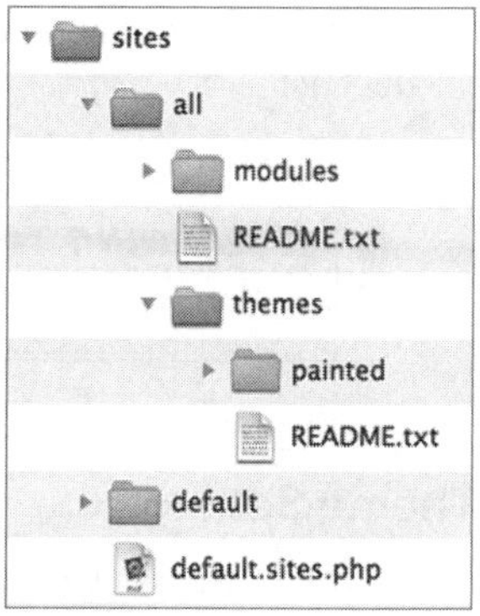

How It Works

A theme alters the look and feel of your site without changing its content or underlying structure. Drupal's design allows a single site to use multiple themes at the same time. When you first enabled the theme your site's appearance did not change; this is because you were within the administrative areas of your site and the administration theme (discussed below) was not modified.

FIGURE 13-1

FIGURE 13-2

Administration Theme

A different theme can be set for the administrative areas of your site. This is because site themes are often set to specific width and height proportions designed to best show off your images, videos, blog posts, or other content. Moreover it is very common to have blocks on the left or right side of a page displays menus, links to related content, or advertisements. The administration theme is designed to reduce the clutter and provide you more space to get your work done.

Set the administration theme alongside your site's theme within Appearance, as shown in Figure 13-3.

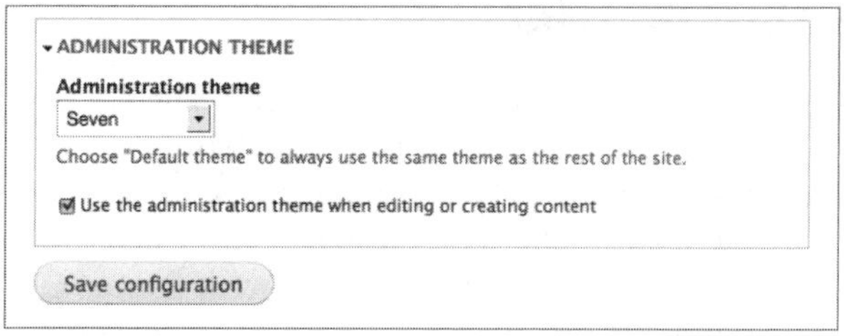

FIGURE 13-3

Configuring Your Themes

The central place of management for all themes is located at Administer ⇨ Appearance or by clicking Appearance in the top administration bar. Themes are enabled and configured in this section. This includes configuring custom theme settings except for the placement of blocks, which is done at Structure ⇨ Blocks.

All installed themes are listed on the theme administration page. As mentioned, a site may have multiple themes enabled to allow users to choose a personalized theme or to set different themes based upon a set of criteria. For example, the Theme Key module (`http://drupal.org/project/themekey`) sets a new theme based upon the taxonomy terms (tags) on a node, the node type, the node language, or even the URL.

> **WARNING** If your site displays unusual or erratic behavior switch back to a core theme, such as Garland, to eliminate the possibility of a broken theme.

Theme Settings

As you learned in Chapter 5, themes share a common collection of settings called the Global settings but can also maintain their own unique settings, as shown in Figure 13-4. Theme developers can pick and choose the global settings they would like to not implement, removing those that are implemented. Theme developers can also add new settings. An example of this is your newly installed Painted theme. Figure 13-5

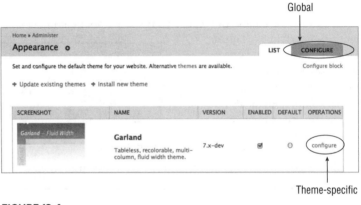

FIGURE 13-4

shows the color module integration, which, if the color module is enabled, allows to easily modify the colors of your theme with a nice color wheel.

CUSTOM THEMING

This is the part of the chapter that gets down to the meat of things. You are here to learn how to customize your site and make it uniquely you (or your client) on the web. Over the next several pages you are going to do exactly that. You'll walk through five exercises, which will transform the plain core Stark theme from that shown in Figure 13-6 to the Drupal and the Chocolate Factory theme shown in Figure 13-7. The exercises are designed to introduce you to theming in a high level overview with details introduced between each of the exercises and more in depth information reserved for after the first set of five exercises.

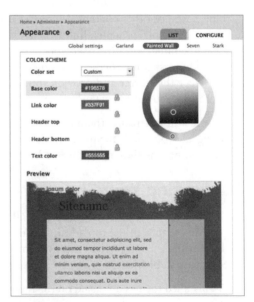

FIGURE 13-5

Theming can be very complex but if you take it slow and dip your toe in first you'll be swimming in no time.

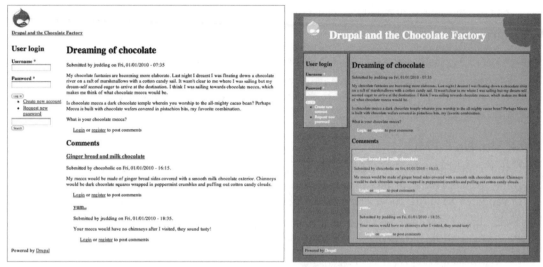

FIGURE 13-6   FIGURE 13-7

Exercise 1: Create the Foundation for Your New Theme

In this exercise you'll use the core Stark theme as the foundation for your new theme.

1. Copy the Stark folder from `/themes/stark` to `sites/all/themes/`.

2. Rename the newly copied Stark folder to `beginning_drupal`.

> **NOTE** When naming your theme be sure to make it unique within your system. Avoid the names of other themes or modules, using spaces or special characters, and numbers in the first part of the theme. You should also avoid the names of themes or modules already on http://drupal.org.

3. Within the newly renamed `beginning_drupal` folder rename `stark.info` to `beginning_drupal.info`. The result should look like that in Figure 13-8.

4. Open `beginning_drupal.info` and modify the name to read Beginning Drupal as shown in the following code then save the file.

Available for
download on
Wrox.com

```
name = Beginning Drupal
description = This theme demonstrates Drupal's default HTML
markup and CSS styles. To learn how to build your own theme and
override Drupal's default code, you should start reading the <a
href="http://drupal.org/theme-guide">Theming Guide</a>.
package = Core
version = VERSION
core = 7.x
```

FIGURE 13-8

```
engine = phptemplate
stylesheets[all][] = layout.css
```

code snippet Chapter 13 beginning_drupal theme

5. Enable your new theme within Appearance.

How It Works

The Stark core theme is a basic stripped down Drupal theme containing only the bits necessary to create a basic structure. It makes a great starting point for your theme as it contains only a small amount of understandable CSS that allows you to see how a theme is built from the ground up.

Look Ma, No HTML!

If you're an experienced web developer you may have searched the theme looking for HTML only to come up empty handed. This is because Drupal's core and contributed modules outputs a strong set of validated XHTML code. Many themes, including stark, can simply use CSS to modify the look of the site.

You may recall the following line from the `beginning_drupal.info` file:

```
stylesheets[all][] = layout.css
```

Using this line the theme is able to add its own custom CSS file(s) to the final HTML output. In the next exercise you'll make and add your own custom CSS file to change the color scheme and begin the major transformation of the site.

TRY IT OUT   **Exercise 2: Add a Custom CSS File to Your Theme**

In this exercise you'll add a custom CSS file to your theme that will modify the color scheme of the site.

1. Within the `beginning_drupal` theme folder create a new file entitled `style.css`.

2. Open `beginning_drupal.info` and underneath the line `stylesheets[all][] = layout.css` add the following line: `stylesheets[all][] = style.css`.

3. Add the following lines to the newly created `style.css` file:

```css
/* Set the background color to a Chocolate brown */
body{
  background: #3b2813;
  height: 100%;
}

/* Color the sections differently than the background to differentiate them */
.section{
  background: #6b3800;
  margin: 5px;
  padding: 10px;
  border: 2px solid #000;
}


/* set the width of the main content area */
```

```
#page{
  width: 960px;
  margin: 20px auto;
}

/* Add the bite image to and set the height of the top header */
#header .section{
  background: url(images/bite.gif) right top no-repeat #6b3800;
  height: 120px;
  border: none;
}
#logo {
  display: inline;
  float: left;
}
#site-name{
  padding: 40px 0 0 100px;
  font-size: 45px;
  margin: 0;
}

/* Change the color of the site's links */
a:link, a:visited{
  color: #fffbe8;
  text-decoration: none;
}
a:hover{
  text-decoration: underline;
}

/* Color the comments differently than the postings to differentiate them */
.comment{
  background: #704928;
  padding: 10px;
  margin-bottom: 10px;
  border: 2px solid #000;
}
```

code snippet Chapter 13 beginning_drupal theme

NOTE *This CSS uses a background image on the header to create the bite mark; it can be downloaded from the book's site.*

4. Rebuild your theme registry by visiting Appearance and clicking the Save configuration button at the bottom of the page.

How It Works

Each theme's `.info` file tells Drupal the CSS files that should be included in the final HTML output created by Drupal. The CSS file you added in this exercise uses Drupal's default CSS IDs and classes to change the color scheme and provide minor alignments that create the chocolate theme shown in Figure 13-8.

After completing the previous exercises your site should look like that shown in Figure 13-8, this major transformation happened with only a few lines of CSS. The exercise should underscore that much of a site's main building blocks can be achieved with only CSS. In the next exercise you'll move beyond pure CSS to explore those changes that require a change of the site's HTML structure. In the third exercise you'll move the submitted by information from the top of the node to the bottom as demonstrated in Figure 13-9.

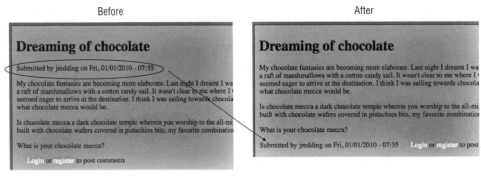

FIGURE 13-9

Before you do this you should review template files.

Template Files

Occasionally you will run into a style design that cannot be implemented with the HTML provided by Drupal's core or contributed modules. In these cases you can override the default HTML and provide your own. Even better, you don't have to provide the entire HTML, you can simply provide the pieces you want to change. As mentioned, Drupal's core and contributed modules provide HTML that, when combined, creates the final rendered page.

A module that generates output will utilize either a template file or a theme function to send their output up to the theme layer (i.e., your theme). The pieces are then assembled into a final rendered page. Consider the example shown in Figure 13-10.

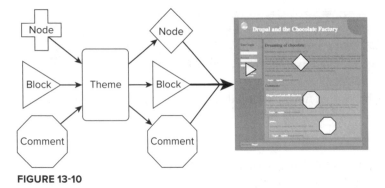

FIGURE 13-10

The node plus sign, block triangle, and comment octagon represent HTML template files used by the node, block, and comment modules respectively. You can see that these are passed into the theme and that the theme lets the comment octagon and block triangle pass without modification. The node plus sign, however, was overridden and turned into a diamond. The final rendered page sent to your site visitors used one of the block triangles to theme the user login block, two of the comment octagons to theme two comments, and one node diamond to theme a node.

Of course this is an oversimplification of the process but it should help to explain that your theme could override each individual piece of the output.

Learning How to Override

The next question to answer is how to do this override, which is to say how do you change the node plus sign into a diamond? To answer this question you should turn to the Theme Developer module, a contributed module that is in every themer's toolkit. Download the Theme developer module as part of the Devel module package available at `http://drupal.org/project/devel`.

After downloading, installing and enabling the Theme developer module set the Development block to appear in your left sidebar, as shown in Figure 13-11. With the Development block shown you can click the Enable Theme developer link exposing the Themer info box, shown in upper right corner of Figure 13-11.

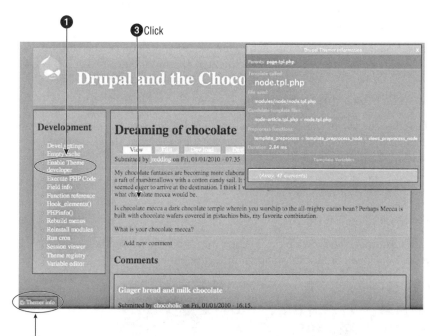

FIGURE 13-11

Taking a look at Figure 13-11 you can see that in step 3 when you clicked on the body of a node the theme developer box showed the exact template file used to theme the output. Take a look at Figure 13-12, the blown up version of the themer info box shown in Figure 13-11.

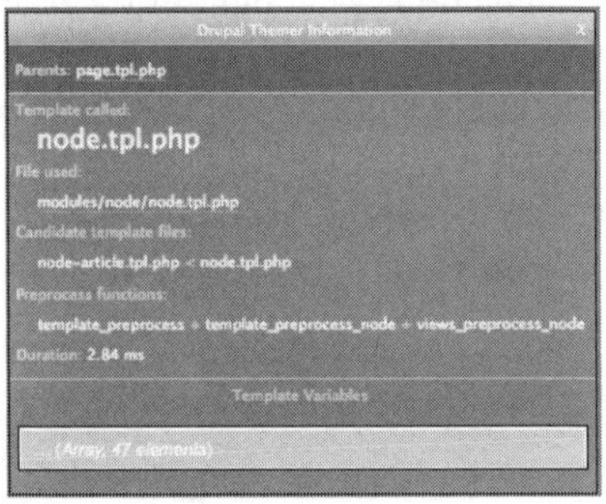

Note that the Template called: is set to node.tpl.php. This is telling you that the node plus sign is a file called `node.tpl.php` and that the file currently being used is at `/modules/node/node.tpl.php` is being used to theme the output. These two lines of information tell you everything you need to know to override this bit of HTML output. The interpretation is roughly, copy the template at `/modules/node/node.tpl.php` to your theme's folder and modify it to suit your needs.

FIGURE 13-12

The Theme Registry

Before you get too far you need to know about Drupal's theme registry. Whenever a new module or theme is enabled Drupal searches it for every themeable element. It then stores a reference to these elements in its registry and refers to its registry whenever it builds a new page. This increases the performance of your site and makes it easy to breakdown how a page was created. Whenever you add a new override, such as a template file, you will need to update the Theme registry. This is a simple process that is done by visiting the Appearance page and clicking the Save configuration button.

In the following exercise you'll add a node override to your `beginning_drupal` theme to move the Submitted by byline from above the node to directly below it as shown in Figure 13-9.

TRY IT OUT **Exercise 3: Move the Byline from Above Each Node to Below It**

In this exercise you will explore the use of the Theme developer module to discover overrideable elements such as node.tpl.php. You will then move the `submitted by` byline from above the node to directly below it, as demonstrated in Figure 13-9.

1. Download, install, and enable the Devel and Theme developer module from `http://drupal.org/project/devel`.

2. Set the Development block to the left sidebar.

3. Navigate to your site's frontpage and enable the Themer info box by clicking the `Enable Theme developer` link in the Development block, as shown in Figure 13-13.

FIGURE 13-13

4. In the lower left corner check the box to display the Themer info box then click anywhere on your frontpage node, you should see a box in the upper right corner that looks similar to Figure 13-14.

5. Using the information from the Themer info box copy the file `/modules/node/node.tpl.php` to your theme's folder at `sites/all/themes/beginning_drupal/node.tpl.php`.

FIGURE 13-14

6. Rebuild the Theme registry to inform Drupal of the `node.tpl.php` override in your theme. Navigate to Appearance then click `Save configuration` at the bottom of the page. (Alternatively you can use the `Empty cache` link in the Development block).

7. Open `sites/all/themes/beginning_drupal/node.tpl.php` in your favorite text editor then find the following lines (starting at line 88):

Available for download on Wrox.com

```php
<?php if ($display_submitted): ?>
  <span class="submitted">
    <?php
      print t('Submitted by !username on !datetime',
      array('!username' => $name, '!datetime' => $date));
    ?>
  </span>
<?php endif; ?>
```

code snippet Chapter 13 beginning_druapl theme

Move these lines down to line 112 just above the following lines:

Available for download on Wrox.com

```php
<?php print render($content['links']); ?>
<?php print render($content['comments']); ?>
```

code snippet Chapter 13 beginning_druapl theme

8. Save the file then refresh your frontpage.

How It Works

Each module you enable will use its own custom template to send its output to your theme resulting in tens if not hundreds of small template files used to generate a single Page. The Theme developer module can quickly pinpoint the right template file for you. Once you have copied a template file you need to inform Drupal of what was overridden by forcing Drupal to update its Theme registry (a cache of all template overrides). You did this by clicking Save configuration within Appearance.

Once Drupal is aware of your override you can modify the template file(s) without having to update the theme registry.

The last exercise might have been a bit lengthy and tedious but once you understand the override process it is quite easy. The basic steps are:

1. Determine the template file to override by using the Theme developer module.

2. Copy the template file to your theme's folder.

3. Update Drupal's Theme registry by navigating to Appearance and clicking Save configuration.

It really is as simple as that. Later in this chapter you'll explore these template files more in depth. Right now add a bit of consistency in your theme by moving the byline information in your comments from the top of the comment to the bottom.

TRY IT OUT | **Exercise 4: Move Comment Byline Information**

In this exercise you'll move the comment byline from the top of the comment to the bottom.

1. Use the Theme developer module to find the template file used to theme comments.

2. Copy `modules/comment/comment.tpl.php` to `sites/all/themes/beginning_drupal/comment.tpl.php`.

3. Rebuild the Theme registry to inform Drupal of the `comment.tpl.php` override in your theme. Navigate to Appearance, then click `Save configuration` at the bottom of the page. Alternatively, you can use the `Empty cache` link in the Development block.

4. Open `comment.tpl.php` and find the lines that are similar to the `submitted` by lines you moved in the previous exercise; they start at line 66:

Available for download on Wrox.com

```
<div class="submitted">
  <?php
  print t('Submitted by !username on !datetime.',
    array('!username' => $author, '!datetime' => $created));
?>
</div>
```

code snippet Chapter 13 beginning_drupal theme

Move these down to line 86 just above:

Available for download on Wrox.com

```
<?php print render($content['links']) ?>
```

code snippet Chapter 13 beginning_drupal theme

How It Works

Similar to the `node.tpl.php` used to theme nodes, `comment.tpl.php` is used to theme comments. After moving the template override to your theme you needed to update the theme registry to inform Drupal of your override. Once the registry has been updated and your template file took over you were free to modify the comment however you wanted.

Theme Functions

In the last two exercises you learned how to use the Theme developer module to discover what templates you can override to customize your page. If you're like most people you also clicked on other areas on the page and in doing so encountered a Themer info box that did not include a template; instead, it looked similar to Figure 13-15.

Notice that near the top the label reads `Function called:` instead of `Template called:` as has been the case in the

FIGURE 13-15

last two exercises. When a module developer is sending data to the user they can choose one of two methods, a template file or a theme function. Both methods can create the same output and vary only in their approach. As you have seen, template files are primarily HTML with a little bit of PHP to display the variables (for example: `<?php print render($content);?>`). Theme functions are the opposite, consisting of primarily PHP and maybe a little bit of HTML.

Drupal contains these two methods to allow developers to choose the one that works best for their application. To be more specific, a theme function typically contains logic that modifies the output based upon a set of criteria. Often the output of a theme function is added to one or more template files. For example, the `theme_username` function shown below will create a link out of a user's name if the `$variables['link_path']` is set, otherwise the user's name will not be linked. This username is then used within `comment.tpl.php` and `node.tpl.php` as $name, which you worked with in the last two exercises.

```php
<?php
function theme_username($variables) {
  if (isset($variables['link_path'])) {
    // We have a link path, so we should generate a link using l().
    // Additional classes may be added as array elements like
    // $variables['link_options']['attributes']['class'][] = 'myclass';
    $output = l($variables['name'] . $variables['extra'], $variables['link_path'],
$variables['link_options']);
  }
  else {
    // Modules may have added important attributes so they must be included
    // in the output. Additional classes may be added as array elements like
    // $variables['attributes_array']['class'][] = 'myclass';
    $output = '<span' . drupal_attributes($variables['attributes_array']) . '>' .
$variables['name'] . $variables['extra'] . '</span>';
  }
  return $output;
}
?>
```

code snippet Chapter 13 beginning_drupal theme

How to Override Theme Functions

You learned that you override a template by placing a template of the same name in your theme's folder. To override a theme function you do the same thing by placing a new function within your theme. These functions are placed within the theme's `template.php` file and named similarly but with the front `theme_` replaced with your theme's name. Table 13-1 shows a few examples:

TABLE 13-1

THEME FUNCTION	YOUR THEME'S OVERRIDE
theme_date	beginning_drupal_date
theme_username	beginning_drupal_username
theme_links	beginning_drupal_links

Template.php

A manually created file, a theme's template.php file contains theme function overrides and preprocess functions. For example, to override `theme_username` your `beginning_drupal` theme's `template.php` would look like:

```php
<?php
function beginning_drupal_username($variables) {
  if (isset($variables['link_path'])) {
    // We have a link path, so we should generate a link using l().
    // Additional classes may be added as array elements like
    // $variables['link_options']['attributes']['class'][] = 'myclass';
    $output = l($variables['name'] . $variables['extra'], $variables['link_path'],
    $variables['link_options']);
  }
  else {
    // Modules may have added important attributes so they must be included
    // in the output. Additional classes may be added as array elements like
    // $variables['attributes_array']['class'][] = 'myclass';
    $output = '<span' . drupal_attributes($variables['attributes_array']) . '>' .
    $variables['name'] . $variables['extra'] . '</span>';
  }
  return $output;
}
?>
```

code snippet Chapter 13 beginning_drupal theme

Preprocess Functions

Before you jump into overriding theme functions, take a second to learn about the power of a preprocess function; it might just save you hours of work. Within nearly every template and theme function are variables that contain the information you want to display. In both the `node.tpl.php` and `comment.tpl.php` file you moved the `submitted by` variable from the top to the bottom of the template. Variables are used in templates like the following:

```php
<?php print render($content['links']); ?>
```

which is displaying the `$content['links']` variable

```php
<?php
  print t('Submitted by !username on
!datetime',
    array('!username' => $name, '!datetime' =>
$date));
?>
```

which contain the variables `$name` and `$date`.

The variables are passed from the modules that create them into theme functions and template files. A preprocess function intercepts these variables before they are used in the function or template file, allowing you to add, remove, or modify their values before they are used, as demonstrated in Figure 13-16.

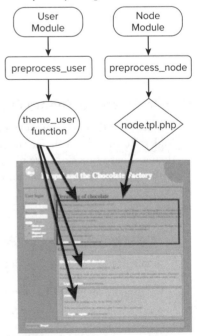

FIGURE 13-16

Preprocess functions are named after the template or theme function they are preprocessing and are preceded by the theme's name. Table 13-2 displays a few examples:

TABLE 13-2

TEMPLATE OR THEME FUNCTION	YOUR THEME'S PREPROCESS FUNCTION
node.tpl.php	beginning_drupal_preprocess_node
comment.tpl.php	beginning_drupal_preprocess_comment
theme_user_signature	beginning_drupal_preprocess_user_signature
theme_username	Beginning_drupal_preprocess_username

Using the word `phptemplate` instead of `beginning_drupal` (theme name) would cause the function to work for all enabled themes including subthemes, discussed later in this chapter.

If this is a bit confusing follow along in the next exercise, which implements a preprocess function within your `beginning_drupal` theme. The exercise modifies Drupal's default behavior of linking all username's to their profile page, instead the username will be simply displayed without a link. The exercise walks you through every step beginning with discovering the theme function using the Theme developer module.

TRY IT OUT   **Exercise 5: Add Template.php and a Preprocess Function**

In this exercise you will modify the usernames on your site so that they do not link to the user's profile page.

1. Log into your site as an administrator and navigate to the frontpage node.

2. Enable the Theme developer and check the box in the lower left corner to display the Themer info box.

3. Click the username within the node's byline as shown in Figure 13-17.

4. The Themer info box should look similar to Figure 13-18 telling you that `theme_user-name` was used to create this element.

FIGURE 13-17 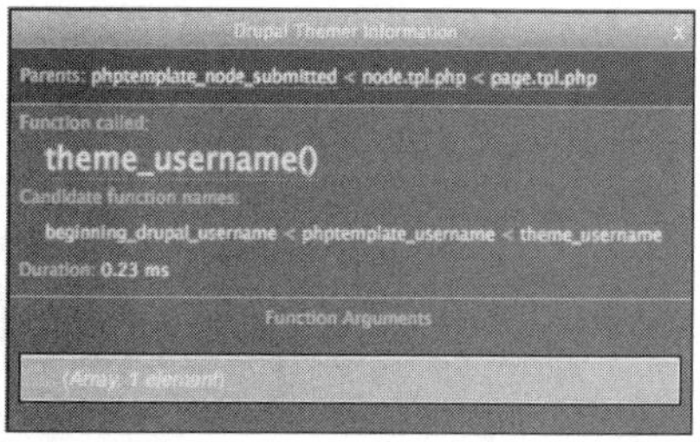   **FIGURE 13-18**

5. Click on the `theme_username` function name, this will link you directly to `http://api.drupal.org`, page dedicated to this function, shown in Figure 13-19.

> ✎ **NOTE** `http://api.drupal.org` *only displays functions included with Drupal's core. You can use the API module available at* `http://drupal.org/project/api` *to display every function on your custom site built including contributed and custom modules.*

6. At the bottom of the API page (Figure 13-19) is the `theme_username` function that was used to create the output shown on your page, shown in Figure 13-20.

Looking at the code, the second and third lines of the function line read:

```
if (isset($variables['link_path'])) {
  //We have a link path, so we should generate a link using l().
```

In plain English: if there is a path, make the username a link. The only thing you need to do is modify the variable so that `$variables['link_path']` is empty (i.e. not set). You can do this with a preprocess function.

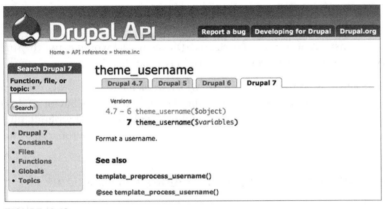

FIGURE 13-19

```php
<?php
function theme_username($variables) {
  if (isset($variables['link_path'])) {
    // We have a link path, so we should generate a link using l().
    // Additional classes may be added as array elements like
    // $variables['link_options']['attributes']['class'][] = 'myclass';
    $output = l($variables['name'] . $variables['extra'], $variables['link_path'], $variables['link_options']);
  }
  else {
    // Modules may have added important attributes so they must be included
    // in the output. Additional classes may be added as array elements like
    // $variables['attributes_array']['class'][] = 'myclass';
    $output = '<span' . drupal_attributes($variables['attributes_array']) . '>' . $variables['name'] . $variables['extra'] . '</span>';
  }
  return $output;
}
?>
```

Code

includes/theme.inc, line 2061

Login or register to post comments

FIGURE 13-20

7. Within the `beginning_drupal` theme folder create a blank file named `template.php`.

8. Type the following into the newly created `template.php` file, then save the file.

```php
<?php
/**
 * Override or insert variables into the username function
 */
function beginning_drupal_preprocess_username(&$variables) {
  unset($variables['link_path']);
}
```

code snippet Chapter 13 beginning_drupal theme

9. Rebuild your theme registry to see the results.

How It Works

A preprocess function runs before a theme function or template file to add, modify, or remove variables before they are used within the function or template file. In the previous exercise you discovered that the `theme_username` function was checking if `$variables['link_path']` was set. To prevent the link from being printed you used a preprocess function to unset `$variables['link_path']`, thus causing the check to fail and preventing the link from being used. When naming the function in `template.php` you only needed to adhere to Drupal's naming convention `themename_prepro-cess_template-or-function-name`, `beginning_drupal_preprocess_user-name`, see Figure 13-21.

FIGURE 13-21

Readers with a bit of PHP experience might have discovered that the same could have been achieved by overriding the `theme_username` function within your `template.php` file instead of using a preprocess function. The following code does exactly this.

```php
<?php
function beginning_drupal_username($variables) {
  $output = '<span' . drupal_attributes($variables['attributes_array']) . '>' .
  $variables['name'] . $variables['extra'] . '</span>';
  return $output;
}
```

In Drupal you will encounter several methods to achieve the same outcome. You'll have to make a decision, which of the methods works best in your environment and is sustainable. Reading the more advanced theming section of this chapter may help you to better understand which of the methods is right for you.

Reviewing the Last Five Exercises

In the last five exercises you reviewed at a high level almost every aspect of theming. You discovered that a page in Drupal is a collaborative effort of all your installed modules, each of them using theme functions and template files to output their data to the theme layer. The theme layer then combines your theme and compares it to the theme registry, checking for overrides. All of these pieces are then rendered into the final page.

Theming, like Drupal, is a complex beast and these exercises have only touched the surface. In the remaining pages of this chapter you'll dig deeper into theming to jump you from the practicing judo student to a stealthy Drupal ninja silently throwing out CSS to knock down any theming component.

Start your journey deeper into the heart with sub-themes.

SUB-THEMES

Imagine that you've just finished your perfect theme. All the elements are in the right positions and it even, miraculously, works in IE6. Your client then comes to you and requests that they would like the same theme except with a color scheme for Christmas. They would also like another theme for New Year's Day, Earth Day, Independence Day, and International Talk-Like-a-Pirate Day including the appropriate eye-patch logo and "Argh, matey" slogan. In hearing all of these requests, you notice a similar thread — the theme is nearly identical, so it may take only a few tweaks to a style sheet and possibly a `.tpl.php` file.

At this point, you have two choices. You could copy and paste the original theme and perform all of these changes. This would leave you with numerous copies of the same data, and if there were ever a bug in the original theme (never happens, right?), you would have to update all copies of your theme. Or, you could create multiple *sub-themes*.

A sub-theme is a child of a parent theme but with its own unique qualities. A sub-theme inherits all style sheets, `.tpl` files, and function overrides from its *base theme*, but it has the ability to override any part of that base theme. If you update the base theme, the sub-theme is automatically updated. Creating a sub-theme is as simple as this:

1. Create a new theme in the same manner as you did back in the first Exercise.

Within the `.info` file, set the variable *base theme* to the *internal* name of the parent theme. For example:

```
base theme = beginning_drupal
```

Follow along in the next exercise to create a White Chocolate sub-theme that is based on the `beginning_drupal` (Chocolate) theme you created in this chapter. The new sub-theme will look identical to the original except that the header will reflect a white chocolate bar instead of a milk chocolate bar.

TRY IT OUT   Create a New Sub Theme

In this exercise you will create a new sub theme that inherits all of the theme elements from the parent theme but modifies a few elements.

1. Within `sites/all/themes` create a new folder entitled `white_chocolate`.

2. Create the `white_chocolate.info` file with the following text:

```
name = White Chocolate
description = A little twist on the usual chocolate
package = Core
version = VERSION
core = 7.x
```

```
engine = phptemplate
base theme = beginning_drupal
stylesheets[all][] = white_chocolate.css
```

code snippet Chapter 13 white chocolate theme

3. Create a `white_chocolate.css` file with the following text:

Available for download on Wrox.com

```
#header .section{
  background: #fffbe8;
}

#site-name a:link, #site-name a:visited{
  color: #3b2813;
}
```

code snippet Chapter 13 white chocolate theme

4. Verify that your theme and theme's folder looks similar to Figure 13-22.

5. Enable your new theme.

How It Works

A `sub-theme` inherits nearly all of the theme elements from the `base theme` named within the sub-theme's .info file, added in Step 2. As you saw, the base theme does not have to be modified or coded any differently to allow for sub-theming. If you were to modify the `beginning_drupal` theme, its changes would automatically be inherited by the sub theme.

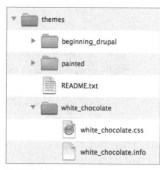

FIGURE 13-22

As mentioned sub-themes inherit nearly everything from the base theme. Table 13-3 breaks down what is and what is not inherited:

TABLE 13-3

INHERITED	NOT INHERITED
Style sheets	
Javascript files	
Template files (*.tpl.php)	
All theme function overrides, preprocess functions, and other functions in the base theme's template.php	Default logo
	Custom theme regions
	Custom theme settings

Zen Base Theme

In the last exercise you used a sub-theme to make a minor change to a new theme that you built from the ground up. Sub-themes built from a solid foundation can dramatically speed up your theme development by predefining the key aspect of a theme leaving you time to focus on the creative and design parts of a theme. In short a solid foundation can leave you more time to bring your theme to nice polished shine. Enter Zen.

Zen is a standards-compliant base theme built and supported by a worldwide team of highly talented web designers. This base theme is designed to provide highly flexible yet semantically correct XHTML that can be stylized purely through CSS. Using Zen allows you to focus on your design and not on the underlying structure that your visitors don't see.

The Zen theme has mounds of great documentation all freely available on Drupal.org it would not make sense to duplicate that information in a book. Zen and the Zen community can be found at `http://drupal.org/project/zen`.

> **NOTE** The Zen Drupal theme pays homage to the amazing CSS Zen Garden that can be found at `http://www.csszengarden.com`. If you're new to HTML and CSS, take a few minutes to visit this site to see how effective CSS can be.

.INFO FILE

As you have experienced, the `.info` file is a very important piece of a theme telling Drupal the theme's name, version, core compatibility, and even what CSS files are being used. It pays to understand this file as it can be pretty powerful.

As you've experienced, the bare minimum required for a theme is:

```
name = Beginning Drupal
description = A simple theme for a complex website
version = 1
engine = phptemplate
core = 7.x
```

If the theme was downloaded from `http://drupal.org`, the `version` and `core` would be automatically added. If you are creating your own theme you need to include these two items.

Removing Theme Settings

If your theme does not implement or does not allow a toggling of the settings at Appearance ⇨ Configure, shown in Figure 13-23, you can remove them from the configuration settings by only naming the settings you do implement.

The default set of settings is similar to the following:

```
features[] = logo
features[] = name
features[] = slogan
features[] = node_user_picture
```

```
features[] = comment_user_picture
features[] = favicon
features[] = main_menu
features[] = secondary_menu
```

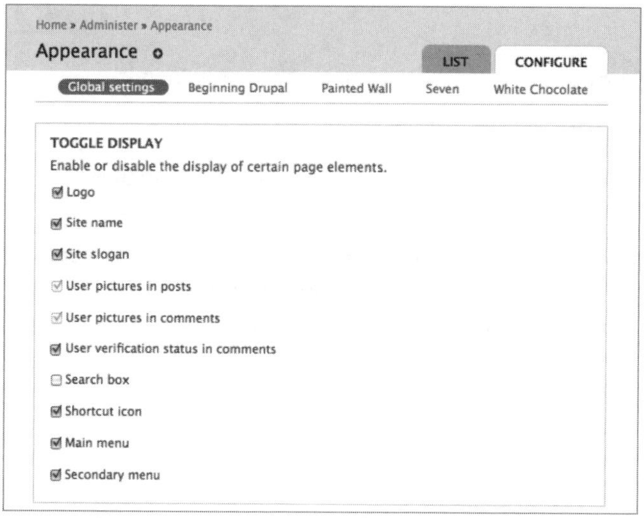

FIGURE 13-23

If your theme only implemented the menus then your .info file would include only:

```
features[] = main_menu
features[] = secondary_menu
```

If you want to remove all settings, simply set this to a blank value:

```
features[] = ""
```

Style Sheets

The stylesheets property provides two important functions. The first is the ability to specify different style sheets for different W3C media types such as a web browser, handheld device, or a printer. Consider the following example:

```
stylesheets[all] = style.css
stylesheets[handheld] = handheld.css
stylesheets[print] = print.css
```

This would render the following output:

```
<link type="text/css" rel="stylesheet" media="all" href="/sites/all/yourtheme/style.css"
/>
<link type="text/css" rel="stylesheet" media="handheld" href="/sites/all/yourtheme/
handheld.css" />
<link type="text/css" rel="stylesheet" media="print" href="/sites/all/yourtheme/print.
css" />
```

The appropriate devices would choose the necessary CSS file.

The second function it provides is to allow the theme to override core or contributed modules' stylesheets. You do this by simply copying the style sheet you want to override into the theme folder and then updating the style sheet property to tell Drupal the new location. Follow along in the next exercise to learn how to do this.

TRY IT OUT   **Overriding a Style Sheet**

Follow these steps to override the suggested node style sheet `node.css`:

1. Ensure that CSS aggregation is turned off at Configuration and modules ⇨ Performance ⇨ Bandwidth Optimization then uncheck Aggregate and compress CSS files into one file.

2. Identify the style sheet you want to override by viewing the source of the website. In this case, you're overriding `node.css`. The source of your site will have a line that reads:

   ```
   <link type="text/css" rel="stylesheet" media="all" href="/modules/node/node.css" />
   ```

3. Copy the `node.css` file from `/modules/node/node.css` to your theme's directory (ex. `/sites/all/themes/beginning_drupal`).

4. Add the following line to the theme's `.info` file:

   ```
   stylesheets[all][] = node.css
   ```

   Note that you use only the filename without the path. You also remove anything that comes after `.css`. For example: `/modules/node/node.css?q` is simply `node.css`.

5. Rebuild the theme registry.

6. Refresh the HTML site. The source should now read as follows:

   ```
   <link type="text/css" rel="stylesheet" media="all" href="/sites/all/themes/beginning_
   drupal/node.css" />
   ```

How It Works

When a new module is enabled Drupal parses the .info file looking for all of its stylesheets. If a stylesheet is identically named as one provided by a core or contributed module Drupal will use the theme's stylesheet thus overriding the original. This allows a theme to have ultimate control over the site's output.

JavaScript

Similarly to style sheets, additional JavaScript/jQuery files can be added via the `.info` file. Use `scripts[] = script.js` to add new files. For example:

```
scripts[] = scripts/user_tweaks.js
scripts[] = scripts/dragdrop.js
scripts[] = scripts/photo_gallery.js
```

Regions

A region is a location on a page wherein blocks may be placed. You interact with regions on the blocks administration page at Structure ⇨ Blocks, as shown in Figure 13-24.

Notice that at the top of the block administration is a listing of all of the enable themes on your site. Each theme controls what regions are used and their placement on the site. Drupal provides each theme with several default regions including: First Sidebar, Second Sidebar, Content, header, Footer, Highlighted content, Help, Dashboard main, Dashboard sidebar. The theme can choose to implement these regions or set its own custom set.

FIGURE 13-24

Creating Custom Regions

The `page.tpl.php` file defines exactly where the output of a region will appear. Regions can be printed on the left side, right side, within a footer or header, or wherever you'd like. Regions can be on all pages or only on selected pages — for example, you can have regions that display only on the frontpage. There are two steps to creating custom regions.

Add the custom region to your theme's `.info` file.

Update page.tpl.php to print the new theme.

For example, to implement a new Advertisements region:

Update the .info file with the following:

```
regions['help'] = Help
regions['highlight'] = Highlight
regions['content'] = Content
regions['sidebar_first'] = Left sidebar
regions['sidebar_second'] = Right sidebar
regions['header'] = Header
regions['footer'] = Footer
regions['ads'] = Advertisements
```

Note that once you define your own regions in your theme, Drupal stops using the default set. If you want to add a region to the default set you have to re-implement the default set in your theme, as shown above.

Add the new region to your `page.tpl.php`. If you don't have a `page.tpl.php` file in your theme copy the file from `modules/system/page.tpl.php` to your theme. The following code would be used:

```php
<?php if ($page['ads']): ?>
  <div id="advertisements" class="ads"><div class="section">
    <?php print render($page['ads']); ?>
  </div></div> <!- /.section, /#ads ->
<?php endif; ?>
```

This code checks to make sure that the region has a block set to it before adding in the `<div>` tags, which is a proper way of doing it. You could skip straight to the chase with only this bit of code:

```php
<?php print render($page['advertisements']); ?>
```

TEMPLATE FILES (.TPL.PHP)

In earlier exercises you explored template files at 5,000 feet; here you'll zoom in and dig a bit deeper. Drupal's core download includes over 40 template files that are as expansive as `page.tpl.php` and as minute as `search-block-form.tpl.php`, which displays the Search text box and button.

This section reviews the most common template files, but first, here are two new terms that you need to understand:

➤ **Core template** — A core template describes what is being themed, such as a page, node, or comment, which defines the name of the template file. For example: `page.tpl.php`, `node.tpl.php`, or `comment.tpl.php`.

➤ **Template Suggestion** — A template suggestion is based on the core template but offers an alternative template file. Suggestions are identical to the core template containing the same variables, but they are used in alternative situations. For example, `node.tpl.php` is used for all nodes unless `node-blog.tpl.php` is present, which will be used for all blog type nodes. Similarly, `page-front.tpl.php` is used for the same purpose as `page.tpl.php` except that it is only used for the frontpage.

Now with an understanding of these terms, take a look at some of Drupal's core and commonly used template files.

page.tpl.php

This is the mother of all templates, because without it, no other template's output is visible. Does this mean that a theme must have a `page.tpl.php` file? No. Remember that Drupal will provide a default template if your theme does not provide an override. `page.tpl.php` displays the cumulated output of all other template files.

Template suggestions include:

➤ `page-front.tpl.php` — This template can be used to theme the frontpage of your site differently than the rest of your site.

➤ `page-path.tpl.php` — `path` is the internal URL to the content and can be multiple levels deep. For example, given the URL `http://localhost/user/register`, Drupal will search for the following template files and use the first one found:

   ➤ `page-user-register.tpl.php`

   ➤ `page-user.tpl.php`

   ➤ `page.tpl.php`

Note that the / in the URL is replaced by - in the template name, and the *internal* URL is used, which may differ from the URL path.

For SEO (Search Engine Optimization) reasons, it is common for a node to be given a path such as `http://localhost/blog/my-first-blog-entry` although the internal URL is something like `http://localhost/node/1`. You can discover the internal URL by simply editing the node and then looking at the browser's address bar.

node.tpl.php

The output of a node is sent to a `node.tpl.php` for processing before it is sent upstream for final rendering to `page.tpl.php`. This template contains only a small amount of HTML necessary to theme a node. Every node uses this template exactly once. If three nodes are displayed on a page, the template is used three times. The accumulated output of the three template file renderings is sent to `page.tpl.php` within the `$content` variable.

Template suggestions include:

➤ `node-id.tpl.php`: Used to theme a specific node; for example: `node-3.tpl.php`.

➤ `node-type.tpl.php`: `type` is the *machine-readable* name of the node. For example, `node-article.tpl.php` or `node-blog.tpl.php`.

comment.tpl.php

Each comment is passed through `comment.tpl.php`.

Template suggestions include:

➤ `comment-type.tpl.php`: Used to theme a comment based on the node type it was responded to. Here are a couple of examples:

   ➤ `comment-article.tpl.php`

   ➤ `comment-blog.tpl.php`

block.tpl.php

All blocks displayed are wrapped with HTML via this template.

Template suggestions include:

➤ `block-modulename-blockname.tpl.php`: A module may provide several blocks, each identified by an *internal* name. You can discover the internal name by using the Theme developer module. An example of a themed block filename is:

   `block-user-online.tpl.php`

➤ `block-modulename.tpl.php`: To theme all blocks from a specific module, use only the module's name as the suggestion. For example:

   `block-user.tpl.php`

➤ `block-region.tpl.php`: Different regions may have different constraints of style patterns. For example:

`block-header.tpl.php`

or

`block-footer.tpl.php`

Template Suggestions

The last few pages highlighted some of the most commonly used template suggestions but there are quite a number more suggestions available. In the next section on preprocess function you'll also discover that you can create more template suggestions.

How do you know what templates suggestions are available?

The Theme developer module tells you all candidate templates (i.e., template suggestions) that could have been used to theme a specific area on your site, as shown in Figure 13-25.

FIGURE 13-25

PREPROCESS FUNCTIONS

Before completing your `beginning_drupal` theme you reviewed `template.php` and preprocess functions. You saw that a preprocess function sits in front of a theme function or template file in order to add, remove, or modify the variables passed to the function or template. Here you dig a little deeper. There are four layers of preprocess functions: Drupal core, modules, the theme engine, and finally, your theme. These layers can override each other. A module can override core, the theme engine can override modules and core, and your theme can override everything.

When implementing a preprocess function the name of it is important. Preprocess functions are named after the theme function or the core template file and preceded by the theme's name. Table 3-4 highlights a few more examples:

TABLE 3-4

TEMPLATE OR THEME FUNCTION	YOUR THEME'S PREPROCESS FUNCTION
node.tpl.php	beginning_drupal_preprocess_node
node-blog.tpl.php	beginning_drupal_preprocess_node
page-front.tpl.php	beginning_drupal_preprocess_page
page-user-login.tpl.php	beginning_drupal_preprocess_page
theme_menu_item	beginning_drupal_preprocess_menu_item

Adding New Variables

To add a new `$weather` variable to all templates, you would add the following code to `template.php`:

```
function beginning_drupal_preprocess(&$variables) {
  $variables['weather'] = 'Sunny';
}
```

If you wanted to restrict this variable to the core template `page.tpl.php` (and its template suggestions) you would use the following `page` hook:

```
function beginning_drupal_preprocess_page(&$variables) {
  $variables['weather'] = 'Sunny';
}
```

The syntax for adding new variables is similar to the syntax for adding regions in the `.info` file. For example:

```
$variables['weather'] = "Sunny";
```

where `'weather'` is the variable name, and `"Sunny"` is its value. Within `page.tpl.php`, this would be utilized with the following code:

```
<div class="weather">
  <?php print $weather; ?>
</div>
```

Template Suggestions

Now let's take a look at providing additional template suggestions. Using the same preprocess function, you can return a variable named `template_file` as follows:

```
function beginning_drupal_preprocess_page(&$variables) {
  $variables['weather'] = "Sunny";
  if ($variables['weather'] == "Sunny") {
    $variables['template_file'] = 'page-sunny';
  }
}'
```

If the weather is indeed sunny, then the template file `page-sunny.tpl.php` would be used instead of `page.tpl.php`. Of course, `page-sunny.tpl.php` must exist. You can provide a range of suggestions by adding `[]` as follows:

```
function beginning_drupal_preprocess_page(&$variables) {
  $variables['weather'] = "Sunny";
  if ($variables['weather'] == "Sunny") {
    $variables['template_file'][] = 'page-sunny';
    $variables['template_file'][] = 'page-sun';
    $variables['template_file'][] = 'page-sol';
  }
}
```

Multiple template file suggestions are processed in LIFO (last in, first out) order. In this example, `page-sol.tpl.php` would be searched for first, then `page-sun.tpl.php`, then `page-sunny.tpl.php`, and, finally, `page.tpl.php` as a last resort. As with all suggestions, once a template is found, the others are ignored.

SWAPPING THEME FUNCTIONS AND TEMPLATE FILES

Drupal's theming layer can pull a really neat trick and swamp a theme function for a template file and vice versa. This trick allows you to put the right tool in place for the job.

Moving a Theme Function to a Template File

Theme functions can be difficult to work with for non-developers. Transferring a function over to a template file could increase productivity, as the designer can focus on HTML and CSS instead of PHP syntax. Follow these steps to transfer a function to a template file, using `theme_user_signature` as an example.

1. Identify the hook (hint: it comes after `theme_`). In this example, the hook for `theme_user_signature` is `user_signature`.

2. Create a template name after the hook, replacing _ with -. So in this example, the hook `user_signature` becomes `user-signature.tpl.php`.

3. Rebuild the theme registry.

4. Modify the template file to contain HTML instead of PHP. In the case of `theme_user_signature`, you need to make the following changes:

ORIGINAL THEME_USER_SIGNATURE

```php
function theme_user_signature($variables) {
  $output = '';
  if ($signature) {
    $output .= '<div class="clear">';
    $output .= $variables['signature'];
    $output .= '</div>';
  }
  return $output;
}

<div class="clear">
  <?php print $variables['signature']; ?>
</div>
```

Moving a Template File to a Theme Function

If your template file has grown from what was once a simple HTML file to a complex and intelligent PHP beast, then it might be time to move your code into a theme function. The purpose of using a template file is to separate PHP and HTML so that it is easier for non-PHP developers to work with. However, if it's too complex, there is no reason to leave it as a template file. Better still theme functions perform faster than template file giving your site a performance boost.

Follow these steps to transfer a template into a function, using `block.tpl.php` as an example:

1. Identify the core template. In this example, the core template for `block.tpl.php` is `block`.

2. Create a function in `template.php` named after the core template, replacing - with _ and prepending `themename_`. In this example, that means `block.tpl.php` becomes `beginning_drupal_block($variables)`.

3. Rebuild the theme registry.

4. Write the code within the function. Here is what `block.tpl.php` as a function would look like:

THE ORIGINAL BLOCK.TPL.PHP

```php
<div id="block-<?php print $block->module . '-' . $block->delta; ?>" class="clear-block
block block-<?php print $block->module ?>">

<?php if (!empty($block->subject)): ?>
  <h2><?php print $block->subject ?></h2>
<?php endif;?>
  <div class="content"><?php print $block->content ?></div>
</div>
```

THE NEW TEMPLATE.PHP FUNCTION

```php
function beginning_drupal_block($block) {
    $output = '<div id="block-'. $block->module .'-'. $block->delta . 'class="clear-block
block block-'. $block->module .'">';
    if (!empty($block->subject)) {
      $output .= '<h2>'. $block->subject .'</h2>';
    }
    $output .= '<div class="content">'. $block->content .'</div>';
    $output .= '</div>';
    return $output;
}
```

THEME REGISTRY

At this point in the chapter I'm sure you have yanked at your hair and yelled "Aaaaahhhhhhhh!" this is usually followed with a frantic darting of the eyes and mumbling something like: "So many tpl files, so many theme functions! How do I know!?!"

Don't go insane just yet — Drupal has a very simple answer. Ripping a page from the Microsoft Windows playbook (or possibly the wedding industry), Drupal maintains a theme registry that, as its name implies, is a registry of all themeable items in Drupal as well as information on how to use them.

In earlier exercises you were already exposed to this theme registry when you revisited the Appearance page in order to rebuild it. You also used the Theme developer module, which uses the theme registry to provide you with information on how to theme every bit of your site. Here you'll learn how to exploit the theme registry and theme developer module to make your life easier.

Consider the theme developer info box shown in Figure 13-26, which is broken down as follows:

Parents: The output of this template file (`comment.tpl.php`) will be sent to `theme_comment_view` and the output of that to `theme_comment_thread_expanded` and so on until its final display within `page.tpl.php`.

Template file: The template file used to theme the output.

Candidate template files: Other template suggestions that could have been used. Listed in the order they would have been used. In this example if `comment-story.tpl.php` existed it would have been used.

Preprocess functions: The preprocess functions that either were used or could have been used to provide or manipulate variables within `comment.tpl.php`. Note that you should change the first part `template_` to `themename_` (for example: `beginning_drupal_preprocess_comment`).

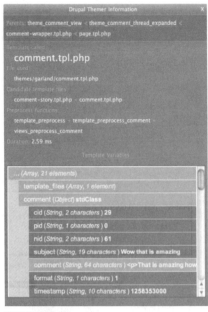

FIGURE 13-26

Template Variables

The second and most powerful half of the themer info box, Template Variables, provides everything you need to create your custom template file. The variables listed here are everything that can be used within the template file. The trick is learning how to read it. Start with a few basic examples, Figure 13-27 is the same themer info box but scrolled down to a different set of variables.

FIGURE 13-27

You can see that the zebra variables is a String that is three characters long and is currently set to odd. You can also see that is_front is a Boolean (meaning either true or false) and is currently false.

How do you use these in your template file?

Zebra would be used with the following code:

```php
<?php print $zebra; ?>
```

You could use `is_front` to do a check to see if the comment is being displayed on the frontpage of your site and if so add a frontpage class.

```php
<?php
if ($is_front) {
  $extra_class = "frontpage";
}
?>
<div class="content <?php print $extra_class; ?>">
  <?php print render($content); ?>
</div>
```

These lines are a bit easy, others might not be as easy. Take for example Figure 13-28 and the line `comment (Object) stdClass`. This line indicates that the variable comment is an Object. The variables cid, pid, nid, subject and comment, are all properties of the object. In order to access these variables you use ->. For example:

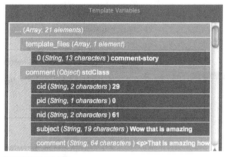

FIGURE 13-28

Available for download on Wrox.com

```
The comment id is <?php print $comment->cid;
?>
The node id that this comment was posted on is
<?php print $comment->nid; ?>
The subject of this comment is <?php print
$comment->subject ?>
```

Also in Figure 13-28 is the variable `template_files`, which is an Array. To access variables inside an array you use `$variable[key]`, in this example the code would be:

```
<?php print $template_files[0]; ?>
```

this would print `comment-story`.

Theme Registry

Using the Devel module you can also access the full Theme registry by clicking Theme registry link within the Development block. Figure 13-29 displays the theme registry for a basic Drupal install. As you can see there are 216 themeable elements. Clicking on any of the lines will open it up to display additional information about the element as shown in Figure 13-30, which shows the same registry information as the themer info box in earlier figures.

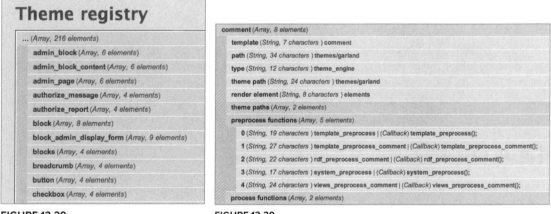

FIGURE 13-29   **FIGURE 13-30**

In this figure the registry is telling us the comment element is themed via a template (comment), which is located at `sites/all/themes/beginning_drupal`.

As you can see much of the information is identical to that of the themer info box. The exception is that the themer info box can show more information such as the candidate template files and the variables used.

Exploring the Theme Registry

In this exercise you'll explore the Theme Registry to get a sense of how you can use it to speed up your theme development.

1. Ensure that the Devel module is installed and enabled and that the Devel block is displayed. (This was done in a previous exercise.)

2. Click the Theme Registry link located in the Development block.

3. On the new page, click Array on the top of the page. This should expand to display a long list of clickable links, as shown in Figure 13-29 (shown earlier).

4. Find the `user_signature` link in the list, and click it to display the `user_signature` properties, as shown in Figure 13-31. Note the following:

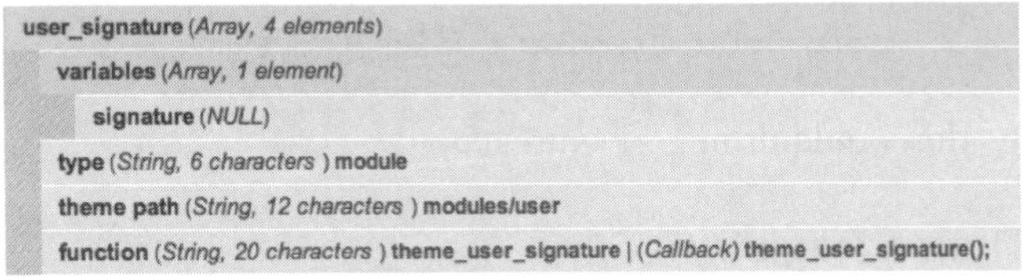

> Its type is Module.

> Its theme path is `modules/user`.

user_signature *(Array, 4 elements)*
   variables *(Array, 1 element)*
      signature *(NULL)*
   type *(String, 6 characters)* **module**
   theme path *(String, 12 characters)* **modules/user**
   function *(String, 20 characters)* **theme_user_signature** | *(Callback)* **theme_user_signature();**

FIGURE 13-31

5. Under `user_signature` click on Variables to reveal $signature, as shown in Figure 13-31.

Note that the function is set to `theme_user_signature`, which is the theme function you can use to override the output.

How It Works

The Theme registry contains a listing for every themeable element on your site. These are discovered whenever a new module or theme is enabled and stored in the registry for quick access to increase the performance of your site. You can use this theme registry to learn how to theme each individual piece of your site.

THEME ENGINES

One last topic before you take your exit and enter the world of theming ninjas, theme engines. Very little of this chapter is dedicated to this topic because a vast majority of themes use a single theme engine: PHPTemplate.

As mentioned previously, Drupal separates the handling of data from the display of data through the use of a *theme layer*. When data is passed from the core and has contributed modules to the theme, it passes through something called the *theme engine*. The theme engine is the mechanism by which the templates are processed into HTML.

If you consider the chocolate factory analogy, the theme engine would sit right before the molds. It would define if the chocolate was placed into the mold by way of a funnel, a tube, or a team of elves dressed in red and white outfits. Consider the following three examples:

EASY TEMPLATE SYSTEM (ETS) THEME ENGINE

```
<div class="content">
  {content}
</div>
```

SMARTY THEME ENGINE

```
<div class="content">
  {$content}
</div>
```

PHPTEMPLATE THEME ENGINE (DRUPAL'S DEFAULT)

```
<div class="content">
  <?php print $content ?>
</div>
```

These three different engines are printing the same data: content. The resulting HTML will be identical. The only difference is the method employed, specifically {content}. {$content}, or <?php print $content ?>. The differences are very subtle in the preceding examples, but the following examples are a little more complex.

EASY TEMPLATE SYSTEM (ETS) THEME ENGINE

```
{if: {links} }
  <div class="links"> {links}</div>
{/if}
```

SMARTY THEME ENGINE

```
{if $links}
  <div class="links">{$links}</div>
{/if}
```

PHPTEMPLATE THEME ENGINE

```
<?php if ($links): ?>
  <div class="links"><?php print $links; ?></div>
<?php endif; ?>
```

Again, the resulting HTML is the same and only the methods are different. Each example is testing to see if the `links` variable has content, and if so, it will print the content of the `links` variable within a set of `div` tags. If you have previous experience with PHP, you probably recognized the syntax in the last example.

The most popular and the only engine included in Drupal's core download is the PHPTemplate engine. Considering that Drupal is written in the PHP language, this shouldn't come as too much of a surprise.

Which Engine Does Your Theme Use?

You're probably wondering how you know what theme engine a theme uses. If you downloaded the theme from `drupal.org`, the theme's project page will note the appropriate theme engine. You can also look at the template file's extension for a clue. PHPTemplate uses `tpl.php` (for example: `node.tpl.php`), and Smarty uses just `.tpl`, (for example: `node.tpl`). Unfortunately ETS, also uses `.tpl`, so a template file's extension is not always the best indicator. The official answer is to peek inside the theme's `.info` file at the `engine` property as in the following example:

```
name = Garland
description = Tableless, recolorable, multi-column, fluid width theme (default).
version = VERSION
core = 7.x
engine = phptemplate
```

Although there are a few reasons why you would choose one engine over another, the main reason is syntax. If your design team has prior experience with the Smarty templating engine, it might make sense to use that. If your designers work closely with your developers, it will probably make more sense to use PHPTemplate so that your developers can use a single language, PHP, for the entire site.

SUMMARY

Theming in Drupal can be a very complex process and, at first glance, daunting. However, taking your time to understand how all the pieces go together will help you become a Drupal theming ninja in no time. This chapter should have helped you discover that Drupal has a very flexible architecture that allows you to mold and manipulate it to meet your design and creative ideas. Your theme has full creative control over the final output sent to your visitors.

Theming is about making your site look good and not about coding. The use of a strong base theme, such as Zen, can provide you with a solid foundation for your theme, allowing you to focus on the unique and creative bits of your site. Getting involved with a design community can provide you with the support you need to create high-end top-notch themes. The community is there to help you but you have to get involved. Navigate over to `http://drupal.org`, login to the `#drupal-themes` IRC channel, and/or post in Drupal's Theming forum to connect with other themers.

In the next chapter you'll switch your focus to finding, evaluating, and using contributed modules and then begin a different Drupal journey, the one to becoming a Drupal module developer.

EXERCISES

1. What is theming?

2. Where are new themes installed?

3. Is it possible for a theme to not have HTML files?

4. What is a region and how are they defined?

5. What is a core and a suggested template?

6. As a themer why is the Theme registry important?

7. Why is the Zen, available on Drupal.org, heavily used and considered a Drupal good practice?

Answers to the Exercises can be found in the Appendix.

▶ WHAT YOU LEARNED IN THIS CHAPTER

➤ Each theme maintains its own configuration within Appearance or use the default global settings.

➤ Individual theme configurations override the global configuration.

➤ Style sheets and JavaScript files are added by the theme's `.info` file.

➤ Use the Theme Developer module to determine how an element is themed and, more importantly, how you can override it.

➤ Template files are overridden by creating a template with the same name or a suggested template name inside your theme's folder.

➤ Theme functions are overridden within your theme's template.php file.

➤ Template.php is used for theme function overrides, preprocess functions, and other theme specific PHP functions.

➤ Preprocess functions are used to add, remove, or modify variables before the variables are sent to a theme template or function.

➤ A preprocess function can also modify the set of available template suggestions.

➤ Whenever a new template, theme function override, or preprocess function is added the theme registry must be updated.

➤ Every piece of a theme's design, look, and feel can be controlled by your theme.

14

Contributed Modules

WHAT YOU WILL LEARN IN THIS CHAPTER:

➤ Discover your module needs

➤ Search for and find contributed modules

➤ Evaluate modules for their quality and support

➤ Utilize Drupal's issue queue to get support and request changes to the module

One of Drupal's greatest advantages is the large collection of contributed modules freely available on `http://drupal.org`. The modules available cover nearly every aspect of Drupal, including modifying comment forms, protecting against spam, and providing newsletter support to building an online store. Generally, the question is not if there is a module that will meet your needs, but rather, how you find the module.

This chapter covers how to find, evaluate, and leverage contributed modules to build your site. The chapter begins with a discussion on how to determine what your needs are and follows through with how to find the module or modules that best meet those needs. You'll explore methods to evaluate modules so that you choose high-quality modules that are well supported. You will also learn how to interact with the module developers by using Drupal.org's issues queue effectively, as well as how to pinpoint the changes you may need to make to a module.

CONTRIBUTED AND CUSTOM MODULES

Modules are chunks of PHP code that hook into and expand Drupal's core to provide new functionality, features, actions, blocks, content types, performance enhancement, and much more. There is almost no limit to what a module can provide for your website. One of the primary reasons why Drupal is so popular is that there are many modules freely available on `http://drupal.org`. The driving reason behind the large number of modules available on `http://drupal.org` is the flexibility of Drupal's underlying framework. This ease and flexibility tempts a lot of new-to-Drupal developers into adding functionality and expanding their website through the use of custom modules rather than contributed modules.

Here's a bit of Drupal terminology that you should become familiar with:

➤ **Contributed module** — A contributed module is any module that is not part of Drupal's core and is downloaded from `http://drupal.org`. Contributed modules, also known as *contrib*, are freely available and licensed under the GNU Public License (GPL).

➤ **Custom module** — A custom module is a module you have developed that is specific to your website. For this reason, custom modules are not available on `http://drupal.org`.

These two terms have a slight but important difference. Because contributed modules are hosted on `Drupal.org`, they have visibility to the entire Drupal community, and from this community, they have a support and maintenance base. If you are using Drupal because of the large community that is supporting it, you should also consider this when deciding whether to use a contributed module or build your own.

DETERMINING YOUR NEEDS

The first step to finding a module that adds the features you need is to identify all the current and potential future features of your website. Ask yourself (or your client) the following questions:

➤ Who is the audience for your website?

➤ What functionality will be provided to the users?

➤ Are there multiple classes of users (such as editors, writers, and readers)?

➤ Will the site provide social-networking features or mainly provide static content?

➤ Is there a forum or other method that users can use to communicate with each other (chatting, comments, and the like)?

➤ What type of media can be added to the sites (such as videos, mp3s, photos, documents, and so on)?

The following is an example of a summary and feature list for an editor/writer website.

This summary and feature list is part of a larger process called *scoping*. Scoping is a vital part of any web-development project, because it identifies

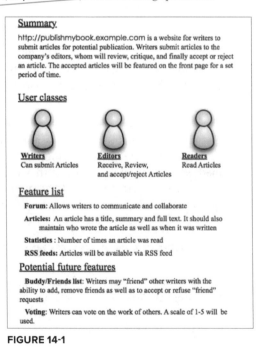

Summary

http://publishmybook.example.com is a website for writers to submit articles for potential publication. Writers submit articles to the company's editors, whom will review, critique, and finally accept or reject an article. The accepted articles will be featured on the front page for a set period of time.

User classes

Writers
Can submit Articles

Editors
Receive, Review, and accept/reject Articles

Readers
Read Articles

Feature list

Forum: Allows writers to communicate and collaborate

Articles: An article has a title, summary and full text. It should also maintain who wrote the article as well as when it was written

Statistics : Number of times an article was read

RSS feeds: Articles will be available via RSS feed

Potential future features

Buddy/Friends list: Writers may "friend" other writers with the ability to add, remove friends as well as to accept or refuse "friend" requests

Voting: Writers can vote on the work of others. A scale of 1-5 will be used.

FIGURE 14-1

all of the pieces of a website that will subsequently be mapped to the module or modules that provide the feature. The creation of a good feature map and scoping document is a skill in itself, and as you take on larger projects, some time should be devoted to this topic.

With your feature list in hand, the next step is to map a website's features to the features you need, provided by Drupal or by one or more contributed modules. Stepping through each feature, ask yourself the following questions:

1. What section does this feature belong to? Is it:

➤ User related?

➤ Content related?

➤ An administrative function?

➤ Voting or evaluative?

➤ Theming (organizing information, modifying the look, and so on)?

2. After the section is determined, what core module most closely addresses this need?

3. If a core module provides partial functionality, what is missing?

4. If a core module doesn't address the need, what part of the core would be the base? For example, the core does not provide a method to vote on content (nodes), but content is what will be voted on. From this, you can determine that the node module is the base for voting.

The answers to these questions will help you navigate the categorization structure on `Drupal.org`, can be used as search terms, and will help you efficiently communicate with other Drupal users and developers. There is always more than one method (or module) to achieve a particular outcome; thus, a thorough understanding of which part of Drupal needs to be enhanced or modified will help you and others find the right solution for your project.

FULFILLING YOUR NEEDS

Before you jump into the modules list on `http://drupal.org`, you should take the time to familiarize yourself with the work of others. The Drupal community has created scores of podcasts, videos, blogs, and recommendation sites to help people like you familiarize yourself with what modules are available and how these modules can be of use. Following are brief descriptions of some of the things that are available to you through this community.

Lullabot Podcast

A long-time and well-respected Drupal shop, Lullabot has created one of the finest podcasts in the Drupal community. If you have decided that Drupal is the right software for you, then you owe it to yourself to take the time to listen to their podcast, which comes out every two weeks to a month. This crew, which includes Drupal 7's lead maintainer, also takes the time to highlight the top Drupal modules at least once a year.

Head over to their site (`http://lullabot.com`) and search for **Top Modules** to find the latest podcast or article highlighting these modules, or sign up for their regular podcast (`http://www.lullabot.com/podcast`).

Top Drupal Modules

Many community members have taken the time to write down what they consider to be the top Drupal modules. Search for **Top Drupal Modules** at `http://google.com`, and you'll get a long list of sites that highlight these modules. The list changes frequently, so this book does not recommend any specific URL.

Showcases

Drupal's showcases are the equivalent of an expedited Drupal education. Many people in the Drupal community have gone above and beyond the call of duty by detailing how they built their sites. The showcases include which modules were chosen, if custom modules were developed, how the theme was designed and built, as well as tips and tricks the developer learned along the way. The best showcases are promoted to frontpage of `Drupal.org`, so it pays to sign up for the RSS feed at `http://drupal.org/rss`.

Here are some of the showcases worth reading:

➤ **Drupalcamp L.A.** — (`http://2009.drupalcampla.com/`)

  Case study: `http://drupal.org/node/519100`

  A well crafted conference website for managing sessions, as well as speaker and attendee sign up. The case details nearly every step used to build the site leaving little out. It is a great roadmap on how to build a high caliber website.

➤ **New York Observer** — (`http://observer.com`)

  Case study: `http://drupal.org/nyobserver`

  Building a magazine site? Check out this case study to see what modules were used and how this magazine transitioned over to Drupal.

➤ **Drupalcon Szeged** — `http://szeged2008.drupalcon.org`

  Case study: `http://drupal.org/node/358129`

  This case study describes how the conference website for Drupalcon was built, including a detailed module list.

All Drupal showcases are available at `http://drupal.org/forum/25`, and also check out the Drupal success stories, most with full outlines of how they were built, here:

  `http://drupal.org/success-stories`

 NOTE *"How'd they build that?" Never ask this question again. Head over to the showcase section at* `Drupal.org` *and read the detailed reports on how live websites were build. After you build your site, submit your own report.*

The fastest method to learn which modules work in what situations is to read the site showcases. You'll soon find out how effective this method is for learning how to build your website.

Planet Drupal

Stay on the pulse of the Drupal community by subscribing to the Planet Drupal RSS feed. Aggregating over 350 different Drupal sources the planet will notify you of the latest websites built on Drupal, new modules, themes, and other newsworthy happenings in the Drupal community:

```
http://drupal.org/planet
```

FINDING MODULES

Looking at lists of top Drupal modules and site showcases that highlight the modules used is a great way to learn how others built their sites, but it may not answer all your questions. With thousands of modules available and more being introduced every day, finding the right module for your job can be akin to a voodoo science. This section describes how to use the following to find elusive modules:

➤ Drupal.org's search engine

➤ Google

➤ Drupalmodules.com

➤ Internet Relay Chat (IRC) and Drupal's forums

➤ RSS feeds

Search Drupal.org

Your first stop should be Drupal's module page located at `http://drupal.org/project/modules`. Three filtering options are available on this page: Sort by, Filter by Compatibility, and Projects.

Filter by Compatibility

Don't forget that modules are specific to the core version for which they were written. Therefore, your first step should be to narrow your results to the specific Drupal version you are using. If you have a bit of programming savvy or would like to gain some experience leave this filter out to show all modules. There is a lot of great code on Drupal.org so if you find a module that hasn't yet been upgraded to Drupal 7 or is abandoned, don't be afraid to get your hands dirty and fix it up.

Sort by

This option allows you to sort by a module's title, creation date, latest release, recent activity, or usage statistics. Usage statistics is a measure of how many installations the module has, not just downloads but actual uses. Sorting by usage statistics (Figure 14-2) helps you understand which modules are most heavily used (and possibly best supported). This option is particularly useful when you are searching within a project category. However don't fall into the popularity trap; some of the greatest modules are the most recently released thus they won't have high usage statistics.

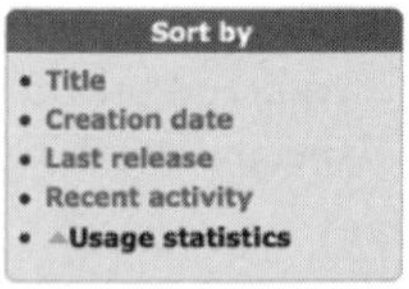

FIGURE 14-2

Recommendations Block

Use the Recommendations block to find related projects and discussions about them. For example, when browsing the Voting API module (`http://drupal.org/project/votingapi`), the Recommendations block, shown in Figure 14-3, displayed a list to Fivestar, Vote Up/Down, and other complimentary modules. When browsing the UserPoints module (`http://drupal.org/project/userpoints`), Figure 14-4, the recommendations included links to voting related as well as Karma modules.

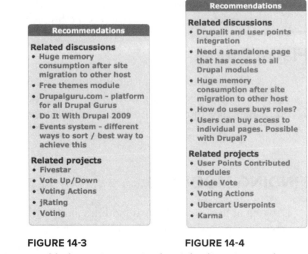

FIGURE 14-3   **FIGURE 14-4**

A quick browse through the related discussions could also point you in the right direction to the module you are truly looking for or how best to configure this module to meet your needs.

Projects

Modules and themes are grouped under one or more categories that are chosen by the module's maintainer. You can use these categories to further narrow down your search results, as shown in Figure 14-5.

Google

Instead of sifting through the numerous modules on `Drupal.org` to find the module you need, or if Drupal's search engine is failing, you can just Google it! The simple trick is to use the site-restricting function. For example, if you were searching for a module that allows users to vote, you could type the following into the Google search box:

```
user voting site:http://drupal.org/project
```

FIGURE 14-5

The `site:http://drupal.org/project` feature restricts Google to the module page of `Drupal.org`, providing you with a powerful way to search through Drupal's modules.

Drupalmodules.com

The `http://drupalmodules.com` site is a community-initiated unofficial website created to help you, and others like you, discover Drupal modules quickly. This website provides a search engine specifically designed to find Drupal modules. You can filter by category or Drupal version, as well as conduct a keyword search on the module's title or description. The website also provides user ratings and comments on the modules.

IRC and the Drupal Community

If you are having a difficult time locating a module for your task, do not hesitate to ask the community. The IRC channel `#drupal-support` is full of people who might have done something similar to what you want to do. Pop in and ask them for a module recommendation. Drupal.org's Post Installation forum (`http://drupal.org/forum/22`) is also teeming with people ready to help you.

The key to asking for a module recommendation is to be detailed yet concise. Avoid unnecessary details about why or for whom you are building the site, and skip straight to what you need. Also be sure to mention any module you may have already tried and other possibly related modules on your site. Try to keep your request to less than two paragraphs.

RSS Feeds

An RSS feed won't help you find the module that you are looking for right now, but it will help keep you apprised of what is available. Several new Drupal modules are released every day, and a quick glance once every few days can help you to discover the vast array of Drupal modules available as well as what is happening in the Drupal community.

New modules posted to Drupal are available at `http://drupal.org/taxonomy/term/14/0/feed`.

Twitter

Like Drupal Planet @drupal_modules on Twitter can help keep you informed for the latest and greatest modules (Figure 14-6). `http://twitter.com/drupal_modules`.

Also follow these other great twitter feeds:

➤ `http://twitter.com/drupal`

➤ `http://twitter.com/drupalcon`

➤ `http://twitter.com/drupal_themes`

➤ `http://twitter.com/drupalsecurity`

FIGURE 14-6

IS IT THE RIGHT MODULE?

`Drupal.org` is a living, breathing website teeming with activity from the community. Community members post new modules, themes, and code snippets every day due to an unspoken single word rule: *share*.

You are able to freely download modules because someone else has shared it. Sharing is not just about uploading themes or modules — it can also be about sharing a little bit of your time and expertise. Modules often develop a small community around them that share new features and bug fixes, and support each other in the use of the module. This sharing philosophy is what is central to the Drupal community and makes it vibrant.

Periodically, you will come across a module that hasn't yet built up a community around it. Sometimes this is because the original developer shared the code but did not have the time to update or support it. This is completely acceptable with the community, because others may be able to build off what the developer started. If you are not a developer, this is something to watch for, because you may not want to start using a module that you are unable to get support on or will never be updated.

The next several pages will demonstrate a few methods to determine if a module is of good quality and has a support and/or maintenance community around it. These are only suggestions. Ultimately, the decision as to if a module will work for you is up to you.

The following topics are covered in this section:

- ➤ Issues queue
- ➤ Usage statistics
- ➤ Developers list and CVS commits
- ➤ Drupalmodules.com
- ➤ Coder module
- ➤ Google

Project Page

Every module and theme is given its own page on `Drupal.org` called the *project page*. This page contains the module's description and download links, so you have most likely already seen it. What you may have missed are the blocks to the side of the project description.

Issues Queue

The *issues queue* is used to communicate directly with the community, developers, and maintainers that are supporting and developing the module. You can request support, report a bug, or request that new features be developed. Reviewing the issues queue can help you determine if support is available, if bugs are being fixed quickly, or if there is a new feature pending that you could benefit from. On the project page is an Issue queue block, similar to that shown in Figure 14-7 for the Views project.

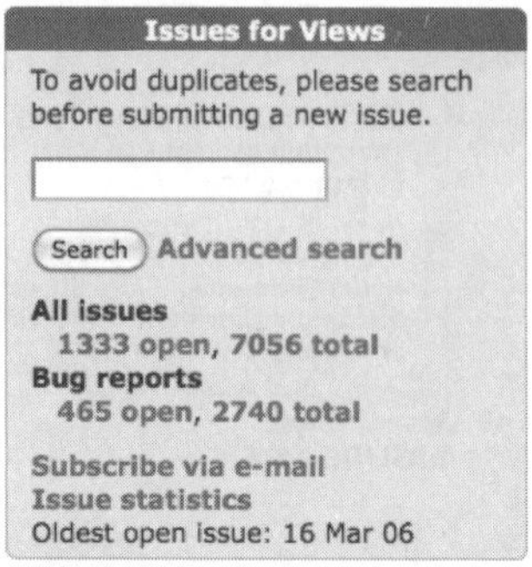

Issues for Views

To avoid duplicates, please search before submitting a new issue.

(Search) Advanced search

All issues
 1333 open, 7056 total
Bug reports
 465 open, 2740 total

Subscribe via e-mail
Issue statistics
Oldest open issue: 16 Mar 06

FIGURE 14-7

Looking at the Issues for View you can see that the project is heavily used with over 7,000 issues submitted and a vast majority of them closed. You can also see that quite a lot of bugs were reported (2,700+). This is Open Source software so bugs are submitted out in the open and a high number doesn't indicate unstable software. In fact the opposite is true. A high number of reported bugs that are subsequently closed (as seen with the Views module) demonstrates a piece of software that has reached a mature state. The great part of having bugs submitted out in the open is that you can search an issue you might be having to see if it is a true bug or just a mis-configuration.

Bug Reports

In the Issues Queue block under Bug reports click on the word Open. Remember that a project's issues queue is also its construction yard so don't be afraid of a high number of "bugs". Many of the bug reports may be against development versions of the module, which is perfectly normal. What you should focus on is what has been reported and their status. Looking at Figure 14-8, a snapshot of the View's issue queue, shows a number of bugs that were reported and subsequently fixed. Each of these bugs also has a number of replies indicating community involvement and a desire to squash the bugs as quickly as possible.

Issues for Views

Login or register to create an issue · Advanced search · Statistics

Search for	Status	Priority	Category	Version	Component
	- Open issues -	- Any -	bug report	- 7.x issues -	- Any -

Summary	Status	Priority	Category	Version	Component	Replies	Last updated▽	Assigned to
Fix js preview	needs work	normal	bug reports	7.x-3.x-dev	User interface		23 hours 2 min	
Relationships defined using wrong base field	fixed	minor	bug reports	7.x-3.x-dev	Views Data	6	23 hours 24 min	
Fix Node: New comments	fixed	normal	bug reports	7.x-3.x-dev	comment data	1	23 hours 29 min	
drupal_build_form needs default build_info parameters	fixed	critical	bug reports	7.x-3.x-dev	Code	3	23 hours 37 min	
Exposed forms are not rendered	fixed	normal	bug reports	7.x-3.x-dev	Code	4	23 hours 37 min	
Saving details returns error, analyze does not display	active	normal	bug reports	7.x-3.x-dev	User interface	1	2 days 10 hours	

FIGURE 14-8

Usage Statistics

Each project maintains statistics on its use around the Web. These statistics are compiled weekly and are uniquely identified by the various versions of the module. Figure 14-9 shows the usage statistics for the Views module. The more a module is used the more likely it is that you'll receive support or be able to find a developer that understands how to use the module. Of course you don't want to use this as your only measure as many great modules are newly released.

Access the statistics by clicking the View usage statistics link at the bottom of the project page. You can also manually navigate to `http://drupal.org/project/usage/<project_name>`.

FIGURE 14-9

Website administrators can disable the reporting of their information, so the usage statistics comprise only a portion of the actual installations. However, usage statistics can provide you with a window to potential size of a module's user base. Just like in high school, you don't want to judge something simply based on its popularity. There are many really great modules that have low usage statistics because they are very niche or newly released.

Developer's List, CVS Commits, and Reputation

Reputation can sometimes play a big role in developing confidence in a module. Every module has one or more maintainers and a single owner (also known as a head or lead maintainer). The owner is listed on the project page at the top left. In Figure 14-10, you can see that the owner of the CCK module is `yched`.

Content Construction Kit (CCK)

| View | CVS instructions |

`yched` - February 7, 2006 - **Administration · Modules · Content · Content Construction Kit (CCK)** 23:35

The Content Construction Kit allows you to add custom fields to nodes using a web browser.

FIGURE 14-10

True to open source form many modules have more than a single developer working on it. Take a look at the Developers block or click the View all committers link on the project page. A committer is someone that has "committed" or given code to the project. Figure 14-11 shows the committer list for the CCK module as of November, 2009.

There is a lot of useful information that you can glean from the developers list. The first is how often development is occurring on the module, which helps to gauge how quickly bugs will be fixed or new features added. A commit is a modification to the programming code. What you can see in Figure 14-1 is that the user *yched* made 2,505 changes to the code over the last two years. The user *KarenS* also made 1,518 changes to the code over the same period. This would be one indication of a well-developed and stable module.

Maintainers for Content Construction Kit (CCK)

- **KarenS - 1518 commits**
  last: 11 hours ago, first: 3 years ago
- **markus_petrux - 346 commits**
  last: 3 days ago, first: 23 weeks ago
- **moshe weitzman - 3 commits**
  last: 9 weeks ago, first: 26 weeks ago
- **yched - 2505 commits**
  last: 16 weeks ago, first: 2 years ago

View all committers

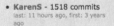

FIGURE 14-11

Several modules do not have a large developer base, but they should not be overlooked. For example, Figure 14-12 shows the developers list for the Mollom module (`http://drupal.org/project/mollom`), which is quite small. Compared to the CCK module, this might seem to be a much poorer module, but nothing could be further from the truth!

FIGURE 14-12

Clicking the user's name (in this case, *Dries*) will whisk you over to their profile. A quick look at this profile will show that not only is Dries the founder of the Drupal project, but he has also committed over 21,000 changes to code on `drupal.org`. His reputation as a developer should provide you with confidence in the Mollom module.

However, you do not want to penalize new developers, so you should use their profiles only as part of your overall assessment.

Google

Pop over to `http://google.com`, type in the module's name along with the word **Drupal**, and see what pops up. You'll frequently find that Drupal-based companies such as Lullabot, Acquia, and Development Seed blog about their favorite modules or modules that don't make the cut.

Coder Module

The Coder module was created to help developers ensure that their code is consistent with Drupal coding standards as well as to check for basic security vulnerabilities. Drupal has stringent quality checking, so it's rare to find a module that will pass all of its tests. Moreover, a 100-percent pass does not indicate a quality module. For example, the module could have code that is perfect but an interface that is difficult to work with.

As an evaluation tool, the Coder module can be useful in determining if a contributed module would make a good starting point to build the module you really want. Remember that the power of Open source means that you can use the source code from one project to build your own custom project.

Tests

Did you know that before Drupal is considered stable it has to pass tens of thousands of tests? It's true. Drupal uses a system called SimpleTest to constantly test the code to ensure that it is stable and bug free. Contributed modules can also use tests to ensure that the module is stable and bug free. You can see if a module has tests by viewing the files of the module and looking for `.test` files. The presence of these tests usually indicates that the developers are working hard to create a stable, bug free module.

Test a module by enabling the testing module on your Drupal installation then navigating to Configuration and modules ⇨ Testing. Testing is discussed further in Chapter 17.

BE A FOLLOWER

Being a follower can help you be a leader. Following others can end up saving you a lot of time and allow you to focus on the creative aspects of your website or application. Try to use well-supported contributed modules. If you are unable to find a module that meets your needs, find the closest match and ask the developer for a new feature or tweak. You may request something that the developer never thought of, or they may respond to your request with a suggestion on another module to use or a tweak to your model. If you are open with your features and how you want your website or application to function, you may find that everything you need has already been developed — you will only need to put the pieces together.

Take It Slow

When you have found the modules you will use for your project, you will need to test them. The first and foremost rule when testing or trying out new modules is: Never use your production site! Newcomers to Drupal often set up only a single site and begin to build it out. They download several different modules and enable them all at the same time. However, they quickly run into a problem and are unable to track down the source because of the large number of modules they just enabled.

Take Your Time

Set up a test site with a clean version of Drupal and no additional modules. Install and enable only one contributed module at a time to take it for a test drive. See what the module can do when it's within the clean environment before you take it to your site. After you have deemed it ready, then consider moving it to your production website, or even better, move it to your development site.

> **NOTE** A quick way to test a module on a clean Drupal install is with the Demo module (`http://drupal.org/project/demo`), which can reset a Drupal site to a former (clean) state.

Uninstall, Don't Just Delete

If you decide to not use a module, be sure to use the Uninstall feature instead of simply deleting the module. Deleting a module from the folder never allows the uninstall routines to run, thus increasing the probability of having the leftover remains of the module on your site forever.

First, disable the module in the Administrative area, and then click the Uninstall tab at the top of the page as shown in Figure 14-13. You will be presented with a list of disabled modules that can be uninstalled. Not all modules support uninstalls. If the recently disabled module isn't listed, then the Uninstall feature is not supported and you can draw one of two conclusions. Uninstall is not necessary, or the developer didn't build an uninstall routine but left a few skeletal remains of its presence on your website. This is when it pays to have done your testing on a development server.

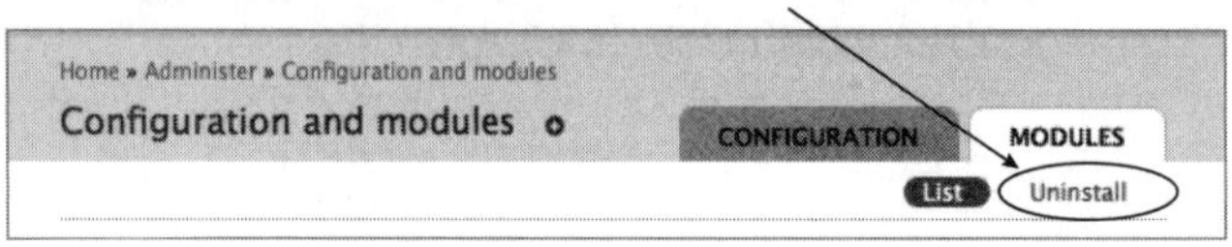

FIGURE 14-13

Set Up a Development Environment

This sounds much more complicated than it is. A development environment is typically little more than a Drupal installation that is roughly similar to what your production (live) site is or will be. The development site allows you to play around with new modules, configuration settings, and other items that might break your actual website. The idea is simple: your live site should only include the modules that you will use. Although most modules include an uninstall routine that cleans up any changes the module made to your website, this is not always the case.

A common development environment looks like the following as shown in Figure 14-14.

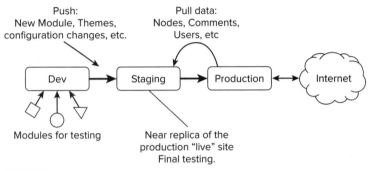

FIGURE 14-14

Modules are tested and vetted on the development site. Modules that make the grade are passed on to the staging server, which is an exact replica of the production site. Further testing is done against the module for compatibility with the site's other modules as well as the site's data. After all tests have passed, then the staging site is pushed over to production.

Team-driven environments typically have one additional layer in front of development for the vetting of new modules. This leaves development as a close replica of the live site, staging as a very near real-time synced version of the live site, and then a final push up to production.

However you set up your environment, one thing should be very clear: Never test modules on a production site!

Avoid the Buffet

Kahlid Bahey, a seasoned Drupal developer, once wrote a blog post entitled "open buffet binge" that fairly accurately describes how some newcomers approach Drupal. He explained that when presented with a large list of useful and free modules, these folks gorged themselves by downloading everything they thought would be useful. There are two problems with this approach.

The first problem pertains to your server. In a very simplistic explanation, each module uses a small portion of your server's memory; thus, the more modules you use, the more memory your server will use. Low-traffic sites may never see a difference, but once traffic begins to pick up, memory usage becomes a big concern and can slow down your site considerably.

Even if you have a big and beefy server, you still have a second problem to worry about. Modules require upkeep and maintenance. The Web is a constant flurry of change, innovation, and, unfortunately, security breaches. First and foremost, you must keep on top of security updates to your site and each of your modules. Your Drupal installation will warn you of updates to your modules, but it is your responsibility to perform the update (see tip).

You can read Kahlid Bahey's article at `http://2bits.com/articles/server-indigestion-the-drupal-contributed-modules-open-buffet-binge-syndrome.html`.

> **NOTE** *The DRUSH module makes keeping all of your contributed modules up to date a breeze. Read more at* `http://drupal.org/project/drush`.

SUMMARY

One of the most daunting tasks facing a new Drupal site builder is determining which modules to use and how to use them. This chapter introduced methods for assessing which modules are right for your job. These methods include reading the `site showcases` on `http://drupal.org`, reviewing "top modules" lists on sites such as `http://lullabot.com` and the module set of `http://acquia.com`, as well as using the other resources available at `drupal.org`. However, these lists will not always have what you are looking for, so learning how to seek out the module gems amongst the pile of modules on `drupal.org` is an essential skill. When you have found the gem, how do you know if it's a diamond in the rough or just an abandoned piece of coal? Using the issues queue, usage statistics, and the other methods introduced in this chapter will help you find the polished gems that will make your website shine.

Unfortunately, you will not always find a contributed module that performs every function or action that you require. It is not uncommon for a website to have one or more custom modules to help clean up the loose ends and really make the site shine. If you think it's time to create your own custom module then continue on to the next chapter and start your Drupal development journey.

EXERCISES

1. What is the difference between a contributed module and a custom module?

2. What is scoping?

3. Where are some of the places you can search for Drupal modules?

4. What is the first and foremost rule when testing or trying out new modules?

Answers to the Exercises can be found in the Appendix.

▶ **WHAT YOU LEARNED IN THIS CHAPTER**

➤ Modules are chunks of PHP code that hook into and expand Drupal's core; they provide new functionality, features, actions, blocks, content types, performance enhancement, and much more.

➤ Before you jump into the modules list on http://drupal.org, you should take the time to familiarize yourself with the work of others, such as the scores of podcasts, videos, blogs, and recommendation sites created by the Drupal community.

➤ Drupal.org's own search engine, Google, Drupalmodules.com, Internet Relay Chat (IRC) and Drupal's forums, and RSS feeds are all places in which you can search for Drupal modules.

➤ Sharing on Drupal.org is not just about uploading themes or modules. It can also be about sharing a little bit of your time and expertise.

➤ The project page, given to every module and theme on Drupal.org, not only contains the module's description and download links but also usage statistics, developers involved, and an issues queue. These areas provide important clues to help you evaluate a module.

➤ Try to use well-supported contributed modules. If you are unable to find a module that meets your needs, find the closest match and ask the developer for a new feature or tweak.

15

Custom Modules

WHAT YOU WILL LEARN IN THIS CHAPTER:

➤ Module basics

➤ Creating a bare-bones module

➤ What a hook is

➤ Building a simple module using a hook

If you have searched drupal.org for a contributed module that meets your needs and came up empty, or have ever uttered the phrase, "But it should do . . .," then this chapter is for you. In this chapter, you will examine the components of a module so that you can modify existing contributed modules to better fit your needs or, if you'd prefer, to build your own custom module. Written without much technical lingo, this chapter is great if want to learn just enough to customize your site or if you plan to become a full-fledged developer.

This chapter starts off by exploring the file components of a module, and then examines a very short and basic module. When you get your feet wet you'll create a more robust module and learn how to track your changes and give back to the community by using the diff command. At the end of this chapter, you will be armed with the knowledge necessary to peer into existing modules and understand how they work. Combine this chapter with the next one, and you will know the secrets of how the majority of Drupal modules operate.

WHAT IS A MODULE?

Many newcomers to Drupal find the word *module* intimidating — as if it were a magic black box of unintelligible gobbledygook that just somehow works. Fortunately, the reality is the exact opposite.

So what is a module? First, the name should be explained. Drupal is built upon a modular structure, meaning that small bits of code can be added to extend the overall functionality of Drupal. These small bits of code are named *modules*. In other systems, these are called *extensions* or *plugins*. Regardless of the name, what should be clear is what they do: extend, enhance, or modify the functionality of Drupal.

So you now have a very textbook definition of the word *module*, but that doesn't tell you what a module really is. The not-so-secret secret is that a module is nothing more than a bunch of text files. These files are not compiled, do not contain secret script, are not compressed or encrypted, or use any other undecipherable method. The only thing tricky about modules is that they are written in the PHP scripting language, which to the uninitiated can be a foreign language.

Modules require just two basic files. The first is the .info file, which is similar to the .info file of a theme. The .info file contains the name, description, core compatibility, and version number of the module. The second item is the .module file, which contains the PHP code. There are several other files that can be used within a module, which are discussed in Chapter 17, but only the .info and .module file are *required*.

Here is a quick reminder of some basic Drupal terminology:

➤ **Core** — Any item that is included with the main Drupal download (stored outside of the sites directory).

➤ **Contributed module** — A module available for download on http://drupal.org.

➤ **Custom module** — A module not included with the core and not available on Drupal.org. This includes any modules that you or others have developed that are specific to your site.

Follow along in this exercise to build your first module.

TRY IT OUT   **Building a Module**

Follow these steps to write the module:

1. Navigate to your site's modules directory (for example, sites/default/modules).

2. Create a new folder and name it beginning_drupal.

3. Within your new folder, create the following two files:

```
beginning_drupal.info
beginning_drupal.module
```

4. Using your favorite text editor, open beginning_drupal.info. Type the following text, and then save the file:

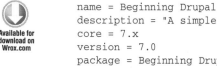
Available for download on Wrox.com

```
name = Beginning Drupal
description = "A simple Drupal module"
core = 7.x
version = 7.0
package = Beginning Drupal
files[] = beginning_drupal.module
```

code snippet chapter 15/beginning_drupal Module beginning_drupal.info

5. Using your favorite text editor, create a file called beginning_drupal.module. Save this new file without entering any text in it.

At this point, your `sites` directory should look like the following:

```
sites/default/modules/beginning_drupal
sites/default/modules/beginning_drupal/beginning_drupal.info
sites/default/modules/beginning_drupal/beginning_drupal.module
```

Note that `beginning_drupal.module` is currently empty.

Next, you need to enable your new module. Follow these steps to do so:

1. Navigate to Administer ➪ Site Building ➪ Modules.

2. Find Beginning Drupal in the list under Modules, select the checkbox to the left, and then click Save.

How It Works

The Beginning Drupal module you just enabled will produce no results, but it does demonstrate how Drupal determines what is and what is not a module. Drupal scans the modules directories looking for folders with a `.info` file and a corresponding `.module` file. The `.info` file must contain specific text to tell Drupal what is the module's name, its version, a short description, and what files are part of the module (`files[] =`). The `.module` file, however, does not have to contain a single word.

Why do an exercise that does not produce results? To demonstrate that module development in Drupal is quite easy. In the next section, you will expand upon this module after a brief introduction to Drupal hooks.

HOOKS

If you are new to Drupal module development, the word *hook* might conjure up images of a recent fishing trip or your Halloween pirate costume. A hook in Drupal, however, is an important and heavily used item. As the name implies, a hook is a method that allows your module to react to an event. Another way to put this is that your module can *hook into* Drupal. For example, you can hook into the creation of a new user account to record additional information about a user's activity, such as what a certain user has created or modified, or notify the administrator of a new user account. Hooks exist for nearly every event, including the creation, modification, and deletion of nodes, comments, and users.

In the following example, you will use the `hook_node_view` hook, simply written as `<module name>_node_view`. This hook will be called every time a node is viewed, allowing your module to act upon the node. Drupal will call this hook once for every node, even if more than one node is displayed on the page. This action is based on the one-way trip the node takes from the database to the user. This means that if you make changes to the node, as you will be doing, the changes are not saved. To save changes through a hook, you would *hook* into the one-way trip from the user back to the database via `hook_node_update`.

In the following exercise, you will utilize `hook_node_view` to change the title of all nodes so that they are preceded by the node type.

TRY IT OUT Using hook_node_view

In this exercise you will implement `hook_node_view` within your module to turn off commenting for all nodes:

1. Open the `beginning_drupal.module` file in your favorite text editor, type in the following code, and then save the file:

```php
<?php
/**
 * Implementation of hook_node_view.
 */
function beginning_drupal_node_view($node, $build_mode) {
  $node->comment = 0;
}
```

> **NOTE** Modules start with a <?php tag but do not end with a ?> as with standard PHP scripts. This is because Drupal is including your module in with other code during runtime thus making the ending ?> tag unnecessary.

2. Rebuild the module cache by visiting the module page and clicking the Save configuration button at the bottom of the page. Configuration and module ➪ modules.

3. Navigate to any node with existing comments to see the changes. Commenting on all of the nodes should be disabled.

How It Works

As you have probably noticed, when using a hook within your module, the word `hook` in the code before `_node_view` is replaced by the module's name, thus `hook_node_view` becomes `beginning_drupal_node_view`. When a hook is implemented (written) in your module, Drupal finds it automatically. The `$node` variable is a PHP object that contains every item of the node. An object is a variable that has many properties. In this example, `$node->comment` is the status of commenting on the node:

　　　　0 = comments disabled and hidden

　　　　1 = comments are visible but read-only

This module modifies the ability to comment on the node but when the node is viewed. This modification is not permanent and is never saved. Thus, if you were to disable the module, commenting would resume at its previous state. `hook_node_view` is a one-way transit from the database to the user, whereas `hook_node_update` is a one-way transit from the user to the database that allows you to permanently alter the node.

> **NOTE** Discover other node properties by using the Devel module (http://drupal.org/project/devel).

More Information

Modifying or acting upon nodes is one of the most common operations in Drupal, and `hook_node_view` is only one of many node-related hooks available. You can find more node hooks at `http://api.drupal.org/api/search/7/hook_node`.

MODULES STEP BY STEP

As you saw in the first exercise, the only two files required in a module are `.info` and `.module`. Modules can consist of a number of files. Here is a partial list of the files you may see in a module:

➤ `.info` (**required**) — Similar to a theme's `.info` file, this file tells Drupal the module's name, description, version, and other useful information.

➤ `.module` (**required**) — This is a collection of hooks and functions that do the actual work of a module.

➤ `.install` — Modules that require database tables or initial configuration perform the operations contained in this file. The `.install` file is processed only when the module is first enabled

➤ `.admin.inc` — This file and others ending in `.inc` contain portions of the `.module` file that have been separated out to enhance readability as well as to increase performance.

➤ `.tpl.php` — Modules that create HTML or other visible items may use a PHP template file to aid the theming process. See Chapter 13 for more information on how these files and functions are used.

➤ `.test` — This is used with the built-in automated testing module, SimpleTest, which is included with Drupal 7. Tests ensure that the module and Drupal are operating correctly.

There are three basic steps to building a module:

1. Choose a name.
2. Create the `.info` file.
3. Create the `.module` file.

Step 1: Choose a Name

A module's name is very important, so care should be taken when choosing one. A module's name is used to name the folder it is contained in, the files associated with it, and its internal functions. It is possible to change the name of your module at a later time, but it is a very tedious process. It is best to save yourself the time and choose a good name from the start.

When choosing a new module name, there are a few naming conventions that you must follow. The first and most important is that a module's name must be unique to the entire website, including themes and other modules. You should do a check on `http://drupal.org` to avoid existing module and theme names. A common mistake is to name a custom module the same as the website's custom theme.

The following guidelines also apply:

➤ Allowed characters include a-z, 0-9 and _ (underscore).

➤ Illegal characters include – (dash) and special characters (such as Ç, á, ?, and à).

➤ The first character cannot be a number.

Table 15-1 gives a few examples of illegal and allowed module names.

TABLE 15-1

INCORRECT	CORRECT
1plus *(first character is a number)*	plus1
hello-world *(includes a dash)*	hello_world
Blog *(conflicts with core module)*	custom_blog

Although uppercase characters are allowed, using all lowercase is considered good practice to avoid confusion.

Step 2: Create the .info File

If you have read Chapter 13, "Theming," then you are already familiar with Drupal's `.info` file format. A `.info` file is required for all themes and modules, because it gives Drupal the specifics about a module, such as its name, version, description, and so on.

The following are the contents of the `.info` file from the custom module you built earlier in this chapter:

```
name = Beginning Drupal
description = "A simple Drupal module"
core = 7.x
version = 7.0
package = Beginning Drupal
files[] = beginning_drupal.module
```

As you can see, a `.info` file can be quite straightforward. Here is a line-by-line breakdown of its contents:

➤ `name` — A friendly name for the module that appears on the administrative pages. This name can contain special characters, spaces, mixed case, or foreign languages.

➤ `description` — A short description of what the module does. This is displayed on the administrative pages.

➤ `core` — Indicates which version of Drupal this module is compatible with. The `.x` indicates compatibility with all minor versions (7.1, 7.2, and so on).

➤   `version` — An arbitrary number that should begin with the version of Drupal and then include a secondary number to indicate its current version. Modules downloaded from `http://drupal.org` have this piece added automatically.

➤   `package` — Modules can be grouped together in packages. In this case, the module is categorized under Beginning Drupal. This is handy to keep related modules together.

➤   `files[]` — This line is required for all files that will be included in your module.

➤   `dependencies[]` — If your module depends upon one or more other modules, being enabled, you should use the `dependencies` parameter to list each one individually in the `.info` file. For example:

```
dependencies[] = taxonomy
```

This will ensure that the Taxonomy module is enabled before your module can be enabled.

The full list of `.info` parameters can be found at `http://drupal.org/node/231036`.

Step 3: Create the .module File

This is a step that is easier said than done. To begin, you first decide where your module will start. Drupal modules do not start from line 1, but rather, from any one of Drupal's hooks. In the second exercise, `hook_node_view` was the starting point for the module, but only when Drupal is displaying a node. If the module also implemented `hook_comment_view`, it would contain two starting points: one when a node is viewed and the other when a comment is viewed.

Drupal is built using the PHP scripting language; thus, all Drupal modules are built using PHP. In order to effectively write Drupal modules, you should invest some time in learning the PHP scripting language. However, understand that PHP is merely the foundation for Drupal. Drupal adds a new layer on top of PHP by providing new functions and functionality. In fact, Drupal adds over thousands of new functions and over 100 hooks to deal with website-specific items such as RSS feeds, comments, user accounts, website content, and so on. This reason alone is why Drupal is considered a content management framework instead of a system.

CREATING A PAGE

PHP is powerful all by itself, but when combined with Drupal, it's awesome.

Capturing a specific URL is one of the most common actions a module performs. Unfortunately, it is also a common frustration point for new Drupal developers who are unaccustomed to how Drupal works. When you're writing custom PHP scripts or static HTML files to create a custom page (for example, `http://localhost/bargains`), you would simply create a new folder called `bargains` and put either `index.php` or `index.html` inside the folder — very simple and straightforward. However, Drupal does things quite differently.

Drupal employs some unusual terminology for this process, but as you use Drupal, it will gradually make more sense. URL paths in Drupal are known as *menu items*. In the `http://localhost/bargains` example, `bargains` is the menu item. This might be confusing because a menu is also a set of links on the left or right side of your website. The `bargains` menu item may or may not be visible in the navigational menu, but it is still considered a menu item.

Capturing Custom URLs with hook_menu

Now that you understand that a custom URL path is a menu item, it should make sense that you would use hook_menu to capture custom URL paths. Drupal modules register their custom URLs by implementing hook_menu and returning a PHP array of URL paths.

In the next exercise, you extend the module to provide a programming classic "Hello world" page at the custom URL path http://localhost/helloworld.

TRY IT OUT   Using hook_menu to Create Custom URLs

In this exercise you will add a custom page at the URL path http://*localhost*/helloworld using hook_menu:

1. Open the beginning_drupal.module file in your favorite text editor, and type in the following code, and then save the file:

Available for download on Wrox.com

```php
<?php
/**
 * Implementation of hook_menu().
 */
function beginning_drupal_menu() {
  $items['helloworld'] = array(
    'title' => 'Hello World',
    'page callback' => 'beginning_drupal_page',
    'access arguments' => array('access content'),
  ); //end $items
  return $items;
}

/**
 * Menu callback to say hello to the world
 */
function beginning_drupal_page() {
  return "Hello world!";
}
```

code snippet Chapter 15 beginning_drupal Module

2. Rebuild the module cache by visiting the module page and clicking the Save configuration button at the bottom of the page at Modules page.

3. Enter http://localhost/helloworld or http://localhost/?q=helloworld if clean URLs is not enabled.

How It Works

Implementing hook_menu allows a module to capture specific URL paths. This is done by returning a PHP array that is "keyed" on the path that you would like to capture and contains an array of information regarding the path. The following is an abbreviation of the previous code, with line numbers added for the purposes of a line-by-line description:

```
1:  function beginning_drupal_menu() {
2:    $items['helloworld'] = array(
```

```
3:       'title' => 'Hello World',
4:       'page callback' => 'beginning_drupal_page',
5:       'access arguments' => array('access content'),
6:     ); //end $items
7:     return $items;
8:   }
9:
10:  function beginning_drupal_page() {
11:      return "Hello world!";
12:  }
```

Here's the explanation of the function behind each line of code:

➤ 1: `function beginning_drupal_menu()` is a PHP function based on the Drupal hook `hook_menu`. Note that the word `hook_` is replaced by the name of the module, which must match the file's name. `beginning_drupal.module` uses `beginning_drupal_menu`. The function is ended on line 8.

➤ 2: `$items['helloworld'] = array(` is the start of a PHP array that ends on line 6 with the `);`symbols. The `'helloworld'` portion is the same as the URL path (see Figure 15-1).

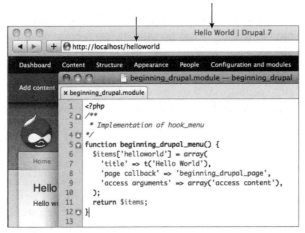

FIGURE 15-1

If you want to capture the URL `http://localhost/hello/world`, you would use `$items['hello/world']`. This syntax does not change if Drupal is located within a subdomain or if clean URLs are disabled.

➤ 3: `'title' => 'Hello World',` is the part of the `$items` array that tells Drupal what the browser's title bar should read.

➤ 4: `'page callback' => 'beginning_drupal_page',` is the name of the PHP function that Drupal will call when a user navigates to the menu location. In this case, when a user navigates to `http://localhost/helloworld`, Drupal will execute the `beginning_drupal_page` function that begins on line 10.

➤   `5: 'access arguments' => array('access content').` An array of permissions the user must have in order to view the menu. In this example the user must have the `access content` permission in order to view this page.

➤   `10: function beginning_drupal_page() {` begins the function that Drupal's menu system was told about on line 4. This function could carry any name, but starting it with the name of your module is good programming practice.

Note that this module does not use the `echo` or `print` functions of PHP, but rather it *returns* information to Drupal. This allows other modules to modify the output as well as to be themed properly. The data is returned to Drupal, which then passes it to other modules, and finally passes it to the theme layer for final output to the user. Note that the output appears in the middle of the Drupal website in the area provided by the `$content` theming variable.

MODIFYING EXISTING MODULES

Open-source software gives you the opportunity to use any module as the foundation for your work. In fact, it is the very nature of open source to take the work of others, improve upon it, and then provide it back to the community. This is how Drupal has become the great piece of software you enjoy today.

If you are like most website creators, you probably have already dived into the source code of the contributed modules you downloaded. In this section, you'll review how you can cleanly modify existing code to meet your needs and give your changes back to the community, thereby helping to improve Drupal.

To Modify or Not to Modify, That Is the Question

Drupal has a few rules concerning when one should modify the code or not. The first and foremost rule is *do not hack core*. This rule is for your own sanity, because almost everything can be done without *hacking* (modifying) the core code of Drupal. Modifying core leaves you open to security vulnerabilities, may have unintended consequences with contributed modules, and makes it difficult to upgrade. If you value your sanity, you'll avoid hacking core.

The second rule is to modify a module through another module. Drupal's core and contributed modules are explicitly written to allow you to modify their output and functionality through another module. For example, the Userpoints contributed module (`http://drupal.org/project/user-points`) provides `hook_userpoints`, which allows a separate module to modify nearly all aspects of the Userpoints module with only a few lines of code.

Rule number three is to always communicate with the community. The Drupal community is extremely active and supportive. If a module doesn't provide the necessary functionality, post your requirements in the issues queue and let the community help you. Each contributed module has an issues queue that is accessible from the module's frontpage.

Patching

As mentioned previously, Drupal is built upon community modifications. Contributed modules are created and improved upon by people like you, so you should not shy away from modifying a contributed module's code. There is, however, a correct way to do this.

The first step is to create a backup of the original code you downloaded from http://drupal.org. Next, make your modifications to the code and create a diff file (also known as a *patch*). The diff file will show the *differences* between the original and your modifications. This file has the following two very important purposes:

> **A diff file can be used to automatically repeat your changes to a module** — When the contributed module you modified is updated on drupal.org, you can simply reapply your diff file without having to remember what it is that you modified.

> **A diff file (patch) can be exchanged with others and posted on drupal.org** — This eliminates the confusing explanations about how to implement the modifications (for example: "Between line 15 and 20 next to the if statement but before the for loop, place an x in the 12th character spot"). In fact, a patch file is the only way that changes are made to Drupal's core. Patch files are tested for conformity to Drupal's coding and security standards as well as their functionality.

Creating a Patch

Patch files are created with the diff command and applied with the patch command. Mac OS X and Linux operating systems include these two utilities, but they must be installed separately on Windows (Cygwin is a great option for Windows users). Optionally, many development applications have this functionality built in, such as Eclipse, Textmate, and others.

In the next exercise, you will create a patch for the beginning_drupal module you created earlier in this chapter.

At its most basic, a patch is created as follows:

```
diff -u original.module modified.module  > changes.patch
```

The created patch file changes.patch could then be applied to the original module with the patch command as shown here:

```
patch -p0 < changes.patch
```

TRY IT OUT   Creating a Patch File

In this exercise, you create a patch file against the beginning_drupal module.

> *NOTE In order to complete this exercise, you will need to have the diff and patch applications installed. Mac OS X and Linux include these utilities, but Windows does not. Windows users can download and install diffutils from http://gnuwin32.sourceforge.net/packages/diffutils.htm. Alternatively the Cygwin shell can be used http://cygwin.org.*

Follow these steps to create the patch:

1. Create a copy of `beginning_drupal.module`, and name the new file `beginning_drupal.module.org`.

2. Open `beginning_drupal.module` in your favorite text editor and modify the function `beginning_drupal_page` to read as follows:

   ```
   function beginning_drupal_page() {
     return "Hello World! Its a brand new day!";
   }
   ```

3. Using the command line, navigate to the `beginning_drupal` folder and use the `diff` command to create a patch file.

   ```
   diff -up beginning_drupal.module.org beginning_drupal.module > bd_changes.patch
   ```

   The resulting file should look similar to this:

   ```
   --- beginning_drupal.module.org
   +++ beginning_drupal.module
   @@ -14,5 +14,5 @@ function beginning_drupal_menu() {
     * Menu callback to say hello to the world
     */
    function beginning_drupal_page() {
   -  return "Hello world!";
   -}
   \ No newline at end of file
   +  return "Hello world! it's a brand new day!";
   +}
   ```

Lines beginning with a – (minus sign) will be removed when the patch is applied and lines beginning with a + will be added.

Testing the Patch

Follow these steps to test the patch you just created:

1. Delete `beginning_drupal.module` and rename `beginning_drupal.module.org` to `beginning_drupal.module` (in other words, revert to the original).

2. At a command line and within the `beginning_drupal` module folder, type in the following command:

   ```
   patch -p0 < bd_changes.patch
   ```

3. Open the `beginning_drupal.module` file to verify that the changes were made.

How It Works

The `diff` command works by comparing two files line by line and creating a separate file containing the differences. The `patch` command reads `diff` files and modifies the referenced files. These two commands can be used to track and recreate the changes to one file, multiple files, or an entire folder. However, it is best to keep the changes to a single file.

The diff utility is used regularly in open source projects to enable developers, aspiring developers, and hackers to create patch files and send them to each other. These patch files make it easy to see what changes were made.

> **NOTE** *When creating patch files try to keep the changes to a minimum and only to those related to each other. For example, if implementing two new features within a module create two separate patches, one for each feature.*

The Value of the Patch

You may be saying to yourself that your PHP and programming skills are not strong enough to post them on the Web for all to see. Patching is not simply about posting your code — it is a method of communication. A patch allows developers to immediately see the changes made to a module, so your ideas and opinions are not lost in a sea of developer lingo. Make your changes, create a patch, and post it. A patch is worth a thousand words.

Aside from sharing your code on drupal.org (which is highly encouraged), patching helps you to keep track of your changes. This is extremely important, because updates will undoubtedly be made to the modules you are using, and you must keep your modules up-to-date in order to avoid security issues. Patch files provide you with a simple way to upgrade your modules and then reapply the changes you made.

When to Modify

The two items you should take away from this section are

➤ Modify contributed modules as a last resort.

➤ Track your changes by creating patch files with the diff command.

And although the following has already been stated several times throughout this book, it warrants repeating: *Do not hack core.* Always try to modify a module with a module. If this is not possible, contact the module's author to request the change, and finally resort to modifying the modules yourself only if all else fails. These may seem like rigid rules, but they are put in place to save your own sanity. The pain of upgrading and maintaining tens of thousands of lines of code is not an easy task.

SUMMARY

This chapter provided you with a taste of what it is like to build a custom module. In the first example, you saw that a module begins with the implementation of a hook. The hook hook_node_view provided your module with the ability to react to the viewing of a node as well as to change the properties of node before it was viewed. This was a one-way trip from the database to the user, so the changes made to the node were not saved. The second example reviewed the use of `hook_menu` to capture a specific URL path and provide a custom page. Although it may seem a bit strange at first, this simple hook provides a lot of power to your modules.

As you discovered in this chapter, hooks are key elements for working with Drupal modules. They provide a module with an ability to react to events such as a node being viewed, a user account created, or a comment being deleted. In the next chapters, you will learn to create custom modules, then review the top 10 hooks used in Drupal modules. These two chapters will guide you through creating the custom modules that will really make your site shine.

EXERCISES

1. What is the definition of a module?

2. Why is choosing a good module name important?

3. What are some rules to follow when choosing a module name?

4. What is the first and foremost rule of Drupal?

Answers to the Exercises can be found in the Appendix.

▶ **WHAT YOU LEARNED IN THIS CHAPTER**

➤ Drupal is built upon a modular structure, meaning that small bits of code can be added to extend the overall functionality of Drupal. Modules extend, enhance, or modify the functionality of Drupal.

➤ A hook is a method that allows your module to react to an event. Hooks exist for nearly every event, including the creation, modification, and deletion of nodes, comments, and users.

➤ Modifying core leaves you open to security vulnerabilities and may have unintended consequences with contributed modules.

➤ Read more about hooks and the full Drupal API at `http://api.drupal.org`.

16

Development Hooks

WHAT YOU WILL LEARN IN THIS CHAPTER:

➤ The top eight Drupal hooks, which allow you to:

- ➤ Create custom pages
- ➤ Add custom permissions
- ➤ Act upon user activities such as new account creations
- ➤ Create custom filters for use in text formats
- ➤ Modify your site's forms
- ➤ Making your modules translatable
- ➤ Adding theming functions to your modules

The previous chapter provided an introduction to Drupal module development, but this chapter dives into the subject. If you are a seasoned developer new to Drupal or simply ready to dive straight into the subject and get to the heart of development, this is the chapter for you. This chapter explains how to use the most common Drupal hooks and theming tasks. In researching this book I wrote a script that analyzed over 2,300 stable modules for Drupal 6, the most active and well-used version of Drupal to date. From this list I chose the top eight most common hooks to introduce you to in this chapter.

These hooks allow you to create custom pages, add administrative settings, custom permissions, new blocks, act on user activities, create custom filters, and modify any of your site's forms. I was pleasantly surprised to find that `hook_help` also made it into the top eight, a hook that provides helpful documentation to your site users.

Why eight? Actually there are over ten. The ninth is `hook_theme`, which is introduced in the theming portion of this chapter. 10, 11, and 12 are `hook_schema`, `hook_install`, and `hook_uninstall` all of which are used for storing custom data and you'll explore these in the next chapter. If you complete Chapters 15, 16, and 17 you will have been exposed to well over 20 of the top hook that are used to power over 90 percent of Drupal's contributed modules.

The hooks covered include:

➤ hook_menu

　　Create's custom pages, tabs, or administrative settings.

➤ hook_permission

　　Custom permissions.

➤ hook_node_* (hook_node_insert, hook_node_delete, etc.)

　　Act on upon nodes being created, edited, viewed, or deleted.

➤ hook_block_*

　　Create new blocks.

➤ hook_user_*

　　Act upon a user account's creation, deletion, user, or profile view.

➤ hook_filter_info

　　Add a custom filter for use within a text format such as the Filtered HTML format.

➤ hook_form_alter

　　Modify any of your site's webforms such as the user login form, or contact page.

➤ hook_help

　　Add custom help to aid your site users.

HOOKS: A MODULE'S STARTING POINT

As you saw in the previous chapter, a module is a PHP script that consists of a set of functions. The starting point for a Drupal module is not line 1, but rather, one of Drupal's many hooks. Hooks allow your module to "hook" into (be triggered by) an action caused by Drupal's core or contributed modules. For example, if you wanted to perform an action whenever a new node is created (i.e., inserted), you would use `hook_node_insert`. Hooks exist for nodes, comments, users, and almost all actions within Drupal. Most hooks allow you to modify the data passed into it (such as modifying a node before it's saved) but a few simply alert your module that an action has occurred.

> **NOTE** For the advanced developers out there hooks are created by using either the Drupal function `module_invoke_all` or simply `module_invoke`. For example, the node module calls `module_invoke_all('node_presave', $node)`, which creates `hook_node_presave`.

COMMUNITY DOCUMENTATION

A printed book is never a substitute for the constantly moving and dynamic nature of community documentation and the Drupal community has some of the best documentation in the open source world. This chapter introduces these hooks to you to help guide your module development and give you a jump-start on becoming a Drupal developer. Each hook, however, could easily have an entire chapter dedicated to its use thus you should not use this as a definitive guide. If you don't see something you're looking for jump over to the Drupal community and ask.

Every hook in Drupal is documented at `http://api.drupal.org` (simply known as a.d.o) a site that you should become very good friends with. You should also read the developer guides at `http://drupal.org/handbooks`, which are constantly updated by the community to give you the most relevant and fresh information.

THE HOOKS

The top eight most used module hooks are outlined over the next several pages. Try out the examples by typing them into the beginning_drupal.module file you created in Chapter 15.

hook_menu

As you learned in the previous chapter, this hook allows your module to register a menu item with Drupal. In Drupal, menus are all items with a specific and unique URL. Menu items may or may not appear in the navigational menu block, but they all must have a unique URL. In order to increase performance, this hook is processed only when your module is enabled and the menu is cached. If you modify your `hook_menu`, you will need to disable and re-enable your module or flush (rebuild) the menu cache.

The `hook_menu` hook expects an array of menu items returned to it. This array will contain the URL to be registered, the title of the page, an array of permissions required to view the page, and the name of a function that Drupal will execute when the page is accessed, which is known as a *page callback*.

```
/**
 * Implementation of hook_menu().
 */
function beginning_drupal_menu() {
  $items['helloworld'] = array(
    'title' => 'Hello World',
    'access arguments' => array('access content'),
    'page callback' => 'beginning_drupal_page',
  ); //end $items
  return $items;
}

/**
 * Menu callback to say hello to the world
 */
function beginning_drupal_page() {
  return "Hello world!";
}
```

code snippet Chapter 16 bdhooks Module

hook_permission

This hook creates a permission set for your module that can be assigned to roles at Configuration ⇨ Permissions.

Permissions are probably the easiest items to implement in your module, because Drupal does all of the work. In this hook, you simply return an array of strings that define your permissions as shown in the following example:

```
function beginning_drupal_permission() {
  $permissions = array(
    'view hello world' => array(
      'title' => t('View the hello world page'),
      'description' => t('Allow a user to modify the hello world message')
    ),
  );
  return $permissions;
}
```

You can use this permission within your module by using with `user_access()`. For example:

```
if (user_access('view hello world')) {
  return $message;
}
```

Adding a new permission created by `hook_permission` to the earlier `hook_menu` example would have the following code. Note that the `view hello world` permission was used in the access arguments of `hook_menu`.

```
/**
 * Implementation of hook_menu().
 */
function beginning_drupal_menu() {
  $items['helloworld'] = array(
    'title' => t('Hello World'),
    'access arguments' => array('view hello world'),
    'page callback' => 'beginning_drupal_page',
  ); //end $items
  return $items;
}


/**
 * Menu callback to say hello to the world
 */
function beginning_drupal_page() {
  return "Hello world!";
}

/**
 * Implementation of hook_permission
 */
function beginning_drupal_permission() {
  $permissions = array(
    'view hello world' => array(
```

```
          'title' => t('View the hello world page'),
          'description' => t('Allow a user to modify the hello world message'),
      ),
      );
   return $permissions;
 }
```

code snippet Chapter 16 bdhooks Module

hook_node_*

Prior to Drupal 7, there was a single hook called `hook_nodeapi`. This hook has been replaced with a series of multiple hooks that each begin with `hook_node`. This series allows you to operate on and modify a node at nearly every stage of its life, starting with its creation all the way to the time it's deleted.

Here is a list of just a few of the `hook_node` hooks that are available for your use:

> `hook_node_presave`
>
> `hook_node_insert`
>
> `hook_node_update`
>
> `hook_node_prepare`
>
> `hook_node_load`
>
> `hook_node_view`
>
> `hook_node_delete`

> **NOTE** *A complete list of the* `hook_node` *hooks can be found at* `http://api.drupal.org/api/search/7/hook_node`.

Choose the appropriate `hook_node` hook for your purposes and implement it in your module. For example, `hook_node_load` is used to react and/or modify nodes after they have been loaded from the database and are in transit to the user (Database ➪ `hook_node_load` ➪ User). The hook catches a node in a one-way transit so changes that you make are displayed to the user but are not saved back to the database. For example, the following code turns commenting off on all nodes:

```
function beginning_drupal_node_load($node, $types) {
  $node->comment = 0;
}
```

If you want to save changes to a node, you could use `hook_node_update`, which operates during a one-way transit from the user to the database (User ➪ `hook_node_update` ➪ Database).

hook_block

The blocks available at Structure ➪ Blocks are provided by `hook_block_*` hooks. You can use these hooks to add a new custom block.

`hook_block` is implemented via the following four hooks:

➤ `hook_block_info` — Returns an array to Drupal with a list of blocks that your module will return.

➤ `hook_block_view` — Displays the block to site visitors.

➤ `hook_block_configure` — Adds custom configuration options to a block.

➤ `hook_block_save` — Saves custom configuration options.

> **NOTE** Only `hook_block_info` and `hook_block_view` are required; the others are optional.

Here's a basic example of how to use a `hook_block`.

```
/**
 * Implementation of hook_block_info()
 */
function beginning_drupal_block_info() {
  $blocks['beginning_drupal']['info'] = t('Beginning Drupal');
  return $blocks;
}

/**
 * Implementation of hook_block_view()
 */
function beginning_drupal_block_view($delta = '') {
  if ($delta == 'beginning_drupal') {
    $block['subject'] = t('Beginning Drupal');
    $block['content'] = t('Hello World');
    return $block;
  }
}
```

code snippet Chapter 16 bdhooks Module

More information about creating blocks can be found at `http://api.drupal.org/api/search/7/hook_block`.

hook_user

Just like `hook_node_*`, prior to Drupal 7 `hook_user` was a single hook that has been branched out to multiple hooks, each beginning with `hook_user`. These hooks allow you to act on the creation, updating, or deletion of a user account as well as the modification of a user's profile, a user's roles, and more.

You first start by choosing the operation on which you want to act. Two examples are `hook_user_presave`, used to act upon or add additional information during initial account creation, and `hook_user_view`, commonly used to add information to the user profile page.

A complete list of all user hooks can be found at `http://api.drupal.org/api/search/7/hook_user`.

The following example demonstrates how to use `hook_user_presave` and `hook_user_view` to record the language of the web browser used when a new account was created. This information will then be displayed on the new user's profile page.

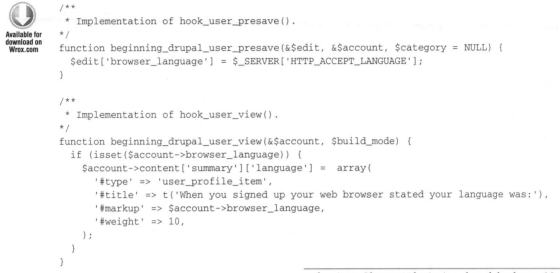

```
/**
 * Implementation of hook_user_presave().
 */
function beginning_drupal_user_presave(&$edit, &$account, $category = NULL) {
  $edit['browser_language'] = $_SERVER['HTTP_ACCEPT_LANGUAGE'];
}


/**
 * Implementation of hook_user_view().
 */
function beginning_drupal_user_view(&$account, $build_mode) {
  if (isset($account->browser_language)) {
    $account->content['summary']['language'] =  array(
      '#type' => 'user_profile_item',
      '#title' => t('When you signed up your web browser stated your language was:'),
      '#markup' => $account->browser_language,
      '#weight' => 10,
    );
  }
}
```

code snippet Chapter 16 beginning_drupal_hook_user Module

hook_filter_info

Text formats such as Filtered HTML are constructed of a series of filters. These filters take in the text entered by the user and output a modified version of the text. Examples of filters include BBCode or Wiki Syntax. You can use `hook_filter_info` to create your own filter for use within text formats.

In the following example, `hook_filter` is used to create a filter which replaces instances of the word Drupal with "I heart Drupal":

```
/**
 * Implementation of hook_filter_info
 */
function beginning_drupal_filter_info() {
  $filters['filter_love_drupal'] = array(
    'title' => t('Love Drupal filter'),
    'description' => t('Converts the word Drupal into the phrase "I heart
Drupal"'),
    'process callback' => '_beginning_drupal_love_filter',
  );
  return $filters;
}

/**
 * Filter processor called from hook_filter_info
 */
function _beginning_drupal_love_filter($text) {
  return str_replace("Drupal", "I heart Drupal", $text);
}
```

code snippet Chapter 16 beginning_drupal_hook_filter Module

hook_form_alter

Easily one of the most powerful hooks within Drupal, this hooks allows you to modify any form on your site such as the user login form, contact form, or the node add form. Drupal creates web forms differently than any other content management system (CMS). Traditionally, forms are created with the `<form>` HTML tag, but in Drupal, they are created through the use of PHP arrays. If you're an experienced HTML user, you might find this strange — until you discover `hook_form_alter`.

Every form array is sent to all modules that implement `hook_form_alter`, allowing the modules to alter the form before the final HTML is rendered. This allows you to add, remove, or modify form elements. For example, you could change a text field into a text box or a drop-down form into a multiple-selection field.

The following example demonstrates the traditional method of creating a form:

```
<form name="helloworld" id="helloworld">
   <input type="textfield" length="30" name="message" value ="Submit your message"/>
   <input type="submit" value="Submit message"/>
</form>
```

And here is the same form created using Drupal's method, which it calls *Forms API* (or *FAPI*):

```
$form = array();
$form['message'] = array(
  '#type' => 'textfield',
  '#default_value' => t('Submit your message'),
  '#length' => 10
);
$form['submit'] = array(
  '#type' => 'submit',
  '#value' => 'Submit your message'
);
return drupal_render_form($form);
```

The advantage of using Drupal to build the forms is twofold. The first is security. Drupal manages the forms and makes sure that no one tampers with or alters the form. It does this through the use of a form token. The second is the ability to provide dynamic forms. Each form array is passed to all modules that have implemented `hook_form_alter` for additional processing. This allows modules to attach new, modify existing, or remove form elements and add attributes such as CSS ids or classes. FAPI and `hook_form_alter` are the two secrets to the dynamic nature of Drupal.

When `hook_form_alter` has been implemented in your module, Drupal will automatically send all form arrays to your module. Your module watches for and modifies the form using FAPI. FAPI is an array syntax that is used to create forms in Drupal. You can find more information on FAPI at `http://api.drupal.org/api/drupal/developer-topics-forms_api.html/7`.

In the following example, `hook_form_alter` is used to modify the user login block to reduce the sizes from the standard 15 to just 10, it also adds custom classes for the name and password fields.

```
/**
 * Implementation of hook_form_alter
 */
function beginning_drupal_form_alter(&$form, &$form_state, $form_id) {
  if ($form_id == 'user_login_block') {
```

```
      $form['name']['#size'] = 10;
      $form['name']['#attributes']['class'][] = 'login-name';
      $form['pass']['#size'] = 10;
      $form['pass']['#attributes']['class'][] = 'login-pass';
   }
}
```

code snippet Chapter 16 hook_form_alter module

By adding the form id into the function name you can target specific forms. For example, the previous example could be written as:

```
function beginning_drupal_form_user_login_block_alter($form, $form_state,) {
   $form['name']['#size'] = 10;
   $form['name']['#attributes']['class'][] = 'login-name';
   $form['pass']['#size'] = 10;
   $form['pass']['#attributes']['class'][] = 'login-pass';
}
```

hook_help

This is a useful function that provides help messages to users of your site. You can use this to create a custom help section located at Administer ➪ Help or to add additional help messages to existing areas of the site. Help messages are returned to Drupal based on the URL path on which they should appear. For example, if you want to add a new help message on the comment administration page, you would use the path /admin/content/comment.

The following example demonstrates how to use hook_help to create two help messages. The first is accessible at Administer ➪ Help ➪ Beginning Drupal, and the second at Administer ➪ Content ➪ Comments:

Available for download on Wrox.com

```
<?php
/**
 * Implementation of hook_help().
 */
function beginning_drupal_help($path, $arg) {
  switch ($path) {
    case 'admin/help#beginning_drupal':
      $output = '<p>' . t('The hook_help demonstration module is a simple module to
understand how hook_help works') . '</p>';
      return $output;
    case 'admin/content/comment':
    return '<p>' . t('You must receive prior approval before deleting or unpublishing
comments.') . '</p>';
  }
}
```

code snippet Chapter 16 hook_help module

MAKING YOUR MODULES THEMEABLE

Part of what makes Drupal a successful CMS is the ability to translate, override, theme, and rearrange nearly all aspects of the system while still maintaining a common system that is in lockstep with hundreds of thousands of others. This system allows developers to focus on creating robust and mature modules and themers/designers to focus on creating attractive looking websites. This flexibility in theming comes from a few simple functions and programming principles.

The guiding principle when writing a Drupal module is that all output needs to be overridable. As described previously, forms can be overridden through the use of `hook_form_alter`. Previous examples also used the `t()` function (meaning translate), to wrap all text strings, enabling Drupal to replace them with translated versions.

The t() Function

This function should be used to wrap all text sent to the user to allow for language translation. The following shows this function's most basic usage:

```
return t('Hello World');
```

If the website language was Spanish this would be translated to "hola mundo."

The `t()` function can also take in other variables as shown in the following example, making translating a website easy. Instead of just translating "The car is green" as a whole sentence, the function translates separate parts of the sentence and pieces it together. "Red" and "blue" can easily replace "green". Likewise, "The bicycle is" can easily replace "The car is."

```
t('The car is !color', array('!color', 'Green'));
```

The advantage of using replacement variables in this way is that the translator can translate each piece independently. For example, the following translations of the code into Spanish and French were pieced together with replacement variables.

Este coche es verde.

Cette voiture est verte.

format_plural

Languages often have different methods of displaying numbers. For example, English uses the concept of singular and plural (such as one *car* but two *cars*). The `format_plural` function not only helps your module use proper grammar by adding the *s* when appropriate, but it also helps translators identify singular/plural formats.

For example, if you're telling a user how many points they have it could output either "You have 1 point" or "You have 5 points".

You can use format plural to make the plural choice for you. The syntax for `format_plural` is:

```
format_plural($count, $singular, $plural, array $args = array(), array $options =
array())
```

Here is how you can use it:

```
$output = format_plural($points, "You have 1 point", "You have @count points");
```

Theme Functions and Template Files

If you have ever themed a website and found it difficult to modify a particular item on that website, then you will understand the importance of the theme functions and theme template files. These two items make it possible for themers and others to modify the output of your module without directly modifying your module. Any output more than a simple string should utilize a theme function or template file. Any output that contains HTML or other markup should *always* be displayed through a theme function.

The decision to use a theme function or a template file is generally based on the amount of programming logic (if statements, while loops, and so on) needed to produce the output. Although care should be taken to minimize or eliminate programming logic within themeable output it is not always possible. Template files should be kept free of all programming logic, whereas theme functions may contain some programming logic.

Drupal maintains a theme registry of all the functions and template files that are used to produce your site. This theme registry helps to make theming easier by providing you a central place to determine how a page or a section on a page was constructed. As a developer you need to register your theme functions or template files before they can be used.

Register your themeable items by implementing hook_theme. All registrations are cached and are only updated when you visit the modules page, the themes page or manually flush the theme cache by using the devel module.

> **NOTE** *Use the Theme developer module to review the theme registry.* http://drupal.org/project/devel_theme.

Theme Functions

Small bits of HTML or output that require some programming logic work best in a theme function. The following three steps are needed to use a theme function:

1. Register the theme function.

2. Write the theme function by preceding the function name with theme_.

3. Utilize the theme function with theme().

To see how a theme function is created, recall the following beginning_drupal_page function introduced in the previous chapter:

```
/**
 * Menu callback to say hello to the world
 */
function beginning_drupal_page() {
  $msg = "Hello world! its a brand new day!";
  return $msg;
}
```

To move the $msg to a theme function, you would need to implement hook_theme and create a theme function as follows:

```
/**
 * Implementation of hook_theme
 */
function beginning_drupal_theme() {
  return array('beginning_drupal_page_msg' => array(
      'variables' => array('msg' => NULL),
    ),
  );
}

/**
 * Theme function for the hello world page
 */
function theme_beginning_drupal_page_msg($variables) {
  $output = '<div class="beginning-drupal-page">'. $variables['msg'] .'</div>';
  return $output;
}

/**
 * Implementation of hook_menu().
 */
function beginning_drupal_menu() {
  $items['helloworld'] = array(
    'title' => Hello World,
    'access arguments' => array('access content'),
    'page callback' => 'beginning_drupal_page',
  ); //end $items
  return $items;
}

/**
 * Menu callback to say hello to the world
 */
function beginning_drupal_page() {
  $msg = "Hello world! Its a brand new day!";
  return theme('beginning_drupal_page_msg', array('msg' => $msg);
}
```

code snippet Chapter 16 hook_theme module

Although the use of a theme function adds a few more lines of code, the flexibility it provides is well worth it.

Template Files

When the output contains large amounts of HTML, a template file may be better suited to your needs than a theme function. Template files utilize the PHP template engine (discussed in Chapter 13). Moving the theme function into a template file requires a change to the hook_theme and the creation of a template file. Here is the change you would need to make to `hook_theme` in `beginning_drupal_page`:

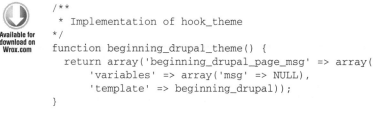

```
/**
 * Implementation of hook_theme
 */
function beginning_drupal_theme() {
  return array('beginning_drupal_page_msg' => array(
      'variables' => array('msg' => NULL),
      'template' => beginning_drupal));
}
```

code snippet Chapter 16 hook_theme module

Note the addition of `'template' => beginning_drupal`.

Here is the `beginning_drupal.tpl.php` template file that you would create:

```
<div class="beginning-drupal-page">
  <?php print $msg; ?>
</div>
```

Note that the syntax for a theme function is different from the syntax of a template file. This is because a theme function begins with PHP and creates HTML, whereas a template file begins with HTML and contains a tiny bit of PHP. For example, the template file uses `<?php print $msg; ?>`; whereas a theme function does not use `print` instead uses the `return` statement.

> ⊗ **WARNING** *After modifying* `hook_theme`, *you must visit the modules page or use the* `devel` *module to rebuild the theme cache.*

hook_theme

Implementing `hook_theme` is the key to making your module themeable, and fortunately, it's easy to use. This hook returns an array that contains the details of the themeable pieces. The format can be copied and pasted with just a few key pieces needing to be changed. For example:

```
1: function beginning_theme() {
2:   return array('beginning_page_msg' => array(
3:       'variables' => array('msg' => NULL),
4:       'template' => 'beginning_drupal'));
5: }
```

Here's what's happening in this example:

➤ `2: return array('beginning_drupal_page_msg' => array(`

This first array is keyed on (named after) the theme function that will be used. In this case, the theme function will be named `theme_beginning_drupal_page_msg` and utilized by calling `theme('beginning_drupal_page_msg')`.

➤   `3: 'variables' => array('msg' => NULL),`

Variables are bits of information passed to the function or template file. The variable is the `$msg` in the theme function, and the `<?php print $msg; ?>` in the template file.

➤   `4: 'template' => beginning_drupal)`

If this line is present, then Drupal will search for a `.tpl.php` file in the module's directory named `beginning_drupal` (i.e. `beginning_drupal.tpl.php`). A theme may override this template file by copying it into the theme folder and modifying it accordingly. In other words your module provides an example/default template for your module's output.

SUMMARY

This chapter provided a lot of information in a mile-high crash course on Drupal module development. Nearly all of Drupal's contributed modules began with one of the hooks covered in this chapter. Each one of the hooks covered could have at least a chapter, if not an entire book, dedicated to its use. The power of these hooks is immense.

In the next chapter, you will create your own module from start to finish. You'll implement many of the hooks introduced in this chapter and expand upon them with other Drupal functions. Proceed to the next chapter to put these hooks to use and explore the missing top hooks `hook_schema`, `hook_install`, and `hook_uninstall`, which create database tables for you to store your own custom data.

EXERCISES

1.   How do you implement a hook?

2.   What are the advantages of using Drupal's Form API to build web forms?

3.   What is one of the guiding principles when writing a Drupal module?

4.   How is the syntax for a theme function different from the syntax for a template file?

Answers to the Exercises can be found in the Appendix.

▶ WHAT YOU LEARNED IN THIS CHAPTER

➤ Hooks are the starting point for a Drupal module. They allow your module to "hook" into (be triggered by) an action caused by Drupal's core or contributed modules.

➤ `http://api.drupal.org` (ado) is the place to go to learn about all of Drupal's hooks and function calls.

➤ Hooks exist for nodes, comments, users, and almost all actions within Drupal. Most allow you to modify the data passed into the hook before that data is viewed, saved, or used.

➤ The `t()` function is used to wrap all text sent to the user to allow for language translation.

➤ `format_plural` is used to format strings or words based upon numeric variables. For example, "You have 1 point" or "You have 5 points."

➤ Your module's output should always be sent from a theme function or theme template file.

➤ Use `hook_theme` to register your module's theme functions and template files.

➤ Theme functions and template files make it possible for themers and others to modify the output of your module without directly modifying your module.

17

Module Development Start to Finish

WHAT YOU WILL LEARN IN THIS CHAPTER:

- ➤ Choosing your hook
- ➤ Offering assistance to site users
- ➤ Adding custom administrative settings
- ➤ Custom permissions
- ➤ Storing data in the database
- ➤ Creating a custom block
- ➤ Testing your module

The previous chapters introduced how modules are built and introduced hooks, the core of a module. Contributed modules contain much more than a hook implementation though. Administrative settings, database tables, custom help text, and permissions are just a few of the pieces of a complete module. In this chapter you'll bring together your knowledge of hooks and Drupal to build a full module from start to finish.

You'll walk step by step through the entire process of building a module. Start off slowly with a few lines of code, implemen a hook and then gradually build on top of it until you have a full module robust enough to be contributed on `drupal.org`, given to a client, or used as a sustainable solution on your own website.

THE MODULE

The module you will be building in this chapter searches for keywords within comments and if present restricts the comment from being posted. You will also create a custom database table to store the number of times the user attempts to post a comment containing restricted keywords.

When you are finished, you will have utilized and practiced the following hooks and APIs:

➤   hook_form_alter and the Forms API

➤   hook_menu

➤   hook_help

➤   hook_permission

➤   hook_install, hook_uninstall, hook_schema and the Schema API

➤   hook_user_view

And finally you will learn how to create a robust module by using SimpleTest to ensure that your module is always working properly.

Although simple this module will teach you the concepts used by a majority of the modules available on Drupal.org. It is meant as a teaching example as similar modules already exist, a few of the modules include:

➤   Word Filter (`http://drupal.org/project/wordfilter`)

➤   Spam (`http://drupal.org/project/spam`)

➤   Akismet (`http://drupal.org/project/akismet`)

➤   Mollom (`http://drupal.org/project/mollom`)

Before You Build That Module

Before you begin writing a module it pays to take time and perform a search on Drupal.org for a similar module. This will not only save you time in writing the module but will save you maintenance time later as you'll be sharing it with the community. You may even pick up additional features and functionality you didn't think about. With over 3,000 modules submitted to drupal.org you are bound to find something that meets your needs. Remember that the Drupal project, its themes, and modules are open sourced. You are free to take the code and use it as the foundation of your module or a part of your module. The heart and soul of open source is sharing with and learning from others.

If you don't find what you need with a search on Drupal.org try asking others in the #drupal-support IRC channel (http://drupal.org/irc), the Post Installation forum (http://drupal.org/forum/22), or perform a custom Google search by appending site:drupal.org/project to your query as demonstrated in Figure 17-1.

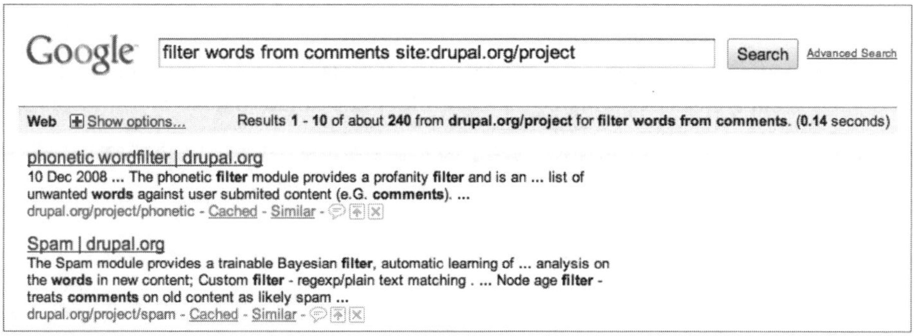

FIGURE 17-1

Beginning Your Module

To begin you will need to create a folder to house the module files and a `.info` file to tell Drupal what this module will do. The name of your module is important and has only a few minor restrictions; no spaces, no special characters, and can't begin with a number. This example keeps it simple: you'll name it `bd_filter` for Beginning Drupal Filter.

TRY IT OUT   **Create Your Module's Foundation**

In this exercise you will create the module's foundation, which is the folder, `.info` file and `.module` file.

1.   Navigate to your site's modules directory (for example, `sites/default/modules`).

2.   Create a new directory and name it `bd_filter`.

3.   Within this folder create the following two empty files:

```
bd_filter.info
bd_filter.module
```

4.   Type the following into the `bd_filter.info` file:

Available for download on Wrox.com

```
name = Beginning Drupal Comment filter
description = "Restricts comments from containing a configured set of keywords."
core = 7.x
version = 7.0
package = Beginning Drupal
files[] = bd_filter.module
```

code snippet Chapter 17 Comment filter module

5.   Save the file then navigate to modules. Note the available module under the Beginning Drupal category at the top of the page.

How It Works

A module's `.info` tells Drupal its name, version compatibility, possible dependencies, and what files the module will use. As you probably guessed, a blank `.module` file is not functional, so continue onto the next exercise to add the first steps of your module.

Implementing a hook

As you have learned the starting point of any module is a hook. A hook is a function located within your module that Drupal will call when a specific action occurs. In the following example you will implement `hook_form_alter`, which is called whenever a form is displayed on your site. Using this hook you will add a new validation routine to the comment form that will prevent comments from being posted that contains a certain keyword.

TRY IT OUT   Implementing a hook

In this exercise you will implement `hook_form_alter` to add a new validation routine to the comment form.

1.   Type the following into the `bd_filter.module` file:

Available for download on Wrox.com

```php
<?php
/**
 * Implementation of hook_form_alter
 */
function bd_filter_form_alter(&$form, &$form_state, $form_id) {
  if ($form_id == "comment_form") {
    $form['#validate'][] = "bd_filter_comment_validate" ;
  }
}

/**
 * Validation routine to prevent keywords from being used within comments.
 */
function bd_filter_comment_validate($form, &$form_state) {
  $word_to_filter = 'cookie';
  if (preg_match('/\b'.$word_to_filter.'\b/i', $form['comment']['#value'])) {
    form_set_error("comment_form", t('Your post contains an offending word, please remove
it and resubmit'));
  }
}
```

code snippet Chapter 17 Comment filter module

2.   Save the file then enable your new module at Modules.

3.   Attempt to add a new comment containing the word `cookie`. If the module is working correctly you will presented with an error message when you preview or save the comment.

How It Works

In the module file you implemented `hook_form_alter`, which allows you to manipulate any form within Drupal. The code added a new validation handler to the comment form, which is called whenever the form is processed. For example when a comment is previewed or saved:

```
function bd_filter_form_alter(&$form, &$form_state, $form_id) {
  if ($form_id('comment_form')) {
    $form['#validate'][] = "bd_filter_comment_validate" ;
  }
}
```

Alternatively you could have written the code this way:

```
function bd_filter_form_comment_form_alter(&$form, &$form_state) {
  $form['#validate'][] = "bd_filter_comment_validate" ;
}
```

Available for
download on
Wrox.com

code snippet Chapter 17 Comment filter module

Note that the form name (`comment_form`) is wedged between `form` and `alter` making the alter function specific to the comment form only.

The validation routine performed a simple search for the word cookie (`$word_to_filter`) and if found an error was raised on the `comment_form` using `form_set_error`; this forces the comment to fail validation and prevents it from being saved.

```
function bd_filter_comment_validate($form, &$form_state) {
  $word_to_filter = 'cookie';
  if (preg_match('/\b'.$word_to_filter.'\b/i', $form['comment']['#value'])) {
    form_set_error("comment_form", t('Your post contains an offending word, please remove
it and resubmit'));
  }
}
```

Available for
download on
Wrox.com

code snippet Chapter 17 Comment filter module

> **NOTE** *The PHP function preg_match uses \b to indicate a word boundary and /i to perform a case insensitive search thus* `preg_match('/\bcookie\b/I',` `$text);` *would search for the whole word cookie within* `$text`. *More information on* `preg_match` *can be found at* `http://php.net/preg_match`.

ADDING CUSTOM CONFIGURATION SETTINGS

At this point you have a fully function module. Unfortunately it is only matching a single word and that word is hard-coded into the module. This is a good time to add a configuration page that will allow you to modify the keyword.

Custom Module Settings

Drupal is designed for rapid module development and does much of the work of saving your module's custom settings for you. Custom module settings are implemented by using `hook_menu` to tell Drupal where your module's configuration page is located. You then provide a settings form with the use of the Forms API (FAPI) and Drupal will do the rest. You do not need to create custom database tables to store simple configuration settings.

The following exercise demonstrates how to do this.

TRY IT OUT Add a Custom Settings Page to Your Module.

In this exercise you will create a custom setting within your module to modify the keyword to be filtered.

1. Open `bd_filter.module` and add an implementation of `hook_menu` as shown in the following code.

Available for download on Wrox.com

```
/*
 * Implementation of hook_menu()
 */
function bd_filter_menu() {
    $items['admin/config/content/bd-filter'] = array(
        'title' => 'Beginning Drupal filter settings',
        'description' => 'Set the keywords to filter',
        'page callback' => 'drupal_get_form',
        'page arguments' => array('bd_filter_admin_settings'),
        'access arguments' => array('administer comments'),
    );
    return $items;
}
```

code snippet Chapter 17 Comment filter

2. Next add the function that will provide the settings

Available for download on Wrox.com

```
/**
 * Menu callback; presents the comment filter settings page.
 */
function bd_filter_admin_settings() {
    $form = array();
    $form['bd_filter_word'] = array(
        '#type' => 'textfield',
        '#title' => t('Disallowed word'),
        '#description' => t('Comments containing this word will be rejected'),
        '#default_value' => variable_get('bd_filter_word', ''),
    );
    return system_settings_form($form);
}
```

code snippet Chapter 17 Comment filter

3. Save the module then revisit the modules page at Administer ⇨ modules and click Save configuration.

> *✎* **NOTE** *To increase performance Drupal caches several key hooks including* hook_menu. *Any changes made to hook_menu after the module has been enabled will not take effect until the cache has been rebuilt. You rebuild this cache by simply visiting the module page and clicking Save configuration. Alternatively you can use the devel module available at* http://drupal.org/project/devel.

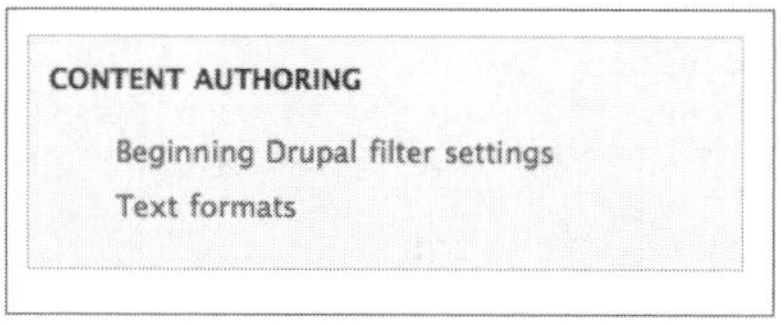

CONTENT AUTHORING

Beginning Drupal filter settings
Text formats

FIGURE 17-2

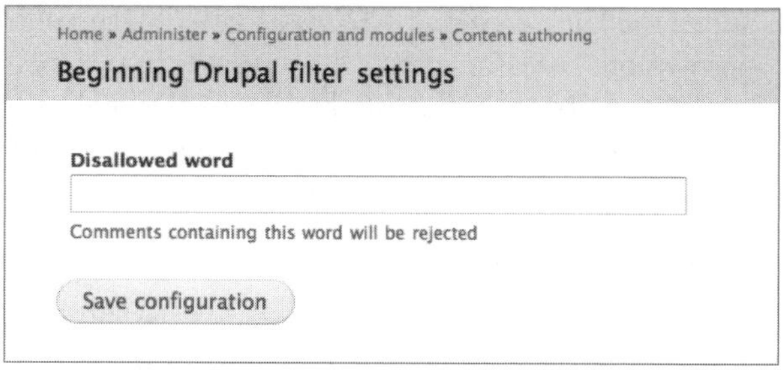

Home » Administer » Configuration and modules » Content authoring
Beginning Drupal filter settings

Disallowed word

Comments containing this word will be rejected

Save configuration

FIGURE 17-3

4. Navigate to the modules page then click Beginning Drupal filter settings under Content Authoring as shown in Figure 17-2. If everything is working properly you will see the configuration options as shown in Figure 17-3.

How It Works

With the implementation of hook_menu, you registered a URL path at /admin/config/content/bd-filter. When this URL is accessed the user is presented with the form created by bd_filter_admin_settings(). Read on to unravel the magic behind this code.

How Did it Become an Option at Configuration?

In Figure 17-2 you can see that a link to the filter settings is presented as an option under the Content Authoring section. Drupal works a bit of assumption magic based upon the URL path to make this happen. Note the first three lines of hook_menu:

```
$items['admin/config/content/bd-filter'] = array(
    'title' => 'Beginning Drupal filter settings',
    'description' => 'Set the keywords to filter',
```

The URL path being registered is `admin/config/content/bd-filter`. The Text formats settings also under this section are located at the URL path `/admin/config/content/formats`. If you had wanted these setting to appear under People and Permission you could change the URL path to read `admin/config/people/bd-filter`.

How Did the Settings Form Appear?

The magic that makes the settings appear is in the second half of hook_menu.

```
    'page callback' => 'drupal_get_form',
    'page arguments' => array('bd_filter_admin_settings'),
    'access arguments' => array('administer comments'),
);
```

When the URL path registered is accessed, Drupal first checks to see if the user has the appropriate permissions listed in `access arguments`. In this example the user must have the `administer com-ments` permission. If the user has access, Drupal calls the function named in the page callback, in this case `drupal_get_form`. It also passes any arguments in `page arguments` to this function. The following execution flow happens:

1. The user navigates to `http://localhost/admin/config/content/bd-filter`.

2. Drupal executes `drupal_get_form('bd_ filter_admin_settings')`.

3. `drupal_get_form()` (a core Drupal function) executes the `bd_filter_admin_settings` function, which returns an array conformant to Drupal's Form API.

4. `bd_filter_admin_settings` uses the `system_settings_form($form)` function to add the Save configuration button to the form (Figure 17-3) and to instruct Drupal to save the data to the module's configuration.

```
    return system_settings_form($form);
```

Where Are the Settings Saved?

The `system_settings_form($form)` core function instructed Drupal to save the settings to Drupal's variables. The saved setting can later be retrieved with `variable_get()` as demonstrated with this line in `bd_filter_admin_settings()`:

```
    '#default_value' => variable_get('bd_filter_word', ''),
```

Note that the variable name is exactly the same as the `$form` key shown here:

```
    $form['bd_filter_word'] = array(
```

Follow the next exercise to put this to work in your module.

Using Saved Configuration Settings in Your Module

In this exercise you will use the custom setting created in the previous exercise within your module.

1. Open `bd_filter.module` and modify the line that reads

```
$word_to_filter = 'cookie';
```
to
```
$word_to_filter = variable_get('bd_filter_word', '');
```

2. Save the module and test it by setting a new word in the configuration settings and attempting to post a comment containing that word.

How It Works

The `variable_get` core function retrieves a module's stored setting by simply naming the variable. The second argument is a default to be used if the variable is not set.

Filtering on Multiple Words

Filtering out a single word helps you understand the concept of the module but it doesn't create a particularly useful module. You'll make a change to the configuration page to allow for multiple keywords and a few lines of code in the validation routine to search for these multiple keywords.

Using Multiple Keywords

In this exercise you will modify your module to handle multiple keywords.

1. Modify the settings form to accept multiple keywords as one per line.

```
$form['bd_filter_word'] = array(
  '#type' => 'textarea',
  '#title' => t('Disallowed words'),
  '#description' => t('Comments containing these words will be rejected. Enter keywords one
per line'),
  '#default_value' => variable_get('bd_filter_word', ''),
);
```

Note that `#type` changed from `textfield` to `textarea`.

2. Modify the `bd_filter_comment_validate()` function to check the comment for multiple keywords.

Available for download on Wrox.com

```
/*
 * Implementation of hook_comment_validate().
 */
function bd_filter_comment_validate(&$form, &$form_state) {
  $words_to_filter = explode("\n", variable_get('bd_filter_word',''));
  foreach ($words_to_filter as $key => $value) {
    $word_to_filter = trim($value);
    if (preg_match('/\b' . $word_to_filter . '\b/i', $form_values['comment'])) {
```

```
        form_set_error('comment', t('Your post contains an offending word, please remove it
and resubmit'));
      } //end if
   } //end foreach
} //end function
```

code snippet Chapter 17 Comment filter

How It Works

The Forms API used by `bd_filter_admin_settings` contains the full breadth of HTML forms. Modifying the type from `textfield` to `textarea` gave the user more room to enter in keywords. Once more keywords were available, you modified the validation routine to handle these keywords.

A Quick Review of the New PHP Code

The validation routine was modified with three new lines. The first line was:

```
$words_to_filter = explode("\n", variable_get('bd_filter_word',''));
```

The `explode` function places each of the words retrieved by `variable_get` into an array. For the next line, use `foreach` to loop through each one of these words:

```
foreach ($words_to_filter as $key => $value) {
```

`trim` is used to remove any erroneous white space the user might have entered:

```
$word_to_filter = trim($value);
```

You now have a functioning module that rejects comments containing any one of the configured keywords. In the next set of exercises you'll add robustness to your module by providing help text to your users, adding custom permissions, logging keyword violations and using automated testing to ensure that you have written a rock-solid module.

HELPING YOUR USERS

One of the greatest things you can do for your users is to provide them with useful help. The first place you should add help is directly within the administrative help section listed on the top administrative bar, shown in Figure 17-4.

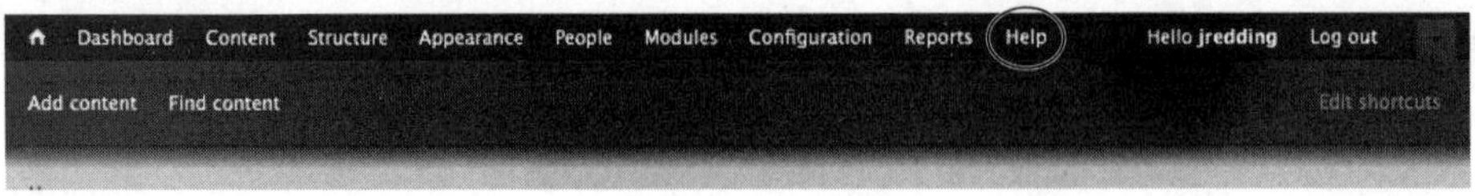

FIGURE 17-4

You can also add help text nearly anywhere on your site. In the following exercise you will also add help text to the comment administration page informing administrators of the keyword restrictions for comment as shown in Figure 17-5.

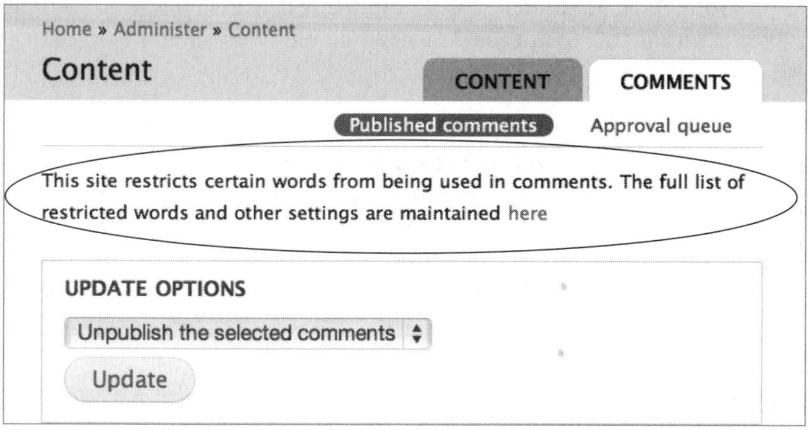

FIGURE 17-5

TRY IT OUT   Implement hook_help

In this exercise you will add an implementation of hook_help to provide help on the main administrative page as well as additional help on the comment moderation page at Content ⇨ Comments.

1.   Add the following function into the bd_filter.module file.

Available for download on Wrox.com

```
/**
 * Implementation of hook_help()
 */
function bd_filter_help($path, $arg) {
  switch ($path) {
    case 'admin/help#bd_filter':
      //Display this help in the administrative help section
      $output = '<p>'. t('The comment word restriction module allows you to define a set of
words that are not allowed within comments. If any of the words are found the comment will
be rejected.') .'</p>';
      return $output;
    case 'admin/content/comment':
      // Display this help above the existing help on the comment moderation page
      $output = t('This site restricts certain words from being used in comments. The full
          list of restricted words and other settings are maintained <a href="@comment-
          filter-admin">here</a>', array('@comment-filter-admin' => url('admin/config/
          content/bd-filter')))
      ;
      return $output;
  }
}
```

code snippet Chapter 17 Comment filter

2. Save the file then rebuild the module cache by visiting Modules and clicking Save configuration.

How It Works

Implementing `hook_help` allows you to add additional help text into any help area on the site simply by stating the URL at which you want the text to appear. You can find out more about `hook_help` at `http://api.drupal.org/api/function/hook_help/7`.

> **NOTE** *The Advanced Help module is a great complementary module to add robust help sections to your modules. http://drupal.org/project/advanced_help.*

PERMISSION HANDLING

Implementing permissions in Drupal sounds intimidating but is in fact quite simple. There are only two steps to implementing custom permissions in Drupal:

1. Declare your permission(s) with `hook_permission`.

2. Check for the permission.

The second point cannot be understated. It is your responsibility to check that a user has the appropriate permission before you perform a secure action. You can use `user_access('permission name')` to determine if a user has the appropriate permission. Drupal will automatically traverse the user roles and permissions then return `true` if access can be granted or `false` if not.

TRY IT OUT   **Implement hook_permission**

In this exercise you will add a new permission entitled `administer comment filter` to restrict access to your module's configuration page.

1. Open bd_filter.module and add the following code:

```
/**
 *  Implementation of hook_permission()
 */
function bd_filter_permission() {
  $perms = array();
  $perms['administer comment filter'] = array (
    'title' => t('Administer comment filter'),
    'description' => t('Manage the word list and configure comment filter settings.'),
  );
  return $perms;
}
```

code snippet Chapter 17 Comment filter

Note that the name of the permission is set in the code above with this line:

```
$perms['administer comment filter'] = array (
```

2. Modify the existing `hook_menu` implementation to restrict access to your module's configuration page unless the requesting user has the `administer comment filter` permission.

```
function bd_filter_menu() {
  $items['admin/config/bd-filter'] = array(
    'title' => 'Beginning Drupal filter settings',
    'description' => 'Set the keywords to filter',
    'page callback' => 'drupal_get_form',
    'page arguments' => array('bd_filter_admin_settings'),
    'access arguments' => array('administer comment filter'),
  );
  return $items;
}
```

code snippet Chapter 17 Comment filter

The only change made here is with this line:

```
'access arguments' => array('administer comment filter'),
```

3. Save the module and rebuild the module cache by visiting modules then clicking Save configuration.

How It Works

Implementing `hook_permission` allows you to add additional permissions that can be assigned to roles. In this exercise you used your new permission as an access argument to `hook_menu`. Elsewhere in your code you can check if a user has the required permission with `user_access('administer comment filter')`. Remember that it is your responsibility as a developer to check for proper security access.

After you have completed this exercise test it by assigning the new permission to a user other than user 1 and logging in as that user.

STORING DATA IN A CUSTOM TABLE

At this point your module is providing nearly all of the necessary functionality. A configurable set of keywords is being restricted from the comments and the module has its own permission set. It's missing just one last feature: the ability to track the users attempting to post these comments.

In the next exercise you will track the users attempting to post offending comments by storing a count of their attempts. You will create a custom table, store data in the database, and create an uninstall routine to clean up the module. The next few pages introduce the following topics:

➤   `.install` file

➤   `hook_install` and `hook_uninstall`

➤ `hook_schema` and the Schema API

➤ `db_merge`

Before you jump into the code, a few topics need to be covered.

Database Abstraction Layer

If you have experience with PHP or have read other programming books you will find that Drupal does things in its own unique way. There are good reasons for this unique Drupal way. Performance is enhanced, you gain database portability, and Drupal provides a more robust development experience.

Drupal 7 includes a database abstraction layer. This means that Drupal can be used with MySQL, SQLLite, or Postgres. Oracle, Microsoft SQL, and other database servers are being added. Abstraction is achieved in two ways with Drupal:

1. The creation, modification, and deletion of database tables is done via Drupal's unique Schema API. Do not use direct SQL queries that you know from previous PHP experiences or books you have read.

2. Retrieving data is done with Drupal's unique database functions. You should never use functions such as `mysql_query` or `pg_query` using these will hinder your site's ability to scale and prevent your module from being database agnostic.

Schema API

If you have a bit of experience with PHP or SQL development you may find Drupal's Schema API a bit baffling. Keep in mind that this Schema API provides you with enormous benefits such as scalability, database portability, and faster development. Examine the differences between using straight PHP and SQL to create a database table and creating the same table using Drupal's Schema API.

PHP + SQL

```
mysql_query("CREATE TABLE bd_filter (
            uid int(11) NOT NULL default '0',
            count int(11) NOT NULL default '0',
          PRIMARY KEY (uid)
            ) /*!40100 DEFAULT CHARACTER SET utf8 */;
        ");
```

DRUPAL 7

```
$schema['bd_filter'] = array(
  'description' => 'Tracks users attempting to posting with restricted words',
  'fields' => array(
    'uid' => array(
      'type' => 'int',
      'not null' => TRUE,
```

```
      'default' => 0,
      'description' => 'The user id of the user attempting to use restricted words',
    ),
    'count' => array(
      'type' => 'int',
      'not null' => TRUE,
      'default' => 0,
      'description' => 'The number of times the user has made an attempt',
    ),
  ),
  'primary key' => array('uid'),
);

drupal_install_schema($schema);
```

The Drupal 7 probably seems intimidating particularly because it includes many more lines of code than using straight PHP + SQL. Note that because the Schema API is self-documenting the database and tables, it is also making the table known to Drupal such that modifications to the table or the removal of your module can happen cleanly.

You can read more about the Schema API at the following websites:

```
http://api.drupal.org/api/group/schemaapi/7
http://drupal.org/node/146843
```

DRUPAL QUERY FUNCTIONS

As with the Schema API, whenever you are adding, retrieving, or manipulating data in your database you should always use Drupal's specific query functions. Amongst other reasons the use of the queries helps with scalability. For example when your site becomes very popular you could employ multiple database servers to handle the increased load. You can only do this if you use Drupal's functions.

Compare the following two sets of code that enter the same data into the same table. One using MySQL specific PHP + SQL code and the other using Drupal's database agnostic code.

PHP + SQL

```
mysql_query("INSERT INTO bd_filter (uid, count) VALUES (1, 4)");
```

DRUPAL 7

```
$fields = array('uid' => 1, 'count' => 4);
db_insert('bd_filter')->fields($fields)->execute();
```

The Drupal method may be a bit strange but there are many reasons why it is preferable. You already read that this helps to create a scalable website. It also helps to keep your site secure. Drupal watches each query for adherence to the database schema (for example, you can't enter a string into an integer field) and for common database attacks such as the infamous SQL injection. By using the Drupal specific functions you not only create a scalable website but a secure one as well.

TRY IT OUT   **Installing a Custom Database Table**

In this exercise you will create a custom database table to store a count of the attempts a user made to post a comment containing the keywords.

1.   Within your module's directory create a new file named `bd_filter.install`.

2.   Type the following code into the newly created `bd_filter.install` file. This code will create both a method to install your database table and to uninstall it.

```php
<?php
/**
 * Implementation of hook_install().
 */
function bd_filter_install() {
  // Create tables.
  drupal_install_schema('bd_filter');
}

/**
 * Implementation of hook_uninstall().
 */
function bd_filter_uninstall() {
  // Remove tables.
  drupal_uninstall_schema('bd_filter');
}

/**
 * Implementation of hook_schema().
 */
function bd_filter_schema() {
  $schema['bd_filter'] = array(
   'description' => 'Tracks users attempting to use restricted words',
   'fields' => array(
   'uid' => array(
     'type' => 'int',
     'not null' => TRUE,
     'default' => 0,
     'description' => 'The user id of the user attempting to use restricted words',
   ),
   'count' => array(
     'type' => 'int',
     'not null' => TRUE,
     'default' => 0,
     'description' => 'The number of times the user has made an attempt',
   ),
   ),
   'primary key' => array('uid')
  );
  return $schema;
}
```

code snippet Chapter 17 Comment filter

3. Save your module, then navigate to the modules administration page, then:

a. Disable your module.

b. Click Uninstall at the top of the modules page and choose to uninstall your module.

c. Enable your module.

How It Works

When a module is first enabled Drupal runs the hook_install function and hook_uninstall when the module is disabled. Each of these functions passes a Schema API array to Drupal's database functions allowing you to define your tables and let Drupal do all the work.

> **NOTE** Drupal will only run hook_install the first time that a module is enabled. You will need to disable, uninstall, and re-enable a module to trigger Drupal to run hook_install again. Fortunately the devel module has a one-click method to make this easy at http://drupal.org/project/devel.

Recording the Count

At this point you have the table necessary to record a count of the number of attempts a user makes. Each user will have a single record in the database with the count field updated after each attempt. Drupal's db_merge function makes this easy because it's designed to handle either an INSERT or an UPDATE query depending on if the user has an existing record. The function also allows for expressions to quickly increment the attempt count.

In your module you will use db_merge with this code:

```
global $user;
db_merge('bd_filter')
  ->key(array('uid' => $user->uid))
  ->fields(array('count' => 1))
  ->expression('count', 'count + 1')
  ->execute();
```

To help you understand what's going on in this code break down its components:

1. ->global is a PHP keyword that pulls in an object or variable that is global in scope. In this case global is pulling in the Drupal-created $user object, which contains information about the currently logged in user.

2. ->db_merge is set to use the bd_filter database table.

3. ->key sets how the database record will be found, db_merge will search for records where the uid is equal to the user's id.

4. `->fields` tell Drupal which field (column) of the database you are updating. If the column is empty a 1 will be placed into it, otherwise the expression will be used.

5. `->expression` runs a mathematical expression on a given field. In this example the field count will be equal to count's previous value plus 1.

6. `->execute()` tells Drupal to execute the query and update the database.

With a general understanding on how to use `db_merge` continue onto to the next exercise to put it into action in your module.

TRY IT OUT   **Update Your Custom Table**

In this exercise you will utilize the `db_merge` function to update your custom table with a count of the user's attempts to post a comment containing restricted keywords.

1. Modify the bd_filter_validate function within the bd_filter.module file with the following code:

Available for download on Wrox.com

```
/**
 * Implementation of hook_comment_filter
 */
function bd_filter_comment_validate(&$form, &$form_state) {
  $words_to_filter = explode("\n", variable_get('bd_filter_word',''));
  foreach ($words_to_filter as $key => $value) {
    $word_to_filter = trim($value);
    if (preg_match('/\b' . $word_to_filter . '\b/i', $form_values['comment'])) {
      form_set_error('comment', t('Your post contains an offending word, please remove it
and resubmit'));
      //Record this attempt
      global $user;
      if ($user->uid > 0) {
        db_merge('bd_filter')
          ->key(array('uid' => $user->uid))
          ->fields(array('count' => 1))
          ->expression('count', 'count + 1')
          ->execute();
      } //end if ($user->uid
    } //end if (preg_match
  } //end foreach
} //end function
```

code snippet Chapter 17 Comment filter

2. Save the file then attempt to post a comment containing a restricted keyword.

How It Works

When a user attempts to post a comment containing a restricted keyword, Drupal will prevent the posting, set an error on the form and then using `db_merge` to record the attempt. Drupal's unique `db_merge` will automatically add or update a database record allowing you to write only a tiny bit of code.

DISPLAYING THE RESULTS ON THE USER'S PROFILE

The module is nearly complete — comments are being tested for restricted words, and the attempts are logged — but one critical element is missing. You can't see the counter. In this next exercise you'll use `hook_user_view` to display a count of each user's attempts on his or her profile page. You could call this shaming them into cleaning up their commentary. A user's profile is accessible by clicking the my account link in the navigational menu.

In the following exercise you'll implement `hook_user_view` and also be introduced to `db_select` and `->fetchField()`.

TRY IT OUT   Display the Count on a User's Profile

In this exercise you will utilize `hook_user_view` to display a user's attempt count.

1. Add an implementation of `hook_user_view` within the `bd_filter.module` file with the following code:

Available for download on Wrox.com

```
/**
 *   Implementation of hook_user_view
 */
function bd_filter_user_view(&$edit, &$account, $category = NULL) {
    $attempts = db_select('bd_filter')
                    ->fields('bd_filter', array('count'))
                    ->condition('uid', $account->uid)
                    ->execute()->fetchField();
    if(is_numeric($attempts)) {
      $account->content['summary']['attempts'] =  array(
        '#type' => 'user_profile_item',
        '#title' => t('Number of attempts'),
        '#markup' => $attempts,
        '#weight' => 2,
      );
    }
}
```

code snippet Chapter 17 Comment filter

2. Save this file then rebuild the module cache by visiting Modules, and clicking Save configuration.

3. Check your profile page by clicking My account in the menu or navigating to `http://localhost/user` while logged in.

How It Works

Implementing `hook_user_view` provides you with the ability to modify or add data to a user's profile page. In this example you are adding a section on the profile's summary page that displays the number of attempts. This number was retrieved from the database using `db_select`.

Recap of db_select

In the exercise db_select was used to retrieve the user's attempt count. The syntax for db_select used is similar to that used with db_merge. Compare the following two methods of using this function:

METHOD 1

```
$attempts = db_select('bd_filter')
                ->fields('bd_filter', array('count'))
                ->condition('uid', $account->uid)
                ->execute()
                ->fetchField();
```

METHOD 2

```
$query = db_select('bd_filter');
$query->fields('bd_filter', array('count'));
$query->condition('uid', $account->uid);
$result = $query->execute()
$attempts = $result->fetchField();
```

Both methods produce the same output with the only difference contained in its syntax. You are free to use the syntax that is the most clear and understandable to you.

To help you better understand the syntax follow method 2 line by line.

First db_select is called to tell Drupal what database table you will be using.

Next fields are added to the query to specify what you want. The count field from the bd_filter table is being requested.

A condition is added to limit the results to those related to the account being viewed ($account->uid).

The query is then sent to the database (executed) and a result sent back and stored in $result.

You retrieve the result for use on the profile page with $result->fetchField().

Why db_select?

If you are familiar with PHP or SQL you may be wondering why a standard SQL statement is not executed with a built-in PHP function such as mysql_query or pg_query. Outlined earlier, Drupal does not use these functions in order to provide scalability, database portability, and to enhance security. Although standard PHP+SQL functions will work you are advised to use Drupal's db_select instead.

The db_select function is incredibly powerful and can implement ranges, query multiple tables, do complex record matching, and a lot more. More information on db_select can be found at http://api.drupal.org/api/function/db_select/7.

DATABASE SUMMARY

When pushing data to or pulling data from Drupal's database, be sure to always use Drupal's unique database functions, including `db_select`, `db_merge`, `db_insert`, and others. These functions make your code flexible, your website highly scalable, increases the security of your site, and makes your code and database portable.

You can read more about Drupal's database abstraction layer and the available database query functions at the following URLs:

```
http://api.drupal.org/api/group/database/7
http://drupal.org/node/213578
```

CREATING A BULLETPROOF SITE WITH SIMPLETEST

Anyone who has used a computer for longer than a few minutes has undoubtedly run into the dreaded *bug* — when an application does something other than what the developer intended it to do. Beginning with Drupal 6 and pushed heavily with Drupal 7, the Drupal community has moved to using a testing application called `SimpleTest` to provide quality control for Drupal's code in order to reduce and ultimately eliminate any bugs.

SimpleTest is an automated way to test Drupal's core and contributed code including your own code. For example, in the module you just built, you will want to test to make sure that the comments are being checked for restricted words as well as to ensure that all attempts are being properly logged. SimpleTest can also make sure that your permissions are being adhered to, test your module with multiple users, thousands of nodes, or other combinations to ensure that you have written rock-solid code.

Test Driven Development

You have been introduced to testing after writing your module because this book is designed for users new to Drupal and/or new to development. Many developers have shifted to writing their tests *before* writing their code to ensure that the code is written correctly and to reduce bugs during development. This is known as *test-driven development (TDD)*.

Before you write your first test take some time to explore Drupal's testing environment.

TRY IT OUT Using SimpleTest

Follow these steps to test your website using SimpleTest:

1. Log into your website as the administrator.

2. Enable the Testing module at Modules.

3. Navigate to newly enabled testing area at Configuration ➪ Development ➪ Testing, shown in Figure 17-6.

4. Open the aggregator section and select several of the tests as shown in Figure 17-7.

5. Click the Run tests button at the bottom of the page.

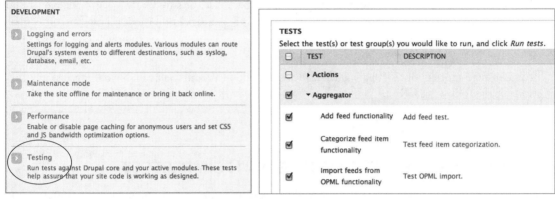

FIGURE 17-6

FIGURE 17-7

As the tests are running you'll be presented with a status report as shown in Figure 17-8.

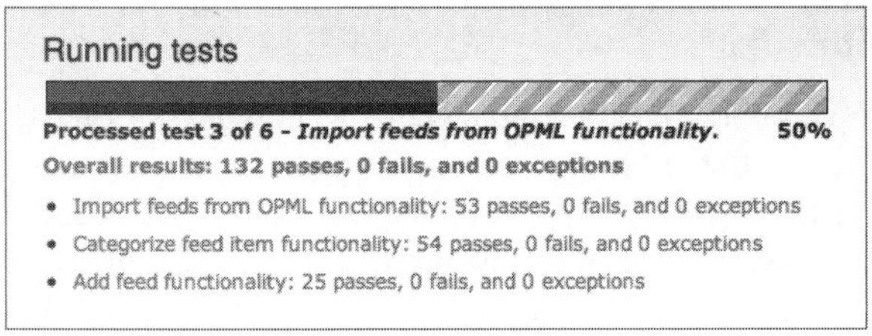

Running tests

Processed test 3 of 6 – *Import feeds from OPML functionality.*   **50%**
Overall results: 132 passes, 0 fails, and 0 exceptions

- Import feeds from OPML functionality: 53 passes, 0 fails, and 0 exceptions
- Categorize feed item functionality: 54 passes, 0 fails, and 0 exceptions
- Add feed functionality: 25 passes, 0 fails, and 0 exceptions

FIGURE 17-8

After the tests complete you'll be provided with a report (shown in Figure 17-9) outlining which tests passed, failed, or had exceptions. This will allow you to pinpoint potential problems on your site.

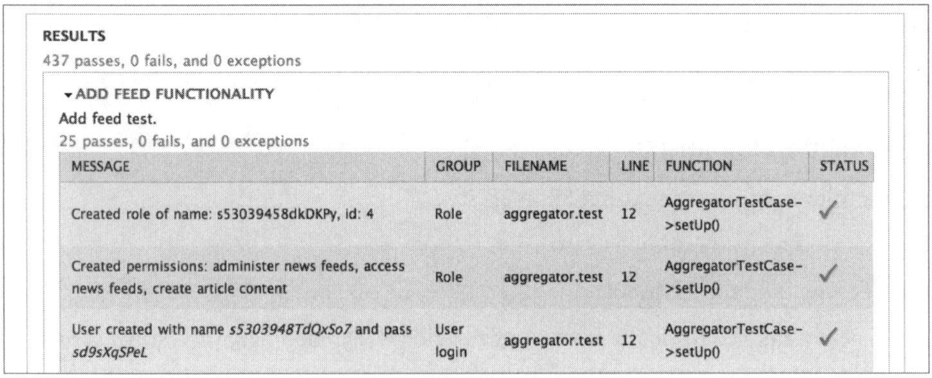

RESULTS
437 passes, 0 fails, and 0 exceptions

▾ ADD FEED FUNCTIONALITY
Add feed test.
25 passes, 0 fails, and 0 exceptions

MESSAGE	GROUP	FILENAME	LINE	FUNCTION	STATUS
Created role of name: s53039458dkDKPy, id: 4	Role	aggregator.test	12	AggregatorTestCase->setUp()	✓
Created permissions: administer news feeds, access news feeds, create article content	Role	aggregator.test	12	AggregatorTestCase->setUp()	✓
User created with name *s5303948TdQxSo7* and pass *sd9sXq5PeL*	User login	aggregator.test	12	AggregatorTestCase->setUp()	✓

FIGURE 17-9

How It Works

SimpleTest works by running tests provided with each module. You'll notice that your module was not included in the list because it does not currently have any tests. Tests are written to ensure that the various pieces of a module are working correctly. Drupal's core ships with thousands of tests, the results of which can help you to pinpoint current or potential problems.

How SimpleTest Performs Its Testing

When SimpleTest begins a testing session it creates a clean, fresh environment within Drupal's database by creating temporary tables and enabling only Drupal's core modules. As SimpleTest performs each of the tests you have chosen, the tests enable other modules potentially creating more temporary tables and a clean install for that module. SimpleTest is not running the tests against your website's data but against a clean installation of Drupal.

After SimpleTest has completed its testing, the temporary tables are removed. If the tests fail the temporary tables may be left behind. You can remove them by using the Clean environment button located at the bottom of the testing page as shown in Figure 17-10.

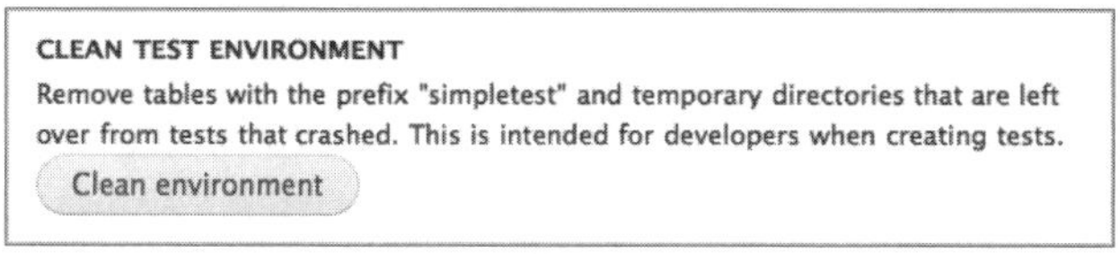

CLEAN TEST ENVIRONMENT
Remove tables with the prefix "simpletest" and temporary directories that are left over from tests that crashed. This is intended for developers when creating tests.

Clean environment

FIGURE 17-10

With this is mind it should come as no surprise that it is not recommended to run tests on a live site. Instead your development site should undergo testing and after passing, the changes can be pushed to your live website. If you suspect problems on your live website, copy it to a development environment and run the tests there.

> ⊗ **WARNING** *Never run SimpleTest on a live website.*

Read more about SimpleTest at `http://drupal.org/handbook/modules/simpletest`.

Writing Your Own SimpleTest

Writing a test for your module to ensure that its bug free not only instills confidence in your module and code-writing ability, it also saves you development time by pinpointing where the problems are and reducing your ongoing maintenance. Tests help you write the module correctly the first time.

Tests are stored in a separate .test file contained with the module. Testing consists of two types of tests: unit tests and functional tests. Unit tests focus on the code itself, or code testing code. Functional tests focus on the user interactivity on the site such as clicking boxes, filling in forms, and so on. As part of your brief introduction to testing you'll write a few unit tests to ensure that the module you wrote in this chapter is functioning correctly.

TRY IT OUT Test Your Module with SimpleTest

In this exercise you will add a test to your module to ensure that it always runs correctly.

Follow these steps to create a stub for your module's tests:

1. Tell Drupal about your new test by adding the following to bd_filter.info:

```
files[] = bd_filter.test
```

2. Within your module's directory create a new file entitled bd_filter.test.

3. Within this file type, in the following code, then save the file:

```php
<?php
class bdFilterTestCase extends DrupalWebTestCase {
    /**
     * Implementation of getInfo().
     */
    public static function getInfo() {
      return array(
        'name' => t('Beginning Drupal Comment Filter'),
        'description' => t('Tests the Beginning Drupal comment filter'),
        'group' => t('Beginning Drupal'),
      );
    } //end function getInfo()
} //end class
```

code snippet Chapter 17 Comment filter

How It Works

What you should notice immediately is that this code looks different from what you wrote earlier. This is because tests are written within objects in what is known as *object-oriented programming* (*OOP*). Take a look at the first line:

```
class bdFilterTestCase extends DrupalWebTestCase {
```

This line creates a new class that extends (builds on top of) DrupalWebTestCase meaning that it will inherit everything from DrupalWebTestCase. SimpleTest will use this class to build an object in order to test your module. If you are new to development and this is a bit confusing, it's sufficient to say that this line is required and your testing functions and code are placed *inside* this class.

The next function, public static function getInfo() operates in a similar manner to Drupal's hooks. It's called by SimpleTest to retrieve your test's information and is therefore required.

SimpleTest Assertions

At this point your test doesn't test anything so you'll pass with flying colors. SimpleTest uses *assertions* to test for certain conditions. A single `.test` file can contain hundreds of assertions with each one testing different items. Each assertion is either true or false to indicate a pass or failure. One of those assertions is `assertEqual`, which is used as follows:

```
$this->assertEqual($variable, "what it should be" , "Message");
```

a bit more clear:

```
$x = 1;
$this->assertEqual($x, 1, t('X was properly set to 1'));
```

If `$x` is indeed `1` then the assertion would return `true` and this portion of the overall test would pass. Each of the assertions is displayed to the user on the test's results page as shown in Figure 17-11.

▾ BEGINNING DRUPAL COMMENT FILTER						
Tests the Beginning Drupal comment filter						
22 passes, 0 fails, and 0 exceptions						
MESSAGE	GROUP	FILENAME	LINE	FUNCTION		STATUS
X was properly set to 1	Other	beginning_drupal_comment_filter_step7.test	19	bdCommentFilterTestCase->testCommentFilter()		✓

FIGURE 17-11

There are assertions to test every aspect of a Drupal module including text, numbers, greater than or less than values, if text appears on a page, if a pattern exists, and many more items. You can find the full list of assertions at `http://drupal.org/node/265828`.

Naming Test Functions

Assertions are the mini-tests that go within a larger test. At this point, your code has merely created the foundation for possible tests. Tests are created through the use of a function within the class and named specifically with the word *test* as the first part of the name. The following code demonstrates how to take the foundation you created earlier and add a simple test to it:

```php
<?php
class bdFilterTestCase extends DrupalWebTestCase {
  /**
   * Implementation of getInfo().
   */
  public static function getInfo() {
    return array(
      'name' => t('Beginning Drupal Comment Filter'),
      'description' => t('Tests the Beginning Drupal comment filter'),
      'group' => t('Beginning Drupal'),
    );
  } //end function getInfo()

  /**
   *  A simple test function
```

```
  */
  function testCommentFilter() {
    $x = 1;
    $this->assertEqual($x, 1, t('X was properly set to 1'));
  } //end testCommentFilter
} //end class
```

Note that the function's name begins with the word test, which is how SimpleTest knows to run this function. If the name does not start with test and is not a reserved function name (such as getInfo()), then SimpleTest will simply ignore it and leave it for your use.

Of course this test isn't very functional. In your test, you want to ensure that comments are being properly blocked and that the logging function is working correctly. Before you do this you need to understand what additional concept, setUp().

setUp()

When SimpleTest begins your tests it will fire a function called setUp before any other work is performed. Keeping in mind that SimpleTest runs on a fresh installation of Drupal and not on your live data; your test will need to ensure that the necessary dependencies and requirements are met. This includes ensuring that the comment module is enabled and that you have user accounts to test your actions with.

In your module, you need the following:

➤ An administrator to set the module's settings

➤ A normal web user to post a comment

➤ A node onto which to post a comment

➤ Commenting enabled for this node and node type

You can perform all of these tasks within a setUp() function as shown in the following code that is placed within the overall class:

```
/**
 * Implementation of setUp()
 */
function setUp() {
  //enable both the bd_filter and comment module
  parent::setUp('bd_filter', 'comment');
  // Create two users; an Administrator and a web user
  $admin_user = $this->drupalCreateUser(array('administer comment filter'));
  $ web_user = $this->drupalCreateUser(
      array('access comments', 'post comments', 'create article content')
      );

  //login as the web user and create a node to post comments on
  $this->drupalLogin(web_user);
  $this->node = $this->drupalCreateNode(array('type' => 'article', 'status' => 1,
'comment' => 2));
  $this->drupalLogout();
}
```

The following functions are used within this code:

➤ `$this->drupalCreateUser`: This function accepts an array of permissions to grant the newly created user.

➤ `$this->drupalLogin($web_user)`: This logs the user into the SimpleTest website (remember that it's a temporarily created website and not your live website). Later you should use `$this->drupalLogout()` to end that user's session.

➤ `$this->drupalCreateNode`: As its name implies, this creates a node according to the array of arguments given. In this example, an article node that is published and has commenting enabled will be created.

There are many more functions available that will help you to properly test your module. You can read more about them and get a complete list at `http://drupal.org/node/265762`.

Adding the Tests to Your Module

Now that you understand what tests do and SimpleTest's `getInfo()` and `setUp()` functions, its your turn to add this into your module. Follow the next exercise to add testing to your module.

TRY IT OUT   Test Your Module with SimpleTest

In this exercise you will add a test to your module to ensure that it always runs correctly. With the code in this exercise you will perform the following functions:

➤ Use `variable_set()` to set the `bd_filter` module's administrative settings.

➤ Attempt to post a comment with the restricted word by using `$this->drupalPost()`.

➤ Use `$this->assertText` to assert that the `bd_filter` module's error message appears on the resulting Drupal page.

➤ Test a second comment without the restricted word and use `$this->assertNoText` to assert that the error message does not appear.

➤ Check the database to make sure that the attempt was logged and logged only once.

1. Modify your module's `bd_filter.test` with the following code.

```php
<?php
class bdFilterTestCase extends DrupalWebTestCase {

  public static function getInfo() {
    return array(
      'name' => t('Beginning Drupal Comment Filter'),
      'description' => t('Tests the Beginning Drupal comment filter'),
      'group' => t('Beginning Drupal'),
    );
  }

  function setUp() {
    parent::setUp('bd_filter', 'comment');
```

```
  }

  /**
   *   Test if a comment with restricted words is properly restricted
   */
  function testCommentFilter() {
    // Create an Administrator account
    $web_user = $this->drupalCreateUser(array('administer comment filter', 'access
comments', 'post comments', 'create article content'));
    //login as the administrator to set the restricted word and comment settings
    $this->drupalLogin($web_user);
    // Set the restricted word to a randomname
    $restricted_word = $this->randomName();
    variable_set('bd_comment_filter_word', $restricted_word);
    // Set the article node type to require a preview on the comment
    variable_set('comment_preview_article', '0');

    //Create a node to post comments on
    $node = $this->drupalCreateNode(array('type' => 'article', 'status' => 1, 'comment' =>
2));

    //Navigate to the node created
    $this->drupalGet('comment/reply/' . $node->nid);

    //Create the comment and place the restricted word in the comment and try to post it
    $edit = array();
    $edit['subject'] = $this->randomName();
    $edit['comment'] = $this->randomName() ." ". $restricted_word ." ". $this-
>randomName();
    $this->drupalPost(NULL, $edit, t('Save'));
    $this->assertText(t('Your post contains an offending word, please remove it and
resubmit'), 'Comment properly blocked');

    //Create a new comment with the restricted word and try to post it
    $edit['subject'] = $this->randomName();
    $edit['comment'] = $this->randomName() . $this->randomName();
    $this->drupalPost(NULL, $edit, t('Save'));
    $this->assertNoText(t('Your post contains an offending word, please remove it and
resubmit'), 'Comment properly allowed');

    $this->drupalLogout();

    //Check to see if the number of attempts was properly logged
    $logged_attempts = db_select('bd_filter', 'bd')
                      ->fields('bd', array('count'))
                      ->condition('uid', $web_user->uid)
                      ->execute()->fetchField();
    $this->assertEqual($logged_attempts, 1, t('Number of attempts made equals the number of
attempts logged'));
  }
} //end class
```

code snippet is part of Chapter 17 Comment filter

2.   Save the file then run your tests at Configuration ➪ Development ➪ Testing.

How It Works

This `.test` file contains only two assertions:

```
$this->assertText(t('Your post contains an offending word, please remove it and
resubmit'), 'Comment properly blocked');
```

and

```
$this->assertNoText(t('Your post contains an offending word, please remove it and
resubmit'), 'Comment properly allowed');
```

When your test is run, however, you will notice that over 200 assertions are tested. Every action within a test spawns a series of other actions that may also contain tests and assertions. For example, using `$this->drupalCreateUser()` will cause a series of tests to be run that ensure Drupal is properly creating a user account. This is desirable because it shows the full flow of Drupal. If a test fails you can pinpoint where it fails and find the root of the problem faster.

Summing Up SimpleTest

At first glance SimpleTest may seem a cumbersome addition to a website that just makes extra work for you. If you take the time to write the tests before or during your development you'll quickly learn that it not only speeds your development, by reducing bugs during development, but it also lessens the ongoing bug fixing and maintenance of your code. Of course, you also have the great benefit of being able to show your boss or client that their site has passed thousands of tests before going live, ensuring a rock-solid website and instilling confidence in your newly developed skills.

Read more about writing tests for SimpleTest at `http://drupal.org/simpletest`.

SUMMARY

This chapter walked you through building a module step by step. You started with only a few lines of code and built upon them adding custom database tables, modifications to a user's profiles and finally topped it off with automated testing to ensure you built a rock solid module. The lessons you have learned in this chapter will help guide you on your path to becoming a Drupal developer. Often a developer will choose a hook and then quickly throw together a module to see if the hook fits their requirements. The remaining items will be built out around the hook to make it a full-fledged module that is configurable and robust.

After reading this chapter you should be ready to create modules for your own site or others. Armed with an understanding of how a module functions you can understand the work of others and participate in the open source community by getting involved with existing modules. Often you will find that a contributed module does nearly everything you need it to do but it lacks a key function. When this happens you'll have a choice to either recreate the module from scratch as a custom module or to simply add in the necessary functionality. The latter choice is almost always the better choice as you'll be reducing your development time and sharing ongoing maintenance of the module with the community. Of course you also get the added benefit of giving back to the Drupal community.

1. What is the starting point of a module?

2 If you would like to add custom settings to your module what hook would you use?

3. What hook do you use to add permissions to your module?

4 What does Drupal use to ensure that Drupal's core, contributed modules, and your module is running properly?

Answers to the Exercises can be found in the Appendix.

▶ WHAT YOU LEARNED IN THIS CHAPTER

➤ A module's starting point is a hook implementation.

➤ Use `http://api.drupal.org` to find available hooks.

➤ Permissions are easily added by implementing `hook_permission` but remember that you must check for the permission by using `user_access('permission name')`.

➤ Forms in Drupal are created Drupal's unique FormsAPI (FAPI) and not with HTML form tags. This method creates secure forms that are easily reusable. Additionally all forms in Drupal can be modified by implementing `hook_form_alter`.

➤ SimpleTest runs automated tests against your site and modules to ensure that everything is running properly. These tests can help to pinpoint any issues.

➤ Drupal uses a unique database abstraction layer and database functions to speed your development, add database portability, and creates a secure and scalable website.

18

Advanced Drupal Installations

WHAT YOU WILL LEARN IN THIS CHAPTER:

➤ Using Drush to manage your Drupal site

➤ Using CVS or SVN to manage your Drupal installation

➤ Installing multiple websites using a single Drupal instance

➤ Sharing users between multiple Drupal websites

➤ Explore the `sites.php` file

➤ An in-depth look at the `settings.php` file

With a base understanding of Drupal's installation process you're ready to explore how to get the most of your Drupal installation. You'll start by learning how to use the Drush module to manage you Drupal site. If you're a developer check out the section on using CVS or SVN to manage your Drupal installation, drastically reducing the amount of time you spend upgrading Drupal. These techniques can be used together or separately to assist your development.

One of Drupal's many tricks is the ability to host more than one website using a single code base (i.e., download). To explore this capability you'll create two independent websites on a single Drupal installation, then two websites that share a set of users, creating a single login and profile for multiple websites. The primary advantage of the multiple-website, single-code base configuration is one point of upgrade for multiple websites and an optional ability to share data between the sites.

In the process of learning how to run multiple websites from a single code base, you will also learn the power of the settings.php file. Later in this chapter you'll dissect this file to learn how to fine-tune your Drupal installation.

DRUSH

At this point in your Drupal journey you may have come to realize the Drupal is much more than a CMS. In fact many people are starting to consider Drupal an operating system because it operates your website (i.e., system). Just like an operating system, Drupal has to be managed, upgraded, and updated to remain a secure, bug free system. To help with this the Drupal Shell (Drush) was created. Drush can automatically update your modules and core to the latest version, install and enable modules, clear your cache, and even run module functions such as cron hooks.

As the module's slogan goes it is the Swiss Army knife of Drupal.

Drush is not a Drupal module and it resides outside of your Drupal installation. Drush is a system for managing a website that is used via the command line. If you are not familiar with the command line this a good time to get started. Follow the next exercise to get started with using Drush by using it to automatically update your existing Drupal installation.

> **NOTE** *Windows users: Some of Drush's commands require Linux/UNIX utilities not available on Windows. You can use Cygwin to get a compatible command line for use with Drush. Cygwin is freely available at* `http://www.cygwin.com.`

TRY IT OUT   Using Drush

In this exercise you will use Drush to automatically update your modules:

1. Download and uncompress Drush from `http://drupal.org/project/drush` into a folder on your hard drive. This should not be the same as your Drupal directory. For example if your Drupal directory is at `/Applications/MAMP/htdocs/drupal` (Mac) or `c:\xammp\htdocs\drupal` (Windows), download Drush to `/Applications/MAMP/drush` (Mac) or `c:\xammp\drush` (windows).

2. Using a command line (called Terminal on a Mac) navigate to your Drupal directory. Example (Mac and Windows):

   ```
   cd /Applications/MAMP/htdocs/drupal
   ```
   or
   ```
   cd c:\xammp\htdocs\drupal
   ```

3. Inside of your Drupal directory type `drush update` (Linux/Mac) or `drush.bat update` (Windows) with its full path. For example:

   ```
   /Applications/MAMP/htdocs/drupal $ > /Applications/MAMP/drush/drush update
   ```
   or
   ```
   C:\xammp\htdocs\drupal> c:\xammp\drush\drush.bat update
   ```

If the command completed successfully you should have seen a screen similar to the following:

```
/Applications/MAMP/htdocs/drupal $ > /Applications/MAMP/drush/drush update
Refreshing update status information ...
Done.
Update information last refreshed: Mon, 01/01/2010 - 09:31

Update status information on all installed and enabled Drupal modules:
  Name                         Installed version  Proposed version  Status
  Drupal                       7.1                7.1               Up to date
```

4. (Optional for Linux/Mac users) Create an alias (shortcut) to the Drush command to make it easier to use.

   a. From the command line type in:

      ```
      /Applications/MAMP/htdocs/drupal $ > alias drush=/Applications/MAMP/drush/drush
      ```

   b. Aliased commands are thrown away when you close the terminal or log out. Add this alias to your /etc/bashrc to ensure it is always available when you use the command line. The completed /etc/bashrc file should look similar to:

   ```
   # System-wide .bashrc file for interactive bash(1) shells.
   if [ -z "$PS1" ]; then
       return
   fi
   PS1='\h:\W \u\$ '
   alias drush=/Applications/MAMP/drush/drush
   ```

   c. With the alias in place you can now simply type drush leaving out the path in front of it. Compare the following command to the one you entered in step 3:

      ```
      /Applications/MAMP/htdocs/drupal $ > drush update
      ```

How It Works

When the drush update command was issued drush began looking for a Drupal installation in the current directory. Drush then compared the Drupal version against the latest version on Drupal.org and downloaded and installed any updates available. It also searched your modules and themes directories looking for updates automatically installing them if available.

In summary drush update makes your life very easy.

But Wait There's More!

Drush is not only useful for keeping your installation up to date it can also be used to download, install, and enable new modules. For example:

```
drush dl views
drush enable views
```

The first command automatically downloads the latest version of views and the second command enables it. Here are a few other commands that you might find useful.

```
drush cron
```

Run your site's cron jobs from the command line.

```
drush cache clear
```

Flushes your site's cache.

```
drush status
```

Returns information about your Drupal site including PHP version, version of Drupal, and database connectivity information.

Find more commands by simply typing in `drush` without any arguments.

USING CVS TO MANAGE DRUPAL

If you have spent time on Drupal's forums or in IRC you have no doubt heard that many people use CVS (Concurrent Versions System) to manage their Drupal installation. But what does this mean? In short, using CVS allows you to automatically update Drupal's core and/or contributed modules with the latest security updates and bug fixes with only a few simple commands.

What is CVS?

CVS is a GPL licensed software application used during software development to track the revisions of files. This form of version control is a necessity when several people are making changes to the same file over a period of time. The Drupal software and all contributed themes, installation pro-files, translations, and modules on `http://drupal.org` are stored in a CVS repository and the community of developers use CVS daily to store their modifications to their software. If you are curious about what has changed from one version to the next, CVS can pinpoint the exact changes for you.

Note that `http://drupal.org` uses CVS. You can learn more about using CVS with the Drupal project at `http://drupal.org/handbook/cvs`.

What is SVN?

SVN is an updated — and some would argue a more popular version — of the CVS application. Whereas the roots of CVS date back to 1984, SVN got its start in 2000; it is the modern equivalent of CVS. There are differences between the two applications and each application has its own cult following, but for the purposes of installing and maintaining a Drupal installation, they are effectively the same and differ only slightly in syntax. Because `http://drupal.org` uses CVS you will be introduced to CVS first, followed by a brief overview of SVN.

Be aware that although http://drupal.org uses CVS, many Drupal professionals, developers, and companies use SVN to manage their software. If you plan on becoming a professional Drupal developer it would be wise to introduce yourself to SVN. The lessons you learn here also apply directly to SVN.

SVN is included standard with Mac OS X starting with version 10.5. Linux and Windows binaries can be downloaded at http://subversion.tigris.org. Similar to CVS, numerous GUI clients exist, although it would be helpful to become familiar with the basics of command line when using it to manage your Drupal installation.

Installing CVS

CVS is a command line application that is not included with Mac OS X or the Windows operating system, although most Linux distributions include it. CVS GUI applications exist, but the command line version is best for managing a Drupal installation. The free Windows application Cygwin (http://cygwin.com) includes CVS, and on Mac OS X CVS is included as part of the developer tools located on the Mac OS X installation DVD.

Installing and Upgrading Drupal using CVS

Follow the next two exercises to learn how to install and upgrade Drupal from the CVS repository.

TRY IT OUT   Installing Drupal from the CVS Repository

Download Drupal from the CVS repository to make upgrades quick and easy.

1. Using the command line navigate to your web root directory. If you are using MAMP (Mac) your web root directory is /Applications/MAMP/htdocs and the XAMPP (windows) web root directory is at C:\XAMPP\htdocs.

2. Type in and execute the following command:

```
cvs -d:pserver:anonymous:anonymous@cvs.drupal.org:/cvs/drupal -z6 co -d cvsdrupal -r
DRUPAL-7-1 drupal
```

If the command executed successfully you should see a screen full of information similar to the following:

```
/Applications/MAMP/htdocs $ >cvs
-d:pserver:anonymous:anonymous@cvs.drupal.org:/cvs/drupal -z6 co -d cvsdrupal -r
DRUPAL-7-1 drupal
cvs checkout: Updating cvsdrupal
U cvsdrupal/.htaccess
U cvsdrupal/CHANGELOG.txt
U cvsdrupal/COPYRIGHT.txt
U cvsdrupal/INSTALL.mysql.txt
U cvsdrupal/INSTALL.pgsql.txt
U cvsdrupal/INSTALL.txt
```

How It Works

CVS downloaded the Drupal source code directly from the drupal.org CVS repository. Examine each piece of the command individually.

`-d:pserver:anonymous:anonymous@cvs.drupal.org:/cvs/drupal` The –d argument stands for Directory and in this case the Directory is a CVS Pserver. You can interpret this line as:

Use the username `anonymous` and password `anonymous` at the Pserver `cvs.drupal.org` to retrieve the source code at `/cvs/drupal`.

> `-z6`: This argument speeds up downloading by using Z compression at level 6.
>
> `co`: Short for checkout. CVS works similar to a library in that code is checked out to a user and any modifications to the code can be traced back to that user when the code is checked back in, known as a commit.
>
> `-d`: This second –d argument tells cvs where to put the downloaded code. If omitted the folder name drupal will be used.
>
> `-r`: DRUPAL-7-1 The revision of Drupal being requested is Drupal 7.1. Drupal 7.2 would be DRUPAL-7-2, Drupal 7.3 DRUPAL-7-3 and so on. In CVS terminology this is known as a tag. If you would like to experiment with the absolute latest Drupal version, bugs and all, simply omit this portion.
>
> `drupal`: This last word tells CVS to download the `drupal` source code.

Putting it all together the plain English interpretation is:

Anonymously log into the cvs.drupal.org/cvs/drupal repository and checkout (download) the 7.1 version of Drupal, oh and use compression (`-z6`).

TRY IT OUT **Update Drupal from the CVS Repository**

Upgrade Drupal to the next available version.

1. Determine the latest version of Drupal by visiting the `http://drupal.org`.

2. Using the command line navigate to the `cvsdrupal` directory created in the last exercise.

3. Type and execute the following CVS command changing DRUPAL-7-2 to the latest Drupal version, for example Drupal 7.3 becomes DRUPAL-7-3.

```
cvs update -r DRUPAL-7-2
```

4. If the command executed successfully you should see a screen full of information similar to the following:

```
/Applications/MAMP/htdocs $ >cvs update -r DRUPAL-7-2
cvs update: Updating .
P .htaccess
P CHANGELOG.txt
P INSTALL.txt
P LICENSE.txt
P MAINTAINERS.txt
```

How It Works

Because CVS downloaded Drupal it remembered the repository, username/password and the previous version. Your command told CVS to `update` the code and what version to update to, in this case

Drupal 7.2. In the resulting output you'll notice that to the left of each file name a P is displayed instead of a U as seen in the first exercise. This indicates that a Patch (an update) has been made to the file alerting you to the files that have been modified between the versions.

Understanding CVS Tags

After completing the last two exercises you may be curious about how Drupal uses versioning and how that corresponds to CVS. Drupal's core, themes, and modules each have official (stable) and development (unstable) versions, as well as major and minor versions. Consider the releases shown in Figure 18-1. You can see that this project has two official releases: one for Drupal 6 (6.x-2.3) and one for Drupal 5 (5.x-1.6). The version for Drupal 7 is still in development, as evidenced by the name 7.x-2.x-dev.

You can probably guess that the far left number is the compatible version of Drupal, meaning that 7.x-2.x-dev is compatible with Drupal 7. The number in the middle is the major version of the project, thus this is version 2 of the Drupal 7 version. The far right portion indicates the project's minor version or its development status. In this case the Drupal 7 compatible version is in development and the Drupal 6 compatible version has had three updates to its version 2 (6.x-2.3).

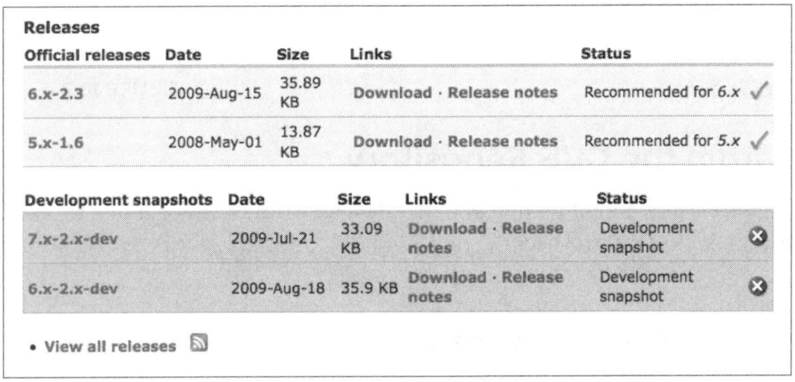

Releases

Official releases	Date	Size	Links		Status	
6.x-2.3	2009-Aug-15	35.89 KB	Download · Release notes		Recommended for 6.x ✓	
5.x-1.6	2008-May-01	13.87 KB	Download · Release notes		Recommended for 5.x ✓	

Development snapshots	Date	Size	Links	Status	
7.x-2.x-dev	2009-Jul-21	33.09 KB	Download · Release notes	Development snapshot	⊗
6.x-2.x-dev	2009-Aug-18	35.9 KB	Download · Release notes	Development snapshot	⊗

• View all releases 🔊

FIGURE 18-1

How Does This Relate to CVS?

Now that you understand how to read Drupal version numbers you can translate these into CVS tags for use within a CVS command. The process is quite simple.

➤ Everything begins with DRUPAL-

➤ The compatibility version is added DRUPAL-7

➤ The major version is added DRUPAL-7-2

➤ Finally stable versions add the minor version DRUPAL-6-2-3

Branches and Tags

As you've already seen, a CVS tag (for example: DRUPAL-7—2) tells CVS what version of Drupal's core, theme, or module you want. Tags are broken into two areas: branches and non-branch tags. Developers use branches and tags to indicate a major change or the stability of their code. A branch indicates that something dramatic has changed with the code, such as compatibility with a new version of Drupal or rewriting of the code base. In short the code has "branched" off. A tag is a simple way of freezing code at a certain point to indicate that no further changes will be made to the code.

Consider the branches and tags used for a Drupal module listed in Figure 18-2. You can see that this module has a compatible version for Drupal 5, 6, and 7. The Drupal 6 compatible version has two versions, 1 and 2, and the Drupal 7 compatible version has only version 2. In the tags you can see that the Drupal 7 compatible version has been tagged as having a stable version 1 release (7.x-2.1).

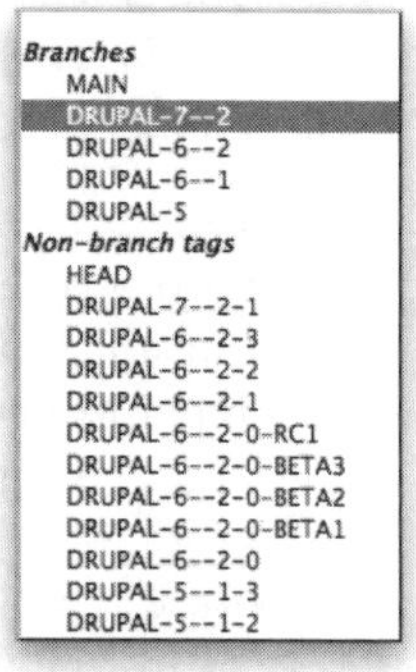

Using CVS, if you wanted a stable version you would use the tag DRUPAL-7—2-1, but if you instead wanted to see all of the latest changes (possibly those about to go into 7.x-2.2), then you would use the tag DRUPAL-7—2.

You will also notice a special branch at the top of Figure 18-2, MAIN. This branch is also known as head and contains the absolute latest code available, which may be for the next version of Drupal.

With an understanding of CVS tags, continue on to learn how to checkout and update modules using CVS.

FIGURE 18-2

Installing Modules from the CVS Repository

This is a great option if you are using a module that is under development or if you'd like to assist in the development. The process is identical to checking out Drupal's core code, with the exception of the repository location.

TRY IT OUT   Install a Module from the CVS Repository

In this exercise you'll install the development version of the Voting API module, using CVS to stay on top of and help with the latest development.

1.   Determine the CVS branch to use by navigating to `http://cvs.drupal.org/viewvc.py/drupal/contributions/modules/votingapi`.

2.   At the top of the page, pull down the Sticky Tag dropdown as shown in Figure 18-3. Note the branch DRUPAL-7—2 and the non-branch tag DRUPAL-7-2-1.

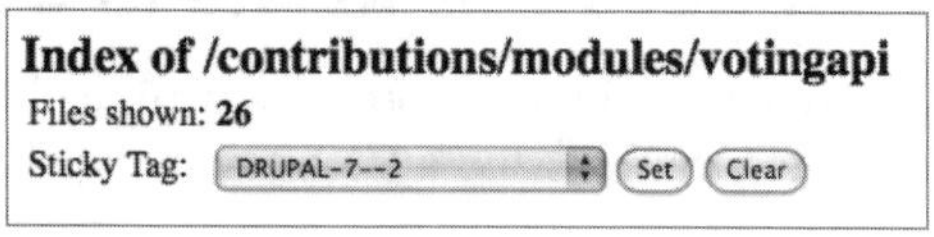

FIGURE 18-3

3.   Using the command line, navigate to your site's modules directory. This is typically `sites/default/modules`. If the `modules` directory doesn't exist, simply create one.

4. Checkout the latest development (unstable) version of the Drupal 7 module by typing in and executing the following command. Note the difference in the pserver's repository directory.

```
cvs -z6 -d:pserver:anonymous:anonymous@cvs.drupal.org:/cvs/drupal-contrib co -r
DRUPAL-7
-2 contributions/modules/votingapi
```

5. You can download the latest updates to the module simply by typing in from inside the `votingapi` directory.

```
cvs update
```

How It Works

Similar to checking out Drupal, CVS remembers where it retrieved the file, so you only need to execute the update command from within the `votingapi` directory. Note the difference with the repository directory, which changed from `/cvs/drupal` to `/cvs/drupal-contrib`.

ONE DRUPAL, MANY WEBSITES

As mentioned before, a single Drupal installation can be used to power multiple websites. This process is known as multi-site. Using Drupal to power multiple websites gives you several advantages, including:

➤ A single point of upgrade when security updates or bug fixes are released for Drupal or any of the modules or themes you are using.

➤ The ability to roll out a module or theme to multiple sites but only installing it once. Also the ability to upgrade the module or theme for all sites by managing only a single instance of it.

➤ Users can login and maintain a single username, password and profile between sites.

➤ Share a single taxonomy between sites.

➤ Share content between sites.

Consider the following example. Suppose you manage the following two websites:

➤ `http://mountainbikes.local`

➤ `http://roadbikes.local`

Using Drupal's multi-site feature, a user who creates an account on `http://mountainbikes.local` can automatically log into `http://roadbikes.local` with the same username and password. When changes are made to the user's account on one website (for example: name, data, etc.), the changes are immediately available on the other website because the two websites share the same user base. The content and user permissions of each website may be completely distinct, which means that a user can be an administrator on one website but not on the other.

You will create these two sites, including sharing a single user base in the second example exercise. In the first example you will learn how to use the multi-site feature of Drupal by creating two web-sites using a single installation of Drupal.

> **NOTE** *The OpenID module, included with Drupal core, allows users to maintain one username and password for use on OpenID enabled websites. Examples of major OpenID providers include Yahoo! and Google.*

Example 1: Multiple Independent Websites

In the following example you'll create two websites using a single installation of Drupal. The keys to this configuration are:

> ➤ A unique site's folder named after the URL

> ➤ A unique database or database table prefix

When hosting multiple websites Drupal separates them by using the respective Sites folder. Each website's folder is named after the URL of the website as described in Chapter 2. Follow the activity to learn more.

TRY IT OUT **Using Drupal for Multiple Websites**

With an existing site already operating at `http://localhost`, you're going to create a new site at `http://mysite.local`.

To complete this exercise, you will need the following:

> ➤ A running Drupal website at `http://localhost`.

> ➤ A new and empty database different from that used on `http://localhost`.

1. Configure your computer to accept the domain name mysite.local.

Add the following line to your HOSTS file:

```
127.0.0.1    mysite.local
```

> ➤ Under Mac or Linux, HOSTS is located at `/etc/hosts`.

> ➤ Under Windows, HOSTS is located at `c:\windows\systems32\drivers\etc\hosts`.

> `http://mysite.local` and `http://localhost` should now display the same website.

2. In your current Drupal's Sites folder, create a new folder named **mysite.local**.

3. Copy `sites/default/default.settings.php` to `sites/mysite.local/` and rename it `settings.php`

4. Navigate to `http://mysite.local`.

5. Install Drupal as normal.

> *NOTE* You can use one database for multiple websites by setting a table prefix within the Advanced options on the Database configuration screen during installation.

How It Works

When Drupal receives a web request it enumerates the Sites folder to look for a folder that matches the URL requested, and then uses the settings.php file within that folder. In this example two URLs were accessed; `http://localhost` and `http://mysite.local`. When Drupal received the request for `http://mysite.local`, it found the `mysite.local` folder and used the `settings.php` file within the folder. Since this file had yet to be configured, (freshly copied from `default.settings.php`) the installation process began. No matching folder was found for the request to `http://localhost` thus the `default` folder was used. For clarity you could rename the `default` folder to `localhost` and achieve the same outcome.

Example 2: Multiple Related Websites

Running two or more websites on a single installation of Drupal is pretty slick and can save you a lot of maintenance time. If your websites are related, Drupal can go one step further and share information between them. The most common use of this feature is a shared user-base — one login for multiple websites. Sharing is accomplished by utilizing a single database for all websites, but separating or sharing data determined by a table prefix.

Sharing data between multiple websites is an advanced installation method and cannot be handled by Drupal's automated installer. You will need to modify the `settings.php` manually. Specifically, the `$databases` and `$db_prefix` arrays in `settings.php` are set to tell Drupal which database you will be using and how to properly name the Database tables during the installation process.

You will need to make a decision to share data between websites before the sites are installed, because Drupal will be creating Database tables or using existing tables during the installation process. Drupal cannot share data between two existing websites because the IDs used throughout the site will overlap. For example, each website will contain a user 1, making it impossible to merge these two user accounts at a later time.

TRY IT OUT **Sharing a Set of Users between Multiple Websites**

In this example, you'll share a set of users between two websites: `http://mountainbikes.local` and `http://roadbikes.local`.

To complete this exercise, you will need the following:

➤   A running Drupal website at `http://localhost`

➤   An empty Database named **bikes**

1. Configure your computer to accept the domain names `roadbikes.local` and `mountainbikes.local`. Add the following lines to your HOSTS file:

   ```
   127.0.0.1    mountainbikes.local
   127.0.0.1    roadbikes.local
   ```

   ➤ Under Mac or Linux, HOSTS is located at `/etc/hosts`.

   ➤ Under Windows HOSTS is located at `c:\windows\systems32\drivers\etc\hosts`.

2. In the Sites directory, create a folder named **mountainbikes.local**.

3. Copy `sites/default/default.settings.php` to `sites/mountainbikes.local` and rename the file to **settings.php**.

4. Open `sites/mountainbikes.local/settings.php` in a text editor and find the following (located at approximately line 153):

   ```
   $databases = array();
   $db_prefix = '';
   ```

5. Replace the line `$databases = array();` with the following, using your own credentials for `'username'` and `'password'`:

   ```
   $databases['default']['default'] = array (
     'driver' => 'mysql',
     'database' => 'bikes',
     'username' => 'username',
     'password' => 'password',
     'host' => 'localhost',
     'port' => '',
   );
   ```

6. Replace the line `$db_prefix = '';` with the following:

   ```
   $db_prefix = array(
       'default'    => 'mountainbikes_',
       'users'      => 'shared_',
       'sessions'   => 'shared_',
       'role'       => 'shared_',
       'authmap'    => 'shared_',
   );
   ```

   The `$db_prefix` line is the important, because it directs Drupal to install the database tables users, sessions, role, and authmap with a prefix of `shared_` so that they will be named shared_sessions, shared_role, shared_authmap, and so on.

7. Navigate to `http://mountainbikes.local` and follow the onscreen instructions. If you have modified the `settings.php` file correctly, you will not be prompted for the database configuration but can configure the other options of your new Drupal website (site name, e-mail address, etc.)

   Drupal should now be installed at `http://mountainbikes.local`.

   With `http://mountainbikes.local` working correctly, you can now create `http://roadbikes.local`.

8. Copy `sites/mountainbikes.local/settings.php` to `sites/roadbikes.local/settings.php`.

9. Open `sites/roadbikes.local/settings.php` in a text editor and modify `$db_prefix` as follows:

```
$db_prefix = array(
      'default'    => 'roadbikes_',
      'users'      => 'shared_',
      'sessions'   => 'shared_',
      'role'       => 'shared_',
      'authmap'    => 'shared_',
);
```

Note that the `'default'` has changed from `'mountainbikes_'` to `'roadbikes_'`.

10. Navigate to `http://roadbikes.local` and follow the onscreen installation instructions to install the road bikes Drupal website. If you modified settings.php correctly you will not be prompted for the database Settings.

You should now have two websites, `http://mountainbikes.local` and `http://roadbike.local`, that are sharing the same set of users.

Test this out to ensure you have everything setup correctly.

1. Navigate to `http://roadbikes.local` and create a new user account by clicking Create new account underneath the user login form.

2. When the new user account is created, navigate to `http://mountainbikes.local` and use the newly created account to log in.

How It Works

There really is no magic to getting Drupal to share content between multiple sites. As discovered in the first exercise, Drupal looks for and uses a settings.php that corresponds to a site's URL. In this example, Drupal was told to use the same database for `http://roadbikes.local` and `http://mountainbikes.local`. The `$db_prefix` is the key to sharing the data.

```
$db_prefix = array(
      'default'    => 'roadbikes_',
      'users'      => 'shared_',
      'sessions'   => 'shared_',
      'role'       => 'shared_',
      'authmap'    => 'shared_',
);
```

Notice that the default variable is unique for the individual websites but the users, sessions, and other variables are set to `shared_`. Each setting directly relates to a table in the database telling Drupal where to find the information. In this example Drupal will look for users in the table named `shared_users`.

It is important to remember that the Database settings had to be placed in settings.php before the website was installed. During a standard installation Drupal automatically configures the settings.php as shown in the first installation example in this chapter.

To expand on the use of the `$db_prefix` variable for the tech minded audience, the following is what occurs. When Drupal searches users it will perform a SQL query similar to the following

```
SELECT uid, name FROM users;
```

In PHP this query might be executed in the following manner:

```
mysql_query("SELECT uid, name FROM users");
```

Drupal developers (i.e., you), however, use a special method for querying data from the database, shown here:

```
$users = db_select('users')
            ->fields('users', array('uid', 'name'))
            ->condition('uid', $account->uid)
            ->execute();
```

This special method allows Drupal to be database agnostic and to modify the table that is being queried., in this example Drupal will replace users with shared_users. This allows you to code once for multiple database types (MySQL, PostgreSQL, etc.) and to allow your modules to be multi-site aware.

Sites.php

Naming each website's folder after its URL is a quick and easy method. But what if you have one website that has multiple URLs? Perhaps you are migrating from one URL to another or are accessing a development version of the site. You could copy the settings.php file to multiple folders but this is very messy and not scalable.

The solution? `sites.php`.

Simply copy the `default.sites.php` file over to `sites.php`, leaving it in the Sites folder and modifying it to map the URLs to the appropriate folder name.

For example, if the following three URLs:

```
http://example.com
http://example.net
http://example.org
```

pointed to the same website, your `sites.php` could read:

```
$sites = array(
  'example.net' => 'example.com',
  'example.org' => 'example.com',
);
```

SETTINGS.PHP

Each Drupal website uses the `settings.php` configuration file contained within the respective Sites folder. As you are now aware, this file is automatically created during the installation process and contains the database settings used by Drupal. When a Drupal site is accessed, this file is one of the first files executed. Because it is executed before modules or themes this file can dramatically affect the way your Drupal site behaves.

You can use this file to set PHP settings including memory settings, block troublesome spammers, modify site variables, and even modify text strings in Drupal.

The settings.php file is very well self-documented, and thus much can be learned from the file itself. Instead of repeating the comments contained within file, the following subsections provide clarification and examples on how you can apply these settings.

$databases

This is the most common setting. It tells Drupal which database server, port, username, and database to use. It can also be used to direct Drupal to use multiple servers for performance reasons or to set up multiple connections. A connection to a single database looks like this:

```
$databases['default']['default'] = array (
  'driver' => 'mysql',
  'database' => 'drupal7',
  'username' => 'username',
  'password' => 'password',
  'host' => 'localhost',
  'port' => '',
);
```

You can also create connections to other databases. This is a nice feature for custom modules because the module does not need to contain the database username and password. Instead you can keep this sensitive information within the secured settings.php file. Better yet you are provided full access to Drupal's API. First you define the connection:

```
$databases['inventory']['default'] = array (
  'driver' => 'mysql',
  'database' => 'non_drupal_inventory_db',
  'username' => 'username',
  'password' => 'password',
  'host' => '192.168.1.1',
  'port' => '',
);
```

Next, you call this database connection from within custom code using db_set_active. For example:

```
db_set_active('inventory');
$sql = "SELECT sku, title, description FROM products WHERE type = '%s'";
$products = db_query($sql, 'toy');
//process data
db_set_active();
```

The first line, db_set_active('inventory'), sets the active database connection to the inventory system. At this point all of Drupal has been switched to using the inventory database so it is very important to switch back to Drupal's database by calling db_set_active() without any arguments. Alternatively you can call db_set_active('default'); to achieve the same effect.

Scalability

If your site grows, and you find yourself needing to add a second database server to gain more performance, the `$database` setting can direct Drupal to select between multiple database servers in a master/slave configuration. The follow example sets `db-master.mysite.com` as Drupal's master database, and `db-slave1.mysite.com` and `db-slave2.mysite.com` as Drupal's slave databases. Drupal will randomize the selection of a slave database to distribute the load. SELECT queries are automatically directed to the slaves whereas INSERT, UPDATE, and DELETE queries are directed to the master.

```
$databases['default']['default'] = array (
  'driver' => 'mysql',
  'database' => 'drupal7',
  'username' => 'username',
  'password' => 'password',
  'host' => 'db-master.mysite.com',
  'port' => '',
);
$databases['default']['slave'][] = array (
  'driver' => 'mysql',
  'database' => 'drupal7',
  'username' => 'username',
  'password' => 'password',
  'host' => 'db-slave1.mysite.com',
  'port' => '',
);
$databases['default']['slave'][] = array (
  'driver' => 'mysql',
  'database' => 'drupal7',
  'username' => 'username',
  'password' => 'password',
  'host' => 'db-slave2.mysite.com',
  'port' => '',
);
```

Note that Drupal does not handle the synchronization between these servers, synchronization should be handled by the respective database software.

$db_prefix

If you are using a single database for multiple websites, placing a prefix before each table name can help distinguish between the websites and to prevent name clashes.

As shown in the earlier exercise you can use `$db_prefix` to set a prefix for all tables with the following:

```
$db_prefix = 'mysite_';
```

Note that any Drupal table can be modified. For example, to share only user roles between sets use the following:

```
$db_prefix = array(
    'default'   => 'mysite_',
    'role'      => 'shared_',
);
```

Or to share a taxonomy structure between sites, use the following:

```
$db_prefix = array(
    'default'                    => 'mysite_',
    'taxonomy_term_data'         => 'shared_',
    'taxonomy_term_hierarchy'    => 'shared_',
    'taxonomy_term_relation'     => 'shared_',
    'taxonomy_term_synonym'      => 'shared_',
    'taxonomy_vocabulary'        => 'shared_',
);
```

Drupal will not rename tables if this setting is modified after installation although it will use the new table names immediately.

$baseurl

This setting directs Drupal to always return the same base URL, regardless of how the user accessed the site. For example, if your site is hosted at `http://mysite.local/drupal7` and is also hosted at `http://mynewsite.local`, you can force Drupal to always return `http://mynewsite.local`.

Set this variable like the following:

```
$baseurl = "http://mynewsite.local";
```

This can be a great setting if you are transitioning a website to a new URL but be aware that Drupal does not send a 301 redirect with this setting. A 301 redirect is a web server directive that tells web browsers and search engines that the content has permanently moved. In short it is a change of address form for the Web. 301 redirects are setup within your web server configuration and not within Drupal.

$ini_set

PHP settings can be modified within Drupal so that they are specific to the Drupal website. The default settings look something like the following:

```
ini_set('session.cache_expire',     200000);
ini_set('session.cache_limiter',    'none');
ini_set('session.cookie_lifetime',  2000000);
```

Killing the White Screen of Death

Two of the most useful settings aren't listed in `settings.php`: the memory limit and error reporting. Drupal requires a bare-minimum of 16MB, but a default PHP installation is often set at only 8MB. If a site does not have enough memory, it will return a blank white screen known as the "White Screen of Death."

The following line will set the memory limit to 32MB per page request:

```
ini_set('memory_limit', 32MB);
```

When you're developing a website, it may be handy to see all of the PHP errors. You can turn error reporting on using the following setting:

```
ini_set('error_reporting', E_ALL );
```

To turn error reporting off, use a 0 (zero) instead of E_ALL.

> **NOTE** *A few web hosting companies may prevent PHP* `ini_set` *from functioning for security and performance reasons. Be sure to check with your web host to ensure that* `ini_set` *is available.*

$reverse_proxy

If you are using a reverse proxy, such as Squid, set this variable to `true`; otherwise, leave it as `false`. Reverse proxies are used to increase performance by placing a caching server in front of your web server.

Variable Overrides

Drupal uses numerous variables to determine items such as which theme to use, the site's name, or even how the frontpage is displayed. Core and contributed modules also set variables for their specific configuration needs. These variables are stored in the Variables database table and can be overridden in `settings.php`.

The following example will change the theme based upon the URL a user has visited:

```
preg_match('/[^.]+\.[^.]+$/',$_SERVER['SERVER_NAME'], $regs);
$url = $regs[0];
if ($url == 'mysite.com') {
  $conf['theme_default'] => 'minnelli';
}
else {
  $conf['theme_default'] => 'garland';
}
```

String Overrides

A nice new feature to Drupal 7 is the ability to replace certain strings (words or sentences) within `settings.php`. This makes the changes fast and doesn't require a separate module. Previously, you had to use either the locale module or the string overrides module (`http://drupal.org/project/stringoverrides`). This setting should only be used to modify a few strings, use the locale module to do mass changes or the i18n module (`http://drupal.org/project/i18n`) or the l10n_client (`http://drupal.org/project/l10n_client`) for language translation.

For example, the following code changes the 'Create new account' and 'Request new password' items on the login block:

```
$conf['locale_custom_strings_en'] = array(
  'Create new account'     => 'Join the community',
  'Request new password' => 'Doh! I forgot my password',
);
```

IP Blocking

Unfortunately, websites are under continuous attacks from spambots and would-be hackers. Drupal has built-in security on its forms and can block IPs through the administrative interface but these mechanisms require Drupal to start up, which can be a drain on precious system resources. Setting $conf['blocked_ips'] within settings.php blocks the IP before Drupal starts saving precious system resources.

The following blocks users originating from the IP 192.168.0.1 or 192.168.0.2 from accessing your website.

```
$conf['blocked_ips'] = array (
  '192.168.0.1',
  '192.168.0.2',
);
```

You may also look into the http:BL module (http://drupal.org/project/httpbl) for advanced IP blocking based on honey pots, or the Troll module (http://drupal.org/project/troll) to prevent abusive users.

Spam can be blocked with either the Mollom or the Spam module at http://drupal.org/project/mollom or http://drupal.org/project/spam respectively.

SUMMARY

Drupal's multi-site features can dramatically reduce the time you spend upgrading to the latest security and bug fixes or deploying new sites. You can also use this feature to share users, taxonomy, or content between sites. The more sites you power with a single instance of Drupal, the more time you will save. The multi-site capability of Drupal is made possible by a combination of the Sites folder and the very powerful settings.php file.

As your Drupal site grows and becomes more complex you will find yourself spending more time in the settings.php file, so it pays to take the time now to explore its functionality. This file is used often to set performance features such as multiple database servers or a reverse proxy. It can also be used to increase performance by setting certain variables immediately when Drupal is accessed instead of relying on a module; which starts up later and requires more system resources.

EXERCISES

1. How can you increase the amount of memory available to Drupal?

2. Consider if your company operates the following four URLs:

```
http://your-company.com
http://also-your-company.com
http://your-company.cn
http://also-your-company.cn
```

How could you configure these sites using Drupal's multi-site capabilities?

3. What are the basic steps to share a set of users between two websites?

4. How many websites can one installation of Drupal power?

5. How can you block a problematic spambot that is originating from a single IP?

Answers to the Exercises can be found in the Appendix.

► **WHAT YOU LEARNED IN THIS CHAPTER**

➤ A website's information should be contained to its respective Sites folder. This makes upgrading Drupal easy.

➤ Drupal can be used to power multiple websites by simply using respective folder names within the Sites folder.

➤ Websites powered by the same version of Drupal can share information within the same Database (Users, content, etc.) by modifying the `$db_prefix` setting.

➤ The `settings.php` file contains numerous settings that can affect your Drupal website such as switching themes, modifying text strings, and blocking IP addresses.

➤ The memory available to Drupal can be increased or decreased by using `ini_set('memory_limit', xxMB)` within `settings.php`.

19

Preflight Checklist

WHAT YOU WILL LEARN IN THIS CHAPTER:

➤ Using a basic checklist for site maintenance, users, Search Engine Optimization (SEO), performance, and disaster recovery to cover all your bases before going live

➤ Overview of SEO

➤ Setting up and optimizing SEO for your site

➤ The importance of clean URLs and URL aliases

➤ Setting up XML Sitemap

➤ An introduction to Google Analytics, and installing the module to monitor your site's activities

➤ Configuring your dashboard

You are nearing the end of your Drupal journey. In the previous chapters, you went from the basics of installing and configuring your site to the challenges of theming, custom development, and advanced installations. You're now set to show the world your creation. Follow the preflight checklist in this chapter to get your site ready for launch.

In this chapter, you will explore the best ways of putting your website before a potential audience of millions. With SEO, you can increase your site's visibility by optimizing your site's content and correctly submitting it to search engines. The chapter introduces you to the SEO Checklist module for Drupal, which helps you properly implement SEO techniques. This chapter also covers the XML Sitemap module, which catalogs your site to help search engines like Google, Yahoo!, and Bing crawl your site more efficiently and retrieve more accurate information.

The chapter ends with an overview of the new Dashboard feature, a function that comes with Drupal 7 in which users can create a customized page with their most commonly used modules.

PREFLIGHT CHECKLIST

Use the following lists as a final run-through of items to complete before launching your site.

Site Information

❏ Set your site name. The site name, which will be your site's identity from the start, can be found in Configuration ⇨ Site Information (System), as described in Chapter 4, "Administration — Configuration, Modules, and Reporting."

❏ Choose a default e-mail address. Set your e-mail address at Configuration ⇨ Site Information (System), as described in Chapter 4.

❏ Make sure your country and time zone are set correctly. Do this at Configuration ⇨ Regional and Language (System), as described in Chapter 4.

❏ Verify that your RSS settings have the correct content and number of items. Do this at Configuration ⇨ RSS Publishing (Web Services), as described in Chapter 4.

❏ Ensure that your contact forms are working. If your site uses contact forms, send yourself an e-mail to test that it is functioning properly, as described in Chapter 3, "Your First Drupal Website."

User Settings

❏ Configure new user account registration settings. User account registration settings can be found at Administer ⇨ Configuration ⇨ Account Settings, as described in Chapter 7, "User Management."

❏ Check permissions for content and comment creation. Default permissions prevent comments and content from anonymous users. Assign permissions by going to Configuration ⇨ People and Permissions ⇨ Permissions, as described in Chapter 7.

❏ Designate user roles and verify all permissions. Roles are created at Configuration ⇨ People and Permissions ⇨ Roles, and a user's default role is assigned within the user account registration settings, as described in Chapter 7.

❏ Tweak user profile settings, such as signatures and user photos. Navigate to Configuration ⇨ People and Permissions ⇨ Profiles, and change the settings as described in Chapter 7.

❏ Check your Text format roles and defaults. Navigate to Configuration ⇨ Text Formats and verify or modify the settings as described in Chapter 4.

Site Maintenance

❏ Make sure Cron is set up and running well. You can manually run Cron by going to Reports ⇨ Status Report or by clicking Status Report directly from the Administrative menu, as described in Chapter 3.

❏ Check your reports. Ensure that your site is up-to-date by checking your status report. You can do this by clicking Reports in the top administration menu or by navigating to Reports ⇨ Available Updates, as described in Chapter 9, "Search, Performance, Statistics and Reporting."

❑ Update notifications. Check to ensure that the Update Manager module is enabled. You should also set an e-mail address where notifications will be sent. This is configured in the same location as the Available Updates report, Reports ⇨ Available updates ⇨ Settings.

❑ Check your file system settings. Ensure that files are being placed in a location large enough to handle your site's growth. Navigate to Administer ⇨ Site Configuration ⇨ File System and modify the settings if necessary, as described in Chapter 4.

❑ Turn off PHP error messages. Navigate to Configuration ⇨ Logging and Errors, and set to Display PHP Messages to None.

❑ Enable Google analytics. Make sure you have downloaded and enabled the Google Analytics module (**http://drupal.org/project/google_analytics**), as described in this chapter (Chapter 19).

SPAM

❑ Configure and test your spam-control module (such as Mollom or the Spam module). A live site without spam protection can be quickly overrun with bogus content. Never launch without protection, as described in Chapter 6, "Content."

SEO

❑ Enable Clean URLs so that search engines can better index your content. Do this at Configuration ⇨ Clean URLs (Search and Metadata), as described in Chapter 4.

❑ Ensure that Pathauto is configured to create automatic URL aliases for all of your content types. Get the Pathauto module at **http://drupal.org/project/pathauto**, and configure it as described in Chapter 14, "Contributed Modules."

❑ Install the XML Sitemap module, and submit your site to various search engines. You can find the XML Sitemap module at **http://drupal.org/project/xmlsitemap**. The module is described later in this chapter.

❑ Download and enable the SEO Checklist. Download the SEO Checklist module from **http://drupal.org/project/seo_checklist**, and use it as described in this chapter (Chapter 19).

❑ Validate your site's HTML. Clean and validated HTML markup is one part of good SEO. Validate your site's markup by using the W3C validator available at http://validator.w3.org/.

❑ Check your site's links. Bad links are bad for SEO. Make sure that all of your links are valid by checking them with the W3C link checker, available at http://validator.w3.org/checklink.

Search

❑ Enable the Search module. Go to Configuration ⇨ Modules, and enable and configure the Search module as described in Chapter 9.

❑ Index your content by running cron. Go to Configuration ⇨ Search settings for the indexing status, run cron as described in Chapter 9.

❑ Grant the Search Content permission to the appropriate role, such as anonymous users. Permissions are set at Configuration ⇨ Permissions. Details can be found in Chapter 7.

Performance

❑ Turn on page caching. Set page caching to Normal at Configuration ➪ Performance (Development), as described in Chapter 9.

❑ Turn on block caching. Enable block caching at Configuration ➪ Performance (under Development), as described in Chapter 9.

❑ Turn on Views caching. If you are using the Views module, each view has a controllable cache setting. Further details can be found in Chapter 11, "Views," under caching.

❑ Aggregate your CSS files. Go to Configuration ➪ Performance (under Development), enable your CSS files for aggregation as described in Chapter 9.

❑ Aggregate your JavaScript files. Go to Configuration ➪ Performance (under Development), enable your JavaScript files for aggregation as described in Chapter 9.

❑ Turn off the Devel module. If you have installed the Devel module, make you sure have disabled it before going live with your site. You do this at Configuration ➪ Modules, as described in Chapter 14, "Contributed Modules."

Disaster Recovery

❑ Test your backups and disaster recovery plan. Test to ensure that your database and site files are properly and consistently backed up.

SEO

Now that your site is ready to go live, it's time to delve deeper into ways to optimize your site's quality and the volume of traffic on it. Not every site needs thousands of visitors a day, but if you are building a commercial site, learning to use a marketing strategy to enhance your search engine visibility is well worth the time.

The basic concept of Search Engine Optimization (SEO) is that the higher your site ranks in search listings, the more visitors it will receive from the search engine. Search engines are text-driven and crawl a website to look for particular items (mainly text) to see what a site is about. Engines use a piece of software called a *spider* to crawl your site, following links to get from one page to another. The spider then indexes every bit of information it finds in a giant database. When a search request comes into an engine like Google, the engine processes it and compares the search string to terms stored in the database.

Of course, search engines have limits to how thoroughly they can search. This is where SEO comes in. Knowing what terms to use and where to place those terms can raise your search engine ranking, but choosing the wrong terms can bury your site deep in the murky depths of search rankings.

This section introduces the concept of SEO and demonstrates some of the most common best practices. SEO is an evolving and ever-moving system that enables you to stay on top of all of the tips and tricks. You can download the SEO Checklist module at `http://drupal.org/project/seo_checklist`. This module lists nearly every SEO best practice and helps you track the ones you've implemented on your site.

SEO Best Practices

How can you tell if your site is adhering to the best SEO practices? Naming is key to SEO. Here are a few pointers to keep in mind:

➤ The keywords that you use should be relevant to site content.

➤ Your page and/or article titles should include targeted keywords.

➤ The names of your site's downloadable files should include targeted keywords.

➤ Your site should have a sitemap.

➤ You should use clean URLs and URL aliases.

➤ Your URLs should be descriptive of the content.

The Importance of URLs

One of the first things you should know about optimizing your site is the importance of having clean, self-describing URLs. For example, if you include an article on your site called "Green Tea in Japanese Culture," Drupal automatically gives it a name like this:

```
http://localhost/index.php?q=node/87.
```

With clean URLS enabled (Configuration ⇨ Clean URLs), it becomes this:

```
http://localhost/node/87
```

With the Path core module enabled, you could manually alias the URL to be this:

```
http://localhost/green-tea-japanese-culture
```

The last URL is self-describing, making it easier for your site visitors and, more importantly, for search engines to understand what the content of the page will contain. As you can probably guess, this last clean, self-describing URL is what you want. To make your life easier, the Pathauto module can automatically create these URL aliases for you based on information like title, taxonomy, and content type. The only thing you need to do is to download, install, and enable the module although you should take a few minutes to configure or verify the default settings.

Clean URLs, URL aliases, and Pathauto are covered in Chapter 4. Pathauto can be downloaded from http://drupal.org/project/pathauto.

XML Sitemap

Search engines such as Google, Yahoo!, and Bing crawl sites all the time, looking for snippets of text that will tell them what a site is about. An engine typically finds a hyperlink that links to a piece of content that in turn links to more content, thus recursively searching a site or sites. This method doesn't allow the search engine to find everything, and it doesn't tell the engine what is and what is not important on your site. For example, if your contact page contains numerous links to other content or other sites, is that considered important? Also, how often should the search engine come back and look for new information? Should it check once a day, once a week, or every few months?

The XML Sitemap module helps search engines find your best and most relevant content by creating categorized and prioritized lists of your site's information. It might help to think of this list as a directory of your site. You then provide this list to the search engines to help them understand your site's content, how often it is updated (which tells them how often they should check back), and where to find your content. In other words, the module helps search engines crawl your site more intelligently and efficiently, which can lead to better search rankings.

After you have created a sitemap with the XML Sitemap module, you can use the Site Verification module to automatically submit this sitemap to Google, Yahoo!, Bing, and other search engines. The Site Verification module also comes with several sub-modules that create sitemap links for menu items, content types, taxonomy terms, and even user profiles.

In the following exercise, you will configure the XML Sitemap and the Site Verification modules.

TRY IT OUT   Creating Your XML Sitemap

In this exercise, you will configure the XML Sitemap module to prepare your site for submission to Google, Yahoo!, Bing, or other search engines.

1. Download and install the following modules:

➤ XML Sitemap (version 2): `http://drupal.org/project/xmlsitemap`

➤ Site Verification: `http://drupal.org/project/site_verify`

2. Enable the following modules, which are a part of XML Sitemap and Site Verification:

➤ XML Sitemap

➤ XML Sitemap Node

3. Navigate to Configuration ⇨ XML Sitemap. Verify that a sitemap is being generated for your site's language under Settings, as shown in Figure 19-1, and write down your site's language-specific URL (for example, `http://localhost/sitemap.xml`) here: _____

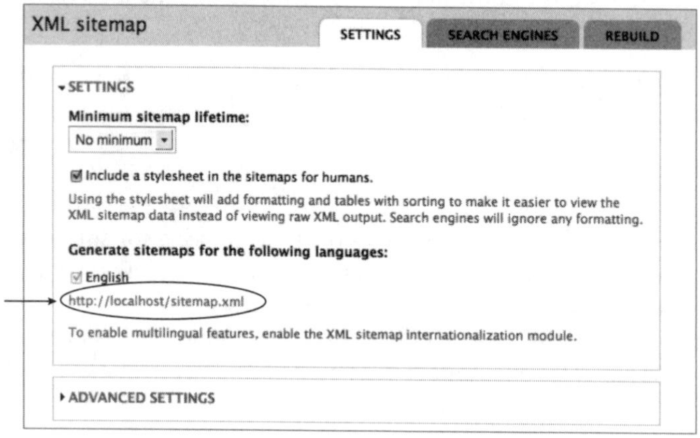

FIGURE 19-1

4. Scroll down the page and open Content Types, as shown in Figure 19-2. Verify that the correct content types are being included in your sitemap.

> **NOTE** *XML Sitemap also contains modules that will include menus or taxonomy terms.*

5. Modify the priority of Articles to be higher than that of Pages. To do this, Navigate to Content types and click edit next to the Article content type. At the bottom of the content type's configuration, modify the XML Sitemap settings to set the Default Priority higher, as demonstrated in Figure 19-3.

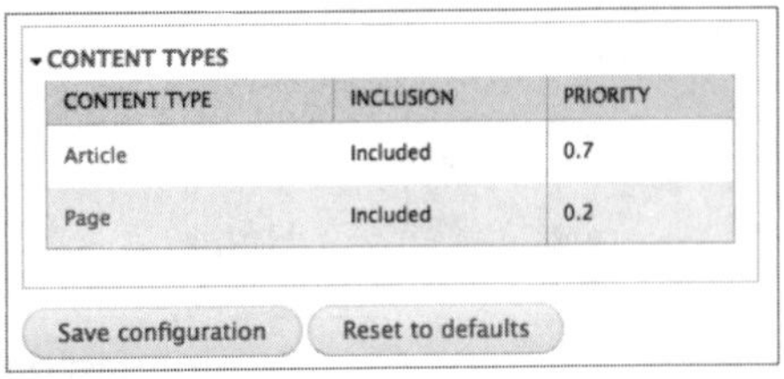

6. Repeat this process for Pages, setting the Default Priority to `0.2`.

7. Run cron manually to create your first sitemap. Navigate to Reports ⇨ Status Report, and then click Run Cron Manually.

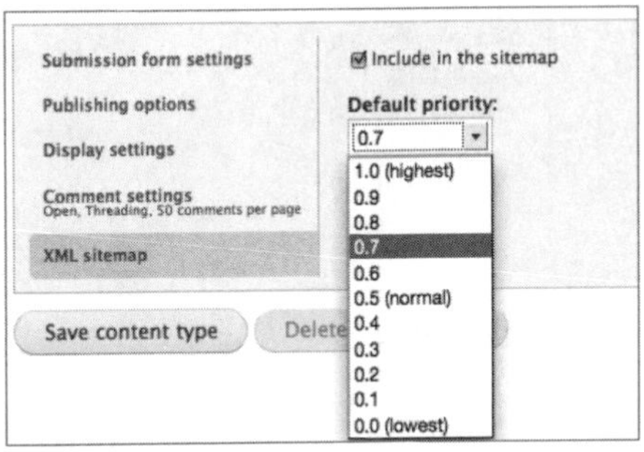

CONTENT TYPES		
CONTENT TYPE	INCLUSION	PRIORITY
Article	Included	0.7
Page	Included	0.2

Save configuration   Reset to defaults

FIGURE 19-2

FIGURE 19-3

How It Works

On each cron run or when content is added, edited, or updated, XML Sitemap will generate a new sitemap according the settings at Configuration ⇨ XML Sitemap. Each piece of content can contain a priority number that tells search engines what content is most relevant on your site. In this exercise, you modified the default for all Articles to be higher than Pages. Note that cron must be routinely running for XML Sitemap to work correctly.

Submitting Your Sitemap to Search Engines

Creating a sitemap is no magic potion to increase search engine rankings. The ugly truth is that search engines won't even know about your sitemap until you tell them. Fortunately, you have tools on your side. XML Sitemaps comes with the search engine sub-module, and each search engine has sets of tools on their site to help you manage your site.

Before you submit a sitemap to a search engine, you must verify that you are the owner of the site and are therefore allowed to provide a sitemap for it. Each search engine has a slightly different method of verification, but they are all roughly the same. In the following exercise, you verify your site with Google in order to submit a sitemap, which you'll do in the exercise directly following this one.

TRY IT OUT   Verifying Site Ownership with Google

In this exercise, you verify ownership of your site within Google Webmaster Tools.

1. Enable the Site Verification module that was installed in the previous exercise.

2. Get your site verification code from Google. Start by navigating to `http://google.com/webmasters` and sign in with your Google account. If you don't have a Google account, you'll need to create one.

3. On your Google's account Home page, click Add a Site and type in your site's URL as shown in Figure 19-4. Click Continue.

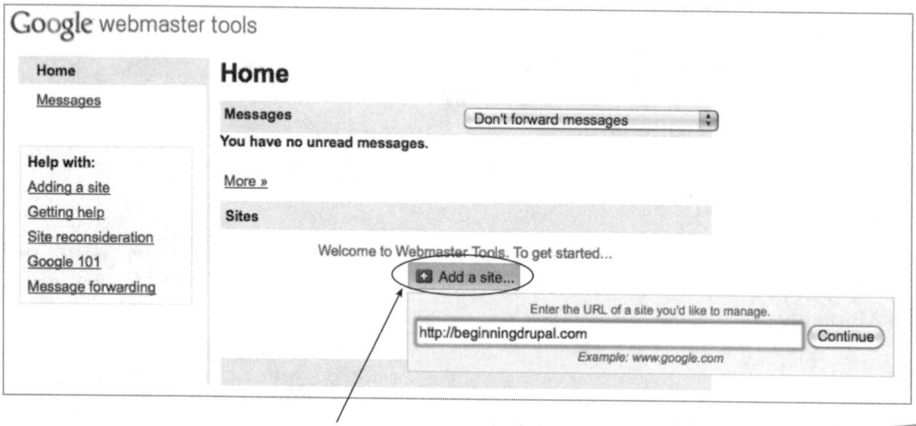

FIGURE 19-4

4. On the next page (Verify Ownership), select Upload an HTML File and download the HTML verification file, as shown in Figure 19-5. Do *not* click Verify.

5. In a new browser tab or window, navigate to your Drupal site, and then navigate to Configuration ⇨ Site Verification.

6. On the Site Verifications page, click the Add Verification tab and select Google as the search engine, as shown in Figure 19-6. Click Next.

7. Upload the verification HTML file you downloaded from Google, as shown in Figure 19-7. Click Save.

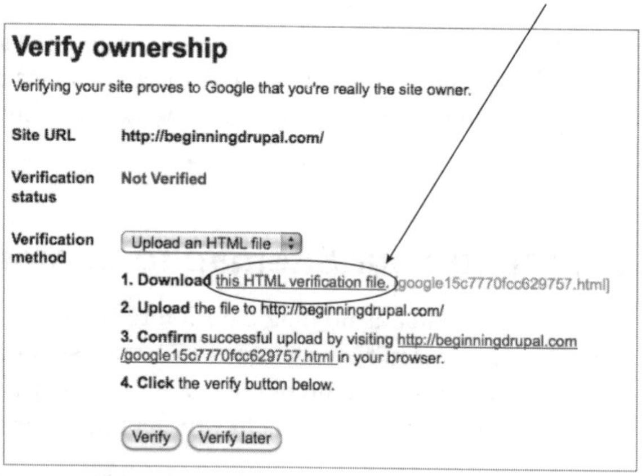

FIGURE 19-5

FIGURE 19-6

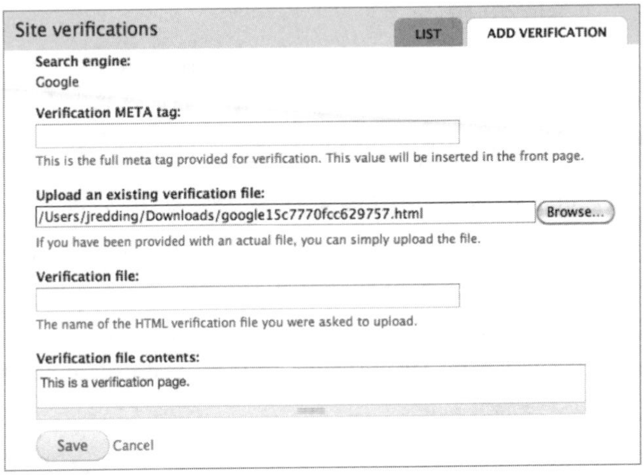

FIGURE 19-7

8. Return to Google's Verify Ownership page (step 4) and click Verify.

9. Still within Google Webmaster Tools, click the Return To Home link to return your account overview. Your site should be listed as either a Pending or Verified.

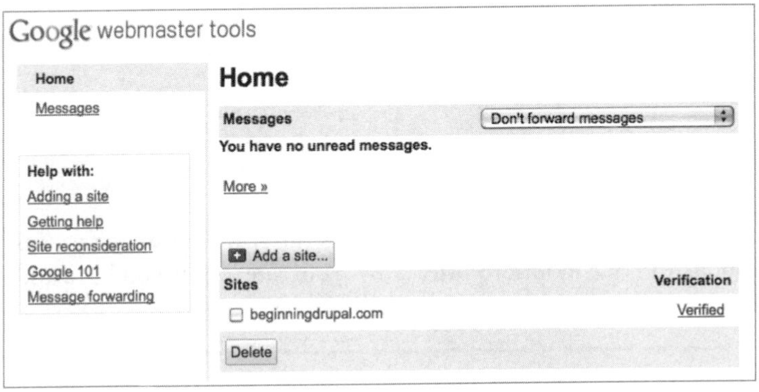

FIGURE 19-8

How It Works

Google and other search engines must verify that you are the site owner before they use your sitemap for indexing purposes. The common methods are uploading an HTML file to your site or adding a meta tag to your site's pages. The Site Verification module makes this process easy and is the preferred method for site verification. Google and other search engines will periodically recheck for site ownership, so do not delete your site verification settings.

CTPRabbit

Adding Your Sitemap to Google

After your site is verified, you can add a sitemap to your Google Webmaster Tools account. Follow the next exercise to add your sitemap.

TRY IT OUT Submitting Your Sitemap to Google

In this exercise, you submit the sitemap created in the previous exercise to the Google search engine.

1. Log into your Google Webmasters Tools account (if you are not still logged in), and click your site's URL on the account homepage (shown previously in Figure 19-8).

2. On the site's page, expand Site Configuration in the left sidebar, click Sitemaps, and then click Submit a Sitemap, as shown in Figure 19-9. Enter the URL of your sitemap, as noted in this chapter's first exercise.

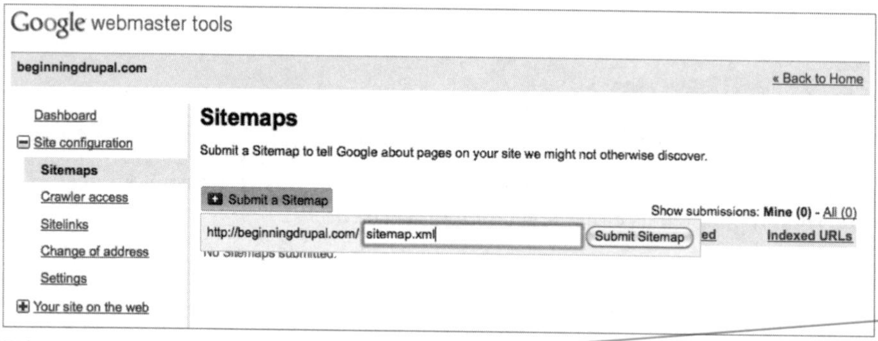

FIGURE 19-9

How It Works

Adding your sitemap to your Google Webmaster Tools account begins the search crawling process. It may take Google between one minute and one month to fully crawl your site. After you have added your site to Google it's a good idea to add your site to other search engines as well.

Keeping Your Site's Information Up-to-Date

After you have verified your site and added your sitemap, your next step is to make sure that the search engine is kept up-to-date. Instead of waiting for search engines to come to your site, you can automatically *ping* them to inform of site updates. XML Sitemap includes the Search Engines submodule, which is used for this exact purpose. Enable it, and then navigate to Configuration ⇨ XML Sitemap, click Search Engines, and select which search engines you want to be automatically informed (pinged) of your site's updates.

ANALYZING YOUR SITE WITH GOOGLE

Few web statistics tracking systems are as user-friendly and versatile as Google Analytics. It enables you to view a wide range of data about traffic to your site, including the top content of the day or month, where your visitors are from, which search engines and sites send the most traffic, and much more. Google Analytics also support something called *goals*, which allow you to set a target (such as a 50-percent increase of traffic to your shopping cart) and track your progress. Using these tools you can pinpoint problem areas on your site, discover what your visitors like, and become more tuned into your audience. The best part is that this is all free!

Google Analytics works by placing a small client-side JavaScript file on your site that records anonymous, public information about your site visitors. The Google Analytics module for Drupal integrates your site with the power of Analytics, and adds a lot more functionality than the default JavaScript provided by Drupal. You can track the activities of individual users or roles, monitor the files that are downloaded from your site, monitor what types of links are tracked, and even collect visit information segmented by user type or profile data. The module also caches the Google Analytics code on your server, giving your site a performance boost compared to manually integrated Google Analytics. Moreover, the module also hooks into other Google features such as Site Search and Google Ads.

The in-depth and daily updated information provided by Google helps you to create a more robust site. To install the module, go to `http://drupal.org/project/google_analytics`. After you download the module and install it, you don't need to do any configuration. But just like with the SEO module, you have to go to Google and sign up for an account in order to get your Google Analytics account number. Follow along in the next exercise to set up site monitoring using Google Analytics.

TRY IT OUT Setting Up Google Analytics

In this exercise, you install the Google Analytics module for your site.

1. Download, install, and enable the Google Analytics module at `http://drupal.org/project/google_analytics`.

2. Create your Google Analytics account by navigating to `http://google.com/analytics` and logging in with your Google account (hint: this can be the same as your Webmaster Tools account).

3. After you are logged in, add your website by clicking the Get Started button and entering your site's information as shown in Figure 19-10. Click Continue.

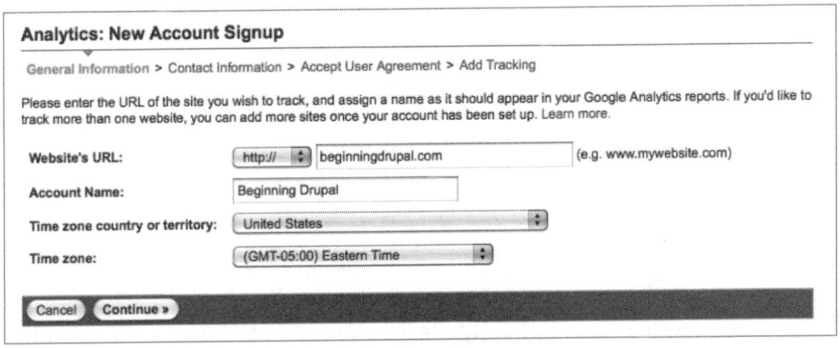

Analytics: New Account Signup

General Information > Contact Information > Accept User Agreement > Add Tracking

Please enter the URL of the site you wish to track, and assign a name as it should appear in your Google Analytics reports. If you'd like to track more than one website, you can add more sites once your account has been set up. Learn more.

Website's URL: http://   beginningdrupal.com   (e.g. www.mywebsite.com)

Account Name: Beginning Drupal

Time zone country or territory: United States

Time zone: (GMT-05:00) Eastern Time

Cancel   Continue »

FIGURE 19-10

4. The next few screens will ask you for your name and require you to accept Google's Terms and Conditions. When you accept, you'll be shown code that Google says need to be pasted on your site. Thanks to the Google Analytics module, you do not need to do this. You only need your site's account number. Find this number in the code by looking for the numbers that begin with UA- as shown in Figure 19-11. Copy this code into your clipboard or write it down here: _____.

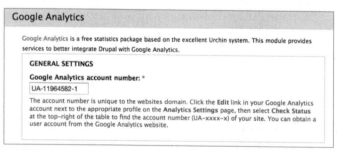

FIGURE 19-11

5. Navigate back to your Drupal site and then to the Google Analytics page at Configuration ⇨ Google Analytics. Enter your site's account number within General Settings, as shown in Figure 19-12. Click Save at the bottom of the page.

FIGURE 19-12

How It Works

Google Analytics performs its magic via a small JavaScript file that is placed within each of your pages. Drupal's Google Analytics module automatically places and manages this JavaScript file, so you do not need to copy and paste any code from Google. To verify that you are the owner of your site and thus authorized to view statistics about its traffic, you must enter in your domain's account number and have it verified.

Google Analytics Module's Configuration Settings

While performing the last exercise, you probably noticed a lot of settings within the Google Analytics module. These settings allow you to track different types of traffic on your site, including by user role, by page, and other options. The defaults are applicable for nearly every site. If you run an e-commerce site or a large user community site, then you can revisit this page — but before you do, take some time to read Google's own document on how to use the Analytics site. This topic is best covered with a dedicated book.

DASHBOARD

Drupal 7 comes with a new feature called Dashboard, an administrative page that can be customized to provide quick access to the tools your site administrators use most. For example, this could be a page that shows all recent comments, recently submitted content, new users, currently logged in users, and links to manage everything displayed.

A *dashboard* is a collection of blocks from your site. These could be Drupal's built-in blocks, blocks provided by contributed modules, or blocks created using the Views module. The dashboard can also be automatically expanded by contributed modules, so look for changes here when you enable a new module.

You can access the Dashboard page by clicking the Dashboard link in the top administration menu or the Dashboard link in the shortcut menu, or by navigating to the admin overview page and clicking the Dashboard link as demonstrated in Figure 19-13.

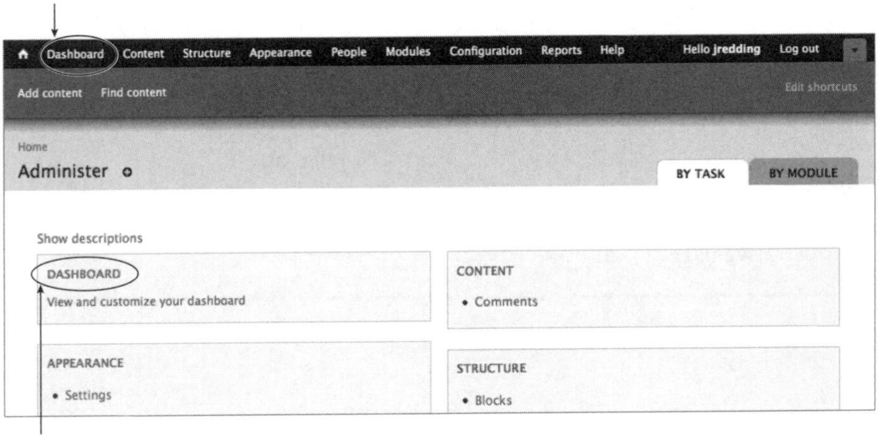

FIGURE 19-13

Follow the next exercise to customize your dashboard.

> **NOTE** *Customizing the dashboard requires the Administer Blocks permission.*

TRY IT OUT   Customizing Your Dashboard

In this exercise, you install and set up the Dashboard module for your site.

1.   Click the Dashboard link in the top administration menu as shown previously in Figure 19-13.

2.   On the Dashboard page, click the Customize link located just below the page title.

3.   Drag and drop the Who's New, Who's Online, and Management blocks into the locations shown in Figure 19-14.

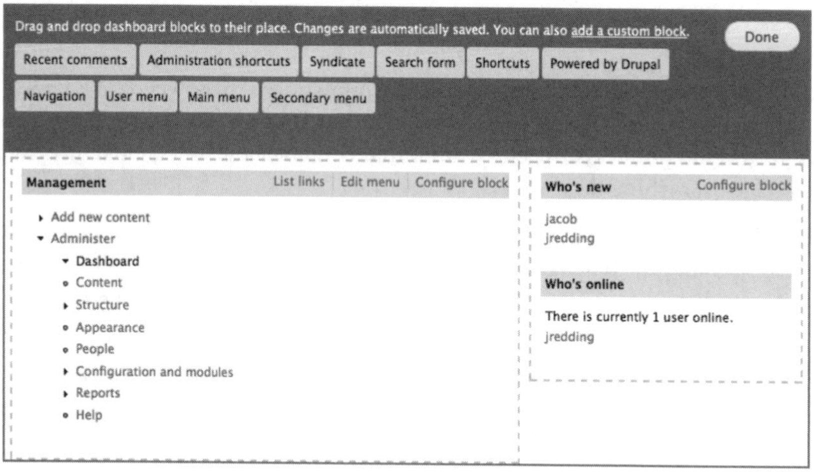

FIGURE 19-14

4.   Click Done.

How It Works

The Dashboard module is designed to provide quick access to commonly performed administrative tasks. A dashboard consists of your site's blocks. You can use Views to create custom blocks to create a highly customized administrative page.

SUMMARY

The hard work of building your site is complete. The Preflight Checklist provides a quick rundown of the important areas to check or tasks to complete before you launch your site. Not only is it important to make sure that basics such as your site title, e-mail, and file folders are properly set, you should also verify that items such as your search index, contact forms, and spam controls are in place and functioning to ensure you have a smooth launch.

Search Engine Optimization (SEO) is a set of techniques used to help search engines find relevant and useful information on your site according to the search terms used. SEO is not guaranteed to bring you thousands of new visitors, but it can greatly enhance your site's visibility on the web. Using good URL aliases set with the Pathauto module and clean URLs are just two ways to optimize your site for search engines. This book barely touches the surface of SEO, so it is best to download the SEO Checklist module at `http://drupal.org/project/seo_checklist`, which will help you implement the most up-to-date SEO techniques.

The XML sitemap module is one SEO technique that will automatically push fresh content to search engines and help those engines discover the most important and relevant data. Analyze your site's traffic with Google Analytics and use the information to tweak and enhance your SEO techniques.

Although these tools are not essential for a basic site, they are helpful if you want a webmaster-friendly experience. You have the tools to track users and activity on your site at your fingertips, and you're in the driver's seat when it comes to displaying your site's content to search engines and readers.

Good luck on your new website, and I hope to see you in the Drupal community, whether it's on the site, in the IRC channels, at a Drupal meetup or camp, or at the next Drupalcon!

EXERCISES

1. Why is it useful to understand the basics of SEO?

2. What does the Pathauto module do?

3. What is the purpose of the XML Sitemap module?

4. How do you create a customized page with the Dashboard module?

Answers to these Exercises can be found in the Appendix.

▶ **WHAT YOU LEARNED IN THIS CHAPTER**

➤ SEO as a marketing strategy can help to increase your site's search engine visibility. Use the SEO Checklist module to stay on top of your site's SEO strategy.

➤ The XML sitemap module helps search engines crawl a site more intelligently and efficiently, and keeps the results up-to-date.

➤ The Pathauto module automatically creates clean, self-describing URL aliases based on information like taxonomy, content type, and the content's title, making it easier for your site visitors and search engines to understand what the content of the page will contain.

➤ Analyze your site's traffic with the Google Analytics module.

➤ Drupal 7's new Dashboard feature can be customized to provide quick access to the most frequently used administrative items.

APPENDIX

Exercises and Answers

CHAPTER 1

1. What website can you use to connect with other Drupal users, developers, and professionals with similar interests or who are located near you?

`http://groups.drupal.org` (aka: GDO) is where thousands of Drupal users, developers, and professionals self-organize into special interest or geographic groups.

2. Where can you communicate with other Drupal users or developers in real time over the Internet?

You can use Internet Relay Chat (IRC) in `#drupal-support` and `#drupal` channels to communicate in real time with users and developers from all over the world. Learn more about IRC at `http://drupal.org/irc`.

3. What nonprofit organization helps to protect the Drupal community's code from GPL copyright infringement, protects the Drupal trademark, and supports the `http://drupal.org` infrastructure?

Created to support the Drupal community the nonprofit Drupal Association (`http://association.drupal.org`) defends against infringements of the Drupal community's GPL-licensed code, manages the hardware infrastructure that powers the `http://drupal.org` websites, and puts on the annual Drupalcon conference. Find out more about how you can get involved at `http://association.drupal.org`.

4. Drupal is a great CMS, but developers also love it because of its great ____? (three letter acronym)

Drupal's API (Application Programming Interface) really helps Drupal stand out from other CMSs because it helps developers extend and customize Drupal to meet their website's needs.

CHAPTER 2

1. What version of PHP does Drupal 7 require?

PHP 5.2 or higher.

2. What is the Sites folder in Drupal used for?

The Sites folder contains items that relate to specific websites. For example a folder named `wrox.com` would power the `http://wrox.com` website. The folder contains a `settings.php` file and modules, themes, and files specific to the website. The Sites folder is what powers Drupal's multi-site capability.

3. How do you install Drupal using a different language?

To install Drupal in a different language, first visit `http://drupal.org/project/translations`, download the translation, and then extract its contents into Drupal's root directory. Start the installation process as normal and select the new language.

4. What is core?

Core is defined as anything outside of the Sites folder.

5. Why should you not modify core?

"Don't hack core" is the Golden Rule of the Drupal community for the sanity of all Drupal developers, support professionals, users, and you. When you modify Drupal's core files, you make it difficult to upgrade your site, troubleshoot your site, and maintain the site. Drupal is build upon a system of APIs and overrides, meaning that all of your customizations can be kept within your Site's folder.

6. If your Drupal site is at the URL `http://www.wiley.com`, what is the name of your site's folder?

Your site's folder should be named `wiley.com`. If Drupal is powering only a single website, you can also use the Default folder.

7. Why is setting a strong password on the first user account created important?

The user account created during installation is known as user one. User one can bypass Drupal's permissions, giving it an all-access pass to your website. This all-access pass is important so that you never lock yourself out of your website, but it can be dangerous if someone discovers your username and password.

CHAPTER 3

1. What is the difference between the Article and Page content types?

Both the Article and Page content types are nodes, so they have the same core functionality. However, they have different preset defaults. The default for Articles is to be promoted to the frontpage and have comments and tags enabled. On the other hand, Pages are not promoted to the frontpage and have comments and tags disabled by default.

2. How does the contact form use categories?

Multiple categories allow those contacting you to specify where their inquiry should be sent. Each category also has a different auto-reply message that can be sent. For example, a user inquiring about Sales can have their inquiry sent to the Sales department, whereas a user reporting a bad link would be directed to the webmaster.

3. What is cron?

Cron is the system that Drupal uses to automate tasks on your website. Tasks could include aggregating RSS feeds from external sites or routine maintenance such as flushing stale cache files and old log entries.

4. How can you deny access to your site's content?

Drupal's permissions assume that a person is denied access unless they have been explicitly granted access. To deny access, simply remove their grant permission by visiting Configuration ⇨ Permissions.

5. What is a theme?

A theme is what controls the look and feel of a website but not its content. A theme can change the color, font type or size, places where the content appears, regions available for blocks, and all other aspects of the look and feel of a website. A theme can neither modify content nor provide additional functionality such as private messaging.

CHAPTER 4

1. Why is it important to set your site's name before you launch?

Your site's name is stored with a user's bookmarks and in their RSS reader. Most browsers do not update these titles after the initial retrieval.

2. The post date of your content is based on what time zone?

The date and time displayed are determined by the viewing user's configured time zone. If the user has not been granted the permission to modify their time zone or simply has not set their time zone, the site's default time zone will be used. This setting is at Configuration ⇨ Regional and Languages ⇨ Regional Settings.

3. What is the difference between a public and a private file?

A public file is accessible by the whole Internet, whereas a private file is only accessible via Drupal. Private files allow you to set permissions on the file or force users to log in before downloading the file.

4. Where should private files be stored?

Private files should always be kept in a non-web-accessible location. This will ensure that Drupal is the only method to retrieve the file and help defend against an insecure server configuration.

5. What is the purpose of a text format?

A text format serves the following three primary purposes:

➤ **Security** — Text formats filter out potentially harmful code.

➤ **Site integrity** — You worked hard on your site's theme, and text formats help keep it looking good by preventing harsh HTML tags that could cause your site to render poorly.

➤ **Ease of use** — Formats can include filters that interpret the text entered. This allows syntax such as Wiki code or BBCode to be entered and gives users a simpler way to write their content.

6. In order for clean URLs to function, what file must exist in Drupal's root directory?

The .htaccess file needs to exist in Drupal's root directory. In the absence of a .htaccess file, the following lines must appear in your site's VirtualHost configuration.

```
RewriteEngine on

#Rewrite URLs of the form 'x' to the form 'index.php?q=x'.
RewriteCond %{REQUEST_FILENAME} !-f
RewriteCond %{REQUEST_FILENAME} !-d
RewriteCond %{REQUEST_URI} !=/favicon.ico
```

7. What is a URL alias?

A URL alias maps one path to another. For example, http://localhost/node/5 can be mapped to http://localhost/about. URL aliases make it easier for visitors to find your site's content and present a well-polished look to your site visitors.

CHAPTER 5

1. What is a block?

A block is a small piece of content that appears within a region of your theme. Examples include the user login form, search form, navigational menu, or links to the latest comments.

2. How many regions does a theme have?

Drupal provides multiple default regions to a theme, such as Left Sidebar, Right Sidebar, Content, and so on. A theme, however, has full control over the regions and may have more or fewer regions than the defaults.

3. If you want a block to appear only on the blog section at http://localhost/blogs, how would you accomplish this?

Use the block configuration's Page Specific Visibility Settings to set it to show on only the pages specified, and then enter the following under Pages (as shown in Figure A-1):

```
blogs
blogs/*
```

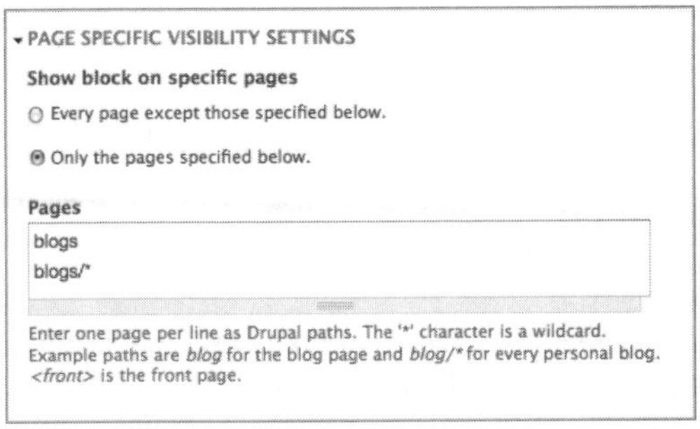

FIGURE A-1

4. Why would you set the Main links and Secondary links to the same menu?

When a Main link is clicked, the child links will appear in the Secondary links area. For example, if the Main link `Add new content` is clicked, the Secondary links will contain a list of content that can be created (Article, Page, and so on).

5. What is a URL alias?

A URL alias is an alternative URL to access a piece of content. For example, `http://localhost/node/1` can be aliased to `http://localhost/about`. Use the Pathauto module to automatically create aliases.

CHAPTER 6

1. What are nodes and how does Drupal use them?

A node is another name for a content type. The term *node* describes the core functionality of a content type, which is to provide basic universal features and the ability to be extended by modules.

2. What is a content type field?

Title and Body are examples of fields on a content type. Drupal allows you to add a near-unlimited number of fields to each content type, providing a lot of flexibility.

3. Explain the difference between a field type and a widget.

A field type defines the type of data being stored, such as text, number, date, files, or images. A widget is how the data is requested from the user — calendar date-pickers, drop-down selection forms, and image upload forms are examples of widgets.

4. How many images can be uploaded using a single image field?

Every field can be set to allow for multiple values. As an administrator, you can choose to limit image uploads to any value between 1 and 10 or unlimited.

5. What is an image style?

An image style can automatically resize, crop, rotate, or desaturate (convert color to black-and-white) uploaded pictures. You can use image styles to create thumbnails, previews, or large versions. Create and use image styles in two steps:

1) Create an image style at Configuration ⇨ Image Styles.

2) Use the newly created image style within the display settings of any image field. Navigate to Structure ⇨ Content Types ⇨ Edit <content type> ⇨ Manage Display.

6. When adding a field with multiple allowed values, what is the purpose of using the following syntax?

```
1|Option A
2|Option B
3|Option C
```

This `key|value` syntax enables you to change the value (for example: `Option A`) without skewing the results of previously stored values, because both values will be tied to the same key.

CHAPTER 7

1. What is OpenID and how is it used in Drupal?

OpenID is a method of authenticating users with a web-centralized username and password. When the OpenID module is enabled, users may add their OpenID to their user account and then use their OpenID provider for authentication. Examples of OpenID providers include Google, Yahoo!, LiveJournal, and Flickr.

2. What is the purpose of a role?

Permissions are assigned to roles. Users are then assigned to one or more roles and receive the cumulative role permissions.

3. How does a private profile field differ from a hidden profile field?

A private field is entered by the user who is creating the profile and is not visible to the general public. A hidden field is only entered by and visible to user administrators.

4. What happens when a user cancels their account?

The account settings at Configuration ⇨ Account Settings determine what happens when a user decides to cancel their account. Their account can be:

➤ Disabled, but the account content is left online

➤ Disabled, and all content is taken offline (unpublished)

➤ Deleted, and all content is deleted

➤ Deleted, and the content is reassigned to the anonymous user

Users with the Select Method for Canceling Account permission can bypass this site-wide default.

CHAPTER 8

1. What is taxonomy and how is it used in Drupal?

Taxonomy is the practice and science of classification. In Drupal, the term describes the overall system that categorizes content on a website. The Drupal taxonomy system uses vocabularies — a collection of terms used on nodes and the settings for how these terms appear.

2. Give an example of parent and child terms.

Parent and child terms allow you to form a hierarchy of terms. A good example is geography: Boston is a child of Massachusetts, which is a child of the United States, which is a child of North America.

3. Why is the taxonomy system so popular and important in Drupal?

Drupal automatically creates a page dedicated to displaying content categorized with the term. Each one of these pages also has a corresponding RSS feed, and the links to these pages are automatically added to each node type. In addition, the taxonomy system works with existing search functionality such as Faceted Search, making for a robust user experience on your site.

4. How does the weight system work in Drupal?

The weight is the order in which the terms appear. For example, a term that is weighted 5 is "lighter" than a term that is weighted 7, so it will float higher. Terms are always ordered first by weight and second alphabetically.

5. What is the advantage of the API (Application Programming Interface)?

When you are writing custom modules or using custom PHP code, you can use the API to save time and code.

CHAPTER 9

1. What is a search index and when is it created?

A search index is a catalog of your site's data that is used to match search keywords to their respective content. A search index is updated during each cron run and is limited only by the site's index throttle set at Configuration ⇨ Search Settings.

2. Why is there a separate permission for the advanced search?

When an advanced search is used, the search query operates more slowly and consumes more system resources.

3. What is a cache?

A cache is storage for pre-rendered blocks or pages to be served to users instead of rebuilding the block or page on every page request. A cache dramatically increases the speed of your site.

4. How does block cache differ from page cache?

Block cache stores only the individual blocks on your website, such as the user login block or a navigational menu. A block cache is used for all users. A page cache stores the fully rendered page of your site and is only used for anonymous users. Authenticated users receive a dynamically rendered page built with cached blocks.

5. Why is CSS aggregation important?

CSS aggregation combines all of your site's CSS files into a single file, removes excess space, and compresses the file. This reduces the transfer speed to the client and reduces the necessary connections from numerous to one. This can have a dramatic positive effect on the client's performance.

CHAPTER 10

1. What is the core Trigger module and how can you use it?

The Trigger module is an example of a module that can perform automated actions. It operates on events such as a post being saved, a comment added, or a new user registered — whenever such an event occurs, the Trigger module can fire off an action, such as sending an e-mail to alert you.

2. Where can you find the Trigger module?

The Trigger module is disabled by default, because not every site will need custom triggers. After you enable the module, it can be found at Administer ➪ Structure ➪ Triggers.

3. What does the Workflow module do?

The Workflow module hooks into triggers and actions, and uses them to create a configurable workflow for your nodes. A workflow is a series of states that a node passes through or between. For example, story nodes may have a workflow that goes through Draft, Peer Review, Editor Review, and Approved/Published states. The Workflow module also tracks who, how, and/or when the change was initiated, and allows commentary on the state change.

4. What is special about the Rules module?

The Rules module, a replacement for the core Trigger module, was created to add some intelligence back to the automation front. The Rules module adds more functionality and flexibility than the core module by adding the ability to trigger actions based upon a set of criteria. For example, with Rules, you can create a trigger that automatically promotes stories to the frontpage, but only if the story was authored by an editor. It's a good module to plug in when you need something more robust than the lightweight but still powerful Trigger module.

5.   What does the Rule Scheduler do?

The Rule Scheduler module straightforwardly schedules rule sets, a collection of rules that will be triggered by something other than a system event. This trigger could be custom PHP code or a schedule.

CHAPTER 11

1.   What is the Advanced Help module?

The Advanced Help module adds numerous pages of documentation directly onto your site alongside the modules and areas you would normally request help on. Download it from `http://drupal.org/project/advanced_help`.

2.   What is the difference between a filter and an exposed filter?

An exposed filter is a form that allows a user to manipulate the settings of a filter to dynamically alter the view.

3.   What permission would you assign a user to allow them to use exposed filters?

If the user has permission to use the view, they can also use the exposed filters. Remember that views often bypass site settings and retrieve data that might normally be inaccessible to a user, so be cautious when allowing users to use exposed filters.

4.   What permissions are available for Views?

The Views module has two types of permissions: all-views and per-view.

The all-view's Access All Views permission permits access to every view on your site regardless of per-view access controls.

Per-view permissions are based on either a user's role or if the user has a certain site permission.

5.   What is the easiest way to increase the performance of your view?

Turn on Views caching.

6.   What is the difference between an exposed filter and an argument?

Arguments do not provide a form or method that a user can manipulate to modify the view. Arguments are often used to provide items such as per-user image galleries, tracker pages, or categorization pages. Arguments allow for very clean URLs such as `/gallery/jredding` or `/comments/jredding`.

Exposed filters provide an easy-to-use form to modify the view in real time. However, they create longer and more confusing URLs such as `/comment&uid=5&post_date=&gt;5`.

7. What is a relationship?

A relationship creates a connection between two items on your site. For example, a comment is related to the node in which the reply was made.

8. What is the difference between a Style and Row Style?

A Row Style setting changes the way an individual row (such as a single node, user, or comment) is styled. The Style setting changes the way all rows appear on your site (such as displaying rows in a grid or an HTML table).

CHAPTER 12

1. How does localization differ from translation?

Localization refers to modifying your site's regional settings, such as the date/time formats and time zones. Localizing also refers to translating the interface to a language other than English. You can translate your interface with the built-in Locale module.

2. What are the basic steps to translating your content?

The basic content translation steps are as follows:

1. Add a second language at Configuration ⇨ Languages.

2. Enable the Content Translation module.

3. Configure each content type to allow for translation. Navigate to Structure ⇨ Content Types ⇨ Article (Edit), and then under Multilingual Support, select Enabled, With Translation.

4. Create a new piece of Content, and then click the Translate tab to add a translation of the content.

3. What does i18n stand for?

Internationalization (based on the fact that there are 18 characters between the first letter, *i*, and the last letter, *n*).

CHAPTER 13

1. What is theming?

Theming is the term used to describe the act of modifying a site's layout, color scheme, and possibly its HTML structure.

2. Where are new themes installed?

New themes are installed either at `/sites/all/themes`, which will make them available to all sites in a multi-site installation, or `/sites/<sitename>/themes` (for example: `sites/example.com/themes`).

3. Is it possible for a theme to not have HTML files?

Of course! Drupal's core and contributed modules include sets of suggested HTML provided by template files and theme functions. You can use CSS to modify the layout, color, and other design elements of the suggested HTML. If you need to modify the suggested HTML you can override it through the use of a template file or theme function.

4. What are regions and how are they defined?

Regions are locations within a theme wherein blocks can be placed, configured at Structure ⇨ Blocks. Within each theme's `.info` file, you can define the regions that are available. The theme must then implement the region within the theme's `page.tpl.php`.

5. What are core and suggested templates?

A core template is the main template used for the theming element. A suggested template is a variation on the template. Here are some examples:

➤ `page.tpl.php`: Core template for all pages

➤ `page-front.tpl.php`: Suggested template for the frontpage

➤ `node.tpl.php`: Core template for all nodes

➤ `node-blog.tpl.php`: Suggested template for the blog content type

6. Why is the theme registry important?

The theme registry contains information about every themeable element, including template files and theme functions. You can use the theme registry to determine what can be themed and how to theme it. It is also important to know about the theme registry, because each new template override and theme function must be registered before it can be used.

7. Why is the Zen theme (available on Drupal.org) heavily used and considered a Drupal good practice?

Zen is a base theme for subthemes to be built from. It provides a solid standards-compliant foundation to quickly build out your custom theme. By using Zen, you are tapping into a community of talented web designers and themers and accessing their pool of Drupal best practices.

CHAPTER 14

1. What is the difference between a contributed module and a custom module?

A contributed module is any module that is not part of Drupal's core. Contributed modues can be downloaded at `http://drupal.org` and have a large support and maintenance base. A custom module is a module that you have developed that is specific to your website.

2.   What is scoping?

Scoping identifies all of the pieces of a website that will subsequently be mapped to the module or modules that provide the feature. It is a vital part of a web development project.

3.   Where are some of the places you can learn more about Drupal modules?

You can search for and learn about Drupal modules on Drupal.org's own search engine, Google, `Drupalmodules.com`, Internet Relay Chat (IRC) channels, Drupal's forums, RSS feeds, and `@drupal_modules` on Twitter. Do a search for **Top Drupal modules** on Lullabot for a great analysis of the most frequented used modules.

4.   What is the first and foremost rule when testing or trying out new modules?

Never use your production site!

CHAPTER 15

1.   What is the definition of a module?

Modules are bits of code that extend, enhance, or modify the functionality of Drupal.

2.   Why is choosing a good module name important?

A module's name is used to name the folder it is contained in, the files associated with it, and its internal functions. It is a very tedious process to change the module name later on, so you should choose a good name from the start.

3.   What are some rules to follow when choosing a module name?

The module's name must be unique to the entire website, including themes and other modules. You should also avoid the names of existing contributed modules and themes available on `http://drupal.org`.

4.   What is the first and foremost rule of Drupal?

Do not hack core! Almost everything can be done without modifying the core code of Drupal. Hacking core leaves you open to security vulnerabilities, may have unintended consequences with contributed modules, and makes it very difficult to upgrade and maintain your site.

CHAPTER 16

1.   How do you implement a hook?

Substitute the word *hook* with your module's name. For example: `hook_node_view` becomes `beginning_drupal_node_view`.

2.   What are the advantages of using Drupal's Form API to build web forms?

The first advantage is security. Drupal manages the forms and makes sure that no one tampers with or alters the form. The second is the ability to provide dynamic forms. Each form array is passed to all modules that have implemented `hook_form_alter` for additional processing, which allows modules to attach new form elements, modify or remove existing elements, and add attributes such as CSS classes.

3. What is one of the guiding principles when writing a Drupal module?

All output needs to be overridable. Always use theme functions, template files, conjunction the `t()` or `format_plural()` functions to allow your output to be overridden.

4. How is the syntax for a theme function different from the syntax for a template file?

A theme function begins with PHP and may contain a bit of HTML, whereas a template file begins with HTML and contains PHP.

CHAPTER 17

1. What is the starting point of a module?

The starting point of any module is a hook. Examples of hooks include `hook_form_alter` to modify Drupal forms, `hook_user_view` to modify a user's profile, and `hook_node_view` to modify the view of a node.

2. If you want to add custom settings to your module, what hook would you use?

`hook_menu` is used to register a URL path that can be used to display your custom settings. Set the page callback to `drupal_get_form` and the page argument to your own custom function. Using the Forms API and the Drupal function `system_settings_form`, you can quickly create a settings page.

3. What hook do you use to add permissions to your module?

`hook_permission` is used to add new permissions to your website.

4. What does Drupal use to ensure that its core and contributed modules and your code are running properly?

Drupal uses SimpleTest to run automated tests against the core and contributed modules. By writing automated tests against your code, you can speed up your development and ensure that you've written rock-solid code.

CHAPTER 18

1. How can you increase the amount of memory available to Drupal?

Within `settings.php`, add in the following line:

```
ini_set('memory_limit', 32MB);
```

2. Consider if your company operates the following four URLs:

➤ `http://your-company.com`

➤ `http://also-your-company.com`

➤ `http://your-company.cn`

➤ `http://also-your-company.cn`

The two URLs that use `.com` are identical, and the two URLs that use `.cn` are different from `.com` but identical to each other — so you have two databases for four websites.

How could you configure these sites using Drupal's multi-site capabilities?

You can use either of the following two methods:

➤ Create two Sites folders: `sites/com` and `sites/cn`.

➤ Create two Sites folders: `your-company.com` and `your-company.cn`. Then use `sites/sites.php` to map `also-your-company.com` and `also-your-company.cn` to their respective peers.

3. What are the basic steps to share a set of users between two websites?

Every website must share the same database and set the `$db_prefix` variable within `settings.php` to separate and share the respective tables.

4. How many websites can one installation of Drupal power?

There is no limit on the number of websites that Drupal can power. However, each website will consume system resources, creating a limitation based upon the server's available resources.

5. How can you block a problematic spambot that is originating from a single IP?

Spambots that are bombarding your website and causing a Denial of Service (DOS) attack can be blocked using the `$conf['blocked_ips']` variable within `settings.php`.

CHAPTER 19

1. Why is it useful to understand the basics of SEO?

Knowing what terms to use for subjects, tags, and other important text, and knowing where to place those terms allow search engines to properly index your site's contents. In addition to making content available to search engines, SEO can help boost your site's rankings so that your content can get higher visibility.

2. What does the Pathauto module do?

    The Pathauto module automatically creates self-describing URL aliases for you based on information such as taxonomy, content type, and/or the content's title, making it easier for search engines and your site visitors to understand what the content of the page will contain.

3. What is the purpose of the XML Sitemap module?

    The XML Sitemap module creates a map or catalog of your site's content for presentation to a search engine. A sitemap helps search engines find your data faster, discover the most relevant content, and keep it up-to-date.

4. How do you create a customized page with the Dashboard module?

    Users with the Administer Blocks permission can click the Customize links above the Dashboard to access the drag-and-drop interface for customizing their dashboards.

INDEX

N